MW01049359

Politically
Correct
Death

Other Works by Francis J. Beckwith

Baha'i (Bethany House, 1985)

David Hume's Argument Against Miracles: A Critical Analysis (University Press of America, 1989)

The Mormon Concept of God: A Philosophical Analysis (with S. E. Parrish) (Edwin Mellen, 1991)

Matters of Life and Death: Calm Answers to Tough Questions about Abortion and Euthanasia (with N. L. Geisler) (Baker, 1991)

Are You Politically Correct?: Debating America's Cultural Standards (co-edited with M. A. Bauman) (Prometheus, 1993)

Politically
Correct
Death

Answering the Arguments
for Abortion Rights

Francis J. Beckwith

 BakerBooks

A Division of Baker Book House Co.
Grand Rapids, Michigan 49516

Copyright 1993 by
Baker Book House Company
P.O. Box 6287, Grand Rapids, Michigan 49506-6287

Printed in the United States of America

All rights reserved. No part of this publication may be reproduced, stored in a retrieval system, or transmitted in any form or by any means—electronic, mechanical, photocopy, recording, or any other—without the prior written permission of the publisher. The only exception is brief quotations in printed reviews.

Library of Congress Cataloging-in-Publication Data

Beckwith, Francis.
    Politically correct death: answering the arguments for abortion rights/Francis J. Beckwith.
        p.   cm.
    Includes bibliographical references (p.) and index.
    ISBN 0-8010-1050-0
    1. Abortion—United States. I. Title.
HQ767.5.U5B43 1993
363.4'6'0973—dc20
                                            92-31659

Earlier versions of parts of this book have appeared elsewhere as either journal articles, newspaper opinion pieces, or papers delivered at professional conferences and public lectures. I would like to thank the journal and newspaper editors for permission to reuse the material, which appeared in the following publications:

"Personal Bodily Rights, Abortion, and Unplugging the Violinist," *International Philosophical Quarterly* 32 (March 1992): 105–18.
"The Misuse of Maternal Mortality Statistics in the Abortion Debate," *Ethics and Medicine* 7 (Summer 1991): 18–19.
"A Critical Appraisal of Theological Arguments for Abortion Rights," *Bibliotheca Sacra* 148 (July–September 1991): 337–55. A popular version of this article appeared as a two-part series, "How Prolife is the Bible?" *Focus on the Family Citizen* 6 (March 16, 1992) and (April 20, 1992).
"Answering the Arguments for Abortion Rights, Part Four: When Does a Human Become a Person?" *Christian Research Journal* 14 (Summer 1991): 28–33.
"Answering the Arguments for Abortion Rights, Part Three: Is the Unborn Human Less than Human?" *Christian Research Journal* 13 (Spring 1991): 8–13, 34.
"Answering the Arguments for Abortion Rights, Part Two: Arguments from Pity, Tolerance and Ad Hominem," *Christian Research Journal* 13 (Winter 1991): 27–32.
"Brave New Bible: A Reply to the Moderate Evangelical Position on Abortion," *Journal of the Evangelical Theological Society* 33 (December 1990): 489–508.
"Answering the Arguments for Abortion Rights, Part One: The Appeal to Pity," *Christian Research Journal* 13 (Fall 1990): 20–26.
"Rights, Filial Obligations, and Medical Risks," *APA Newsletter on Philosophy and Medicine* 89:2 (Winter 1990): 86–88.
Abortion and Public Policy: A Response to Some Arguments," *Journal of the Evangelical Theological Society* 32 (December 1989): 503–18.
"Abortion and Argument: A Response to Mollenkott," *Journal of Biblical Ethics in Medicine* 3 (Summer 1989): 48–56.
"Utilitarianism, Abortion Rights, and Justice Blackmun's Dissent in *Webster*: Some Philosophical Observations," *Simon Greenleaf Review of Law and Religion* 8 (1988–89): 5–24.
"Socrates Meets Dukakis," *Las Vegas Review Journal* (30 October 1988): 1AA, 4AA.
"Answering the Pro-choice Arguments," *Las Vegas Sun* (30 June 1989): Opinion page.

"Defense of Legal Abortion Ignores Logic," *Las Vegas Review-Journal* (10 August 1989): Opinion page.
Michael Bauman, "The Euphemisms of Abortion Hide the Crime," *Orange County Register* (9 January 1989): Opinion page.

The papers delivered at either professional conferences or public lectures were:

"Tolerance, Religious Pluralism, and Abortion Rights," annual meeting of the Evangelical Philosophical Society, San Francisco, California, 19–21 November 1992.
"Pulling the Plug on the Violinist: A Critique of Thomson's Argument for Abortion Rights," annual meeting of the American Philosophical Association, Pacific Division, San Francisco, California, 27–30 March 1991. Also presented at the national meeting of the University Faculty for Life, Georgetown University, Washington, D.C., 8–10 June 1991.
"Personal Bodily Rights, Abortion, and Unplugging the Violinist," annual meeting of the Evangelical Philosophical Society, New Orleans Baptist Theological Seminary, New Orleans, Louisiana, 15–17 November 1990.
"Abortion Rights and Utilitarian Arguments: A Philosophical Analysis," annual meeting of the Evangelical Philosophical Society, Bethel Theological Seminary West, San Diego, California, 16–18 November 1989. Also presented at the sesquicentennial symposium, "Health Care Ethics: The Work of the Catholic Community," sponsored by Loras College's Bioethics Resource Center, Loras College, Dubuque, Iowa, 5–7 April 1990.
"Sound Bites and Unsound Reasoning: Critical Thinking and Popular Moral Rhetoric," University Forum Lecture Series, University of Nevada, Las Vegas, Beam Hall, 30 October 1989.
"Abortion, Public Policy and Religious Conviction," annual Far West Region meeting of the Evangelical Theological Society, The Master's Seminary, Sun Valley, California, 7 April 1989.

I would also like to thank the publisher and author for permission to use:

A chart, which I slightly amended in this book, from Stephen D. Schwarz, *The Moral Question of Abortion* (Chicago: Loyola University Press, 1990), 23–25.

To my wife,

Frankie Rozelle Dickerson Beckwith.

You always remind me
that blood is thicker than water
and more difficult in which to sink.

Contents

Acknowledgments

Although I did much reading and research in the writing of this book, certain works stand out as especially influential in shaping my views concerning abortion, public policy, and the law. Although I do not necessarily agree with every aspect of each work (in fact, I am critical of some), the influence of each work should be acknowledged: Baruch Brody, *Abortion and the Sanctity of Human Life* (Cambridge, Mass.: M.I.T. Press, 1975); Stephen D. Schwarz, *The Moral Question of Abortion* (Chicago: Loyola University Press, 1990); Robert Wennberg, *Life in the Balance: Exploring the Abortion Controversy* (Grand Rapids: Eerdmans, 1985); Dennis J. Horan, Edward R. Grant, and Paige C. Cunningham, eds., *Abortion and the Constitution: Reversing* Roe v. Wade *Through the Courts* (Washington, D.C.: Georgetown University Press, 1987); Laurence Tribe, *Abortion: The Clash of Absolutes* (New York: Norton, 1990); Francis A. Schaeffer and C. Everett Koop, *Whatever Happened to the Human Race?* (Old Tappan, N.J.: Revell, 1979); Harold O. J. Brown, *Death Before Birth* (Nashville: Thomas Nelson, 1977); Jeff Lane Hensley, ed., *The Zero People* (Ann Arbor: Servant, 1983); John Jefferson Davis, *Abortion and the Christian* (Phillipsburg, N.J.: Presbyterian and Reformed, 1984); Stephen M. Krason, *Abortion: Politics, Morality, and the Constitution* (Lanham, Md.: University Press of America, 1984); Marvin Olasky, *The Press and Abortion: 1838–1988* (Hillsdale, N.J.: Lawrence Erlbaum Associates, 1988); and Marvin Olasky, *Abortion Rites: A Social History of Abortion in America* (Wheaton, Ill.: Crossway, 1992).

There are many people who I wish to thank: my wife, Frankie R. D. Beckwith, to whom this book is dedicated, who remained patient, loving, and encouraging during the writing of this work; my brother-in-law, Mark Wiegand (and his wife, Lexi, who tolerated our late-night jogging/debates), who was and continues to be instrumental in helping me to more clearly respond to abortion-rights arguments in both popular debate and written form; my good friend and former UNLV colleague, Dr. J. David Turner, whose sage insights into the proper application of communication theory in popular moral debate have been helpful in the formation of my own thoughts; Dr. J. P. Moreland, professor of philosophy of religion, Talbot School of Theology, Biola University, whose friendship, and whose writings and lectures in the areas of moral reasoning and medical ethics, have had a tremendous impact in bringing to fruition some of the arguments I put forth throughout this book (especially in chapter 6); Dennis Irby, whose critical comments of this text proved to be useful; the president of UNLV, Dr. Robert Maxson, whose continued support and encouragement is most appreciated; my department chairman, Dr. Maurice Finocchiaro, professor of philosophy, UNLV, whose own scholarship and academic success have served as a model I hope to emulate; the director of my university's Greenspun School of Communication, Dr. Gage Chapel, professor of communication studies, UNLV, whose advice and encouragement are always appreciated and taken to heart; my former teacher and current colleague, Dr. Craig Walton, professor of philosophy and director of the Institute for Ethics and Policy Studies, UNLV, who first made me aware of the importance of sound moral reasoning in public policy decision-making and whose disagreement with me on the abortion issue has provoked me to think deeper and do more research in order to better articulate my views; two UNLV graduate students in our M.A. program in ethics and policy studies, who also double as "part-time" logic instructors, Jeanette Catsoulis and David Day, whose probing questions and love for sound reasoning have no doubt contributed to the sharpening of the arguments presented in this text; Elliot Miller, Dr. Robert M. Bowman, Jr., and Dr. Ron Rhodes, who did an excellent job in editing the portions of this book that originally appeared in *Christian Research Journal*; the American Civil Liberties Union of Las Vegas, Nevada, whose invitation to be part of a panel discussion on whether *Roe v. Wade* should be overturned (Community College of Southern Nevada, February 18, 1988) first spurred my scholarly interest in abortion, which eventually resulted in this book; my fellow Fordham alumnus, Dr. Michael Bauman, professor of theology and culture, Hillsdale College, whose keen insights, profound wit, and transcontinental friendship have been both a scholarly

and a spiritual encouragement in my study of the abortion debate; Dr. Stephen D. Schwarz, professor of philosophy, University of Rhode Island, for his helpful suggestions and valuable insights; Dr. Nigel Cameron, professor of theology, Trinity Evangelical Divinity School, for his wise counsel on how best to articulate pro-life theological arguments; Dr. Pat Leary, professor of biology, Community College of Southern Nevada, for his valuable help in deciphering biological concepts; Bob and Gretchen Passantino, for the illuminating discussions we had in April 1991 that eventually changed my mind about Operation Rescue; the UNLV faculty committee, which allocates the Barrick Faculty Development Funds that fully financed the delivering of a paper (at Bethel Theological Seminary West, San Diego, California, 16 November 1989), much of which is included in this book; my students at UNLV ("Contemporary Moral Issues" and "Introduction to Ethics" classes), Christian Life Community Church's adult education program ("Ethics, Abortion, and Argument" class), and Crisis Pregnancy Center ("Responding to Abortion Rights Arguments" module), whose questions, papers, disagreements, and enthusiasm have been a constant source of intellectual and spiritual growth; Howard Hoffmann, M.D., who has been gracious enough to financially support my travels and scholarly activities; and my parents, Harold and Elizabeth (Guido) Beckwith, and their children, James, Patrick, and Elizabeth Ann, who have been the mortal source of my appreciation for family and community, two institutions whose existence is imperiled by an abortion ethic that places utility over obligation and artificial license above natural bonds.

Although these persons, in greater and lesser degrees, were influential, supportive, and/or instrumental in the formation of this work, I take full responsibility for its contents. Although many of them agree with my position on abortion, some of them do not. Hence, my acknowledgment of any person should not imply total or even partial agreement with my views.

Introduction

We live in a political world
Love don't have any place
We're livin' in times when men commit crimes
And crime don't have a face.

We live in a political world
Courage is a thing of the past
Houses are haunted, children aren't wanted
The next day could be your last.
                    Bob Dylan (1989)

Abortion has become the most divisive political and religious issue in late twentieth-century America. The arguments for abortion rights are being put forth in the political arena with greater vigor and rhetorical hostility than ever before. What is apparent, however, is that both pro-life spokespersons and political candidates have for the most part responded inadequately. They have either toned down their pro-life position, caved into the opposition, or permitted the abortion-rights movement to control the terminology and framework of the debate.[1] I hope that this book will serve to reverse this trend by providing a rigorous intellectual defense of the pro-life position that will be helpful to policy makers, political consultants, pro-life leaders, and ordinary Americans. Of course, as a professional philosopher and ethicist, I am also writing for respected colleagues on both sides of the debate. I hope, however, that they forgive me for my occasional excursions into the morass of popular rhetoric. But if we are to live and believe Socrates' dictum that the unexamined life is not worth living, then we must be prepared to walk down Madison Avenue, watch "Nightline," and read *People* magazine. In such arenas the thinking of ordinary men and women is nurtured.

A recent issue of *Newsweek* (17 December 1990) speaks critically of a movement on American college campuses that brands anyone who does not accept the "politically correct" views of the academic far left (i.e., affirmative action, radical feminism, neo-Marxism, gay rights, animal rights) as racist, sexist, homophobic, speciesist, or whatever demagogic scarlet letter is currently applied under this new "Mc-

Carthyism."[2] Although "sensitive" to the political needs of nearly every interest group, this movement tolerates *natalism*: the denial of the fundamental human right to life to a segment of human beings simply because they are not post-uterine. Just as skin color (racism), ethnic origin (ethnocentrism), gender (sexism), national power (imperialism), and birth date (ageism) are irrelevant to one's possession of fundamental human rights, so is one's degree of development and location inside or outside the womb (natalism). Unfortunately, this politically correct prejudice, manifested in the practice of abortion, nearly always results in the death of its victim. Hence, the title of this book: *Politically Correct Death*. It is my hope that this work will play a part, however small, in abolishing this last great American prejudice.

In this book I will present a clear defense of the pro-life position on abortion. This position can be defined in the following way: since the unborn entity is fully human from the *moment of conception*, and abortion typically results in the unborn entity's death, therefore abortion ordinarily entails the unjustified killing of a human being who has a full right to life. If, however, there is a strong probability that a woman's pregnancy will result in her death, as in the case of a tubal pregnancy, abortion is justified. For it is a greater good that one human should live (the mother) rather than two die (the mother and her child). This is the pro-life position I will be defending in this book. This position can be put in the following argument-outline:

1. The unborn entity, from the moment of conception, is fully human.
2. It is prima facie wrong to kill an entity which is fully human.
3. Almost every act of abortion is intended to kill the unborn entity, an entity which is fully human.
4. Therefore, almost every act of abortion is prima facie wrong.

In this book I hope to show that each one of the premises of this argument is true or at least more likely true than not. In chapter 9 I will review this argument outline and summarize the conclusions reached in chapters 3 through 8 concerning the truth of its premises.

It should be kept in mind that even if the reader does not find compelling the case for human personhood beginning at conception and that almost all abortions are not morally justified, it does not follow that she is required to accept the radical abortion-rights position that a fetus is not a person at any moment prior to birth and that the choice to abort needs no moral justification. In other words, the reader may conclude that human personhood begins at the onset of detectable brain waves (forty to forty-two days after conception) or when the fetus looks like a miniature baby (seven weeks after conception), or she may believe that abortion is morally justified in cases of rape, incest, or severe fetal deformity. But since most women do not discover they are pregnant until the end of the second month of pregnancy, and rape, incest, and severe fetal deformity abortions make up only a tiny percentage of abortions, the reader should consider herself a moderate pro-life advocate who opposes the radical abortion-rights position that is currently the law in the United States. Although I would like such a reader to accept all my arguments, it is not necessary to do so in order to oppose almost all abortions performed in this country.

At this juncture, it is important to define some terms. First, when I say that the unborn entity is *fully human*, I mean that she is just as human as either you or I and hence deserving of all the rights which go along with such a status. Second, when I say that killing a being who is fully human is prima facie morally wrong, I mean to say that in ordinary circumstances no one is morally justified in killing another human being. However, this does not mean that it is *always* wrong in *every* circumstance to kill someone who is fully human. There could be circumstances in which killing or letting die is justified because one has a duty to a higher good. For example, a vast majority of people believe that it is all right to kill someone in the act of self-defense or in a just war, and many also believe that one is justified in letting someone die if that someone is brain-dead and his bodily organs are kept alive by a machine that is not doing him any medical good.[3] And as I noted earlier, in the case of abortion, the killing of an unborn entity is justified if her presence in her mother's womb poses a significant threat to her mother's life. For if the unborn entity is not surgically removed (which will undoubtedly result in her death if performed early on in the pregnancy), then both mother and child will die. The specific intention is not to kill the child but to save the life of the mother. The child's death is an unfortunate consequence which, although anticipated, cannot be avoided unless one is willing to let both mother and child die. But since it is prima facie a higher good that one human should live rather than two die, abortion to save the life of the mother is justified.

The news media often inaccurately refer to the pro-life position as *antiabortion*. Even though the pro-life advocate *prefers* to be called pro-life, the media still insist on calling him antiabortion. On the other hand, the abortion-rights advocate prefers to be called pro-choice, and is courteously referred to as such. But aside from the obvious bias of such selective courtesy,[4] the reason why the media are incorrect in calling the pro-life position antiabortion is because the pro-life advocate would have no problem with the "pro-choice" position of abortion on demand—abortion for the entire nine months of pregnancy for any reason the pregnant woman deems fit[5]—if the pregnant woman's choice to abort did not result in the death of her unborn offspring. Hence, it is not abortion per se that the pro-life advocate opposes, but the killing of an unborn human being who has a full right to life.

This book is divided into three main parts. In part 1, which contains two chapters, the focus of our attention will be on moral reasoning and the U.S. Supreme Court's *Roe v. Wade* decision. Chapter 1 is a brief defense of the importance of moral reasoning. I will argue that contrary to popular opinion there are values that have universal application, and for this reason, moral reasoning and argumentation is possible. Furthermore, it is

not the question of the reality or nonreality of these values that divides both sides of the abortion debate, but rather, disagreement over both the application of these values and the truth of some important facts. Chapter 2 is a brief essay explaining why the landmark Supreme Court decisions on abortion, *Roe v. Wade* (1973) and *Doe v. Bolton* (1973) support abortion on demand for all nine months of pregnancy and how the Supreme Court's recent decisions, *Webster v. Reproductive Health Services* (1989) and *Planned Parenthood v. Casey* (1992), could affect abortion law in this country. If the reader is interested in reading the actual decisions without making an extended trip to a law library, I have included *Roe, Bolton,* and *Webster* as appendices in a book I coauthored, *Matters of Life and Death: Calm Answers to Tough Questions about Abortion and Euthanasia.* An abridged version of *Casey* appears as Appendix G in this book.

In part 2 of this book I will critically analyze the major arguments for abortion rights. However, prior to this analysis, in chapter 3, I will present the scientific facts of prenatal development as well as the different methods physicians use in performing abortions and whether these methods cause the unborn to feel any pain. In chapters 4 through 8 I will critique more than sixty arguments that are used to justify abortion at some stage during pregnancy. I will argue that with the exception of intending to save the mother's life abortion is not justified.

There are four questions fundamental to the abortion debate that I hope to answer in these chapters: Do the popular arguments really support abortion as a fundamental *right* (chaps. 4 and 5)? Is there any decisive moment in the unborn's development at which it becomes "fully human" (chap. 6)? Even if the unborn entity is not fully human, is it possible to *still* morally justify most abortions (chap. 7)? Which position (pro-life or abortion rights) is grounded better theologically (chap. 8)?

Chapters 6 and 7 discuss different ways ethicists attempt to answer the second and third questions and how they often reach positions on abortion other than the two polarized positions that are most familiar (pro-life and abortion rights). And when we discuss the fourth question in chapter 8, the reader will no doubt be surprised that both the pro-life position and the abortion-rights position are defended by some as consistent with the Hebrew-Christian Scriptures.

Part 3 is a brief section in which I make a few concluding remarks. In chapter 9 I will sum up my case for the pro-life position by briefly reviewing the conclusions arrived at in the first eight chapters of this work. The epilogue is a fictional dialogue concerning the controversial question of civil disobedience and the abortion issue, a question that has come to the attention of the nation through the group Operation Rescue. The use of dialogue in this chapter, which is a significant departure from the first nine chapters of the book, is intended to help the reader to understand in an entertaining way why I take the stand I do and why certain other pro-lifers take an opposing view.

I have also included seven appendices that I hope will be helpful. Appendix A is a list of all the abortion-rights arguments presented and where one can find responses to them in this book. Appendix B lists strange and unusual quotes by abortion-rights activists concerning such topics as infanticide and the nature of the family, and is preceded by the reason why I included these quotes. Appendix C is a brief dialogue I wrote for the *Las Vegas Review-Journal* in 1988. Appendix D contains another article that originally appeared in the *Las Vegas Review-Journal* in the summer of 1989, written in response to an article by a southern Nevada physician who owns an abortion clinic, Dr. Sol DeLee. Appendix E is a short critique of the abortion-rights movement's use of language in the abortion debate written by Professor Michael Bauman of Hillsdale College. Appendix F is a list of pro-life organizations the reader may want to contact for more information or involvement. Appendix G is an abridged version of the 1992 *Casey* decision.

I should also say what I am *not* going to do in this book. First, I will *not* argue for the pro-life position by appealing to theological reasoning. The main thrust of this work is philosophical. Hence, if my arguments are sound, an atheist, agnostic, or humanist is intellectually obligated to become pro-life. Although I do address theological arguments for abortion rights in chapter 8, my arguments in that chapter stand apart from the rest of the book. The purpose of chapter 8 is to address the specific concerns of Christians and Jews who are confused about their traditions' view on abortion. In other words, one could completely ignore chapter 8 without missing any aspect of my philosophical case for the pro-life position. It should be mentioned, as well, that the stereotyping of the pro-life position as a "religious view" will be discussed in chapter 5.

Second, I will not critically analyze the Supreme Court's decisions on abortion, although I will on occasion criticize arguments employed by particular justices when these arguments are relevant to the issues we are discussing in this book. Since legal scholarship, both pro-life and pro-choice, has been quite harsh in its criticism of the Court's decisions, especially from a historical point of view, I refer the reader to these important works.[6] I critique the Court's legal reasoning in chapter 2 of *Matters of Life and Death*.

Third, I will avoid the exclusive use of statistics either to establish or to discount my opponents' ethical arguments, since I believe that the use of statistics is valuable only *after* one's ethical position is already established. For example, abortion-rights advocates frequently cite the number of women who died due to illegal abortions prior to *Roe v. Wade* as evidence for the ethical legitimacy of abortion rights. But since the pro-life advocate believes that legal abortions have resulted in a far greater number of unjustified homicides than *illegal* ones, she finds this abortion-rights argument to be extremely unpersuasive. Now of course, if the unborn are *not* fully human, the abortion-rights advocate makes an excellent point, a point that any truly moral person must seriously consider (an argument dealt with in greater detail in chap. 4).

Pro-life advocates also misuse statistics. In response to the abortion-rights argument that abortion is justified because there are too many unwanted children, the pro-life advocate will often cite statistics that support the fact that there are a great number of childless couples seeking children for adoption.[7] There are several problems with this pro-life response. First, why should this point even matter? If there were no such couples, would abortion ipso facto become morally correct? If the unborn have an inherent right to life, a principle that is the foundation of the pro-life position, why should the absence or presence of a couple who wants a child make a difference? Second, a sophisticated abortion-rights advocate would remain unconvinced, since according to his position a woman has a right to an abortion but has no obligation to make sure other people can adopt children. Why should the abortion-rights advocate accept pro life assumptions? And third, it follows from these two points that the pro-life advocate's appeal to adoption puts him in the odd position of appearing to support the abortion-rights assumption that only if the unborn are wanted do they have a right to life. This is a fatal concession for the pro-life cause. Although there may be a social good in advocating adoption, just as there is a social good in advocating charity, the adoption option has little to do with the morality of abortion per se if one accepts from the outset either the pro-life position ("the unborn have an inherent right to life") or the abortion-rights position ("the unborn do not have an inherent right to life"). Hence, statistics are not rationally persuasive unless one first establishes the moral framework in which they are to be employed.

This is not to say that statistics are never important. For instance, some defenders of abortion rights argue that a first-trimester abortion is morally justified, even if the unborn has a full right to life, because childbirth is *statistically* more risky than a first-trimester abortion and it is immoral to ask anyone to risk her life for another against her will.[8] When I discuss this argument in chapter 7 I will point out, among other things, that it is doubtful whether a first-trimester abortion is safer than childbirth, but even if it were, the lack of significant risk in ordinary childbearing makes this argument's use of statistics entirely moot. I will on occasion cite

statistics and critique their use, but I will do so only to confirm or disconfirm a factual claim (not a value claim) that may be helpful in evaluating the application of certain moral values, as in the argument from maternal risk.

Fourth, I will not sidestep either the sophisticated arguments of professional ethicists and philosophers or the arguments that dominate popular moral rhetoric. Concerning the former, it is too often the case that many defenders of the pro-life position concern themselves only with the rhetoric of popular moral debate. Although obviously important for one's success in the political arena, this approach ignores the highly sophisticated defenses and rebuttals of the abortion-rights position by ethicists and philosophers on all sides of the debate. It is my contention that in order to achieve true political success and to influence one's culture in the long run, one must present intellectually convincing arguments that may not be fully understood by everyone, but will be taken seriously by the legal, medical, and philosophical communities. Since it is inevitable that the ideas that are prevalent in these communities will trickle down to the masses, as evidenced by the apparent success of the intelligentsia-supported abortion-rights movement,[9] it is no exaggeration to claim that to influence the legal, medical, and philosophical communities is to influence the world.

On the other hand, philosophers and ethicists, with few exceptions,[10] have not involved themselves with the popular abortion debate, although there seems to be widespread agreement by many abortion-rights philosophers that the popular arguments for their position are extremely weak.[11] For this reason, it is rare to find a full-blown serious and sophisticated critique of the popular arguments by an ethicist or philosopher. In chapters 3 through 8 of this book I will deal with both the popular arguments and the ones put forth by philosophers and ethicists. Hence, this book is intended to provide a defense of the pro-life position that will address both the concerns of scholars and the rhetoric that predominates the popular debate.

Finally, I will *not* propose a grandiose social policy as a possible solution to the problems that abortion is often used to "solve," for example, unwanted teenage pregnancy or poor women who can't afford more children. For I believe that the question of whether or not abortion is immoral is entirely independent of whether or not one can solve the problems for which abortion is ordinarily employed to eliminate (although recent studies have shown that abortion does not solve these problems and may even precipitate them[12]). This observation, however, is not often appreciated by abortion-rights activists. For example, when confronted with pro-life arguments that are put forth to show abortion's immoral status, abortion-rights advocates often respond: "If the pregnant woman cannot have an abortion, are you going to take care of the child after it is born?" This bit of rhetoric can be distilled into the following assertion: unless the pro-lifer is willing to help bring up the children he does not want aborted, he has no right to prevent a woman from having an abortion. As a principle of moral action, this seems to be a rather bizarre assertion. Think of all the unusual precepts that would result: unless I am willing to marry my neighbor's wife, I cannot prevent her husband from beating her; unless I am willing to adopt my neighbor's daughter, I cannot prevent her mother from abusing her; unless I am willing to hire ex-slaves for my business, I cannot say that the slave owner should not own slaves. By illegitimately shifting the discussion from the morality of abortion to whether one has a "solution" to certain social problems, the abortion-rights advocate avoids the point under question. Although a clever move, it has nothing to do with whether or not abortion results in the death of human beings who have a full right to life or whether or not abortion is immoral. As we shall see in chapters 4 and 5, when I evaluate this argument and similar ones, there is a fundamental difference between "eliminating a problem" and "finding a solution."

Moral Reasoning and Abortion Law

Part 1

The Possibility of Moral Reasoning

We are all faced throughout our lives with agonizing decisions—moral choices. Some are on a grand scale; most of these choices are on lesser points. But we define ourselves by the choices we have made. We are, in fact, the sum total of our choices.
  Professor Louis Levy, a character in Woody Allen's *Crimes and Misdemeanors* (1989)

We have been trying, like Lear, to have it both ways: to lay down our human perogative and yet at the same time retain it. It is impossible. Either we are rational spirit obliged for ever to obey the absolute value of the Tao [i.e., natural law], or else we are mere nature to be kneaded and cut into new shapes for the pleasures of masters who must, by hypothesis, have no motive but their own 'natural' impulses. Only the Tao provides a common human law of action which can overarch rulers and ruled alike. A dogmatic belief in objective values is necessary to the very idea of a rule which is not tyranny or an obedience which is not slavery.
  C. S. Lewis (1947)

In addition to the abortion controversy, other ethical, moral, and social issues are taking over the headlines of our major newspapers and the front covers of our leading magazines. Take the following issues as examples. Is animal experimentation justified and should animals have rights in the same moral sense that humans do under the Constitution? In light of the recent financial scandals involving PTL and the subsequent conviction of Jim Bakker, should the government monitor the monetary practices of television evangelists, or would such a monitoring constitute a violation of the separation of church and state? Should school boards have the right to ban certain books from school curricula and school libraries, or is such an activity a violation of the First-Amendment right of freedom of expression? Does the Constitution protect "the right to die"? Is surrogate motherhood ever ethically justified?

The purpose of this chapter is to point out why I believe that, as thoughtful Americans, we have a difficult time rationally discussing such issues, including the abortion issue. I will limit my discussion to four areas. First, I will discuss the problem of moral relativism, a problem I believe impedes our ability as a people to critically and rationally discuss issues of great moral and ethical importance. Second, I will discuss the nature of argumentation and how it is possible to argue for a particular moral position. Third, if moral relativism is false, how do we reconcile values when two or more of them apparently conflict with each other? And fourth, I will point out that the pro-life and abortion-rights movements hold a number of values in common, and that the differences between these two movements are not in their values but in disagreements over both the application of these values and the truth of certain facts.

It is unfortunate that we have assumed rationality and logic have no place in evaluating moral questions and that there is no way such questions can be answered. We believe that we are simply stuck with our opinions, and all opinions are relative and have no basis in any absolute or unchanging moral values. I know that this is a rather harsh indictment, but as we shall see in our analysis of some of the popular abortion-rights arguments, most moral rhetoric in America is not very thoughtful or tough-minded. So often persuaded by image and not taking the time to investigate substance, we tend to fall for such rhetorical devices as gory pictures, stick-whipped orangutans, cats with wires in their heads, and radical leftists burning flags, rather than critical argumentation. A long time ago Plato warned us that appearance is not reality. It is time we heed Plato's timeless warning.

Moral Relativism

In his important and influential work, *The Closing of the American Mind*, Allan Bloom observes that "there is one thing a professor can be absolutely certain of: almost every student entering the university believes, or says he believes, that truth is relative. . . . The students, of course, cannot defend their opinion. It is something with which they have been indoctrinated."[1] By dogmatically asserting that there is no truth, we have become closed-minded to the possibility of knowing the truth if in fact it does exist. Consequently, lurking behind most of the moral rhetoric in America today is moral relativism, the belief that there are no mind-independent moral values that transcend culture or the individual. This is why many people begin or end their moral judgments with such phrases as, "It is only my personal opinion," "Of course I am not judging anyone's behavior," or "If you think it is all right, that is okay, but I'm personally against it." Although such assertions certainly have their place, we often use them inappropriately. Take a common ploy used by politicians who are absolutely petrified to take a stand on the abortion issue. They often resort to saying, "I'm personally against abortion, but I don't object if a woman believes it is right for her to have one." The problem with this assertion is that it doesn't tell us why the politician is personally against abortion. Since most people oppose abortion because they believe that the unborn are fully human and have all the rights that go along with such a status, my guess is that the politician is personally against abortion for the same reason. Now this makes the politician's personal opposition and public permission of abortion somewhat perplexing, since the reason he is probably personally against abortion is the reason why he should be against publicly permitting it, namely, that an entity which he believes is fully human has a right to life. After all, what would we think of the depth of the convictions of an individual who claimed that he was personally against the genocide of a particular race, but if others thought this race was not human they were certainly welcome to participate in the genocide if they so choose? The nature of some "personal" opinions warrant public actions, even if these opinions turn out to be wrong, while other opinions, such as one's personal preference for German chocolate cake, do not.

Another example of how ethical relativism affects the way we approach a public moral issue can be seen in the arguments concerning the rights of certain groups to boycott products that are advertised on television programs that these groups find to be inconsistent with the public good. The usual argument in response to these groups is the following, "If you don't like a particular program, you don't have to watch it. You can always change the channel." But is this response really compelling? After all, these groups are not only saying that they personally find these programs offensive; rather, they are arguing that the programs themselves convey messages and create a moral climate that will affect others, especially children, in a way they believe is adverse to the public good. Hence, what bothers these groups is that *you* and *your children* will not change the channel. Furthermore, it bothers these people that there is probably somewhere in America, an unsupervised ten-year-old listening to and watching MTV while Aerosmith sings about the virtues of oral sex on an elevator. Most of these people fear that their ten year-olds may have to socially interact someday with the unsupervised MTV-watching ten-year-old. Frankly, I do not believe that such a parental concern is totally unjustified, especially in light of what we know about how certain forms of entertainment and media affect people. Therefore, the question cannot be relegated to a question of one's personal preference. The appropriate question is what sort of social action is permissible and would best serve the public good.

As long as these groups do not advocate state censorship, but merely apply social and economic pressure to private corporations (which civil rights groups and feminist groups have been doing for nearly two decades), a balance of freedoms is achieved. Both are free to pursue their interests within the confines of constitutional protection, although both must be willing to suffer the social and economic consequences of their actions. This seems to best serve the public good. Notice that my response does not resort to ethical relativism, but takes seriously the values of freedom, the public good, and individual rights, and attempts to uphold these values in a way that is consistent and fair.

Arguments for Moral Relativism

People have put forth two popular arguments to defend ethical relativism. Argument 1 states: Since cultures and individuals differ in certain moral practices, there are no objective transcultural values.

There are several problems with this argument. First, the fact that people disagree about something does not mean that there is no truth. For example, if you and I disagree as to whether or not the earth is round, this is certainly not proof that the earth has no shape. In moral discussion, the fact that a skinhead (a type of young neo-Nazi) and I may disagree as to whether we should treat people equally and with fairness is certainly not sufficient evidence to say that equality and fairness have no objective value. Even if individuals and cultures hold no values in common, it does not follow from this that nobody is right or wrong about the correct values. That is, there could be a mistaken individual or culture, such as Adolf Hitler and Nazi Germany.

Another problem with this first argument is that though cultures and individuals differ in moral practices it does not follow that they do not share common values. For example, the fact that female islanders who live in the South Seas bare their breasts and British women do not does not mean that the former do not value modesty. Due to the climate, environmental conditions, and certain religious beliefs, the people of the South Seas have developed certain practices that manifest the transcultural value of modesty. Although cultures may differ as to how they manifest such values as honesty, courage, or preservation of life, none promote dishonesty, cowardice, or arbitrary killing.

Second, sometimes apparent moral differences are not moral differences at all but factual differences. During the Salem witch trials, certain individuals were put to death who were believed to be practicing witchcraft. We don't execute witches today, but not because our moral values have changed. We don't execute witches today because we don't believe that the practice of their craft has a fatal effect upon the community—contrary to what the residents of Massachusetts believed in the seventeenth-century. But suppose that we had good evidence that the practice of witchcraft does affect other people in the same way that cigarette smoke affects the nonsmoker. We would alter the practice of our values to take into consideration this factual change. We may set up non-witch sections in restaurants and ban the casting of spells on interstate airplane flights. The upshot of all this is that the good of the community is a value we share with the seventeenth-century residents of Salem, but we simply believe that they were factually wrong about the effect of witches upon that good.

Consider a second example. Many people who live in India do not eat cows, because they believe in the doctrine of reincarnation—that these cows possess the souls of deceased human beings. In the United States we do not believe that cows have human souls. For this reason, we eat cows but we do not eat Grandma. It appears on the surface, therefore, that there is a fundamental value difference between Indians and Americans. But this is a hasty conclusion, for both cultures do believe that it is wrong to eat Grandma; the Indians, however, believe that the cow may be Grandma. Thus it is a factual, not a value, difference that divides our culinary habits.

Philosopher James Rachels presents another example of how the knowledge of certain facts can help us understand why it seems that other people have different values.[2] He points out that the practice of infanticide (of primarily female babies) was common among the Eskimos. On the surface, this Eskimo practice seems to indicate that they have a radically different value of human life than we do. And since one's view of human life is fundamental, it seems to follow from this that ethical relativism is correct. Rachels does not agree. He explains that once one realizes that certain factual considerations have made the practice of infanticide a necessary evil for the Eskimos, one sees that the Eskimos' value of human life is not all that different from ours. Writes Rachels:

But suppose we ask *why* the Eskimos [practice infanticide]. The explanation is not that they have less affection for their children or less respect for human life. An Eskimo family will always protect its babies if conditions permit. But they live in a harsh environment, where food is often in short supply. . . . Infant girls are readily disposed of because, first, in this society the males are the primary food providers—they are the hunters, according to the traditional division of labor—and it is obviously important to maintain a sufficient number of food gatherers. But there is an important second reason as well. Because the hunters suffer a high casualty rate, the adult men who die prematurely far outnumber the adult women who die early. Thus if male and female infants survived in equal numbers, the female adult population would greatly outnumber the male adult population. Examining the available statistics, one writer concluded that "were it not for female infanticide . . . there would be approximately one-and-a-half times as many females in the average Eskimo local group as there are food-producing males."

So among the Eskimos, infanticide does not signal a fundamentally different attitude toward children. Instead, it is a recognition that drastic measures are sometimes needed to ensure the family's survival. Even then, however, killing the baby is not the first option considered. Adoption is common; childless couples are especially happy to take a more fertile couple's "surplus." Killing is only the last resort. I emphasize this in order to show that the raw data of the anthropologists can be misleading; it can make the differences in values between cultures appear greater than they are. The Eskimos' values are not all that different from our values. It is only that life forces upon them choices that we do not have to make.[3]

This is not to say that the Eskimos are right or that we should not try to persuade them to believe that their practice is wrong. Rather, this example simply shows that one can better understand so-called value differences, and conclude that they are not really value differences at all, when one carefully examines why a certain practice, such as female infanticide, is performed. Other examples can be produced to show why this first argument for moral relativism is inadequate,[4] although I believe that what we have covered thus far is sufficient for our purposes. It should be noted, however, that there are some common values among peoples and cultures does not mean that all cultures share all the same values. It is obvious that certain peoples and cultures may have developed some values that others have not developed. Hence, the discovering of a unique value in a particular society does not in any way take away from my central thesis that there are certain values to which all societies either implicitly or explicitly hold.

Third, the argument from differing practices puts an undue emphasis on differences while ignoring similarities, in addition to giving the mistaken appearance that all moral conflicts are in some sense insoluble. In discussing moral conflicts in the United States we tend to focus our attention on contemporary issues, such as abortion, euthanasia, and affirmative action, over which there is obviously wide and impassioned disagreement. However, we tend to ignore the fact that the disputants in these moral debates hold a number of values in common, that there are a great number of moral issues on which almost all Americans agree (e.g., "it is wrong to molest six-year-old girls"), and that a number of past moral conflicts have been solved (e.g., slavery, women's suffrage). Hence, by focusing our attention on disagreements, our perception is skewed. Rachels points out how such a mistaken focus can also be applied to other disciplines:

> If we think of questions like *this* [i.e., abortion, euthanasia, affirmative action], it is easy to believe that "proof" in ethics is impossible. The same can be said of the sciences. There are many complicated matters that physicists cannot agree on; and if we focused our attention entirely on *them* we might conclude that there is no "proof" in physics. But of course, many simpler matters in physics *can* be proven, and about those all competent physicists agree. Similarly, in ethics there are many matters far simpler than abortion, about which all reasonable people must agree.[5]

Argument 2 states: Since ethical relativism promotes tolerance of certain cultural practices that we, as members of Western civilization, may think are strange, ethical relativism is a good thing. There are several problems with this argument. First, the value of tolerance presupposes the existence of at least one real nonrelative, objective value: tolerance. Bioethicist Tom Beauchamp observes:

> If we interpret normative relativism as *requiring* tolerance of other views, the whole theory is imperiled by inconsistency. The proposition that we ought to tolerate the views of others, or that it is right not to interfere with others, is precluded by the very strictures of the theory. Such a proposition bears all the marks of a *non-relative* account of moral rightness, one based on, but not reducible to, the cross-cultural findings of anthropologists. . . . But if this moral principle [of tolerance] is recognized as valid, it can of course be employed as an instrument for criticizing such cultural practices as the denial of human rights to minorities and such beliefs as that of racial superiority. A moral commitment to tolerance of other practices and beliefs thus leads inexorably to the abandonment of normative relativism.[6]

Second, tolerance can be a virtue only if you think the other person, whose viewpoint you're supposed to tolerate, is mistaken. That is to say, if you do not believe that one viewpoint is better than another, then to ask someone to be tolerant of other viewpoints makes no sense, since to tolerate another's viewpoint implies this other person has a right to his viewpoint despite the fact that others may think that it is wrong. To be tolerant of differing viewpoints involves just that—*differing viewpoints*, all of which cannot be equally correct at the same time (although they certainly may all be equally wrong at the same time). If one thinks that one can be tolerant while at the same time believe that nobody is either right or wrong about any moral value, one would be no more virtuous than the man who thought his chastity was virtuous even though he was born with no sexual organs. Consequently, real tolerance

23

presupposes that someone is right and someone is wrong (and in the latter case, especially the person who is intolerant), a viewpoint that implicitly denies moral relativism.

It must be acknowledged, however, that there is a noble motive behind the relativist's appeal to tolerance. He believes that his view of tolerance will help us to better understand other cultures and other people without being hypercritical about their practices or forcibly imposing our own cultural practices upon them, such as putting blouses on the bare-breasted women of the South Seas or forcing polygamous families to divide and become monogamous. I do not disagree with this view of transcultural tolerance. However, a cultural practice is different from a cultural value. For it does not follow from different practices that people have different values.

The same goes for popular moral debate in the United States today. For example, both those who favor capital punishment and those who oppose it agree that human life is in some sense sacred. Where they disagree is in the application of this value. Most proponents of capital punishment argue that since human life is so sacred, an individual who takes another's innocent life should forfeit his own life. Arguing from the same value, most opponents of capital punishment claim that it should be forbidden, since the sacredness of human life makes it never justifiable for the state to execute a human being.

The local controversies surrounding the elimination of certain books from public school curricula and libraries is another example of how people can agree on values and yet disagree on practice. Those who favor conservative guidelines, and who are often referred to as advocating censorship, usually propose that certain materials are not suitable for certain age groups. They argue that parents, not educational administrators, are best suited to know what is best for their children. On the other hand, their opponents, who are often referred to as advocating freedom of expression, usually propose that teachers and educational administrators should choose what is suitable material, although they do believe that a line should be

drawn somewhere. For example, none of these defenders of freedom of expression defend the placing of hardcore pornography in the hands of fourth graders. This, of course, makes the debate all the more interesting, since it means that both sides agree on the following general principles: a line must be drawn, certain materials are suitable for certain age groups, and education is important and valuable. Where they disagree is on who should make the decisions surrounding these issues. Both advocate some kind of censorship. They just disagree on who should be the censors and what should be censored. Therefore, they both hold to the same values, but they disagree as to the application of these values.

Although this distinction between practice and value helps us to be tolerant of unusual cultural practices, we are still able to make valuable moral judgments about others and ourselves. First, we are free to criticize those intolerable cultural practices that do conflict with basic human values, such as in the cases of genocide in Nazi Germany and apartheid in South Africa. Second, we are able to admit to real moral progress, such as in the case of the abolition of slavery. And third, there can exist real moral reformers, such as Martin Luther King, Jr., and the prophets of the Old Testament, who served as prophetic voices to reprimand their cultures for having drifted far from a true moral practice based on basic human values. These three points that follow from a belief in transcultural values do not follow from a belief in ethical relativism. That is to say, in order to remain consistent the ethical relativist cannot criticize intolerable moral practices, believe in real moral progress, or acknowledge the existence of real moral reformers. For these three forms of moral judgment presuppose the existence of real transcultural nonrelative objective values.

Although much more can be said about the justification and existence of certain values,[7] what we have covered thus far is sufficient to show that ethical relativism is enormously problematic and that we can rationally discuss and argue with each other about right and wrong without resorting to the claim that ethical judgments are merely subjective or relative and that all such judgments have equal validity. For to claim the latter logically leads one to the judgment that Mother Teresa is no more and no less virtuous than Adolf Hitler. I believe that this example is sufficient to show ethical relativism to be bankrupt.

What Happens When Values Conflict?[8]

Some people argue that because so-called objective values sometimes conflict, this disproves that such values actually exist. The problem with this argument is that it assumes that all objective moral values are of equal value. But they are not. For example, the value of preserving life is a higher value than that of telling the truth, and if these values conflict, one should perform the moral act that is consistent with the higher value. Consider the following story.

Suppose that you are a German non-Jew in Nazi Germany and you are hiding Jewish people in your home. If these Jews are found by the Nazis, they will most likely be cruelly tortured and executed in a concentration camp. Two Gestapo agents come to your door and ask whether you are hiding anybody or if you know of anybody who is hiding Jewish people. What do you say? If you tell the truth, then you are fulfilling the moral requirement of truth-telling, but you are violating the moral value of preserving life, for the people you are hiding will probably be murdered. If you don't tell the truth, you are fulfilling the moral requirement of preserving life, but you are violating the moral value of truth-telling. This seems to be quite a dilemma. I believe, however, that this dilemma is soluble, since the moral value of preserving life is a higher value than truth-telling, and when two values conflict with each other one should act in a way consistent with the higher value. Therefore, if the Gestapo comes to your door and asks whether you are hiding Jews, you should not tell them the truth. I am not saying that this is an *exception* to the requirement of truth-telling, but rather, that one is *exempted* from the obligation of truth-telling

since one has a *greater* obligation to preserve life.

One can easily see how such moral deliberation can apply to the abortion issue. Suppose that a woman is two weeks pregnant and if she continues with the pregnancy there is little doubt that she will die. The pro-life advocate must deal with two values that seem to conflict: the unborn's right to life and the mother's right to life. For if the woman is forced to carry her child, she will die, but if she does have an abortion, her unborn offspring will die. The way out of this problem is to consider which action will produce the highest good. If the pregnant woman does not have the abortion, then it is likely that both she and her unborn child will die, since the unborn's life is solely dependent upon his mother for about the first twenty-four weeks of pregnancy. But if she does have the abortion, then the unborn entity will die but the mother will live. Hence, it is clear that the second course of action, to have the abortion in order to save the life of the mother, is the highest good one can perform in such a difficult situation.

Morality and Some Basic Rules of Argumentation[9]

At this juncture it is important that we go over some basic rules of argumentation and see how one can apply them to moral debate. An argument is made up of two parts, a premise and a conclusion. In the following argument, 1 is the premise and 2 is the conclusion:

A
1. John is a bachelor.
2. Therefore, John is not married.

The premise serves as the reason why the conclusion is true. When an argument is valid, such as A, the conclusion must be true assuming the premises are true. Another way of putting it is to say that the conclusion follows from the premises. That is, you cannot imagine the conclusion being false if you suppose that the reasons are true. The following is another example of a valid argument:

B
1. All men love football.
2. Bill Clinton is a man.
3. Therefore, Bill Clinton loves football.

The premises in this argument are 1 and 2. And since this argument is valid, assuming its premises are true, the conclusion must be true. But there is something wrong with B, namely, premise 1. It is not true that all men love football. Some men haven't even heard of football. But since premise 1 is not true, argument B is unsound. So even though B is valid it is unsound because one of its premises is false. Another type of argument is one which is invalid, such as C:

C
1. Mary is not home.
2. John is not home.
3. Therefore, John and Mary are out together.

Assuming that premises 1 and 2 are true, the conclusion does not follow. For it is possible that Mary and John are both not home and that they are not out together. That is, one can easily imagine both premises being true and the conclusion being false. So an invalid argument is one in which the conclusion does not follow from the premises even if the premises are true. An invalid argument is automatically unsound.

Of course, an ideal argument is one which is both sound and valid (sound arguments are automatically valid), such as D:

D
1. All bachelors are unmarried men.
2. Arsenio Hall is a bachelor.
3. Therefore, Arsenio Hall is unmarried.

This argument is valid, for if both premises are true, the conclusion cannot be false. But since both premises are in fact true, this argument is also sound. In sum, there are three different basic types of arguments, the first of which is the correct form of argumentation:

1. a sound argument—an argument that is valid and has true reasons (e.g., A, D).
2. an unsound/valid argument—an argument that is valid but at least one of its reasons is false (e.g., B).

3. an unsound/invalid argument—an argument in which the conclusion does not follow from the premises even if the premises are true (e.g., C).

Now how does this apply to moral argumentation? Suppose someone who is anti-capital punishment presents the following argument:

E
1. 50 percent of all convicts on death row were unjustly convicted.
2. It is unjust to execute people who were unjustly convicted.
3. Therefore, to execute these convicts would be unjust.

This argument is valid; that is, the conclusion follows from the premises. However, the first premise can be challenged. For it does not seem true that 50 percent of all convicts were unjustly convicted. And if it were true, why are they all still on death row? Wouldn't the state release them upon hearing the evidence of injustice? Furthermore, even if it is admitted that some people have been unjustly convicted, it seems incredible that this number includes 50 percent of those on death row. Hence, argument E is a bad argument, for although valid it is unsound. The following is another example of a moral argument:

F
1. Adolf Hitler is responsible for killing six million innocent Jewish people, many of whom were women and children.
2. All things being equal, one is immoral if one kills innocent people.
3. Therefore, Adolf Hitler was an immoral person.

This argument is both valid and sound. Concerning its validity, there does not seem to be any way that both premises can be true and the conclusion false. As to the truth of the premises, 1 and 2 seem indisputable. Premise 1 has been historically established and premise 2 is a well-founded moral intuition[10] in the same way that my belief that there exists a world outside my mind is a well-founded sensory intuition. Argument F is sound since it is valid and its premises are true.

Many of the arguments we will go over in this book cannot be easily put in this outline form. Furthermore, not every premise in every argument is either absolutely true or absolutely false. Some premises may be more likely true than not or more likely false than not or somewhere in between. In addition, not every argument is either absolutely valid or absolutely invalid. Some arguments have a higher degree of validity than others, but are still not absolutely valid (these are often called inductive arguments). Yet despite these nuances, the arguments we will cover in this book can still be critically analyzed by examining whether the premises are true or highly probable and whether the arguments are valid or have a high degree of validity (or as some logicians say, inductive strength). Sometimes an argument's invalidity or unsoundness can be exposed by showing that it commits a logical fallacy (a fallacy is a type of mistake in reasoning). You will learn some of these fallacies when we critique some abortion-rights arguments. In any event, this brief lesson in logic shows that one can reason about moral topics and that one must follow some basic logical rules in order to reason correctly.

Some Common Values in the Abortion Debate

Even if one is not convinced that there exist transcultural and transpersonal values and believes that some sort of relativism is correct, one cannot deny that at least in our culture both sides of the abortion debate have a great deal more in common than meets the eye. In fact, the differences between the two positions lie not in their values but in certain factual disputes and the application of these common values.

First, both sides of the abortion debate believe that all human persons possess certain inalienable rights regardless of whether their governments protect these rights. That is why both sides appeal to what each believes is a fundamental right. The pro-life advocate appeals to "life." The abortion-rights advocate appeals to "liberty."

Second, each side of the abortion debate believes that its position best exemplifies its opponent's fundamental value. The abortion-rights advocate does not deny that "life" is a value, but argues that his position's appeal to human liberty is the necessary ingredient by which an individual can pursue the fullest and most complete life possible. Furthermore, most sophisticated abortion-rights advocates argue that the unborn are not fully human. And for this reason, they do not have a right to life if their life hinders the liberty of a person who is fully human (i.e., their mother). Others, such as Judith Jarvis Thomson,[11] argue that even if the unborn entity is fully human, it has no right to use the body of another against that person's will, since such a usage of another's body demands of that person great risk and sacrifice, one that goes beyond any ordinary moral obligation. Hence, since a pregnant woman is not morally obligated to put herself at great risk and to make a significant sacrifice for another, she is morally justified in removing her unborn offspring even if such a removal results in its death. (See chaps. 6 and 7 for responses to these views.)

On the other hand, the pro-life advocate does not eschew "liberty." He believes that all human liberty is limited by another human person's right to life. For example, I have a right to freely pursue any goal I believe is consistent with my happiness, such as attending a UNLV basketball game. However, I have no right to freely pursue this goal at the expense of another's life or liberty, such as running over pedestrians with my car so that I can get to the game on time. And of course, the pro-life advocate argues that the unborn are fully human and have a full right to life. And since the act of abortion typically results in the death of the unborn, abortion, unless the mother's life is in danger (since it is better that one human should live rather than two die), is not morally justified.

It is apparent then that the main dispute in the abortion debate does not involve differing values, but disagreement about both the application of these values and the truth of certain facts. The abortion-rights advocate does not deny that human beings have a fundamental right to life. He just believes that this right to life is not extended to the unborn since they are not fully human and/or their existence demands that another (the pregnant woman) is asked to make significant non-obligatory sacrifices. The pro-life advocate does not deny that human persons have the liberty to make choices that they believe are in their best interests. He believes that this liberty does not entail the right to choose abortion since such a choice conflicts with the life, liberty, and interests of another human person (the unborn entity).

In summary, since there is a common ground between two moral positions that are often depicted as absolutely polarized, we can coherently reason and argue about this issue. And since there is a common ground of values, the question as to which position is correct rests on which one is best established by the facts and is consistent with our common values.

Why Abortion on Demand Is Legal in America

The care of human life and happiness, and not their destruction, is the first and only legitimate object of good government.
Thomas Jefferson

In the 1973 cases [Roe v. Wade and Doe v. Bolton], Justice Douglas agreed that the unborn has no right to live. Yet, in 1972, in the case of Sierra Club against Morton (405 U.S. 727 - 1972), Justice Douglas argued that the Sierra Club had a sufficient interest to contest in Federal court the building of the Mineral King Recreational Development in California, because the Sierra Club should be allowed to assert the right to sue of the inanimate objects and wildlife in the Mineral King area. Justice Douglas conferred legal rights on, and I quote his opinion, "valleys, alpine meadows, rivers, lakes, estuaries, beaches, ridges, groves of trees, swampland or even air that feels the destructive pressures of modern technology and modern life." (405 U.S. at 743) The inanimate objects were argued by Justice Douglas to have the right to speak on behalf of wildlife such as, and I quote him again, "the pileated woodpecker as well as the coyote and bear, the lemmings as well as the trout in the streams." (405 U.S. at 752) And I quote Justice Douglas, "The voice of the inanimate object, therefore," he said, "should not be stilled." (405 U.S. at 749).

But the voice of the unborn child, according to Justice Douglas, may be stilled any time his mother so desires. So swamps and trees have rights, but the human child in the womb has no rights.

Dr. Charles Rice, professor of law, Notre Dame University (1974)

In order to fully grasp the nature of abortion law in the United States, it is important to look at at least four different but interrelated topics: the political problem and the public's perception of abortion law; the legality of sex-selection abortions; what the law really says about abortion on demand; and the effect of *Webster v. Reproductive Health Services* (1989) and *Planned Parenthood v. Casey* (1992) on that law.

The Political Problem and the Public's Perception of Abortion Law

There seems to be a widespread perception that the Supreme Court decisions, *Roe v. Wade* (1973) and *Doe v. Bolton* (1973), were moderate decisions that do not support abortion on demand, meaning the right to an unrestricted abortion for all nine months for virtually any reason the woman deems fit. One false claim that I often hear is that the Supreme Court permitted abortions only up to twenty-four weeks and after that time only to save the life of the mother. Another typical false claim was recently broadcasted in a news story on KNUU 970 AM radio in southern Nevada (October 16, 1990). The story asserted that abortions are legal only in the "early stages of pregnancy." Even a philosopher of such erudition as Mortimer Adler does not seem to fully understand the legal implications of *Roe* and *Bolton*: "Mr. Justice Blackmun's decision in the case of *Roe v. Wade* invokes the right to privacy, which is *nothing but the freedom of an adult woman to do as she pleases with her own body in the first trimester of pregnancy*"(emphasis added).[1]

In the 1990 pro-life campaign in Nevada to defeat an abortion-rights referendum, KLAS-TV, a CBS affiliate, refused to air a commercial that featured former UNLV basketball star (and son of its former coach, Jerry Tarkanian) Danny Tarkanian. In the commercial, Danny, a practicing attorney, claimed that current Nevada law permits abortions for all nine months of pregnancy for reasons as trivial as sex-selection (i.e., a woman having an abortion because the child is the "wrong" gender). KLAS management claimed that Tarkanian's comments were "inflammatory" and "untrue," despite the fact that his claims are well-documented and supported by the scholarly literature. The station did air, however, an abortion-rights commercial in which a "typical" housewife says she supports abortion rights in order to keep the abortion decision between "the woman, her physician, and her family." It never occurred to KLAS that this commercial is inflammatory and untrue, especially in light of two well-known legal facts: 1) a woman can have an abortion performed on her by a physician she has known for less than thirty seconds, and 2) her family has no legal right to forbid, permit, or be informed about her abortion (the Supreme Court has consistently struck down state statutes that have required

involvement by other family members in the abortion decision of an adult female; see, for example, *Planned Parenthood of Missouri v. Danforth*, 428 U.S. 52 [1976]).

In a letter I hand-delivered to KLAS for station manager Richard Fraim (3 November 1990) I pointed out and documented these two well-known legal facts. I also included most of what is in this chapter concerning the legality of abortion on demand. As of the publication of this book, I have yet to receive a response from Mr. Fraim. Since I have published widely in this area in scholarly publications (see the bibliography) and teach ethics and contemporary moral issues at the city's only university, you would think that Mr. Fraim would have taken the time to respond to my letter, or at least to thank me for expressing my concern. He has not.

Do Sex-Selection Abortions Really Occur?

An article in the nonpartisan and highly respected *Hastings Center Report* by Drs. Dorothy C. Wertz and John C. Fletcher[2] clearly shows that sex-selection abortions can and do happen and are legal under *Roe* and *Bolton*, the abortion decisions that are currently in force in most every state in the union. Wertz and Fletcher point out that in a 1985 study, two-thirds of 295 geneticists surveyed would either perform prenatal diagnosis (28 percent) or refer the parents to someone who would (34 percent) even if the parents had clearly said that they would choose to abort if the child were not the desired gender. Some argue "that as long as abortion is available on demand, it should not be denied for specific purposes."[3]

Dr. Laird Jackson, director of Thomas Jefferson University's (Philadelphia) medical genetics division, pointed out in 1987 that about 10 of the 2,500 women who underwent prenatal diagnosis chose abortion solely because the fetus was not the desired gender. Officials at the Michael Reese Medical Center in Chicago and the University of California at San Francisco each claim that about 1 out of 1,000 women who have undergone their testing programs abort for the reason of sex selection. And Baylor University officials at the institution's Houston-based medical school state that 4 out of the 320 women who have undergone CVS procedures (chorionic villus sampling: a method that involves the laboratory analysis of a small sample of placenta tissue and is ordinarily employed to diagnose fetal abnormalities in the first three months of pregnancy) have had abortions solely because their unborn child was not the "correct" gender.[4]

But those who favor abortion rights and yet find sex-selection abortions abhorrent have no legal principle to which to appeal. Since the Supreme Court in *Roe, Bolton,* and *Thornburg v. American College of Obstetricians and Gynecologists* (1986) has allowed abortion on demand for virtually any reason, sex-selection abortions are legal as well as consistent with the abortion-rights moral rhetoric that sees a pregnant woman's right to bodily autonomy as absolute. As Dr. Mitchell Golbus of the University of California at San Francisco points out: "It is very hard to make a moral argument about terminations for sex when you can have abortions for any reason."[5]

According to Dr. Mark Evans, a Wayne State University (Detroit) obstetrician and geneticist, unborn girls are those most often selected to be killed in sex-selection abortions: "Probably 99 percent of nonmedical requests for prenatal diagnosis are made because people want a boy."[6] The media have pointed out that tens of thousands, perhaps hundreds of thousands, of unborn children in some Third World and Asian countries have been executed for only one reason: they were female. In a study cited in *Newsweek,* "out of 8,000 cases of abortion in Bombay, 7,999 involved a female fetus."[7]

Although some in the abortion-rights movement abhor sex-selection abortions (even though such abhorrence is inconsistent with a truly pro-choice ethic), many are willing to not take any legal action against the practice. For example, Barbara Radford, executive director of the National Abortion Federation, comments: "The information about a woman's pregnancy has to be made available to her. We can't legislate what a man or woman will do with medical information

[such as getting a sex-selection abortion]. Physicians with problems with the way a patient will use information they give them should let the patient know so they can go elsewhere."[8] Patricia Brogan, director of community relations for Planned Parenthood of Lancaster County, Pennsylvania, argues: "Individuals need to be given the right—and they have the capacity to act—as their own moral agents. It would be inconsistent to say [referring to sex-selection abortions] that 'this is appropriate' or 'this is inappropriate.'"[9] Dr. Michael A. Roth of Detroit, an obstetrician who performs abortions, has no problem with performing the prenatal diagnosis to determine the unborn's sex as well as the abortion used to kill the unborn if it is not the preferred gender. "I have no ethical problems with it, absolutely not. I think abortion should be available on demand."[10]

Even though there are no national data on the number of women who choose abortion based on sex selection or who receive prenatal diagnoses for that reason, "every one of more than a dozen geneticists interviewed" for a *New York Times* article on the subject "said they regularly receive requests for prenatal diagnosis for sex selection."[11]

What the Law Really Says about Abortion on Demand

The false perceptions about the legality of abortion have been fueled in large part by abortion-rights groups that want to hide their radical agenda from the general public. Unfortunately, these false perceptions have been uncritically accepted by the media. The fact is, however, that the current law in nearly every state does not restrict a woman from getting an abortion during the entire nine months of pregnancy. In order to understand why this is the case, a little history lesson is in order.

In *Roe* Justice Blackmun divided pregnancy into three trimesters. He ruled that aside from normal procedural guidelines (e.g., an abortion must be safely performed by a licensed physician) a state has no right to restrict abortion in the first six months of pregnancy. Thus a woman could have an abortion during the first six months of pregnancy for any reason—unplanned pregnancy, gender-selection, convenience, rape—she deems fit. In the last trimester (after fetal viability, the time at which the fetus can live outside the womb even with technological assistance) the state has a right, although not an obligation, to restrict abortions to only those cases in which the mother's health is jeopardized, since, according to Blackmun, the state may have a legitimate interest in prenatal life. In sum, *Roe* does not prevent a state from allowing unrestricted abortion for the entire nine months of pregnancy.

But since Blackmun said that a state only has an interest in protecting prenatal life after it is viable (which in 1973 was between twenty-four and twenty-eight weeks), and since the viability line is being pushed back in pregnancy (now it is between twenty and twenty-four weeks) because of the increased technological sophistication of incubators and other devices, Justice Sandra Day O'Connor made the comment in her dissent in *Akron v. Akron Center for Reproductive Health, Inc.* that *Roe* is on a "collision course with itself."[12] In other words, if viability is pushed back far enough, the right to abortion will vanish and *Roe* will cease to have any legal weight. That is to say, in principle a state's interest in a viable fetus can extend back to conception. Furthermore, Blackmun's choice of viability as the point at which the state has interest in protecting prenatal life is based on a circular argument (see chap. 6).

But there is a loophole to which abortion-rights supporters can appeal. Consider the following example of a state law written within the framework of *Roe*. Nevada restricts abortion by permitting abortions after the twenty-fourth week of pregnancy only if "there is a substantial risk that the continuance of the pregnancy would endanger the life of the patient or would gravely impair the physical or mental health of the patient."[13] But this restriction is a restriction in name only. For the Supreme Court so broadly defined health in *Roe*'s companion decision, *Doe v. Bolton* (1973), that the current law in nearly every state allows for abortion on demand. In *Bolton* the court ruled that health

must be taken in its broadest possible medical context, and must be defined "in light of all factors—physical, emotional, psychological, familial, and the woman's age—relevant to the well-being of the patient. All these factors relate to health."[14] Since all pregnancies have consequences for a woman's emotional and family situation, the court's health provision has the practical effect of legalizing abortion up until the time of birth if a woman can convince her physician that she needs the abortion to preserve her emotional health. This is why the U.S. Senate Judiciary Committee, after much critical evaluation of the current law in light of the Court's opinions, confirmed this interpretation when it concluded that "no significant legal barriers of any kind whatsoever exist today in the United States for a woman to obtain an abortion for any reason during any stage of her pregnancy."[15]

Even former Chief Justice Warren Burger, who originally sided with the majority in *Roe* because he assumed that abortion after viability would occur only if the mother's physical life and health were in imminent peril, concluded in his dissent in *Thornburg v. American College of Obstetricians and Gynecologists* (1986) that *Roe* did, contrary to his own interpretation of the decision, support abortion on demand: "We have apparently already passed the point at which abortion is available merely on demand. . . . The point at which these [state] interests become 'compelling' under *Roe* is at viability of the fetus. . . . Today, however, the Court abandons that standard and renders the solemnly stated concerns of the 1973 *Roe* opinion for the interests of the States mere shallow rhetoric."[16] A number of legal scholars have come to the same conclusion.

The concept of "health," as defined by the Supreme Court in *Doe v. Bolton*, includes all medical, psychological, social, familial, and economic factors which might potentially inspire a decision to procure an abortion. As such, "health" abortion is indistinguishable from elective abortion. Thus, until a more narrow definition of "health" is obtained, it may not be possible to limit effectively the number of abortions performed.[17] (Victor Rosenblum and Thomas Marzen)

The apparently restrictive standard for the third trimester has in fact proved no different from the standard of abortion on demand expressly allowed during the first six months of the unborn child's life. The exception for maternal health has been so broad in practice as to swallow the rule. The Supreme Court has defined "health" in this context to include "all factors—physical, emotional, familial, and the woman's age—relevant to the well-being of the patient." *Doe v. Bolton*, 410 U.S. 179, 192 (1973). Since there is nothing to stop an abortionist from certifying that a third-trimester abortion is beneficial to the health of the mother—in this broad sense—the Supreme Court's decision has in fact made abortion available on demand throughout the prenatal life of the child, from conception to birth.[18] (U. S. Senate Judiciary Committee)

. . . according to the Court's opinion, not only physical but emotional, psychological, and familial factors, as well as the woman's age, are relevant for diagnostic purposes. So the pressure is very great to perform the abortion she insists on. And remember, too, that "[i]nduced abortions are a source of easy income for doctors." All this adds up to abortion on demand.[19] (Thomas O'Meara)

As it turns out, a state has scant power to proscribe [forbid] the abortion of a viable fetus because of the broad manner in which the Court defines the legitimate dangers to the mother's health, including all factors— "physical, emotional, psychological, familial, and the woman's age—relevant to the well-being of the patient . . ." Thus, although the Court affirmed that "the State may assert interests beyond the protection of the pregnant woman alone," it is indeed difficult to determine what fetal interest is protected since a pregnant woman now has sufficient latitude to obtain a legal abortion for virtually any reason.[20] (Stanley M. Harrison)

Since, under the Court's expansive definition of "health" virtually any maternal interest may be sufficient to overcome the state's compelling interest in preserving prenatal life, it cannot be argued that the Court

considered such life important enough even to be included in the balancing which did take place.[21] (Robert A. Destro)

Under *Roe*, abortion is always permissible when a woman's life or health is at stake. The Court never clearly articulated what it meant by "health," but it is a word which effectively transcends any authority which might have been given to the state to proscribe [that is, forbid] post-viability abortions.[22] (Jacqueline Nolan Haley)

[A]fter viability the mother's life *or health* (which presumably is to be defined very broadly indeed, so as to include what many might regard as the mother's convenience . . .) must, as a matter of constitutional law, take precedence over . . . the fetus' *life*.[23] (John Hart Ely)

Abortion-on-demand after the first six or seven months of fetal existence has been effected by the Court through its denial of personhood to the viable fetus, on the one hand, and through its broad definition of health, on the other.[24] (Judge John T. Noonan, Jr., Ninth Circuit Court of Appeals, San Francisco)

The health of the mother, said the Court in *Bolton*, includes "psychological as well as physical well-being" and "the medical judgment may be exercised in light of all factors—physical, emotional, psychological, familial, and the woman's age—relevant to the well-being" of the mother. The mental health of the mother is such an elastic ground for abortion that the Supreme Court decisions effectively permit elective abortion right up until the time of normal delivery.[25] (Charles E. Rice)

Since *Roe*, the Supreme Court's interpretation of the Constitution, requiring the national legalization of abortion on demand, has created the swelling abortion dispute.[26] (Lynn Wardle and Mary Anne Q. Wood)

Roe . . . allows abortion when the fetus is viable, if necessary for the preservation of the life or health of the mother. The result of this standard could be that which Chief Justice Burger assured us would not occur: abortion on demand. . . . We get a better idea of what "health" means when the Court in *Roe* discusses the potential harm to pregnant women of a strict abortion statute: "There is also the distress, for all concerned, associated with the unwanted child, and there is the problem of bringing a child into a family already unable, psychologically and otherwise, to care for it. . . . [T]he stigma of unwed motherhood may be involved." We are thus left with the specter, of an unwed mother bearing a child capable of now living outside its mother's womb obtaining an abortion because she fears the stigma of unwed motherhood.[27] (William R. Hopkin, Jr.)

In actual effect, *Roe v. Wade* judicially created abortion on demand in the United States.[28] (John Warwick Montgomery)

[In *Doe v. Bolton*] the Court moved from one argument to another, presenting its holding and reasoning. It used the early part of the section to make its one crucial addendum to the *Wade* decision: the meaning of the "health" exception which legitimizes abortion to birth.[29] (Stephen M. Krason)

I would not deny that the use of viability [in *Roe*] as a compelling point is defensible and reasonable, though I defy anyone to show it to be uniquely so. Nor would I deny the propriety of abortion to prevent the mother's death or injury to her health if the state's interest in protecting maternal health is superior to its interest in protecting potential life. Of course, many will protest when Justice Douglas informs us in his concurring opinion, which refers to the *Vuitch* decision, that "health" must here be construed to "give full sweep to the 'psychological as well as the physical well-being' of women patients." With that construal, a woman who wants a late-term abortion will usually be able to find a physician willing to certify it as necessary for her health.[30] (Roger Wertheimer)

So it is safe to say that in the first six months of pregnancy a woman can have an abortion for no reason, but in the last three months she can have it for any reason. This is abortion on demand.

Those who defend abortion rights do not deny these horrendous ramifications but often dismiss them by claiming that 0.9 percent of all abortions are performed after viability (from about the twenty-second week of pregnancy until birth[31]), and almost always because the pregnant woman's life is in jeopardy. There are several problems with this statistical dismissal. First, the fact that late-term abortions are permitted for nearly any reason and that unborn children are left unprotected is significant, regardless of whether a small percentage of total abortions have taken place during this time. Second, since there were about 1.6 million abortions in 1992 in the United States, it follows that 14,400 (or 0.9 percent) of them were performed after viability. This means that 1,200 of them were performed every month (about 40 a day). Since the odds of any woman surviving pregnancy are very good (a 99.991 percent chance of maternal survival[32]), it stretches credibility to the limit to believe that all these post-viability abortions were done to save the life of the mother.

For those who still find it difficult to believe that abortion on demand for any reason is the law, consider the following. In an affidavit I wrote for the pro-life citizens of Nevada who sued the Secretary of State for biased ballot language,[33] I used some of the same arguments as well as some of the legal scholarship cited in this chapter. Keep in mind that an affidavit is equivalent to sworn courtroom testimony. If I were not telling the truth about the law, the Attorney General (who at that time was Brian McKay, an abortion-rights supporter who undoubtedly favored our opponent's position in the election) could have easily indicted and convicted me for perjury. With just one phone call to the Attorney General, the Secretary of State (the defendant in this case) could have called for my head. None of this ever happened, and for a good reason. My affidavit and its arguments and citations could not be challenged in a court of law.

The Effect of Recent Court Decisions on *Roe*

On 3 July 1989 the U.S. Supreme Court gave its opinion on *Webster v. Reproductive*

Health Services (1989). In a 5 to 4 vote, the Court reversed a lower-court decision and upheld a Missouri statute that contains several provisions, one of which forbids physicians to perform abortions after the unborn is twenty weeks old. In order to determine this, the statute requires physicians to test a pregnant woman seeking an abortion if the physician believes that she may be twenty weeks pregnant.

Furthermore, this decision modified *Roe* in at least two significant ways. First, the *Webster* court rejected the trimester division of pregnancy that is found in *Roe*. Chief Justice Rehnquist writes in *Webster* that "the key elements of the *Roe* framework—trimesters and viability—are not found in the text of the Constitution or in any place else one would expect to find a constitutional principle. . . . In the second place, we do not see why the State's interest in protecting potential human life should come into existence at the point of viability, and that there should therefore be a rigid line allowing state regulation after viability but prohibiting it before viability."[34]

Second, the *Webster* Court concluded that the portion of the Missouri statute that forbade use of government funds and employees in performing or counseling for a nontherapeutic abortion is constitutional. The Court claimed that although a pregnant woman still has a legal right to an abortion, the government is not obligated to support it.

Although the *Webster* decision neither overturned *Roe* nor affected the *Roe*-modeled statutes in states other than Missouri, it did invite other states to pass restrictive abortion laws that may be legally challenged and eventually serve as the impetus to finally overturn *Roe*. Keep in mind, however, *Webster* did not make abortion unconstitutional or overturn the right to privacy on which *Roe* was partially based.

In *Planned Parenthood v. Casey* (1992) the Supreme Court had an opportunity to overturn *Roe*. In this case, the Court was asked to consider the constitutionality of five provisions of the Pennsylvania Abortion Control Act of 1982. This act requires that 1) "a woman seeking an abortion give her informed consent prior to the procedure, and

specifies that she be provided with certain information at least 24 hours before the abortion is performed." 2) The act "mandates the informed consent of one parent for a minor to obtain an abortion, but provides a judicial bypass procedure." 3) It also "commands that, unless certain exceptions apply, a married woman seeking an abortion must sign a statement indicating that she has notified her husband." 4) However, the act defines and allows for "a 'medical emergency' that will excuse compliance with foregoing requirements." 5) The act also imposes "certain reporting requirements on facilities providing abortion services."[35]

Because of "principles of institutional integrity [i.e., the Court's integrity] and the rule of *stare decisis* [i.e., the principle that the Court respect precedent]" the Court, in a 5 to 4 decision, upheld and reaffirmed what it considers *Roe*'s three parts: "(1) a recognition of a woman's right to choose to have an abortion before fetal viability and to obtain it without undue interference from the State, whose previability interests are not strong enough to support an abortion prohibition or the imposition of substantial obstacles to the woman's effective right to elect the procedure; (2) a confirmation of the State's power to restrict abortions after viability, if the law contains exceptions for pregnancies endangering a woman's life or health; and (3) the principle that the State has legitimate interests from the outset of the pregnancy in protecting the health of the woman and the life of the fetus that may become a child."[36]

However, the court upheld as constitutional four of the five provisions of the Pennsylvania act. The only one rejected as unconstitutional was the provision requiring notification of husbands, based on what it calls the "undue burden" standard. *Roe* affirms abortion as a fundamental constitutional right and thus makes any possible restrictions subject to strict scrutiny (that is, possible restrictions must be essential to meeting a compelling public need in order to be valid). However, the Court in *Casey*, by subscribing to the undue burden standard, does not support the right to terminate one's pregnancy as fundamental. That is to say, requiring that a woman's husband be notified of her abortion decision places on her an undue burden since it would prevent a number of married women from having abortions. The other provisions, on the other hand, do not place on the woman undue burden, although they do not meet a compelling public need and thus do not withstand strict scrutiny. Consequently, the states can enact abortion restrictions that may not be able to withstand strict scrutiny but nevertheless do not place on the woman an undue burden. Admitting that the undue burden standard "has no basis in constitutional law," Justices O'Connor, Kennedy, and Souter suggest that when courts apply this standard in order to evaluate abortion regulations, "judges will have to make the subjective, unguided determination whether the regulations place 'substantial obstacles' in the path of a woman seeking an abortion, undoubtedly engendering a variety of conflicting views."[37]

The Court, in agreement with *Webster*, rejected *Roe's* trimester framework. Although the Court also claimed to reject the apparent liberalizing of *Roe* in decisions such as *Thornburgh v. ACOG* (1986), it is not clear whether states will pass legislation that will make late-term abortions more difficult to obtain; states are not required by the Court to do so. It should also be noted that in *Casey* the Court still upheld *Roe's* view that the unborn are not full persons until they pass through the birth canal. Throughout the opinion the unborn are referred to as "potential persons."

Even though the majority rejected *Roe's* trimester framework, its requirement that regulations be subjected to "strict scrutiny," and that a woman has a fundamental right to abortion, the justices nevertheless claimed that *Roe* as a precedent must be respected. Now a gutted decision which for the most part still upholds abortion on demand, *Roe* is best described by Chief Justice Rehnquist in his dissenting opinion in *Casey*: "*Roe* continues to exist, but only in the way a storefront on a western movie set exists: a mere facade to give the illusion of reality."[38]

In late 1992 the Supreme Court refused to hear a case involving Guam's restrictive law, which forbade abortions through all nine months of pregnancy except to save the life of the mother. The Court let stand a lower court ruling which declared the law unconstitutional.

Conclusion: Virtually No Abortions Are Illegal under *Roe*

From the preceding analysis it follows that several types of abortions, abortions that a great majority of Americans say should be made illegal,[39] are legal under the current law in almost all jurisdictions if a pregnant woman can obtain the services of a willing physician: sex-selection abortions; abortions for birth control, those performed not for difficult situations (such as rape or incest) but because contraception has failed; abortions for pregnancies out of wedlock that do not involve rape or incest; abortions for eugenic reasons, such as in the case of the couple who intentionally conceived a child in order to use its bone marrow to help their older child, but would have been perfectly within the law to abort if the unborn child's bone marrow did not match her older sibling's; and late-term abortions, those performed after the thirteenth week of pregnancy, when the unborn, who "by the end of the seventh week" is "a well-proportioned small-scale baby,"[40] can feel pain (see chap. 3).[41]

Of course, many abortions occur for reasons other than these and early on in pregnancy. However, the purpose of bringing out these legal facts is not to manipulate the reader, as has been the accusation of some abortion-rights proponents against pro-lifers who have pointed out these same facts,[42] but rather to understand the logic of the pro-life position: If it is wrong to kill a six-month unborn child, why is it all right to kill the same being four months earlier? He is only less mature than he would be at six months in terms of development, dependency, and size, considerations that are not morally relevant when it comes to the right to life of born people (i.e., a two-year-old does not have a lesser right to life than an adult simply because he differs from the adult in terms of development, dependency, and size). Furthermore, if it is wrong to kill a three-month-old unborn child for eugenic reasons or sex selection, why is it not wrong to kill the same child for other reasons such as rape, the mother's poverty, or genetic defect? After all, the right to life of born people is not dependent on their origin, income, or level of intellectual or physical ability. Why are these factors relevant to the unborn's right to life? We will address these points in greater detail in chapters 4 through 7.

Answering the Arguments for Abortion Rights

Prenatal Development, Abortion Methods, and Fetal Pain

We of today know that man is born of sexual union; that he starts life as an embryo within the body of the female; and that the embryo is formed from the fusion of two cells, the ovum and the sperm. . . . This seems so simple and evident to us that it is difficult to picture a time when it was not part of common knowledge.
   Dr. Alan F. Guttmacher, Planned Parenthood (1933)

Scientifically all we know is that a living human sperm unites with a living human egg; if they were not living there could be no union. . . . Does human life begin before or with the union of the gametes, or with birth, or at some intermediate time? I, for one, confess, I do not know.
   Dr. Alan F. Guttmacher, Planned Parenthood (1973)

A person is a person no matter how small.
   Dr. Seuss

In order to properly evaluate both the popular and the philosophical arguments for abortion rights, it is important to understand prenatal development, since many of the arguments for abortion rights try to show that the unborn becomes "fully human" sometime during its prenatal development (though some, such as Michael Tooley and Peter Singer, argue that full humanity is not attained until sometime after birth). In this chapter we will consider the scientific facts of prenatal development, abortion methods, and fetal pain.

Human Life at Conception and the Facts of Prenatal Development[1]

While presenting the facts of prenatal development I will lay a foundation for the pro-life view that full humanness begins at conception. However, philosophical objections to this view will be reviewed when I critique the decisive moment and gradualist views in chapter 6.

First Month

Pregnancy begins at conception, the result of the process of fertilization in which the male sperm and the female ovum unite. That is to say, fertilization is a process that culminates in conception. And what results is an entity called a zygote, a one-celled biological entity, a stage in human development through which each of us has passed (just as we have passed through infancy, childhood, and adolescence). It is a misnomer to refer to this entity as a "fertilized ovum." For both ovum and sperm, which are genetically each a part of its owner (mother and father, respectively), cease to exist at the moment of conception. There is no doubt that the zygote is biologically alive. The zygote fulfills the four criteria needed to establish biological life: metabolism, growth, reaction to stimuli, and reproduction. (There is cell reproduction and twinning, a form of asexual reproduction, that can occur after conception. For more on twinning, see chap. 6.) But is this life an individual human life? I believe that the facts clearly reveal that it is.

First, the human conceptus, that which results from conception and begins as a zygote, is the sexual product of human parents. Hence, insofar as having human causes, the conceptus is human.

Second, resulting from the union of the female ovum (which contains twenty-three chromosomes) and the male sperm (which contains twenty-three chromosomes) the conceptus is a new, although tiny, individual with its own genetic code (with forty-six chromosomes), a code that is neither her mother's nor her father's. From this point until death no new genetic information is needed to make the unborn entity a individual human. Her genetic makeup is established at conception, determining to a great extent her own individual physical characteristics—gender, eye color, bone structure, hair color, skin color, susceptability to certain diseases. That is to say, at conception, the genotype—the inherited characteristics of an individual human being—is established and will remain in force for the entire life of this individual. The unborn individual, sharing the same nature with all human beings, is unlike any individual who has been conceived before and is unlike any individual who will ever be conceived again (unless she is an identical twin; see chap. 6). The only thing

necessary for the growth and development of this human organism, as with the rest of us, is oxygen, food, and water, since this organism, like the newborn, the infant, and the adolescent, needs only to develop in accordance with her already-designed nature that is present at conception. This is why French geneticist Jerome L. LeJeune, while testifying before a Senate subcommittee, asserted: "To accept the fact that after fertilization has taken place a new human has come into being is no longer a matter of taste or opinion. The human nature of the human being from conception to old age is not a metaphysical contention, it is plain experimental evidence."[2]

LeJeune's conclusion is substantiated by a host of other authorities, some of which were cited in a U.S. Senate subcommittee report to the U.S. Senate Judiciary Committee (1981). The following is a limited sample:

> I think we can now also say that the question of the beginning of life—when life begins—is no longer a question for theological or philosophical dispute. It is an established scientific fact. Theologians and philosophers may go on to debate the meaning of life or purpose of life, but it is an established fact that all life, including human life, begins at the moment of conception.
>
> I have never ever seen in my own scientific reading, long before I became concerned with issues of life of this nature, that anyone has ever argued that life did not begin at the moment of conception and that it was a human conception if it resulted from the fertilization of the human egg by a human sperm. As far as I know, these have never been argued against.[3] (Dr. Hymie Gordon, professor of medical genetics and physician at the Mayo Clinic)

> [A]ll organisms, however large and complex they may be when fullgrown, begin life as but a single cell.
>
> This is true of the human being, for instance, who begins life as a fertilized ovum.[4] (Dr. M. Krieger, *The Human Reproductive System* 88 [1969])

> The formation, maturation and meeting of a male and female sex cell are all prelimi-

nary to their actual union into a combined cell, or *zygote*, which definitely marks the beginning of a new individual.[5] (Dr. B. Patten, *Human Embryology* 43 [3d ed., 1968])

So, therefore, it is scientifically correct to say that an individual human life begins at conception, when egg and sperm join to form the zygote, and this developing human always is a member of our species in all stages of its life.[6] (Dr. Micheline Matthews-Roth, a principal research associate in the Department of Medicine, Harvard Medical School)

It is interesting to note that the U.S. Senate subcommittee, which cited these authorities in its report, made the telling observation that "no witness [who testified before the subcommittee] raised any evidence to refute the biological fact that from the moment of conception there exists a distinct individual being who is alive and is of the human species. No witness challenged the scientific consensus that unborn children are 'human beings,' insofar as the term is used to mean living beings of the human species." On the other hand, "those witnesses who testified that science cannot say whether unborn children are human beings were speaking in every instance to the value question rather than the scientific question. . . . [T]hese witnesses invoked their value preferences to redefine the term 'human being.'" The committee report explains that these witnesses "took the view that each person may define as 'human' only those beings whose lives that a person wants to value. Because they did not wish to accord instrinsic worth to the lives of unborn children, they refused to call them 'human beings,' regardless of the scientific evidence."[7] I will critique these value arguments in chapters 6 through 8.

So from a strictly scientific point of view, there is no doubt that the development of an individual human life begins at conception. Consequently, it is vital that the reader understand that she did not come from a zygote, she once was a zygote; she did not come from an embryo, she once was an embryo; she did not come from a fetus, she once was a fetus; she did not come from an adolescent, she once was an adolescent. Consequently,

each one of us has experienced these various developmental stages of life. None of these stages, however, imparted us with our humanity.

Since the conceptus can be brought into existence in a petri dish, as evidenced in the case of the so-called test-tube baby, and since this entity, if it has white parents, can be transferred to the womb of a black woman and be born white, we know conclusively that the conceptus is *not* part of the woman's body. It is amazing how many people are ignorant of this fact, including those who are well educated. Take for example the comments of the philosopher and scholar Mortimer Adler, who, evidently in ignorance of the biological facts, asserted: "If the [unborn] cannot live by itself as an independent organism [before viability], it does not have a life of its own. The life it has is as a part of the mother's body, in the same sense that an individual's arm or leg is a part of a living organism."[8] Adler's claim is false, as we have seen and shall see throughout this chapter as well as in chapter 6 when I deal with the argument that full humanness begins at viability.

Although the zygote is a one-celled organism, it is not just a cell like the rest of the cells of either the mother's or the father's body. It is an individual human organism whose cells all have the same genetic code—just like those in her mother's body as well as in our own—except the zygote is a human being at a stage in her development at which her body happens to have only one cell. But the fact that the zygote is a one-celled entity should not take away from the intricate complex information found in her genetic code. Bart T. Hefferman, M.D., tells us:

The new combination of chromosomes [i.e., the zygote's genetic structure] sets in motion the individual's life, controlled by his own individual code (genes) with its fantastic library of information projected from the past on the helix of . . . DNA. A single thread of DNA from a human cell contains information equivalent to six hundred thousand printed pages with five hundred words on a page, or a library of one thousand volumes.

The stored knowledge at conception in the new individual's library of instruction is fifty times more than that contained in the *Encyclopedia Britannica*. These unique and individual instructions are operative over the whole of the individual's life and form a continuum of human existence even into succeeding generations.[9]

As Gordon writes, "Even at that early stage, the complexity of the living cell is so great that it is beyond our comprehension. It is a privilege to be allowed to protect and nurture it."[10]

Within one week after conception, implantation occurs, the time at which the conceptus "nests" or implants in her mother's uterus. During this time, and possibly up to fourteen days after conception,[11] a splitting of the conceptus may occur that results in the creation of identical twins. In some instances the two concepti may recombine and become one conceptus. (I will respond in chapter 6 to the argument that the possibility of the conceptus twinning and the subsequent concepti recombining refutes the pro-life claim that full humanness begins at conception.) At about three weeks a primitive heart muscle begins to pulsate. Other organs, such as a liver, primitive kidneys, a digestive tract, and a simple umbilical cord, begin to develop during the first month. This developing body has a head with a developing face with primitive ears, mouth, and eyes, despite the fact that it is no larger than half of the size of a pea. Toward the end of the first month (between twenty-six and twenty-eight days) the arms and legs begin to appear as tiny buds. A whole embryo is formed by the end of the first month.

From the eighteenth day after conception substantial development of the brain and nervous system occurs. Krason points out, "This is necessary because the nervous system integrates the action of all the other systems. By the end of the twentieth day the foundation of the child's brain, spinal cord, and entire nervous system will have been established."[12]

A vast majority of abortions are performed during this time, despite the scientific facts that clearly show that an individual human life is developing, as it would after birth from infant to child to adolescent to adult.

Second Month

Despite its small size, the unborn child by the beginning of the second month *looks* distinctly "human" (though it *is* human from conception), and yet it is highly likely that the mother does not even know she is pregnant. During the second month, the eyes, ears, nose, toes, and fingers make their appearance. The child's skeleton develops, her heart beats, and her blood, with its own type, flows. The unborn at this time has reflexes and her lips become sensitive to touch. "By the sixth week, [the central nervous] system will have developed so well that it is controlling movements of the baby's muscles, even though the woman may not be aware she is pregnant. At thirty days the primary brain is seen. By the thirty-third day the cerebral cortex, the part of the central nervous system which governs motor activity as well as intellect, may be seen."[13] Brain waves can be detected at about forty to forty-three days after conception, although they could very well be occurring earlier. "*By the end of the seventh week we see a well proportioned small scale baby* [emphasis mine]. In its seventh week, it bears the familiar external features and all the internal organs of the adult, even though it is less than an inch long and weighs only 1/30th of an ounce."[14] By the eighth week her own unique fingerprints start to form along with the lines in her hands. As the heart beats sturdily, the unborn's stomach produces digestive juices, her liver manufactures blood cells, and her kidneys begin to function by extracting uric acid from her blood stream. "After the eighth week no further primordia will form; *everything* is already present that will be found in the full term baby. . . . From this point until adulthood, when full growth is achieved somewhere between 25 and 27 years, the changes in the body will be mainly in dimension and in gradual refinement of the working parts."[15]

Third Month

Movement characterizes the third month of pregnancy. Although she weighs only one ounce and is no smaller than a goose egg, the unborn begins to swallow, squint, and swim, grasp with her hands, and move her tongue. She also sucks her thumb. Her organs undergo further development. The salivary glands, taste buds, and stomach digestive glands develop, as evidenced by her swallowing and utilization of the amniotic fluid. She also begins to urinate. Depending on the unborn's sex, primitive sperm or eggs form. Parental resemblance may already be seen in the unborn's facial expressions. "The vocal chords are completed. In the absence of air they cannot produce sound; the child cannot cry aloud until birth although he is capable of crying long before."[16]

Fourth and Fifth Months

Growth is characteristic of the fourth month. From the twelfth to the sixteenth week, the weight of the unborn increases six times, to about one-half her birth weight. Her height is between eight and ten inches long, and she can hear her mother's voice.

In the fifth month of pregnancy the unborn becomes viable. That is, she now has the ability, under our current technological knowledge, to live outside her mother's womb. Some babies have survived as early as twenty weeks. The fifth month is also the time at which the mother begins to feel the unborn's movements, although mothers have been known to have felt stirrings earlier. This first movement was traditionally called quickening, the time at which some medieval and common-law scholars thought the soul entered the body. Not having access to the biological facts we currently possess, they reasoned that prior to quickening it could not be proven that the unborn was alive. Current biology, which has conclusively demonstrated that a biologically living human individual is present from conception, has decisively refuted this notion of "quickening," just as current astronomy has refuted the geocentric solar system.

During the fifth month, the unborn's hair, skin, and nails develop. She can also dream (rapid eye movement [REM] sleep). It is, however, legal under *Roe v. Wade* and *Doe v. Bolton* to kill this unborn human being by abortion for any reason her mother so chooses.

In the remaining four months of pregnancy the unborn continues to develop. The child's chances of survival outside the womb increase as she draws closer to her expected birthday. During this time she responds to sounds, her mother's voice, pain (see more on this subsequently), and the taste of substances placed in the amniotic fluid. Some studies have shown that the child can actually learn before it is born.[17] The child is born approximately forty weeks after conception.

In summary, the pro-life advocate believes that full humanness begins at conception for at least four reasons: (1) At the moment of conception a separate human individual, with its own genetic code and needing only food, water, shelter, and oxygen in order to grow and develop, comes into existence. (2) Like the infant, the child, and the adolescent, the conceptus is a being who is in the process of becoming. She is not a becoming who is striving toward being. She is not a potential human life but a human life with great potential. (3) The conceptus is the sexual product of human parents, and a developing conceptus that is the sexual product of members of a particular mammalian species is itself an individual member of that species. (4) The same being that begins as a zygote continues to birth and adulthood. That is to say, there is no decisive break in the continuous development of the human entity from conception until death that would make this entity a different individual before birth. This is why it makes perfect sense for any one of us to say, "When *I* was conceived. . . ."

It is certainly possible that the early fetus is qualitatively different from the later fetus, even if we cannot pinpoint a decisive moment; otherwise, I would be committing the fallacy of the beard. However, it is apparent from the biological facts that although the unborn develops from a less complex to a more complex creature, it does not follow from this fact that it changes from one being into another. Consequently, it would appear that the burden of proof is on the one who claims that a qualitative change does take place. In order to meet this burden, a number of thinkers have defended certain theories, which I will critique in chapter 6.

Of course, many people who argue for abortion rights do not believe that unborn human beings deserve legal protection. In popular rhetoric they often use emotional arguments that are not well thought-out and do not really address the question of whether abortion is in fact unjustified homicide. I will evaluate those in chapters 4 and 5. Yet, as we saw in the citation from the U.S. Senate subcommittee report, more sophisticated defenders of abortion rights admit without reservation that the unborn is a human being, and agree with the accuracy of the facts presented so far in this chapter. Some argue, however, that the unborn, although genetically a human being, is not fully human or a person. I will critically analyze these arguments in chapter 6, as well as respond to some common questions often asked about the pro-life position I am defending. On the other hand, some argue that even if the unborn is fully human, he has no right to occupy his mother's body without prior consent, just as one cannot demand to use another's kidney to save one's life without prior consent. This and similar arguments will be evaluated in chapter 7. In any event, it is clear that even sophisticated abortion-rights proponents agree that the unborn entity is an individual human being from the moment of conception. This factual concession, to the peril of the abortion-rights position, plays an important part in my dismantling of the arguments of those who believe that the unborn is a human being but not a person.

Abortion Methods

It is true that some forms of birth control are not contraceptives (i.e., that which prevent conception) but abortifacients, substances that produce an early-term abortion that results in the killing of the embryo or early fetus. The IUD and the abortion pill,

RU-486, are among several different types of abortifacients that may be used in the earliest stages of pregnancy.

However, when it comes to abortions performed by physicians at either a clinic or hospital, the following common methods are used: dilation and curettage (D & C), suction abortion, saline abortion, hysterotomy, dilation and evacuation (D & E), and prostaglandin.

Former Surgeon General C. Everett Koop, M.D., a world-renowned pediatrician, describes the first four of these popular methods.

Dilation and Curettage (D & C)

The technique used most often to end early pregnancies [between 7 and 12 weeks] is called D & C or *dilation and curettage*. In this procedure, usually before the twelfth or thirteenth week of pregnancy, the uterus is approached through the vagina. The cervix is stretched to permit the insertion of a curette, a tiny hoelike instrument. The surgeon then scrapes the wall of the uterus, cutting the baby's body to pieces and scraping the placenta from its attachments on the uterine wall. Bleeding is considerable.[18]

In order to insure that the aborted woman does not bleed after the abortion procedure or get an infection, the operating nurse reassembles the unborn's parts to make sure the woman's uterus has been emptied. (This may also take place after D & E abortions [see p. 47].

Suction Abortion

A method used as an alternative to D & C during the same period of pregnancy is the suction abortion:

The principle is the same as in the D & C. A powerful suction tube is inserted through the dilated cervix into the uterus. This tears apart the body of the developing baby and the placenta, sucking the pieces into a jar. The smaller parts of the body are recognizable as arms, legs, head, and so on. More than two-thirds of all abortions performed in the United States and Canada apparently are done by this method.[19]

Sometimes physicians perform menstrual extractions, a very early suction abortion, often before the woman's pregnancy test is positive.

Saline Abortion

Saline abortion or "salting out" is a method used in later pregnancy when either suction abortion or D & C might result in too much bleeding for the pregnant woman.

This method is usually carried out after sixteen weeks of pregnancy, when enough amniotic fluid has accumulated in the sac around the baby. A long needle is inserted through the mother's abdomen directly into the sac, and a solution of concentrated salt is injected into the amniotic fluid. The salt solution is absorbed both through the lungs and the gastrointestinal tract, producing changes in the osmotic pressure. The outer layer of skin is burned off by the high concentration of salt. It takes about an hour to kill the baby by this slow method. The mother usually goes into labor about a day later and delivers a dead, shriveled baby.[20]

Hysterotomy

If a woman chooses an abortion when it is too late to accomplish it by saline, suction, D & C, or D & E, doctors may employ a technique known as hysterotomy, though this method is rarely used today because of the increased risk to the patient (though it is a *legal* procedure).

A hysterotomy is exactly the same as a Cesarean section with one difference—in a Cesarean section the operation is usually performed to save the life of the baby, whereas a hysterotomy is performed to kill the baby. These babies look very much like other babies except that they are small and weigh, for example, about two pounds at the end of a twenty-four week pregnancy. They are truly alive, but they are allowed to die through neglect or sometimes killed by a direct act.[21]

Dilation and Evacuation (D & E)

Stephen Schwarz, an ethicist in the University of Rhode Island's philosophy department, explains D & E or dilation and evacuation:

Used between 12 and 24 weeks. Here ... the child is cut to pieces by a sharp knife [or a pliers-like instrument], as in D & C, only it is a much larger and far more developed child, weighing as much as a pound, and measuring as much as a foot in length.[22]

Prostaglandin

Performed after the twelfth week of pregnancy, prostaglandin abortions involve the "uses of chemicals developed and sold by the Upjohn Pharmaceutical Company. . . . The hormone-like compounds are injected or otherwise applied to the muscle of the uterus, causing it to contract intensely, thereby pushing out the developing baby. Babies have been decapitated during these abnormal contractions. Many have been born alive."[23]

Fetal Pain

Do these methods of abortion cause the unborn to feel pain? This question can only be answered by examining three important questions: What is physiologically necessary for pain to be felt? If the unborn is able to feel pain beginning at some point in her prenatal development, do the methods of abortion cause her to feel pain? If the unborn is able to feel pain during some abortions, what is the percentage of total abortions performed during this time? I will conclude this section with brief responses to some objections.

The Physiological Factors Necessary to Feel Pain

It is beyond a reasonable doubt that the unborn can feel pain possibly as early as eight weeks after conception and definitely by thirteen and a half weeks. Vincent J. Collins, M.D., professor of anesthesiology at Northwestern University and the University of Illinois as well as author of *Principles of Anesthesiology*, one of the leading medical texts on the control of pain, writes: "Certain neurological structures are necessary to pain sensation: pain receptive nerve cells, neural pathways, and the thalamus [two egg-shaped masses of nerve tissue located deep within the brain at the top of the brain-stem]." Since these requisite neurological structures begin developing at eight weeks after conception and are completely in place as well as functioning by thirteen and a half weeks, "as evidenced by the aversive response of the human fetus, it may be concluded with reasonable medical certainty that the fetus can sense pain at least by 13½ weeks." But since "the neurological structures are at least partially in place between 8 and 13½ weeks, it seems probable that some pain can also be felt during this time of gestation."[24]

Abortion Methods and Fetal Pain

Since the evidence indicates with near certainty that pain can be felt by the unborn after the thirteenth week and quite possibly as early as eight weeks after conception, "induced abortion will cause pain to a fetus with a functioning nervous system if the method used stimulates the pain receptors, excites the neural pathways, and the impulse reaches the thalamus." Techniques employed after the twelfth week—dilation and evacuation (D & E), abortion by saline amnio-infusion, and prostaglandin abortions—are all capable of stimulating pain receptors as well as exciting neural pathways.[25]

Since it involves the crushing, slicing, and dismembering of the unborn, D & E abortion no doubt excites pain receptors as well as neural pathways. Saline abortion burns "away the upper skin layers of the fetus. The esophagus and mouth are also burned when the fetus swallows amniotic fluid polluted by the saline. By the time the fetus is expelled there is extensive edema and submembranous degeneration." Moreover, "by damaging the surface of the fetus in this fashion, saline would excite pain receptors and stimulate the neural pathways of a functioning central nervous system during the course of the abortion until the fetus dies. It is well-known that the fetus reacts with aversive re-sponses when saline is introduced into amniotic fluid," as evidenced by the chilling fact that the "aborting mother can feel her baby thrashing in the uterus during the approximately two hours it usually takes for the saline solution to kill the fetus." Prostaglandin abortion "may bring about death of the fetus by constricting the circulation of the blood and/or impairing the heart function." This pain, many physicians have reasonably inferred, is very much like the one experienced by a person suffering a heart attack.[26]

The Number of Abortions Performed When the Unborn Can Feel Pain

Using a typical year, 1980, as an example, a large number of the total number of abortions performed that year (1.5 million), were performed when we are almost certain that the unborn can feel pain: approximately 113,500 abortions (9 percent of all abortions) were performed in the second and third trimesters of pregnancy (after thirteen weeks), using the D & E, saline amnio-infusion, and prostaglandin techniques. Approximately 9,600 of them were prostaglandin abortions, approximately 24,000 were abortions by the saline amnio-infusion method, and approximately 80,000 were D & E abortions. Moreover, approximately 480,500 (33 percent) of the total number of abortions were performed after the eighth and before the thirteenth weeks when the unborn child is usually killed by suction abortion, which tears it part by part. Consequently, we are quite certain that in 9 percent of all abortions the unborn suffer "the greatest of bodily evils, the ending of their lives. They are undergoing the death agony. However inarticulate, however slight their cognitive powers, however rudimentary their sensations, they are sentient creatures undergoing the disintegration of their being and the termination of their vital capabilities. That experience is painful in itself."[28] And there is a good chance that as many as another 33 percent of the total number of aborted unborn (after eight and before thirteen weeks old) are undergoing the same agony. It is quite possible, therefore, that more than four out of ten abortions (42 percent) result in the sort of excruciating torture of a sentient being that many people would find morally repugnant if performed on animals.

Possible Objections to the Reality of Fetal Pain

At least two possible objections can be raised against my presentation of the facts of fetal pain.[29]

The fact of fetal pain is not morally relevant if the unborn is not fully human. In response to such an objection, one can argue that even if the unborn is not fully human, it does not logically follow that the unborn's pain is morally irrelevant. Consider the following. On the same grounds that we claim that it is not morally appropriate to torture puppies and other animals even though they are not fully human, it seems morally appropriate to assert that it is wrong to burn, smother, dismember, and/or crush an unborn human (and thus causing it excruciating pain), even if we assume that it is *not* fully human. Hence, if we are going to make sure that young canines, which are not potential persons, are not tortured, then we should at least grant the same courtesy to preborn humans, who are surely at least potential persons.

But suppose the pro-lifer is correct that the unborn is fully human. Then the factor of fetal pain makes a horrible evil (i.e., the unjustified killing of an innocent person) even more horrible and morally repugnant: the unjustified killing of an innocent person by means of torture manifested in the burning, smothering, dismembering, and/or crushing of the victim. Hence, it seems to follow from this that if there is a small probability that the unborn is fully human (as most abortion-rights advocates concede when they argue that "no one knows when life begins"—that is, the unborn *may be* fully human), and that abortion causes the unborn excruciating pain, at least after the thirteenth week and possibly earlier, then it is possible that a great many abortions make the womb into nothing more than a torture chamber in which innocent human persons are burned, smothered, dismembered, and/or crushed to death. In light of this horrible possibility, isn't it better to err on the side of life and against violence and not keep open the possibility of this horror being repeated every day throughout America?

Maybe abortion-rights supporters who do not believe that the unborn are fully human, but are nevertheless morally disturbed by the reality and/or the strong possibility of fetal pain, should propose that abortions be performed only if the unborn human being is anesthetized.

Although the requisite physical conditions are definitely present by thirteen and a half weeks, the child cannot feel pain because she lacks higher psychological functions, since her cerebral cortex is not fully developed. Pain is both a cognitive and a physical experience.[30] On the contrary, Dr. Collins points out that "the presence of a functioning cortex is not necessary to pain sensation. Even complete removal of the cortex does not eliminate the sensation of pain; no portion of the cortex, if artificially stimulated, results in pain sensation." Therefore, "neither the presence of the cortex nor transmission of pain impulses to the cortex are essential to pain sensation. When the cortex (which develops and functions later in human gestation than the thalamus) is involved in a pain response, it generates elaborated aversive behavior and adds psychological and cognitive components to pain sensation."[31]

Second, the lack of a fully developed cerebral cortex may increase the intensity of pain:

> While the likelihood of weak participation by the cerebral cortex will work against the magnification of the pain, there will also be an absence of the inhibitory imput from the brain which modulates and balances the sensory imput in more developed beings. Consequently, the possibility exists of smaller and weaker sensory imputs having the same effect which later is achieved only by larger and stronger sensations.[32]

Third, all the evidence, which is overwhelming, points to the fact that the unborn is able to feel pain—the requisite neurological structures begin developing at eight weeks after conception and are completely in place as well as functioning by thirteen and a half weeks, as evidenced by the aversive response of the human fetus to needles and other sharp instruments as well as pain causing substances such as saline. Thus the burden of proof is on the skeptic to prove that the unborn does not feel pain. This is an unenviable task, since the same reasons why we believe that in particular instances animals and infants feel pain—they possess the requisite neurological structures as well as apparently resisting instruments of pain (i.e., knives, needles, chemicals) by making hurried movements and/or sounds when these instruments are inflicted upon them—are the same reasons why we believe that the unborn feel pain. If one denies the evidence for the unborn's pain, one is forced to deny that animals and infants feel pain. But if one believes that animals and infants feel pain, one is forced to admit that the unborn feel pain. *Reductio ad absurdum.*

Keep in mind that the pro-life position is not contingent upon the unborn experiencing pain when aborted. Why then use the facts of fetal pain? I believe that they help us all to realize that the unborn human is not "a blob of cells," as many abortion-rights activists like to describe her, but a living sentient being of the species *homo sapiens* who is able through most of its gestation to experience excruciating pain and torture. In any event, let it not be forgotten that the pro-life position hinges on the full humanness of the unborn regardless of whether it experiences pain while being aborted.

Tying It All Together

In order to fully grasp the correlation between prenatal development, abortion techniques, and fetal pain, I have provided a table that originally appeared in Schwarz's *The Moral Question of Abortion*. I have slightly amended it for my purposes here. The chart clearly describes each level of prenatal development as well as presenting the appropriate level of development at which types of abortion techniques are performed.[33]

Number of Weeks	Status of Development	Type of Abortion	
2.5	Blood cells, heart		
3	Foundation for child's brain, spinal cord, and entire nervous system. Eyes begin to form.		
3.5	Heart starts first pulsations.		
4.5	The three parts of the brain are present. Eyes, ears, nasal organs, digestive tract, and gall bladder are forming.		
5.5	Heartbeat essentially like that of an adult. A one-inch miniature doll, gracefully formed arms and legs, an unmistakably human face.		
6	Brain waves noted.	Suction	D&C
7	A "well-proportioned small scale baby." Brain configuration like adult brain sends impulses that coordinate functions of other organs. Nervous system well-developed. The heart beats sturdily. Familiar external features and all internal organs of the adult. If the area of the lips is stroked, he responds by bending his upper body to one side and making a quick backward motion with his hand.		
8.5	Eyelids and palms of hand sensitive to touch. If eyelid is stroked, child squirms. If palm is stroked, fingers close into a small fist.		
9	All structures completed; only development and growth from now on. Entire body sensitive to touch, except sides, back, and top of head. Child moves spontaneously without being touched.	↓	↓

Number of Weeks	Status of Development	Type of Abortion
10	Threefold increase in nerve-muscle connections. If forehead is touched, he can turn his head away. Arm movements, bending the elbow and wrists independently.	
11	Facial expressions similar to his parents. Fingernails appear. Eyelids close over eyes.	
12	Baby can move his thumb in opposition to his fingers. He swallows regularly. He moves gracefully. (All this before the mother feels any movement.)	
13	He can kick his legs, turn his feet, curl his toes, make a fist, suck his thumb, bend his wrist, turn his head, frown, open his mouth, press his lips tightly together. He drinks amniotic fluid.	D&E Saline Prostaglandin
16	Weight increases six times since week 12. He is 8–10 inches tall.	
22	He is now about one foot tall, weighs one pound. Fine baby hair begins to grow on his eyebrows and his head. He sleeps and wakes just as he will after birth.	
24		Hysterotomy
38	End of time in the womb; some babies are born before 38 weeks.	

Conclusion

In this chapter we saw that an individual human life is present from the moment of conception; and all the major methods of abortion, when performed after the thirteenth week of pregnancy and quite possibly as early as the eighth week, cause the unborn agonizing pain.

51

Arguments from Pity

The most merciful thing a large family can do for one of its infant members is to kill it.
    Margaret Sanger, founder of Planned Parenthood (1920)

. . . [W]e are still unable to put babies in the class of dangerous epidemics, even though this is the exact truth.
    Dr. Mary Calderone, former president of Planned Parenthood (1968)

rguments for abortion rights have been put forth by many diverse groups and individuals in our culture. In this chapter I will present and critique those arguments that are best classified as appeals to pity. Of course, not every defender of abortion rights holds to all or any of these arguments. Some of the more sophisticated defenders of abortion rights eschew much of the popular rhetoric and defend their position on other grounds. But since most people will come into contact with these arguments in both the popular media and abortion-rights literature, and since some of these arguments figured prominently in the dissenting opinions of Supreme Court Justices Blackmun and Stevens in the 1989 *Webster* case, it is necessary that they be carefully analyzed.

Arguments from Pity

An argument from pity is an attempt to show the plausibility of one's position on any issue by trying to move another emotionally, although the reasonableness of the position really stands or falls on the basis of other important factors. In his textbook *Thinking Logically*, philosopher James B. Freeman states that one appeals to pity when "one pulls on the 'heartstrings,' presents a most pathetic, tear-jerking story to obtain agreement—not because any good reason has been given but because the hearer feels sorry."[1] Freeman cites a letter to the editor as an example:

Dear Sir:
    As a mother of nine children I would like to speak out on the draft everyone is talking about.

I am one that is very much against it. I lost a husband in Korea and if they draft from age 18 to 26 I stand to lose four sons and one daughter.

As a mother in poor health I don't think I could take that.

Why can't [the president] leave well enough alone and try and find our boys missing or being held some place?

Mrs. L.T.[2]

The problem with Mrs. L.T.'s argument is not that it does not accurately convey to us her true feelings, but that it fails to present any relevant reasons to support her position that draft registration is not the correct public policy. After all, one could readily admit to Mrs. L.T. that she may be correct that she would not be emotionally capable of handling a situation in which all her children were war fatalities. But this fact alone is insufficient to establish that draft registration as a public policy is a bad idea. Another mother could argue in the same manner that it is unjust to send her money-embezzling children to prison on the basis that she will not be able to handle it emotionally. But whether or not they morally and legally deserve prison is independent of their mother's emotional ability to handle their prison term.

There is no doubt that an appeal to pity is sometimes appropriate if it helps to make us aware of true moral obligations and rights, although these obligations or rights themselves are not based on pity. For example, in order to gain political support for the elimination of a nuclear dump site, someone may point out that people who live near such sites have a significantly greater risk of getting cancer in comparison to people who don't live near such places. Therefore, since the government has an obligation not to put the public at significant risk, the dump site should be eliminated. But in order to prick the consciences of the general public so that they may truly understand the devastating impact of cancer upon a family, it may be necessary for political opponents of the dump site to tell of particular cases in which beloved family members were cut down in the prime of life. Notice that this moral cause is not based on pity, but is based on an appeal to a government's fundamental obligation to protect its citizens from significant harm. The emotional stories help to convey to the general public the type of harm from which the government is obligated to protect us. Of course, the use of these stories would be a fallacious appeal to pity if there was no statistical evidence to show that living near a nuclear dump site posed significant risk to the citizenry. In that case the government would not have an obligation to eliminate nuclear dump sites. Hence, in a moral argument, an appeal to pity is inappropriate when one argues for a position primarily on that basis and ignores relevant facts or philosophical insights that would make such an appeal almost irrelevant, as in the case of Mrs. L.T. The following eight arguments for abortion rights are examples of such inappropriate appeals to pity.

Argument from the Dangers of Illegal Abortions

Anyone who keeps up with the many abortion-rights demonstrations in the United States cannot help but see on abortion-rights placards and buttons a drawing of the infamous coat hanger. This symbol of the abortion-rights movement represents the many women who were either harmed or killed because they performed illegal abortions on themselves (i.e., the surgery was performed with a coat hanger) or went to unscrupulous physicians (or back-alley butchers). Hence, as the argument goes, if abortion is made illegal, then women will once again be harmed. Needless to say, this argument serves a powerful rhetorical purpose. Although the image of a young woman being aborted with a coat hanger is to say the least unpleasant, powerfully persuasive, and emotionally charged, it does not a good argument make. Joseph McCarthy taught us that a number of decades ago, as do the demogogues of today. This argument fails for at least two reasons, one moral and the other factual: it begs the question; and it is based on questionable, if not clearly false, statistics.

This argument begs the question. As we shall see, this fallacy seems to lurk behind a good percentage of the popular arguments for the abortion-rights position. One begs the question when one assumes what one is trying to prove. Another way of putting it is to say that the arguer is reasoning in a circle. For example, if one concludes that the Boston Celtics are the best team because no team is better, one is not giving any reasons for this belief. To claim that a team is the best team is exactly the same as saying that no team is better. Sometimes this fallacy is committed in a more subtle way. For instance, an unsophisticated Christian may argue that he believes in God because the Bible says that God exists and the Bible is God's Word. The Christian is assuming that there is a God who inspired the Bible, but this is the Being whose existence is in question. Hence, by implicitly assuming his conclusion to be true in his appeal to the Bible's authority, the Christian commits the logical fallacy of begging the question.

The question-begging nature of the coat hanger argument is easy to discern. That is to say, only by assuming that the unborn are not fully human does the argument work. For if the unborn are not fully human, then the abortion-rights advocate has a legitimate concern, as one would have in overturning a law forbidding appendicitis operations if countless people were needlessly dying of both appendicitis and illegal operations. But if the unborn are fully human, this abortion-rights argument is tantamount to saying that because people die or are harmed while killing other people (i.e., unborn people), the state should make it safe for them to do so. Hence, only by assuming that the unborn are not fully human does this abortion-rights argument work. Therefore, it begs the question.

Even some abortion-rights advocates, who argue for their position in other ways, admit that the coat hanger/back-alley argument is fallacious. For example, abortion-rights philosopher Mary Anne Warren clearly recognizes that her position on abortion cannot rest on this argument if it is not first demonstrated that the unborn entity is not fully human. She writes that

the fact that restricting access to abortion has tragic side effects does not, in itself, show that the restrictions are unjustified, since murder is wrong regardless of the consequences of prohibiting it.[3]

This argument is based on highly questionable statistics. Although it is doubtful whether statistics can establish a particular moral position, there has been considerable debate over both the actual number of illegal abortions and the number of women who died as a result of them.[4] Prior to *Roe* abortion-rights activists were fond of saying that in the several decades prior to *Roe*, one to two million women every year obtained illegal abortions that resulted in thousands of fatalities. Consequently, safe, legal abortions (1.5 million per year) numerically replaced unsafe, illegal ones, resulting in no increase in the number of abortions.

But consider the following. Bernard Nathanson, one of the original leaders of the American pro-abortion movement and cofounder of N.A.R.A.L. (the National Association for the Repeal of Abortion Laws, now known as the National Abortion Rights Action League) who has since become pro-life, admits that he and others in the abortion-rights movement intentionally fabricated the number of women who allegedly died as a result of illegal abortions. He writes:

How many deaths were we talking about when abortion was illegal? In N.A.R.A.L. we generally emphasized the drama of the individual case, not the mass statistics, but when we spoke of the latter it was always "5,000 to 10,000 deaths a year." I confess that I knew the figures were totally false, and I suppose the others did too if they stopped to think of it. But in the "morality" of the revolution, it was a *useful* figure, widely accepted, so why go out of our way to correct it with honest statistics. The overriding concern was to get the laws eliminated, and anything within reason had to be done was permissible.[5]

Lawrence Lader, one of the leaders in the early days of the contemporary abortion-rights movement, once tried to support the figure cited by Nathanson when he claimed that "one study at the University of California's School of Public Health estimated 5,000 to 10,000 abortion deaths annually. Dr. [Christopher] Tietze places the figure nearer 1,000."[6] In response, Dr. James T. Burtchaell writes that "it is enlightening to consult the sources to which Lader refers the reader. No University of California study is cited. Instead, Lader refers to a source that depends on a deputy medical examiner of Los Angeles, who simply passes on a conjecture of 5,000 to 10,000 deaths annually. As for Tietze, the article to which Lader refers contains no estimate of or comment upon national abortion mortality."[7] Hence, Lader lied as to the identity of one source, a source who nevertheless provided Lader with a made-up figure. The second source, although real, provided no evidence whatsoever for Lader's position.

Second, Nathanson's observation is borne out in the best official statistical studies available. According to the U.S. Bureau of Vital Statistics, 39 women died from illegal abortions the year before *Roe v. Wade*, 1972.[8] Dr. Andre Hellegers, the late professor of obstetrics and gynecology at Georgetown University Hospital, has pointed out that there has been a steady decrease of abortion-related deaths since 1942. That year there were 1,231 deaths. Due to improved medical care and the use of penicillin, this number fell to 133 by 1968.[9] The year before the first state-liberalized abortion, 1966, there were about 120 abortion-related deaths.[10] This is not to minimize the undeniable fact that such deaths were significant losses to the families and loved ones of those who had died. But one must be willing to admit the equally undeniable fact that if the unborn are fully human, these abortion-related maternal deaths, which one abortion-rights scholar, Christopher Tietze, said numbered on the average of about 500 per year,[11] pale in comparison to the 1.5 million pre-born humans who on the average die every year. And even if we grant that there were more abortion-related deaths than the low number confirmed, there is no doubt that the 5,000 to 10,000

deaths cited by the abortion-rights movement is a gross exaggeration.[12]

These facts, however, do not prevent abortion-rights advocates from making false, and clearly absurd, claims. For example, Dr. E. Hakim-Elahi, while medical director of Planned Parenthood of New York City, stated that "when it was illegal for a woman to end her pregnancy, *one out of every 40 women who had abortions died*."[13] This means, of course, that if the 5,000 to 10,000 yearly figure for pre-*Roe* abortion-related deaths is correct, which Nathanson and Lader at one time defended, then there were 200,000 to 400,000 illegal abortions per year, far below the 1.5 million legal abortions performed every year and the 1 to 2 million ordinarily claimed by abortion-rights advocates to have occurred illegally prior to *Roe*. This means, of course, that contrary to abortion-rights proponents, legal abortions did not replace illegal abortions, but rather the legalization of abortion resulted in an eight to fourfold increase of the number of abortions. Consequently, making abortion illegal *did* prevent many abortions. But if the statistics from the U.S. Bureau of Vital Statisitics are correct (which is probably the case, since the bureau is not an abortion-rights or pro-life activist group), then the total number of illegal abortions prior to *Roe* is even smaller if we accept Hakim-Elahi's 1 in 40 abortion-related mortality rate: 1972, 1,560; 1968, 5,320; 1966, 4,800; 1942, 49,200. And even if we were to accept the figure provided by Tietze of 500 deaths per year, this would mean that there were 20,000 illegal abortions every year. Although these estimates are clearly low, they show how difficult it is for abortion-rights activists to sustain some of their claims.

On the other hand, if there were 1 to 2 million illegal abortions per year in the decades prior to *Roe*, as claimed by many in the abortion-rights movement,[14] the situation becomes more absurd if we assume Hakim-Elahi's claim that 1 in 40 women died from illegal abortions. For this would mean that about 25,000 to 50,000 women died from illegal abortions every year. But this poses an interesting problem. For example, in a typical pre-*Roe* year, 1965, 50,456 women aged

15 to 44 (the childbearing years) died of *all* causes.[15] This means that, according to pro-choice mathematics, in 1965 between 49.5 percent (25,000) and 99 percent (50,000) of women aged 15 to 44 died of illegal abortions. That, my friend, is absurd.

In a speech before the American Bar Association's annual meeting in 1990, former Planned Parenthood president Faye Wattleton claimed that in the 1960s the majority of women receiving abortions were "my poor, African-American sisters." Wattleton claimed that there were 600,000 to 1,200,000 illegal abortions per year prior to *Roe*.[16] Authors Robert Marshall and Charles Donovan apply Hakim-Elahi's rates to Wattleton's claim:

Using Hakim-Elahi's rates and Wattleton's figures for black abortions and black abortion deaths produces a complete absurdity. . . . The numbers of black women dying aged fifteen to forty-four in 1965 was 13,056. Using Wattleton's unspecific claim, black women must have had at least 51% of all abortions. Applying this figure to Hakim-Elahi's death rate would yield a minimum of 7,650 abortion deaths for black women, or 58.6% of all deaths among black females aged fifteen to forty-four [assuming Wattleton's low figure of 600,000 illegal abortions per year]. If Wattleton's higher abortion figure is the correct one [1.2 million], then 15,300 black women aged fifteen to forty-four died from illegal abortion, or, *almost 2,000 more black women than died from all causes in that age bracket during 1965*.[17] (emphasis added)

When abortion-rights supporters, such as Wattleton, start claiming that it is probable that more black women have died from illegal abortions than black women have died, it's time for the media, the medical community, and the legal system to start making abortion-rights proponents accountable for their claims.[18]

Third, it is an exaggeration to claim that there were one to two million illegal abortions per year prior to legalization. In addition to the problems already outlined, there is no reliable statistical support for this claim.[19] On the other hand, a highly so-phisticated recent study has concluded that "a reasonable estimate for the actual number of criminal abortions per year in the pre-legalization era [prior to 1967] would be from a low of 39,000 (1950) to a high of 210,000 (1961) and a mean of 98,000 per year."[20]

Moreover, one can reasonably argue that the claim of one to two million abortions a year is nearly impossible to sustain just from extrapolating the pre-*Roe* abortion-related death rates proposed by abortion-rights supporters. Consider the following proposals offered by abortion-rights supporters (the rate is the number of abortion-related deaths per 100,000 abortions):[21]

Author	Date(s)	Rate
Willard Cates, Jr.[22]	1972–74	30/100,000
Christopher Tietze[23]	1973	40/100,000
Christopher Tietze[24]	1960	66/100,000
Steven Polgar[25]	1965–67	3,416/100,000

The interesting thing about these statistics is that the higher the mortality rate, the lower the total number of illegal abortions. Take the example provided by Marshall and Donovan: "the National Center for Health Statistics (NCHS) has classified 114 maternal deaths in 1960 as resulting from illegal abortion. Applying the above maternal death rates would produce the following estimates for illegal abortions in 1960:"[26]

Cates at (30/100,000)	=	373,333 illegal abortions
Tietze at (66/100,000)	=	169,696 illegal abortions
Polgar at (3,416/100,000)	=	3,279 illegal abortions[27]

This means that the the figure of one to two million abortions a year is probably an exaggeration. Yet many people, including respected scholars who should know better, keep citing statistics somewhere between this number. For example, Harvard law professor Laurence Tribe in one place speaks of "the real risks to their lives and health undertaken by the *one million* women who had illegal abortions each year prior to *Roe*" (emphasis added). In another place Tribe uncritically accepts the statistic that "by the late 1960's as many as 1,200,000 women were undergoing illegal abortions each year; more than one criminal abortion a minute,"[28] despite the fact that the source on which he relies, Professor James Mohr, actually says "by the late 1960s estimates of the number of illegal abortions performed in the United States each year ranged from 200,000 to 1,200,000."[29] By not citing the lower end of the spectrum (200,000) and literally ignoring the scores of scholarly works that have been critical of the higher estimates, Tribe overstates his case and deceives the reader.

A recent study by David C. Reardon supports the view that there were a far less number of illegal abortions than the one to two million claimed by the abortion-rights movement. This can be inferred from the fact that Reardon found that if abortion were illegal, three-quarters of the women he interviewed who had undergone legal abortions would not have sought an abortion. Reardon writes:

> Given their doubts about the morality of abortion, most aborting women are strongly influenced by the legal status of the abortion option. When asked, "Did the knowledge that abortion was legal influence your opinion about the morality of choosing abortion?" 70 percent said that the law had played a major role in their moral perception of abortion. . . . *Asked whether or not they would have sought an illegal abortion if a legal abortion had not been available, 75 percent said they definitely would not have sought an illegal abortion. . . .*[30] (emphasis added)

Fourth, it is misleading to say that pre-*Roe* illegal abortions were performed by back-alley butchers with rusty coat hangers. Dr. Mary Calderone, while president of Planned Parenthood, pointed out in a 1960 article in the *American Journal of Public Health* that Dr. Alfred C. Kinsey showed in 1958 that 84 to 87 percent of all illegal abortions were performed by licensed physicians in good standing. Accepting Kinsey's conclusions, Calderone, as editor of the Planned Parenthood conference proceedings, wrote that

the conference estimated that *90 percent of all illegal abortions are done by physicians.* Call them what you will, abortionists or anything else, they are still physicians, trained as such; and many of them are in good standing in their communities. . . . Whatever trouble arises usually comes after self-induced abortions, which comprise approximately 8 percent, or with *the very small percentage that go to some kind of non-medical abortionist.* Another corollary fact: physicians of impeccable standing are referring their patients for these illegal abortions to the colleagues they know are willing to perform them.[31] (emphasis added)

It seems that the vast majority of back-alley butchers eventually became the "reproductive health providers" of our present day.

To give the reader an idea of how Planned Parenthood and other abortion-rights groups have no regard for truth, consider the contents of a 22 January 1979 letter from former Planned Parenthood president Faye Wattleton to members of Congress: "Illegal abortions have virtually disappeared. Estimates are that fewer than two percent of all abortions in 1975 were conducted illegally by unlicensed practitioners (compared with 95 percent in the 1960s)."[32] With only a typewriter and not a shred of evidence in support of her claim, Wattleton turned Calderone's and Kinsey's authoritative estimate that 90 percent of all illegal abortions were performed by physicians into a mere 5 percent.

Despite all the facts cited, facts to which abortion-rights supporters have access, the misinformation continues unabated. For example, novelist Sally Quinn, in a 1992 opinion piece that originally appeared in the *Washington Post*, writes about "the days when abortion was unsafe and illegal (and *the annual death rate was in the thousands*)" (emphasis added).[33] Of course, we know that 90 percent of these "unsafe and illegal" abortions were performed by physicians in good standing and that thousands of deaths did not result from them yearly. But Quinn and those of her ilk have no time to quibble with the facts, for they have a revolution to promote.

And fifth, due to advances in pharmacology and medical technology, it is extremely unlikely that if abortion is made illegal many women will be harmed. As Nathanson points out:

> The practice was revolutionized at virtually the same moment that the laws were revolutionized, through the widespread introduction of suction curettage in 1970. (Even before this, antibiotics and other advances had already dramatically lowered the abortion death rate.) . . . Though it is preferable that this be done by a licensed physician, one can expect that if abortion is driven underground again, even non-physicians will be able to perform this procedure with remarkable safety. No woman need die if she chooses to abort during the first twelve weeks of pregnancy. . . . As for self-induced abortion, by thrusting a coat hanger or other dangerous objects into the womb, this will be a thing of the past. Compounds known as prostaglandins can now be used to bring on contractions and expel alpha [the unborn], and would readily be available for do-it-yourself abortions in vaginal suppository form. . . . This may sound cynical, but this is what would now happen in practice if abortion were illegal.[34]

It should be kept in mind that my criticism of the use of statistics by the abortion-rights movement should in no way imply that any of its members may not be correct about certain numbers. My purpose is merely to show that certain statistical claims are inconsistent with each other, and that on several occasions abortion proponents, relying on dubious statistical claims, have spoken speculatively under the guise of presenting accurate information.

However, from a completely moral perspective, as noted in my first criticism of this argument, the number of illegal abortions prior to *Roe* is irrelevant to the debate. After all, if the unborn are human persons, then it makes no sense to claim that the state ought to make it safer to kill such persons because people participating in the killing may be harmed.

Argument from Economic Inequity

Abortion-rights advocates often argue that prior to abortion being legalized, pregnant women who did not go to unscrupulous physicians or back-alley butchers traveled to foreign nations where abortions were legal. This was an option open only to rich women. Hence, *Roe v. Wade* has made the current situation fairer for poor women. Therefore, if abortion is prohibited it will not prevent rich women from having safe and legal abortions elsewhere.[35]

This argument is fallacious. For it assumes that legal abortion is a moral good that poor women will be denied if abortion is made illegal. But since the morality of abortion is the point under question, the abortion-rights proponent assumes what he is trying to prove and therefore begs the question. One can think of a number of examples to better understand this point. To cite one, we would consider it bizarre if someone argued that the hiring of hit men to kill one's enemies should be legalized, since, after all, the poor do not have easy economic access to such a practice.

In the abortion debate the question of whether abortion entails the death of a being who is fully human must be answered before the question of fairness is even asked. That is to say, since equal opportunity to kill an innocent human person is rarely if ever a moral good, the question of whether it is fair that certain rich people will have privileged access to abortion if it becomes illegal must be answered *after* we answer the question of whether abortion in fact is *not* the killing of an innocent person. For it is not true that the vices of the wealthy are virtues simply because the poor are denied them.

Furthermore, the pro-life advocate could turn this argument on its ear by admitting to the abortion-rights advocate that indeed something economically unjust will occur if abortion on demand is made illegal, namely, that rich unborn humans will not have the same right to life as poor unborn humans. But this is more preferable than what is currently occurring, namely, that both rich and poor unborn humans do not have a right to life. Of course, the pro-life advocate is assuming that the unborn entity is fully human and the abortion-rights advocate is assuming that it is not. Therefore, the real issue is not one of economic inequity but whether the unborn are fully human and hence deserving of the right to life enjoyed by those of us who are already born.

Argument from Population, Poverty, and Financial Burden

Some abortion-rights advocates make much of both the use of abortion as a means of population control and the financial and emotional burden a child may put on a family. It is argued that in such situations abortion is justified. A number of abortion-rights advocates argue that if abortion is forbidden, then the poor will keep producing more children to draw more welfare. Hence, there is an economic incentive in permitting abortion. There are two major problems with this argument, one factual and the other moral: it is based on the false assumption that population increase is bad; it is based on bad moral reasoning.

This argument is based on the false assumption that population increase is bad. The so-called population problem has little to do with the number of people in a particular nation but rather with its economic system and whether the government provides incentives for growth. In fact, under a free-market economic system, there is evidence to suggest that population growth is actually healthy and desirable, resulting in an increase in the standard of living. Economist P. T. Bauer argues for this thesis:

> Since the 1950s rapid population increase in densely-populated Hong Kong and Singapore has been accompanied by large increases in real income and wages. The population of the Western world has more than quadrupled since the middle of the eighteenth century. Real income per head is estimated to have increased by a factor of five or more. Most of the increase in incomes took place when population increased as fast as, or faster than, in the contemporary less developed world. . . .

> In both the less developed world and in the West some of the most prosperous countries and regions are extremely densely populated. Hong Kong and Singapore are probably the most densely populated countries in the world, with originally very poor land. . . . In the advanced world Japan, West Germany, Belgium, and Holland are examples of densely populated countries. Conversely, many millions of extremely backward people live in sparsely populated regions amidst cultivable land. Examples include the backward peoples in Sumatra, Borneo, Central Africa and the interior of South America. They have ready access to vast areas of land—for them land is a free good. In South Asia, generally regarded as a region suffering from over-population, there is much uncultivated land, land which could be cultivated at the level of technology prevailing in the region.[36]

It is no coincidence that the Far Eastern and Western nations mentioned by Bauer, nations that are densely populated and/or have experienced large increases in population as well as economic growth, have free-market (capitalist) economies, whereas the nations that are sparsely populated, rich with natural resources, and yet largely impoverished, have for the most part rejected a free-market economic system.

Second, E. Calvin Beisner lends support to Bauer's thesis by arguing that abortion is economically harmful to future generations in the United States, especially the elderly. He argues that "on average, children are an economic liability from conception to age eighteen, after which they become, on average, an economic asset until sixty-five, after which they become, on average, an economic liability again." Extrapolating from numbers estimated by economist Marvin DeVries and reported by Allan C. Carlson in *Family Reflections: Reflections on the American Social Crisis* ([New Brunswick, N.J.: Transaction, 1988], 59–60), Beisner concludes "that the average person (this average takes into account *all* people, whether they ever work or never work, and regardless of income) will represent a combined liability, or economic cost, of $192,600 during his first eighteen years plus his lifetime after retirement at age sixty-five." On the other hand, "the same average person will occasion the production, directly and indirectly, of goods and services with average worth, if a male, of $55,277 per year, or, if a female, of $26,680 per year, every year from age eighteen to age sixty-five."[37]

It follows from these numbers that "the average male will occasion the production (either through his own direct work or through his multiplication effect on others' productivity—cooperation increases productivity geometrically, not arithmetically) of $2,598,019 worth of goods and services during his lifetime, and the average female will occasion the production of $1,253,960 worth of goods and services in her lifetime." Subtracting the economic cost of both a male's and female's first eighteen years and retirement, $192,600, "the average male's net worth to society . . . will be $2,405,419, and the average female's will be $1,061,360." Consequently, "abort the average male and you rob society, over the span of his lifetime, of $2,405,419; abort the average female and you rob society, over the span of her lifetime, of $1,061,360. (Actually, you can tag on about another $400 to each of those figures—for the cost of the abortion, which the aborted person can never repay by his productivity.)"[38]

Since these figures are the person's net worth, arrived at after the person's costs to society have been subtracted from his benefits, one cannot object to Beisner's argument on the grounds that it does not take into consideration how much these people will cost us in unemployment insurance, education, or health care. Yet, aborting these individuals will result in significantly less revenue for both Social Security and the Internal Revenue Service, since these individuals will not exist to be productive. If 14.5 percent of personal earnings are taxed to fund Social Security and this percentage does not increase in a person's lifetime (which is highly unlikely), during each of their lifetimes the average male's productivity will contribute $348,785 and the average female's productivity will contribute $153,897. Since about 20 percent of the gross national product (GNP) is taxed

by the federal government, during each of their lifetimes the average male's productivity will contribute $481,084 to the federal budget and the average female's productivity will contribute $212,272. It follows from these numbers that abortion is contributing to America's budget deficit as well as the disintegration of the Social Security fund. Abortion for economic health is utterly absurd.[39]

Third, Humboldt University economist Jacqueline R. Kasun argues that the natural resources of the world are more than capable of sustaining the world's current population of four billion. The problem lies in the nations with economic systems not conducive to either economic growth or efficiently harnessing the world's resources. Kasun writes:

> Colin Clark, former director of the Agricultural Economic Institute at Oxford University and noted author of many books on population-resource questions, classified world land types by their food-raising capabilities and found that, if all farmers were to use the best methods now in use, enough food could be raised to provide an American-type diet for 35,100,000,000 people, almost ten times as many as now exist! Since the American diet is a very rich one, Clark found that it would be possible to feed three times as many again—30 times as many people as now exist—at a Japanese standard of food intake. Nor would these high levels of food output require cropping every inch of available land space. Clark's model assumed that nearly half of the earth's land area would remain conservation areas. The noted city planner, Constantin Doxiadis, arrived independently at a similar estimate of the world's ability to feed people and to provide conservation areas. . . . It is of some interest at this point to compare the current UN [United Nations] forecast of the eventual size of the world population—between 10 and 16,000,000,000 at the end of the 21st century—a figure viewed with alarm in some quarters, with the carefully estimated world capability of feeding between 35 and 100,000,000,000 people, using *presently known* methods.[40] (emphasis added)

Some people argue that increased congestion is evidence that population growth is a worldwide problem. But this is a deceptive argument, since congestion is found exclusively in the urbanized seacoasts and major cities. The fact is that most of the earth is still largely empty. As Francis Felice points out, "We could put the entire world population [4 billion] in the state of Texas and each man, woman and child could be allotted 2,000 square feet [the average home ranges between 1,400 and 1,800 square feet] and the whole rest of the world could be empty."[41]

This argument is based on bad moral reasoning. There are at least three reasons why this argument is based on bad moral reasoning. First, it does not really support the "pro-choice" position that abortion is a fundamental right the pregnant woman can exercise for any reason she deems fit during the entire nine months of pregnancy.[42] That is to say, if this argument is successful it only establishes the right to an abortion in the cases of overpopulation, poverty, and financial burden—*not* "for any reason the pregnant woman deems fit." Futhermore, suppose that the world was overpopulated but that the pregnant women in such a world refused to have abortions. Would the abortion-rights advocate force these women to have abortions? If yes, then appealing to overpopulation is not a pro-*choice* argument, since it entails compulsory abortions. If the answer is no, then abortion for population control is not relevant to establishing the pro-*choice* position, since it is obvious that women can always choose to not have abortions in the face of overpopulation.

Second, this argument is morally problematic, since, like the other arguments we have gone over, it also begs the question. That is, only if the abortion-rights advocate assumes that the unborn poor are not fully human does his policy carry any weight. For if the unborn poor are fully human, the abortion-rights advocate's plan to eliminate overpopulation and poverty by permitting the extermination of the unborn poor is inconsistent with his own ethic of personal rights. Thus, the question of aborting the unborn poor, like the arguments brought up earlier,

hinges on the status of the unborn. Furthermore, if the unborn are fully human, then this is also a good argument for infanticide and the killing of all humans we find to be financially burdensome or emotionally taxing. Therefore, only by assuming that the unborn are not fully human does the abortion-rights advocate avoid such horrendous consequences. Thus in order for this argument to work, the abortion-rights advocate must beg the question.

This is not to say that the human race may not reach a time in its history at which overpopulation becomes a problem so severe that it must significantly curtail its birthrate. At such a time it would be wise to try to persuade people either to willingly use contraceptive devices or to practice sexual discipline. If such a tactic does not work, then forced sterilization may be a viable, albeit desperate, option, since it does not entail the death of the unborn. In any event, if the unborn are fully human, abortion is not a solution to population problems even in the most dire of circumstances. Hence, the real question is whether or not the unborn are fully human.

Third, underlying this type of abortion-rights argument is a fundamental confusion between the concept of "finding a solution" and the concept of "eliminating a problem." For example, one can eliminate the problem of poverty by executing all poor people, but this would not really solve the problem, since it would directly conflict with our basic moral intuition that persons should not be gratuitously exterminated for the sake of easing economic tension. This "solution" would undermine the very moral sentiments that ground our compassion for poor people—namely, that they are humans of great worth and should be treated with dignity regardless of their predicament. Similarly, one can eliminate the problem of having a headache by cutting off one's head just as a society can eliminate a lifetime of wife-beating by legalizing newlywed wife-killing, but these are certainly not real solutions. Therefore, the argument of the abortion-rights advocate is superfluous unless he can first show that the unborn are not fully human and hence do not deserve to be the recipients of our basic moral sentiments. Rice University philosopher and bioethicist Baruch Brody comments:

> In an age where we doubt the justice of capital punishment even for very dangerous criminals, killing a fetus who has not done any harm, to avoid a future problem it may pose, seems totally unjust. There are indeed many social problems that could be erased simply by destroying those persons who constitute or cause them, but that is a solution repugnant to the values of society itself. In short, then, if the fetus is a human being, the appeal to its being unwanted justifies no abortions.[43]

This is not to minimize the fact that there are tragic circumstances, such as the poor woman with four small children who has become pregnant by her alcoholic husband. But once again we must ask whether or not the unborn entity is fully human, for hardship does not justify homicide. For example, if I knew that killing you would relieve me of future hardship no moral person would say that that would be sufficient justification for me to kill you. Do you suppose that if an abortion-rights supporter knew that his death would help heal a dysfunctional family, he would argue that the members of this family have a right to kill him in order to achieve this goal? I think not. But if the abortion-rights supporter is not obligated to die for others who perceive his death as a benefit for them, why is the unborn child obligated to do so?

In rare cases in which a child may bring extra hardship, those in the religious and charitable communities should help lend financial and emotional support to the family, as they will do and have done in many cases. And it may be wise, if it is a case of extreme hardship, for the woman to put her baby up for adoption, so that she may give to others the gift of parenthood. But in any event, if the unborn child is fully human, killing her is never a morally viable option, just as killing born children, who we know are fully human, is never a morally viable option for parents who seek relief from the burdens of parenthood.

Argument from the Unwanted Child and Child Abuse

It is argued by many people in the abortion-rights movement that legal abortion will help eliminate unwanted children. They believe that unwantedness is indirectly responsible for a great number of family problems, such as child abuse. Hence, if a family can have the "correct" amount of children at the "proper" times, then these family problems will be greatly reduced if not eliminated.[44] There are several serious problems with this argument.

First, it begs the question, because only by assuming that the unborn are not fully human does this argument work. For if the unborn are fully human, like the abused born children that we readily admit are fully human, then to execute the unborn is the worst sort of child abuse imaginable. Would the killing of three-year-olds be morally acceptable if it would eliminate the abuse of five-year-olds? Of course not. But what morally distinguishes the unborn from the born infant, the three-year-old, or the five-year-old? So that is the real question—"Are the unborn fully human?"—not, "Does abortion help curb child abuse?"

Second, it is very difficult to demonstrate that the moral and metaphysical value of a human person is dependent on whether someone wants or cares for that human person. For example, no one disputes that the homeless have value even though they are for the most part unwanted. But suppose the abortion-rights advocate responds to this by saying, "But you are treating the unborn as if they were as human as the homeless." And this is exactly my point. The question is not whether the unborn are wanted; the question is whether the unborn are fully human.

Third, abortion on demand has been legal in America for twenty years. And yet reports of child abuse have increased dramatically. Former Surgeon General C. Everett Koop points out:

> [I]n 1972 there were 60,000 child-abuse incidents which were brought to official at-

tention in the United States. Just four years later, in 1976, the number that received official attention passed the half-million mark. *Reported* cases of child abuse probably represent only half of what really occurs.

Child abuse is the fifth most frequent cause of death among children. In *U.S. News and World Report* (May 3, 1976) it was reported that Dr. Irwin Hedlener, investigating child abuse at Jackson Memorial Hospital in Miami, said: "If child abuse were polio, the whole country would be up in arms looking for a solution."[45]

David Reardon points out that this is an international phenomenon:

Since *Roe v. Wade*, child abuse has increased proportionately with the skyrocketing rate of legal abortions. The same pattern of increased child battery following legalization of abortion has also been observed in many other countries, including Canada, Britain, and Japan. During 1975 alone, the rate of child battery in New York increased 18 to 20 percent, leading to estimates that during the 1980s there would be 1.5 million battered children, resulting in 50,000 deaths and 300,000 permanent injuries.[46]

Unfortunately, this trend does not seem to be letting up. In a lecture she gave at Brown University (March 8, 1989), Anne H. Cohn, executive director of the National Committee for the Prevention of Child Abuse, told the audience that "about 2.25 million child abuse cases were reported last year [1988], half of which required some form of treatment; 1,130 deaths were attributed to child abuse last year; the number of reported cases has risen 50 percent in the last 5 years."[47]

Although it seems clear that abortion is no solution to child abuse, it may very well help to precipitate it, as Philip Ney, M.D., a professor of psychiatry, has concluded in his studies on the subject.[48] After all, if it is all right to brutalize one's offspring before birth, why not after?

Fourth, an unwanted child almost never turns out to be a resented baby. This seems to be borne out statistically: there is no solid evidence that unwantedness during pregnancy produces child abuse; according to one study, 90 percent of battered children were wanted pregnancies;[49] and some writers have argued that there is a higher frequency of abuse among adopted children—who were undoubtedly wanted by their adoptee parents—than among those who are not adopted.[50] In his voluminous and scholarly study on the moral, political, and constitutional aspects of the abortion issue, Stephen Krason summarizes his findings concerning the argument from unwantedness by pointing out that "the factors causing child abuse cited most frequently by the researchers are not 'unwantedness,' but parents' lack of social support from family, friends and community, hostility to them by society, based on a disapproved sexual and social pattern of existence, and—most commonly—their having been abused and neglected themselves when they were children."[51]

Fifth, the unwantedness of children in general tells us a great deal about our psychological and moral makeup as a people, but very little about the value of the child involved. For it is a self-centered hedonistic people who do not consider it a self-evident obligation to care for the most vulnerable and defenseless members of the human race. A lack of caring is a flaw in the one who ought to care, not in the person who ought to be cared for. Hence, whether or not abortion is morally justified depends on whether the unborn are fully human, not on their wantedness.

Sixth, the appeal to wantedness for determining value only applies to things that have economic value based on demand for them. For example, tickets to the Super Bowl are valuable because they are desired by people. If nobody cared about the Super Bowl, ticket prices would be lowered in order to attract more people to the game. Hence, their value would decrease as demand decreased. The skills of Larry Bird are another example of such a "thing." The Boston Celtics were willing to pay Bird several million dollars a year simply because his abilities helped his team win, attracted ticket-paying fans, and brought in revenue through multimillion dollar television contracts. Now Bird's value as a human person is the same regardless of whether or not his skills as an athlete were wanted. To say that his human value is equal to the economic value of his skills would be to undermine the very system of rights and obligations that serves as the foundation for our claim that civil and human rights are universal in scope and no respecter of persons. Hence, only if the unborn entity is not fully human does its wantedness have a bearing on its value. Therefore, the question is not whether the unborn entity is wanted but whether it is fully human, for if it is fully human its wantedness is irrelevant to its intrinsic value.

Psychologist Sidney Callahan has observed that the problem with the abortion-rights argument from "unwantedness" is that it sets a terrible social precedent, for it is clearly implying that "the powerful" (in this case, parents) can determine at will the worth of "the powerless" (in this case, their unborn children). She writes:

> The powerful (including parents) cannot be allowed to want and unwant people at will. . . .
>
> It's destructive of family life for parents even to think in these categories of wanted and unwanted children. By using the words you set up parents with too much power, including psychological power, over their children. Somehow the child is being measured by the parent's attitudes and being defined by the parent's feelings. We usually want only objects, and wanting them or not implies that we are superior, or at least engage in a one-way relationship, to them.
>
> In the same way, men have "wanted" women through the ages. Often a woman's position was precarious and rested on being wanted by some man. The unwanted woman could be cast off when she was no longer a desirable object. She did not have an intrinsic dignity beyond wanting.[52]

It seems, then, that abortion-rights feminists have espoused the least virtuous and most repulsive aspect of "machoism"—"I can snuff you out because I'm bigger."

Argument from the Deformed and Mentally Handicapped Child

Since it is now possible to detect through amniocentesis and other tests whether the unborn entity will turn out to be physically or mentally handicapped,[53] some abortion-rights advocates argue that abortion should remain a choice for women who do not want to take care of such a child. Another reason cited for advocating the aborting of the defective unborn is that it is better for such children to never be born rather than to live a life with a serious mental or physical handicap. There are several problems with this argument.

First, this argument, like many of the appeals to "hard cases," does not really support the abortion-rights position, the position that abortion is a fundamental right the pregnant woman can exercise for any reason she deems fit during the entire nine months of pregnancy.[54] In other words, if this argument is successful in showing that abortion is justified in the case of a woman pregnant with a deformed or a mentally handicapped fetus, it only establishes the right to an abortion in such cases, not "for any reason the pregnant woman deems fit." And almost all abortions performed in America are of healthy fetuses.

Second, like many of the abortion-rights arguments, this argument begs the question by assuming that the unborn entity is not fully human. If the unborn are fully human, then to promote the aborting of the handicapped unborn is tantamount to promoting the execution of handicapped people who are already born. But such a practice is morally reprehensible. Are not adults with the same deformities human? Then so too are smaller people. In fact, abortion-rights advocates Peter Singer and Helga Kuhse, who argue for their position in other ways, admit that "pro-life groups are right about one thing: the location of the baby inside or outside the womb cannot make such a crucial moral difference. . . . The solution, however, is not to accept the pro-life view that the fetus is a human being with the same moral status as yours or mine. The solution is the very opposite: to abandon the idea that all human life is of equal worth."[55] Although I do not agree with this conclusion, and will argue against it in chapter 6, Singer and Kuhse make an important observation: the question is not whether a particular unborn entity is physically or mentally handicapped, but whether it is fully human and deserving of all the rights of such a status.

Third, it is amazingly presumptuous to say that certain human beings are better off not existing. For one thing, how can one compare nonexistence with existence when they do not have anything in common? How can one be better off not existing if one is not there to appreciate the joy of such a "state" (whatever that means)? Koop, who worked for years with severely deformed infants as a pediatric surgeon at Philadelphia's Children's Hospital, has made the observation that "it has been my constant experience that disability and unhappiness do not necessarily go together."[56] He goes on to state:

> Some of the most unhappy children whom I have known have all of their physical and mental faculties, and on the other hand some of the happiest youngsters have borne burdens which I myself would find very difficult to bear. Our obligation in such circumstances is to find alternatives for the problems our patients face. I don't consider death an acceptable alternative. With our technology and creativity, we are merely at the beginning of what we can do educationally and in the field of leisure activities for such youngsters. And who knows what happiness is for another person?[57]

This is not to say that there are not tragedies in life and that having a handicapped child is not difficult. But it is important to realize that if the unborn entity is fully human, homicide cannot be justified simply because it relieves one of a terrible burden. It is fundamental to correct moral reasoning that it is better to suffer evil rather than to inflict it.[58] If this moral precept were not true, all so-called moral dilemmas would be easily solved by appealing to one's own relief from suffering. But in such a world the antidote would be worse than the poison, for

people would then have a right to harm another if it relieved them of a burden. None of us has a right to expect someone else, whether it is an unborn child or a full-grown adult, to forfeit his or her life so that we may be relieved of a burden. I, and a great number of other people, would find such a world morally intolerable.

Moreover, it should not be forgotten that a handicapped child can give both society and the family into which it has been born an opportunity to exercise true compassion, love, charity, and kindness. It is an assault upon our common humanity to deny our capacity to attain virtue in the presence of suffering and/or disability.

Fourth, many handicapped people, for obvious reasons, are vehemently opposed to this argument. In fact, not a single organization of handicapped people is on record in favor of abortion of those who may be handicapped. Koop cites the following letter, which appeared in the London *Daily Telegraph* (8 December 1962) at a time when European newspapers were seriously discussing the use of abortion as an effective means by which to avoid the birth of children who became defective *en utero* due to their mother's use of thalidomide (a tranquilizer used by European women in the 1950s and 1960s but never approved by the FDA for sale in the U.S.):

> Trowbridge
> Kent
> Dec. 8, 1962
>
> Sirs:
> We were disabled from causes other than thalidomide, the first of us having two useless arms and hands; the second, two useless legs; and the third, the use of neither arms nor legs.
> We were fortunate . . . in having been allowed to live and we want to say with strong conviction how thankful we are that none took it upon themselves to destroy us as useless cripples.
> Here at the Debarue school of spastics, one of the schools of the National Spastic Society, we have found worthwhile and happy lives and we face our future with confidence. Despite our disability, life still has much to offer and we are more than anx-

ious, if only metaphorically, to reach out toward the future.

This, we hope will give comfort and hope to the parents of the thalidomide babies, and at the same time serve to condemn those who would contemplate the destruction of even a limbless baby.

Yours faithfully,
Elaine Duckett
Glynn Verdon
Caryl Hodges.[59]

Fifth, if there were a correlation between happiness and handicap, it would seem natural to find more suicides among the handicapped than the general public. But this is not the case. Krason points out that "no study . . . has found that handicapped persons are more likely than nonhandicapped persons to want to be killed or to commit suicide." Citing a study by Hellegers, Krason writes that "of 200 consecutive suicides by the Baltimore Morgue . . . none had been commited by people with congenital anomolies."[60] Eugene F. Diamond, M.D., reinforces this point when he writes:

There is no evidence that the handicapped child would rather not go on living. As a matter of fact, handicapped persons commit suicide far less often than normal persons. An interesting study was done at the Ana Stift in Hanover, Germany, a center where a large number of children with phocomelia, due to thalidomide, are cared for. Psychological testing on these children indicated that they do indeed value their lives, that they are glad that they were born and they look forward to the future with hope and pleasant anticipation.[61]

A society whose ethic asserts that certain pre-born human beings forfeit their right to life simply because they have a certain physical deformity or mental handicap is a society that will inevitably see those with the same features who have already been born as having lives "not worth living." Passing through the birth canal, as passing through the Panama Canal, does nothing to change who one is. The chilling logic of this conclusion was played out in a real-life situation in

1982. That year, an Indiana newborn, Infant Doe, who was born with Down's syndrome and a congenital defect that prevented food from reaching her stomach, was permitted to die at the request of her parents, who asked the attending physician to withhold food and water from the infant. This parental decision was upheld by an Indiana court. Her stomach problem was correctable by surgery, and if Infant Doe had not been "retarded," there is no doubt that the parents would have requested the necessary surgery. It was not her inability to eat that killed Infant Doe, but parents who neglected her simply because she had Down's syndrome. Commenting on this case, columnist George Will writes about his own son, Jonathan, who is a Down's syndrome citizen:

When a commentator has a direct personal interest in an issue, it behooves him to say so. Some of my best friends are Down's syndrome citizens. (Citizens are what Down's syndrome children are if they avoid being homicide victims in hospitals).

Jonathan Will, 10, fourth-grader and Orioles fan (and the best Wiffle-ball hitter in southern Maryland), has Down's syndrome. He does not "suffer from" (as newspapers are wont to say) Down's syndrome. He suffers from nothing, except anxiety about the Orioles' lousy start. He is doing nicely, thank you. But he is bound to have quite enough problems dealing with society—receiving rights, let alone empathy. He can do without people like Infant Doe's parents, and courts like Indiana's asserting by their actions the principle that people like him are less than fully human. On the evidence, Down's syndrome citizens have little to learn about being human from people responsible for the death of Infant Doe.[62]

Someone may respond by asking, "But how can you force someone to bring a handicapped child into the world?" This question, of course, assumes that the unborn human is only a potential person. Thus, like other arguments, it begs the question. But suppose the unborn is fully human—a human person with great potential and not just a potential person—then the child in the womb is already in the world. Hence, the question would be misguided, since nobody would be forcing anyone to bring a handicapped child into the world; the child is already in the world. Pro-lifers want the handicapped children who are already in the world, born and unborn, to be protected from murder.

The humanness of some entities that are sometimes present in the womb, such as a tertatoma or an anencephalic baby, is more controversial. The tertatoma is simply a tumor with some human genetic material that has gone awry. Sometimes it may contain hair, teeth, skin, or even fingers, but it is not an unborn human entity and does not have the natural inherent capacity to develop under any conditions into a human infant. Furthermore, the tertatoma is part of the woman's bodily tissue, not a separate human individual.[63]

According to the *American Medical Association Encyclopedia of Medicine*, anencephaly is the "absence at birth of the brain, cranial vault (top of the skull), and spinal cord. Most affected infants are stillborn or survive only a few hours." Anencephaly occurs "due to a failure in development of the neural tube, the nerve tissue in the embryo that eventually develops into the spinal cord and brain." A woman can know early in pregnancy that she is carrying an anencephalic baby "by measurement of *alphafetoprotein*, by *ultrasound scanning*, and by *amniocentesis*."[64]

We may or may not be dealing with human beings in the case of anencephalic babies. Relying on the work of Germain Grisez, Krason argues that "there are two ways we may view the 'anencephalic monster,' depending on when the abnormality originates." One way, "when the abnormality or the genetic certainty of it is present from conception, is to view the organism as human in its conception, but incapable of developing beyond a few hours, a few days, or a few weeks." He argues "that in such cases, especially if the specifically human genetic pattern is greatly transformed, we may not consider the conceptus a human individual."[65]

Or, we could view the anencephalic as we would an individual who has had his head blown off by a shotgun. "Such a person is human and remains such until he dies." Since "the anencephalic originated as a human and developed normally up to the point when the neural tube failed to close . . ., he thus can be viewed as a human being, albeit a damaged one, whose abnormality will cause his death shortly after birth, like the gunshot wounded person will die a short while after his wound."[66] A damaged human is not a nonhuman.

It should be remembered, however, that the anencephalic is a "hard case," and cannot be used to justify the vast majority of abortions that involve the killing of healthy preborns for any reason the pregnant woman deems fit.

Argument from Interference in Career

This argument has been used by many abortion-rights advocates in popular debate. It has been put forth in a scholarly forum by Virginia Ramey Mollenkott.[67] She begins her article by pointing out the perils of being a woman in today's society. She cites the fact that even if a sexually active woman uses the most effective contraceptives available, failure can occur and she can still get pregnant. Mollenkott then asks, "How is a married woman able to plan schooling or commit herself to a career or vocation as long as her life is continually open to the disruption of unplanned pregnancies?" She concludes, "Unless, of course, she can fall back on an abortion when all else fails."[68]

The fundamental problem with this argument is that it begs the question by assuming that the unborn are not fully human. What would we think of a mother who murdered her two-year-old because he interfered with her ability to advance in her occupation? We would find such an act morally reprehensible. Therefore, the abortion-rights position hinges on its ability to show that the unborn are not fully human, not on appeals to careers or occupations.

Argument from Rape and Incest

A woman who becomes pregnant due to rape or incest is a victim of a horribly violent and morally reprehensible crime. Although pregnancy as a result of either rape or incest is extremely rare,[69] pregnancy does occur in some instances. Bioethicist Andrew Varga summarizes the argument from rape and incest:

> It is argued that in these tragic cases the great value of the mental health of a woman who becomes pregnant as a result of rape or incest can best be safeguarded by abortion. It is also said that a pregnancy caused by rape or incest is the result of a grave injustice and that the victim should not be obliged to carry the fetus to viability. This would keep reminding her for nine months of the violence committed against her and would just increase her mental anguish. It is reasoned that the value of the woman's mental health is greater than the value of the fetus. In addition, it is maintained that the fetus is an aggressor against the woman's integrity and personal life; it is only just and morally defensible to repel an aggressor even by killing him if that is the only way to defend personal and human values. It is concluded, then, that abortion is justified in these cases.[70]

There are several problems with this argument. First, this argument is not relevant to the case for abortion on demand, the position defended by the popular abortion-rights movement. This position states that a woman has a right to have an abortion for nearly any reason she prefers during the entire nine months of pregnancy.[71] To argue for abortion on demand from the hard cases of rape and incest is like trying to argue for the elimination of traffic laws from the fact that one might have to violate some of them in rare circumstances, such as when one's spouse or child needs to be rushed to the hospital. Proving an exception does not prove a general rule. (For more on this, see "Abortion Rights and Utilitarian Arguments.")

Second, the unborn entity is not an aggressor when its presence does not endanger its mother's life (as in the case of a tubal pregnancy). The rapist is the aggressor. The unborn entity is just as much an innocent victim as its mother. An abortion will not change the fact that the woman was raped.

Hence, abortion cannot be justified on the basis that the unborn is an aggressor.

Third, this argument begs the question by assuming that the unborn is not fully human. If the unborn is fully human, then we must weigh the relieving of the woman's mental suffering against the right to life of an innocent human person. But homicide of another is never justified to relieve one of emotional distress. Although such a judgment is indeed anguishing, we must not forget that the same innocent unborn entity that the career-oriented woman will abort in order to avoid interference with a job promotion is biologically and morally indistinguishable from the unborn entity that results from an act of rape or incest. And since abortion for career advancement cannot be justified if the unborn entity is fully human, abortion cannot be justified in the cases of rape and incest, since in both cases abortion results in the death of an innocent human person. As Nathanson has written, "The unwanted pregnancy flows biologically from the sexual act, but not morally from it."[72] Hence, this argument, like the others, is successful only if the unborn are not fully human.

Fourth, if the unborn is fully human (which is the real question), to request that its life be forfeited for the alleged benefit of another (its mother) is to violate a basic principle of ethics: "we may never kill innocent person B to save person A." For example, "we cannot kill John by removing a vital organ in order to save Mary, who needs it. This is not a lack of compassion for Mary; it is the refusal to commit murder, even for a good cause. John has a right not to be killed to benefit Mary, even to save her life. Mary has the same right. We could not kill the woman to benefit the child. Equally, we cannot kill the child to benefit the woman." In abortion, "the child is being sacrificed for the benefit of another. He has no duty to do this; it is not right to force him. Would those who favor abortion for rape volunteer their lives so that another may be benefited in a similar way? If not, is it right to force this on another person? If yes, at least they have the opportunity to make a choice; the child does not?"[73]

Simply because some people believe that an unborn child's death may result in the happiness of another does not mean that the child has a duty to die.

Some abortion-rights advocates claim that the pro-lifer lacks compassion, since the pro-lifer's position on rape and incest forces a woman to carry her baby against her will. Nothing could be further from the truth. It is the rapist who has forced this woman to carry her child, not the pro-lifer. The pro-life advocate merely wants to prevent another innocent human person (the unborn entity) from being a victim of another violent and morally reprehensible act, abortion (see the section on fetal pain in chap. 3 as well as the arguments for fetal personhood in chaps. 3 and 6), for two wrongs do not make a right. What makes abortion evil is the same thing that makes rape evil: an innocent human person is brutally violated and dehumanized. Surely refusal to sanction murder is no lack of compassion. As Schwarz points out, sometimes the moral thing to do is not the most pleasant:

> A person in a concentration camp may have the opportunity to become an informer, which means a better life for him. But it also means betraying his friends and causing them additional suffering. Morally, he is forced to remain in his present, pitiable state, rather than do a moral evil, namely, betraying his friends, perhaps causing their deaths. If a woman is forced to continue a pregnancy, the case is similar in this respect, that she too is forced to remain in a pitiable state because the alternative is a moral evil, the killing of an innocent child.[74]

Fifth, theologian and ethicist Michael Bauman has observed: "A child does not lose its right to life simply because its father or its mother was a sexual criminal or a deviate."[75] Bauman also points out that in using the rape/incest argument the abortion-rights advocate is making the highly questionable assumption that the rape victim is the one best suited to administer justice and should be permitted to kill the criminal's offspring. But if the unborn entity is fully human (which is the real question in the abortion debate), this type of justice is nothing resembling what reasonable people have thought of as justice, for "a civilized nation does not permit the victim of a crime to pass a death sentence on the criminal's offspring. To empower the victim of a sex offense to kill the offender's child is an even more deplorable act than the rape that conceived it. The child conceived by rape or incest is a victim, too. In America, we do not execute victims."[76] Bauman concludes:

> Because ours is a government of laws and not of men, we must not consign justice and morality to the pain-beguiled whims of victims. They, of all people, might be the least able to render a just verdict or to identify the path of highest virtue. I am convinced that the more monstrously one is mistreated, the more likely it is that revenge and personal expedience will look to that person like goodness. While rape victims most certainly know best the horror and indignity of the crime in question, being its victims does not confer upon them either ethical or jurisprudential expertise. Nor does it enable them to balance the scales of justice or satisfy the demands of the moral imperative with care, knowledge, finesse, or precision. If one was an uninformed or inept ethicist or penologist before the crime, as most of us undoubtedly are, being a victim does not alter that fact at all. Justice is traditionally portrayed as blind, not because she was victimized and had her eyes criminally removed, but because she is impartial. Rape victims, like all other crime victims, rarely can be trusted to be sufficiently impartial or dependably ethical, especially seeing that they so often decide that the best alternative open to them is to kill the criminal's child.[77]

Sixth, aside from its moral shortcomings, the argument from rape and incest makes the questionable factual assumption that abortion is the only or best way a pregnant woman can be relieved of the trauma and violation of rape. For one thing, the anguish and psychic suffering caused by rape and incest has been treated quite effectively for those women who choose to carry their children to term. Krason points out that "psychological studies have shown that, when given the proper support, most pregnant rape victims progressively change their attitudes about their unborn child from something repulsive to someone who is innocent and uniquely worthwhile."[78] The pro-life advocate believes that help should be given to the rape victim "to make it as easy as possible for her to give up her baby for adoption, if she desires. Dealing with the woman pregnant from rape, then, can be an opportunity for us—both as individuals and society—to develop true understanding and charity. Is it not better to try to develop these virtues than to countenance an ethic of destruction as the solution?"[79]

Some therapists argue that aborting a pregnant rape victim is most likely to exacerbate her trauma, not relieve it: "Because it is likely that the victim already harbors feelings of guilt as a result of the assault, medicosocial pressures which encourage and result in abortion could compound the woman's feelings of guilt and self-blame."[80] David Reardon, in his survey of 225 women who were pregnant due to rape or incest and had abortions, concluded:

We have found that abortion proponents have used these "hard" cases to elicit sympathy for their cause, but they have failed to consider the real desires and health needs of the women who face these difficult circumstances. In fact, the urging of abortion on women in these cases is most often a paternalistic attempt to conceal their problems, rather than to aid them through their difficulties.

The "exceptions" of rape and incest, which in fact represent special cases, involve psychiatric stresses which are ill-treated with abortion. The evidence shows that pressures to abort in these cases arise primarily from outside sources, from the superstition and prejudice that friends, family, and society hold against "tainted" women. When the desires of the victims are examined, it is found that the vast majority of women pregnant from rape or incest actually desire to carry their children to term. *Psychologists confirm that this is a healthy response and is the most productive path these women can take in reestablishing their self-images and renewing control over their lives.* It is the social pressure to hide (abort) these pregnancies which

needs to be eliminated, not the innocent children who are "conceived in sin."

These "hard" cases all support our contention that the more sympathetic the circumstances indicating abortion, the less likely it is that abortion will solve those problems. Indeed, in what are generally very difficult psychological circumstances, abortion almost invariably tends to aggravate and complicate the woman's problems. Therefore, a more "conscientious physician" would be obliged to strongly recommend against abortion, especially in these "hard" cases.[81] (emphasis added)

Reardon's conclusions are echoed in the insights of Fred E. Mecklenburg, professor of obstetrics and gynecology at the University of Minnesota Medical School and member of the American Association of Planned Parenthood Physicians:

There are no known psychiatric diseases which can be cured by abortion. In addition there are none which can be predictably improved by abortion. . . . [Rather], it may leave unresolved conflicts coupled with guilt and added depression which may be more harmful than the continuation of the pregnancy.

Furthermore, there is good evidence to suggest that serious mental disorders arise following abortions more often in women with real psychiatric problems. *Paradoxically, the very women for whom legal abortion may seem most justifiable are also the ones for whom the risk is highest for post-abortion psychic insufficiency. . . .*

When abortion is substituted for adequate psychiatric care—and there is ample evidence to suggest that this is already happening—then there is a distinct danger of minimizing established psychotherapeutic principles. Unfortunately, it is the distressed woman who ultimately faces the dulling impact of this minimization. She is the one who cries for help, and she is also the one who is turned away.[82] (emphasis added)

Since there are no known psychiatric disorders for which abortion is a cure, it is puzzling that women who have undergone the traumatic experience of rape should be encouraged to have an abortion, as if the procedure itself, which results in the death of a human fetus, could heal the trauma of rape. Perhaps this is why an official statement of the World Health Organization says: "Thus the very women for whom legal abortion is considered justified on psychiatric grounds are the ones who have the highest risk of post-abortion psychiatric disorders."[83]

Argument from Pity for the Women Prosecuted, Convicted, and/or Sentenced for Murder if Abortion Is Made Illegal

According to abortion-rights supporters, if abortion is made illegal, then many women will be prosecuted, convicted, and/or sentenced for murder (a capital offense in some states), because the changed law will entail that abortion in almost every circumstance entails the unjustified and premeditated killing of an innocent person (the unborn). Abortion-rights activists argue that such a situation will unnecessarily cause emotional and familial harm to women who are already in a desperate situation (i.e., seeking an illegal abortion). Such laws, if they are instituted, will lack compassion. But, according to the abortion-rights supporter, if the pro-lifer is to remain consistent with her position that the unborn are human persons, then she must institute such compassion-lacking laws. On the other hand, if the pro-lifer does not institute such laws, then it is highly doubtful that she really believes that the unborn are human persons. In any event, the pro-life position appears to be inconsistent.

There are several problems with this argument. First, if this argument is correct about the pro-lifer's inconsistency, it does not prove that the unborn are not human persons or that abortion is not a great moral evil. It simply proves that pro-lifers are unwilling to consistently apply their position. The fact that pro-lifers may possess this character flaw does not mean that their arguments for the unborn's full humanity are flawed.

Second, this argument clearly ignores the pre-legalization laws and penalties for illegal abortion and possible reasons why they were instituted. Although it is clear that these laws considered the unborn human persons,[84] in most states women were granted immunity from prosecution and in other states the penalties were very light. In *Roe* the Supreme Court used these latter two facts and ignored the former to conclude that state antiabortion statutes were not intended to protect the unborn's life but only to protect maternal health, and that this was not consistent with the view that the unborn is a human person under the Fourteenth Amendment to the Constitution.[85] The problem with the Court's conclusion is that it did not take into consideration the possible reasons why the statutes granted women immunity and light sentences, especially in light of the fact that in other places the law considered the unborn to be persons. Legal scholar James Witherspoon suggests three reasons:

First, they [the legislatures] might have considered that the woman who would attempt such an act would only do so out of desperation, and that it would be inhumane to inflict criminal penalties on her after having suffered through such an experience. That legislators were moved by such considerations is indicated by the fact that legislatures which did incriminate the woman's participation generally imposed less severe penalties on the woman for this participation than on the person who actually attempted to induce the abortion.

Second, it is also possible that this immunization of women from criminal liability for participation in their own abortions was a result of the paternalism of the era, which limited criminal responsibility of women at the same time that it limited their civil rights. Despite her consent to the act, the woman was considered a victim rather than a perpetrator of the act.

Third, the immunity might have been motivated in part by practical considerations. Often the only testimony which could be secured against the criminal abortionist was that of the woman on whom the abortion was performed; perhaps the woman was granted complete immunity so that she would not be deterred from revealing the crime or from testifying against the abortionist by any risk of incurring criminal liability herself. That the non-incrimination of the woman's participation was motivated by this practical consideration is indicated by the fact that those states which *did* incriminate the woman's participation often enacted statutes granting a woman immunity from prosecution in exchange for her testimony, or providing that this evidence would not be admissible in any criminal prosecution against her.[86]

Abortion historian Marvin Olasky, a University of Texas journalism professor, concurs:

> Some states gave immunity to women from all criminal liability, partly because women pregnant after seduction were considered desperate victims rather than perpetrators, and partly because of the search for any kind of edge in prosecution. New Jersey, New York, and other states gave women immunity from prosecution in exchange for testimony. Wisconsin was among the states that applied a relatively light penalty for abortion of a non-quickened child—three months to one year—and then provided the woman who had an abortion with a one- to six-month sentence and/or fine. By providing either no or low penalties, so that a woman *would* testify that she had been pregnant, prosecutors had a chance to leap the evidentiary hurdles of convincing a jury an abortion actually had occurred.[87]

Thus it makes sense to say that by prudently balancing the unborn's right to life, the evil of abortion, the desperation of the woman, and the need for testimonial evidence in order to insure a conviction, jurists and legislators in the past believed that the best way to prevent abortions from occurring and at the same time uphold the sanctity of human life is to criminalize abortion, prosecute the abortionist,[88] grant immunity or a light penalty to the woman, and show her compassion by recognizing that in most cases she is indeed the second victim of abortion.

Consequently, if abortion is made illegal because the law again comes to recognize the unborn as human persons with a right to life, legislatures, while creating laws and penalties, and courts, while handing out sentences, will have to take into consideration the fol-

lowing important facts. (1) It is a reality that unborn humans are persons and to kill them is no different than killing a newborn baby, an infant, a small child, an adolescent, or an adult. (2) Because of both the lack of education concerning prenatal development and the miseducation of abortion-rights propaganda that permeates the media (see chaps. 4 and 5), both men and women are often ignorant of the true nature of the unborn child (see chap. 3) and the philosophical arguments that support it (chap. 6). (3) The woman who will seek and obtain an illegal abortion is really a second victim. Women who seek illegal abortions will probably do so out of desperation. Not realizing at the time of the abortion that the procedure kills a real person who, in many cases, suffers excruciating pain (see chaps. 3 and 6), many women often suffer from depression and guilt feelings after finding out about these facts.[89] And since both those who may encourage these women to seek an illegal abortion (family, friends, or lovers) as well as the abortionist who will be paid for performing this deed have no intention of discouraging her, it is likely that the pregnant women will be lied to (e.g., "You're not carrying a baby, it's a 'product of conception,' 'blob of tissue,' 'a bunch of cells'") and unlikely that true facts will be provided to them. Thus, the woman who seeks and obtains an illegal abortion is really a second victim. (4) Even if his intention may be to help the woman, the abortionist is a hired killer who is knowledgable about his victim's nature and should be treated as such. (5) The government has an interest in preventing unjustified and premeditated killing of persons, whether born or unborn, who live within its jurisdiction. Legislators and jurists who intend to pass and enforce laws and penalties prohibiting almost all abortions, if they are to be just, fair, and compassionate, must take into consideration these five points, as did legislators and jurists in the past. There is no doubt, therefore, that the law will reflect this sentiment if abortion is made illegal again.

Third, it follows from my second objection that the defender of this argument has a distorted view of the purpose of criminal law and the penalties for violating it. For sometimes the purpose of a penalty is not to make a value judgment about the nature of the act prohibited or about its victim, but to provide an incentive for the realization of the best possible circumstances for societal elimination of the prohibited act and protection of its victim, precisely because the act in question and the violation of its victim so morally transgresses what is indeed valuable and good. For example, in some states it is a capital offense to kill a police officer in the line of duty but not an ordinary citizen on the job, but this does not mean that the ordinary citizen has less value as a person than the police officer. Consequently, precisely because there is great value in prohibiting the act of abortion, since it entails the killing of an unborn human person, a prudent legislature will take into consideration all the variables and types of individuals ordinarily involved in the act, such as those presented in the above five points, in order to protect as many unborn children as possible.

Abortion Rights and Utilitarian Arguments

Philosophers and ethicists, attempting to avoid the fallacies associated with the type of popular moral argumentation we have examined in this chapter, have for the most part distanced themselves from the rhetoric employed by abortion-rights activists. For example, one finds in the literature rigorous discussions of what constitutes human personhood and whether the unborn are fully human.[90] One rarely if ever finds discussions of coat hangers or back-alley butchers. However, Supreme Court Justice Harry Blackmun uses such popular argumentation in his dissenting opinion in the case of *Webster v. Reproductive Health Services* (1989).[91] In this section I will argue that such argumentation has little if anything to do with abortion rights, if one understands the concept of a "right" as ordinarily understood in our American legal tradition.

What Is a Right?

There has been much discussion as to what is a right and what rights an individual may or may not exercise.[92] Although important, such discussion is not necessary for our present purposes. I intend to merely outline in broad terms what the American legal tradition has looked upon as the nature of rights. The American document that first addresses this question of rights is the Declaration of Independence:

We hold these truths to be self-evident: that all men are created equal; that they are endowed by their Creator, with certain unalienable rights, that among these are life, liberty, and the pursuit of happiness. That to secure these rights, governments are instituted among men, deriving their just powers from the consent of the governed; that whenever any form of government becomes destructive of these ends, it is the right of the people to alter or abolish it, and to institute new government, laying its foundation on such principles, and organizing its powers in such form, as to them shall seem most likely to affect their safety and happiness.[93]

Although not a legal document per se, the Declaration is important in our understanding of the nature of the rights outlined in the Constitution of the United States. The passage from the Declaration makes several claims about rights: because all men are created equal by their Creator, they possess certain *inalienable* rights; among these rights are life, liberty, and the pursuit of happiness; since these rights are *inalienable*, the role of the state is not to create these rights, but to secure them and make sure they are not trampled upon; the state derives its power to secure these rights from the consent of the governed; and the people have a right to either abolish or alter the government and form a new one if the performance of the former government is destructive to the purpose of securing these rights. Notice that these rights are not justified by their utility. One does not, for example, establish the freedom of religion as a natural right because it has some social benefit. But rather, freedom of religion has a social benefit because it is a natural right.

The Constitution outlines the structure of a government that will secure the basic rights found in the Declaration. It is an attempt to put these rights in a framework that will "establish Justice, insure domestic Tranquility, provide for the common Defence, promote the general Welfare, and secure the Blessing of Liberty to ourselves and our Posterity."[94]

Furthermore, the Constitution outlines how these three basic rights—life, liberty, and the pursuit of happiness—are best secured in the securing of more specific rights, such as those found in the First Amendment: freedom of religion, speech, press, assembly, and petition. These basic rights are also secured in the specific rights outlined in the Ninth and Fourteenth Amendments, the amendments from which the Supreme Court argued that the right to privacy is found.[95] And it is from the right to privacy that the Court argued in *Roe v. Wade* and *Doe v. Bolton* (1973) that a woman has a right to an abortion for any reason she deems fit during the entire nine months of pregnancy.[96] In sum, it is accurate to say that the right to abortion is claimed by abortion-rights proponents to be ultimately derived from the inalienable rights put forth in the Declaration of Independence.[97]

Utilitarian Arguments

Most of the arguments that we covered in this chapter could be broadly classified as *utilitarian*. Utilitarianism is a moral theory (with different versions) that states that an act or a rule is morally justified if and only if it produces pleasing results. As we saw earlier, in popular moral debate abortion-rights advocates oftentimes argue for their position by citing either hard cases, in which childbirth and subsequent childrearing would place a tremendous psychological and/or physical burden upon the mother, or the horrible results for women who would undergo illegal abortions. The burden relieved by the legal termination of the pregnancy morally justifies the termination. Consequently, allowing abortion rights is justified because there will

be fewer women who either will be harmed or will have to bear the burden of motherhood. The ends achieved by permitting abortion justify its permission. I will argue that such argumentation is irrelevant, if it is claiming to be in the tradition that we have examined, a tradition that holds to the belief that there exist fundamental inalienable rights.

In his dissenting comments in the *Webster* decision, Justice Blackmun employs utilitarian arguments typical of popular abortion-rights rhetoric:

> Thus, "not with a bang, but a whimper," the plurality discards a landmark case of the last generation [i.e., *Roe v. Wade*], and casts into darkness the hopes and visions of every woman in this country who had come to believe that the Constitution guaranteed her the right to exercise some control over her unique ability to bear children. The plurality does so either oblivious or insensitive to the fact that millions of women, and their families, have ordered their lives around the right to reproductive choice, and this right has become vital to the full participation of women in the economic and political walks of American life. The plurality would clear the way once again for government to force upon women the physical labor and specific and direct medical and psychological harms that may accompany a fetus to term. The plurality would clear the way again for the State to conscript a woman's body and to force upon her a "distressful life and future." *Roe*, 410 U.S., at 153.
> The result, as we know from experience, see Cates & Rocket, Illegal Abortion in the United States: 1972–1974, 8 Family Planning Perspectives 88, 92 (1976), would be that every year hundreds of thousands of women, in desperation, would defy the law, and place their health and safety in the unclean and unsympathetic hands of back-alley abortionists, or they would attempt to perform abortions upon themselves, with disastrous results. Every year, many women, especially poor and minority women, would die or suffer debilitating physical trauma, all in the name of enforced morality or religious dictates or lack of compassion, as it may be.[98]

Blackmun argues that because the Supreme Court in the *Webster* decision has given the states greater leverage in restricting abortion rights, all types of horrible consequences will eventually result. But suppose that none or few of the consequences that Blackmun predicts will in fact occur. Suppose that for the most part people obey the new restrictions, and these restrictions do not hinder the "full participation of women in the economic and political walks of American life." Suppose further that *Roe v. Wade* is fully reversed and the pro-life movement gains enormous momentum and convinces a vast majority of Americans of the full humanity of the unborn and our special responsibility in caring for them. If so, would Blackmun recant and say that he was wrong in dissenting in *Webster,* or would he continue to defend a woman's right to abortion because this right is in his view found in the Fourteenth and Ninth Amendments to the Constitution, as he argued in *Roe*? If he opts for the latter and chooses to defend the right to abortion regardless of whether or not the consequences he warned us about would occur, then these consequences are not relevant to the question of abortion rights. If, however, Blackmun opts for the former and claims that his views are contingent upon these consequences, then abortion is not a right found in the Ninth and Fourteenth Amendments to the Constitution. It seems that the utilitarian arguments for abortion rights, although a source of powerful rhetoric, have little to do with the real question of rights.

It is important to note that by discounting the evidence for the unborn's humanness from the outset, Blackmun's argument is reduced to a highly emotional appeal that merely begs the question as to the unborn's personhood, just as it would beg the question as to the black man's personhood if it were employed in a defense of slavery:

Thus, "not with a bang, but a whimper," the Congress in passing the Fourteenth Amendment discards a landmark case of the last generation (*Dred Scott*), and casts into darkness the hopes and visions of every property owner in the South who had come

to believe that the Constitution guaranteed him the right to exercise some control over his God-given right to own property. The plurality does so either oblivious or insensitive to the fact that millions of property owners, and their families, have ordered their lives around the right to ownership of property, and that this right has become vital to the full participation of Southern gentlemen in the economic and political walks of American life.

Feminism and the Social Necessity of Abortion for Equality

Blackmun echoes the call of popular abortion-rights rhetoric, which asserts that women cannot achieve social and political equality without "control" of their reproductive lives. Consider the following comments put forth by other abortion-rights supporters:

Laws restricting abortion so dramatically shape the lives of women, and only of women, that their denial of equality hardly needs detailed elaboration. While men retain the right to sexual and reproductive autonomy, restrictions on abortion deny that autonomy to women. *Laws restricting access to abortion thereby place a real and substantial burden on women's ability to participate in society as equals.*[99] (emphasis added) (Laurence Tribe, Tyler Professor of Constitutional Law, Harvard Law School)

We have to remind people that abortion is the guarantor of a woman's . . . right to participate fully in the social and political life of society.[100] (Kate Michelman, president of the National Abortion Rights Action League [NARAL])

This right [to abortion], of necessity *must* be absolute, for if it is not, women will never truly have the ability to plan and to control their own lives.[101] (Nancy S. Erickson, abortion-rights attorney)

But the assumption behind this rhetoric—that equality can be achieved only through special surgery (abortion)—implies that women are naturally inferior to men, that they need abortion (a form of corrective surgery) in order to become equal with men.

This is hardly consistent with any feminism that claims that men are not naturally superior to women. As one feminist publication has pointed out: "How can women ever lose second-class status as long as they are seen as requiring surgery in order to avoid it? . . . [This] is the premise of male domination throughout the millenia—that it was nature which made men superior and women inferior. Medical technology is offered as a solution to achieve equality; but the premise is wrong. Nature doesn't provide for inequality, and it's an insult to women to say women must change biology in order to fit into society."[102]

Conclusion

If one holds to the existence of real fundamental human rights and values, utilitarian arguments for abortion rights are question-begging and their success is contingent upon the success of abortion-rights activists in showing that the unborn are not fully human. Realizing that this is the case, some sophisticated abortion-rights advocates argue that the unborn entity is not fully human. They argue for this position by making a distinction between *human being* and *person*. They admit that the unborn entity is *genetically* human but they argue that it does not possess the full attributes of personhood until some time prior to or after birth.[103] Hence, to kill an unborn entity before it achieves personhood (ethicists dispute when this point arrives) is not to violate anyone's rights, since there is no one whose rights are being violated. We will critically examine the arguments for this position in chapter 6.

Other ethicists take a different approach.[104] They argue that even if the unborn is fully human, it is not immoral for a woman to obtain an abortion if she does not want to be pregnant. The unborn entity is using another's body against her will, and this is obviously immoral, just as it is immoral for an individual to force another to donate his kidney in order to save that individual's life. That is, one does not have an obligation to act heroically for another's sake. By conceding the full humanness of the unborn and arguing that abortion is justified on other grounds, the defender of this argument seemingly avoids the question-begging nature of the appeals to pity we have covered in this chapter. We will critically examine this argument in chapter 7.

But in terms of our legal tradition, the utilitarian arguments for abortion rights are not successful if the unborn are fully human, because the abortion-rights movement claims that its position is based on rights outlined in the Constitution (the Ninth and Fourteenth Amendments) that are grounded in the inalienable rights found in the Declaration of Independence. These rights would also apply to the unborn if they are fully human. Strangely enough, Blackmun admits to this in *Roe v. Wade*: "If this suggestion of personhood [of the unborn] is established, the appellant's case, of course, collapses, for the fetus' right to life is then guaranteed specifically by the [Fourteenth] Amendment."[105] This admission makes Blackmun's use of the utilitarian arguments in his *Webster* dissent all the more perplexing and, by implication, irrelevant to abortion rights.

Arguments from Tolerance and Ad Hominem 5

> *The Roman Catholic bishops of the United States are currently campaigning for passage of an amendment to the Federal Constitution [i.e., Human Life Amendment] which would write Catholic doctrine into constitutional law. They want to change the traditional American position that a person legally exists at birth to their theological position that a person exists from the moment of conception.*
> Professor John M. Swomley, Jr., Methodist Seminary professor (1976)

> *Things have come to a pretty pass when religion is allowed to invade public life.*
> Lord Melbourne (opposing abolition of the slave trade)

> *Remember that opposition to torture in Brazil does not become a religious moral position just because that opposition is now being led by the Catholic bishops.*
> Dr. Baruch Brody, Rice University bioethicist and philosophy professor (1978)

In this chapter I will present and critique those arguments that are best classified as appeals to tolerance and ad hominem (literally, against the person). Not every defender of abortion rights holds to all or any of these arguments. But unlike the arguments in chapter 4, which are found almost exclusively in popular rhetoric, the arguments we will analyze in this chapter are put forth in both scholarly and popular circles.

Arguments from Tolerance

Many people in the abortion-rights movement argue that their position is more tolerant than the pro-life position. After all, they reason, the abortion-rights movement is not forcing pro-life women to have abortions, but the pro-life movement *is* trying to deny all women the option to make a choice. Abortion-rights advocates use at least six arguments to articulate this position.

Argument from Religious Pluralism

It is sometimes argued that the question of when protectable human life begins is a religious question that one must answer for oneself. Justice Blackmun writes in *Roe v. Wade*, "We need not resolve the difficult question of when life begins. When those trained in the respective disciplines of medicine, philosophy, and theology are unable to arrive at any consensus, the judiciary, at this point in the development of man's knowledge, is not in a position to speculate."[1] Hence, the state should not take one theory of life and force those who do not agree with that theory to subscribe to it. Blackmun writes in *Roe*, "In view of all this, we do not agree that, by adopting one theory of life, Texas may override the rights of the pregnant woman that are at stake."[2] In his dissenting opinion in *Webster*, Justice Stevens goes even further than Blackmun; "The Missouri Legislature [which said that life begins at conception] may not inject its endorsement of a particular religious tradition in this debate, for 'the Establishment Clause does not allow public bodies to foment such disagreement.'"[3] Thus for the pro-life advocate to propose that women should be forbidden from having abortions, on the basis that personhood begins at conception or at least sometime before birth, not only violates their right to privacy but also violates the separation of church and state. Such a separation is supposedly necessary to sustain tolerance in a pluralistic society. As abortion-rights advocate Virginia Ramey Mollenkott argues:

> Women who believe that abortion is murder may *never* justly be required to have an abortion. Anti-abortion laws would not affect such women for obvious reasons. But for women whose religious beliefs do permit them to consider abortion (and under certain circumstances require them to do so), anti-abortion legislation would forbid their following these religious convictions.[4]

There are several problems with this argument. First, it is self-refuting and question-begging. To claim, as Justices Blackmun and Stevens do, that the Court should not propose one theory of life over another, and that the decision should be left up to each pregnant woman as to when protectable human life begins, is to propose a theory of life that hardly has a clear consensus in this country.[5] Once one claims that certain individuals (pregnant women) have the right to bestow personhood on unborn humans, one implies that the bestowers are fully human. This is a theory of life held by a number of religious denominations and groups, whose amicus briefs Stevens oddly enough cites in a footnote in his *Webster* dissent.[6] Moreover, what if a religious group arose that believed that personhood did not begin until the age of two and prior to that time parents could sacrifice their children to the devil. By forbidding child-killing after birth, the Court would be infringing upon the religious beliefs of this group, would it not? And in doing so, the Court would obviously be proposing one theory of life over another. Hence, in attempting not to propose one theory of life, Blackmun and Stevens in fact assume a particular theory of life, and by doing so clearly beg the question and show that their opinions cannot abide by their own standard of not proposing one theory of life.

Second, the fact that a particular theory of life is consistent with a religious view does not mean that it is exclusively religious or that it is in violation of the Establishment Clause of the Constitution. For example, many pro-life advocates argue for their position by emphasizing that there is nontheological support for their position,[7] while many abortion-rights advocates, such as Mollenkott,[8] argue that their position is theologically grounded in the Bible. Hence, the pro-life advocate could argue that the fact that a philosophically and scientifically plausible position is also found in religious literature, such as the Bible, does not make such a view exclusively religious. If it did, our society would have to dispense with laws forbidding such crimes as murder and robbery simply because such actions are prohibited in the Hebrew-Christian Scriptures. Furthermore, some public policies, such as civil-rights legislation and elimination of nuclear testing—policies supported by many clergymen who find these policies in agreement with and supported by their doctrinal beliefs—would have to be abolished simply because they are believed by some to be supported by a particular religious theory of life. It is well-known that those who sought to abolish slavery in nineteenth-century America were unashamed to admit that their moral convictions were based almost exclusively on their Christian beliefs. Even abortion-rights advocate Laurence Tribe agrees that simply because one's morality originates in a religious tradition does not mean that one cannot help shape public policy:

> But as a matter of constitutional law, a question such as this [abortion], having an irreducibly moral dimension, cannot properly be kept out of the political realm merely because many religions and organized religious groups inevitably take strong positions on it. . . . The participation of religious groups in political dialogue *has never been constitutional anathema in the United States.* Quite the contrary. The values reflected in the constitutional guarantees of freedom of religion and political expression argue strongly for the inclusion of church and religious groups, and of religious beliefs and arguments, in public life.[9] (emphasis added)

Hence, the pro-life position is a legitimate public policy option and does not violate the Establishment Clause of the Constitution.

Third, this argument asks the pro-life movement to act as if its fundamental view of human life is incorrect and to accept the abortion-rights view of what constitutes both a just society and a correct view of human life. This asks too much of the pro-life movement, as philosopher George Mavrodes shows:

> Let us imagine a person who believes that Jews are human persons, and that the extermination of Jews is murder. Many of us will find that exercise fairly easy, because we are people of that sort ourselves. So we may as well take ourselves to be the people in question. And let us now go on to imagine that we live in a society in which the "termination" of Jews is an everyday routine procedure, a society in which public facili-

ties are provided in every community for this operation, and one in which any citizen is free to identify and denounce Jews and to arrange for their arrest and termination. In that imaginary society, many of us will know people who have themselves participated in these procedures, many of us will drive past the termination centers daily on our way to work, we can often see the smoke rising gently in the late afternoon sky, and so on. And now imagine that someone tells us that if we happen to believe that Jews are human beings then that's O.K., we needn't fear any coercion, nobody requires us to participate in the termination procedures ourselves. We need not work in the gas chamber, we don't have to denounce a Jew, and so on. We can simply mind our own business, walk quietly past the well-trimmed lawns, and (of course) pay our taxes.

> Can we get some feel for what it would be like to live in that context? . . . And maybe we can then have some understanding of why they [the right-to-lifers] are unlikely to be satisfied by being told that they don't have to get an abortion themselves.[10]

Since the abortion-rights advocate asks the pro-life advocate to act as if his fundamental view of human life is false, the pro-life advocate may legitimately view his adversary's position as a subtle and patronizing form of intolerance. When the "pro-choicer" rails at the pro-lifer, "Don't like abortion, don't have one," the pro-lifer hears, "Don't like murder, don't commit one" or "Don't like slavery, don't own a slave."

Argument from Imposing Morality

Some abortion-rights advocates argue that it is wrong for anyone to force his or her own view of what is morally right on someone else. They argue that pro-lifers, by attempting to forbid women from having abortions, are trying to force their morality on others. Aside from the fact that this argument makes the controversial assumption that all morality is subjective and relative (see chap. 1), there are at least three other problems with it.

First, it does not seem obvious that it is always wrong to demand that people behave in accordance with certain moral precepts. For instance, laws against drunk driving, murder, smoking crack, robbery, and child molestation all are intended to impose a particular moral perspective on the free moral agency of others. Such laws are instituted because the acts they are intended to limit often obstruct the free agency of other persons. For example, a person killed by a drunk driver is prevented from exercising his free agency. These laws seek to maintain a just and orderly society by limiting some free moral agency so that free moral agency is increased for a greater number. Therefore, a law forbidding abortion would unjustly impose a moral perspective upon another only if the act of abortion does not limit the free agency of another. That is to say, if the unborn entity is fully human, forbidding abortions would be just, since nearly every abortion limits the free agency of another (i.e., the unborn human).

Although it does not seriously damage their entire position, it is interesting to note that some abortion-rights advocates do not hesitate to impose their moral perspective on others when they call for the use of other people's tax dollars (many of whom do not approve of this use of funds) to help pay for the abortions of poor women.

Second, although he presents his position in the rhetoric of freedom, the abortion-rights advocate nevertheless imposes his perspective on others. All rights imply obligations on the part of others, and all obligations impose a moral perspective on others to make them act in a certain way. Thus, the abortion-rights advocate, by saying that the pro-lifer is obligated not to interfere with the free choice of pregnant women to kill their unborn offspring, is imposing his moral perspective upon the pro-lifer who believes it is her duty to rescue the unborn because these beings are fully human and hence deserve, like all human beings, our society's protection. Therefore, every right, whether it is the right to life or the right to abortion, imposes some moral perspective on others to either act or not act in a certain way.

Third, it follows that the abortion-rights advocate begs the question. If the unborn are

not fully human, the abortion-rights advocate is correct in saying that the pro-lifers are trying to force their morality onto women who want abortions. But if the unborn are fully human, a woman receiving an abortion is imposing her morality upon another. Therefore, unless the abortion-rights advocate assumes that the unborn are not fully human, his argument is not successful. Hence, the question of whose morality is being forced upon whom hinges on the status of the unborn.

Argument against a Public Policy Forbidding Abortion

There is another variation on the first argument from pluralism. Some people argue that it is not wise to make a public-policy decision in one direction when there is wide diversity of opinion within society. This argument can be outlined in the following way:

1. There can never be a just law requiring uniformity of behavior on any issue on which there is widespread disagreement.
2. There is widespread disagreement on the issue of forbidding abortion on demand.
3. Therefore, any law that forbids abortion on demand is unjust.

One way to show that this argument is wrong is to show that premise 1 is false. There are several reasons to believe that it is. First, if premise 1 is true, then the abortion-rights advocate must admit that the United States Supreme Court decision, *Roe v. Wade*, is an unjust decision, since the Court ruled that the states, whose statutes prior to the ruling disagreed on the abortion issue, must behave uniformly in accordance with the Court's decision. If, however, the abortion-rights advocate denies that *Roe* was an unjust decision, then he is conceding that it is false that "there can never be a just law requiring uniformity of behavior on any issue on which there is widespread disagreement." Second, if premise 1 is true, then the abolition of slavery was unjust because there was widespread disagreement of opinion among Americans in the nineteenth century. Yet nobody would say that slavery should have remained as an institution. Third, if premise 1 is true, then much of civil-rights legislation, about which there was much disagreement, would be unjust. Fourth, if premise 1 is true, then a favorite abortion-rights public policy proposal is also unjust. Some abortion-rights advocates believe that the federal and/or state government should use the tax dollars of the American people to fund the abortions of poor women. Large numbers of Americans, however, some of whom support abortion rights, do not want their tax dollars used in this way. And fifth, if premise 1 is true, then laws forbidding pro-life advocates from preventing their unborn neighbors from being aborted would be unjust. One cannot say that there is not widespread disagreement concerning this issue. But these are the very laws which the abortion-rights advocate supports. Hence, this argument is self-refuting, since by legislating the "pro-choice" perspective the government is "requiring uniformity of behavior on an issue on which there is widespread disagreement." That is to say, the abortion-rights advocate is forcing the pro-lifer to act as if she were a pro-choicer. By making "no law," the government is implicitly affirming the view that the unborn are not fully human, which is hardly a neutral position.

Another way to show that this argument is not successful is to challenge the second premise and show that there is not widespread disagreement on the question of whether abortion on demand should be forbidden. Recent polls have shown that a great majority of Americans, although supporting a woman's right to an abortion in the rare "hard cases" (such as rape, incest, and severe fetal deformity), do not support abortion on demand, the abortion-rights position that asserts that abortion should remain legal during the entire nine months of pregnancy for any reason the woman deems fit (see chap. 2). According to one poll, taken by the *Boston Globe* and WBZ Broadcasting,[11] the vast majority of Americans would ban abortions in the following circumstances: "a woman is a minor" (50 percent), "wrong time in life to have a child" (82 percent), "fetus not desired sex" (93 percent), "woman cannot afford a child" (75 percent), "as a means of birth control" (89 percent), "pregnancy would cause too much emotional strain" (64 percent), "father unwilling to help raise the child" (83 percent), "father absent" (81 percent), "mother wants abortion/father wants baby" (72 percent), "father wants abortion/mother wants baby" (75 percent).[12] This is why the journalist who reported this poll concluded that "most Americans would ban the vast majority of abortions performed in this country. . . . While 78 percent of the nation would keep abortion legal in limited circumstances, according to the poll, *those circumstances account for a tiny percentage of the reasons*"[13] (emphasis added). Therefore, the second premise in this argument is wrong. There is not "widespread disagreement on the issue of forbidding abortion on demand."

Argument from the Impossibility of Legally Stopping Abortion

Suppose a person makes the more subtle point that because there is widespread disagreement on the abortion issue, enforcement of any laws prohibiting abortion would be difficult. In other words, abortions are going to happen anyway, so we ought to make them safe and legal. There are several problems with this argument (for more detailed responses, see "Argument from the Dangers of Illegal Abortion" in chap. 4).

First, it totally begs the question, because it assumes that the unborn are not fully human. If the unborn are fully human, this argument is tantamount to saying: since people will murder other people anyway, we ought to make it safe and legal for them to do so. But murder is never justified, even if there is a social penalty in forbidding it.

Second, since the vast majority of Americans are law-abiding citizens, they will probably obey the law as they did prior to *Roe v. Wade*. A recent study supports this notion:

Given their doubts about the morality of abortion, most aborting women are strongly influenced by the legal status of the abortion option. When asked, "Did the knowledge that abortion was legal influence your opinion about the morality of choosing abortion?" 70 percent said that the law had played a major role in their moral perception of abortion. . . . Asked whether or not they would have sought an illegal abortion if a legal abortion had not been available, 75 percent said they definitely would not have sought an illegal abortion. . . .[14]

Furthermore, one study concluded that "a reasonable estimate for the actual number of criminal abortions per year in the pre-legalization era [prior to 1967] would be from a low of 39,000 (1950) to a high of 210,000 (1961) and a mean of 98,000 per year."[15] Contrasting this with the fact that 1.6 million abortions were performed in 1992, one can only conclude that the pre-*Roe* anti-abortion laws were quite effective in limiting the number of abortions.

Now if the abortion-rights advocate claims that a law cannot stop all abortions, he makes a trivial claim, for this is true of all laws which forbid illegal acts. For example, since both hiring paid assassins and purchasing child pornography are illegal, some people have no choice but to acquire them illegally. But there is no doubt that their illegality does hinder a number of citizens from obtaining them. Should we then legalize child pornography and assassinations because we can't stop all people from obtaining such "goods" and services? Such reasoning is absurd.

Third, pro-life advocates do believe that changing the law itself will help create a climate of opinion in which people's attitudes concerning abortion will become more sympathetic toward the pro-life position, just as public opinion became more sympathetic toward the abortion-rights position after abortion was legalized. The function of law is not always to reflect the attitudes and behavior of society. This has been borne out by the study that states 75 percent of the women who had legal abortions said they definitely would not have sought an illegal abortion.

Consequently, sometimes laws "are also a mechanism by which people are encouraged to do what they know is right, even when it is difficult to do so."[16] David C. Reardon points out that "studies in the psychology of

morality reveal that the law is truly the teacher. One of the most significant conclusions of these studies shows that existing laws and customs are the most important criteria for deciding what is right or wrong for most adults in a given culture."[17] Citing legal philosopher John Finnis, Dr. Bernard Nathanson writes that "sometimes the law is ahead of public morality. Laws against dueling and racial bias preceded popular support for these attitudes."[18]

Argument from "Compulsory" Pregnancy

Some abortion-rights advocates, wanting to get a rhetorical edge in public debate, refer to pro-life legislation as "tantamount to advocating compulsory pregnancy."[19] This is not really an argument in a technical sense, since it has only a conclusion and contains no premises to support the conclusion. It is merely an assertion that begs the question, since it assumes the nonpersonhood of the unborn—the point under question. To cite an example, a man who murdered his wife and children would be begging the question as to the personhood of his victims if he referred to the laws that forbid murder as tantamount to advocating *compulsory marriage* and *compulsory fatherhood*. Can you imagine a father or a mother arguing that he or she is not obligated to obey child-support laws because they are "tantamount to advocating *compulsory parenthood*"? A rapist could argue on the same grounds and conclude that laws against rape are "tantamount to advocating *compulsory chastity*." And the slave owner, the pro-choicer of the mid-nineteenth-century political scene, could easily conclude that Lincoln's Emancipation Proclamation, since it robbed him of slave ownership, was "tantamount to advocating compulsory government-mandated relinquishing of private property."

In sum, a law that forbids the brutal victimizing of another person is inherently a just law, whether the victim is an unborn child, an adult woman, a youngster, or an African-American. Hence, the real question is whether the unborn are fully human, not whether pro-life legislation advocates "compulsory pregnancy."

A more sophisticated version of this argument ("Argument from Unplugging the Violinist") is defended by philosopher Judith Jarvis Thomson. I will critique this argument in chapter 7.

Argument from Privacy

Much of abortion-rights literature argues that pro-life legislation is wrong because the abortion decision is a private and intimate one that should be made by a woman, her physician, and her family, since they know what is best for the woman. There are, however, several problems with this argument.

First, from a legal perspective this argument is dishonest (see chap. 2), especially when it is used in abortion-rights television and radio advertising, as it was used by the "Campaign for Choice" in Nevada's 1990 abortion referendum battle. A woman can have an abortion performed by a physician she met thirty seconds ago; no law requires that it be performed by *her* regular physician. And legally she is not obligated to either inform or receive consent from any family members, including her husband if she is married; the U.S. Supreme Court has consistently struck down statutes that require spousal notification (see, for example, *Planned Parenthood of Missouri v. Danforth*, 428 U.S. 52 [1976]).

Second, as with the other arguments in this chapter and in the previous one, this argument begs the question. The fact that a decision is intimate and private has no bearing on the question of whether the unborn entity who is killed by abortion is fully human and deserving of legal protection. If the unborn is fully human, then killing her, even in the most intimate and private of settings, is still morally repugnant. If the unborn is not fully human, then her death is of little moral significance, whether or not it is performed in the most intimate and private of settings. Consequently, the privacy and the intimacy of the decision are irrelevant to the morality of abortion.

It may, however, have a bearing on the moral culpability of the parents who have chosen to abort. They may have chosen abortion in almost complete ignorance of the unborn's true nature, as is true of so many people who wrestle with this choice. Or, within the intimacy and privacy of marriage, they may have chosen to abort out of loving concern for each other, society, and/or their born children. In such a case, the parents are not murderers but well-meaning people who, while pursuing what they believed was the correct decision, acted without informed consent. A murderer is someone who intentionally and knowingly kills an innocent human person. The parents did not do this. For this reason, they are the second victims of abortion and deserve our continued counsel, support, and love. This, of course, does not mean that the *act* of killing the child was not murder, just that the parents, because of their ignorance and noble intentions, are not murderers.

Third, assuming that the unborn entity is fully human, University of Rhode Island ethicist Stephen Schwarz makes an excellent point: Since the unborn child is the mother's, "entrusted to her, residing in her, nourished in her, protected by her," it follows that "it is abortion, not the prohibition of it, that violates the intimate realm of a woman who is pregnant. It is abortion that intrudes into this beautiful sanctuary, where a small, innocent, defenseless child is nestled and protected." The fact that it is the woman who requests the abortion does not disprove Schwarz's point. Since the abortion "is objectively a violent sundering of this natural, intimate relationship," by requesting the abortion the mother "becomes a part of this terrible evil, and often suffers from it as the second victim."[20] Schwarz goes on, "Yes, there is something private and intimate that we should protect: the child. Abortion is a violation of the child's privacy, and intrusion into what is intimate for him, his own person. The methods of abortion and the pain they cause are violations of intimacy and privacy."[21]

It seems, then, that the appeal to intimacy and privacy drives one to the opposite conclusion of the abortion-rights position: abortions should be forbidden. After all, "the child's right to live, not to be killed, especially by the painful methods of abortion, . . . surely outweighs anyone's claim to a right to privacy. And the state must protect that right, just as it protects other civil rights."[22] Men cannot beat their wives in the name of privacy and neither can parents molest or physically abuse their children because the family circle is "a private and intimate sanctuary." Therefore, it is the personhood of the unborn that is the real question, not appeals to privacy, intimacy, or any other politically correct "neutral zone."

Conclusion: The Impossibility of "Tolerance" on the Abortion Issue

In summary, if one holds to the existence of real fundamental human rights, these arguments from tolerance are question-begging and their success is contingent upon the success of abortion-rights activists in showing that the unborn are not fully human.

Sophisticated abortion-rights advocates realize that such arguments are question-begging. For this reason, they argue that the unborn entity is not fully human. They argue for this position by making a distinction between *human being* and *person*. They admit that the unborn entity is genetically human but argue that it does not possess the full attributes of personhood until some time prior to or after birth.[23] Hence, to kill an unborn entity prior to its achievement of personhood (ethicists dispute when this point arrives) is not to violate anyone's rights, since there is no one whose rights are being violated. I critique these arguments in chapter 6.

Other ethicists, such as Judith Jarvis Thomson and Jay Kantor,[24] argue that even if the unborn is fully human, it is not immoral for a woman to obtain an abortion if the woman does not want to be pregnant. For the unborn entity is using another's body against her will, and this is obviously immoral, just as it is immoral for an individual to force another to donate his kidney in order to save that individual's life. That is, one does not have an obligation to act heroically for another's sake. By conceding the full humanness of the un-

born and arguing that abortion is justified on other grounds, the defender of this argument seemingly avoids the question-begging nature of the appeals to tolerance we have covered in this chapter. I critique this argument in chapter 7.

But in terms of our legal tradition, the arguments from tolerance are indeed question-begging if the full humanness of the unborn has not been determined. The legal advocates of abortion-rights claim that their position is based on rights outlined in the Constitution (the Ninth and Fourteenth Amendments), which would also apply to the unborn if they are fully human. Strangely enough, Blackmun admits to this in *Roe v. Wade*: "If this suggestion of personhood [of the unborn] is established, the appellant's case, of course, collapses, for the fetus' right to life is then guaranteed specifically by the [Fourteenth] Amendment."[25]

I believe that the impossibility of appealing to "tolerance" to "solve" the moral and legal questions of abortion is best illustrated by the actions of the radical pro-life group, Operation Rescue (OR), which disobeys trespassing laws by peacefully blocking the entrances of abortion clinics in order to rescue unborn children from certain death. (For a defense of the moral right of OR to engage in civil disobedience, see the dialogue in this book's epilogue, "Socrates to the Rescue.")

Regardless of what one thinks about OR, there is no doubt that OR's actions have convinced many of the intellectual bankruptcy of such bumper-sticker slogans as "Pro-choice, but personally opposed," "Don't like abortion, don't have one," or "Abortion is against my beliefs, but I would never dream of imposing my beliefs on others." These slogans attempt to articulate in a simple way a common avenue taken by politicians and others who want to avoid the slings and arrows that naturally follow a firm position on abortion. It is an attempt to find a compromise or a middle ground; it's a way to avoid being labeled an extremist of either camp.

During the 1984 presidential campaign, when questions of Geraldine Ferraro's Catholicism and its apparent conflict with her abortion-rights stance were prominent in the media, New York Governor Mario Cuomo, in a lecture delivered at the University of Notre Dame, attempted to give this middle ground intellectual respectability. He tried to provide a philosophical foundation for his friend's position. He failed miserably. One cannot appeal to the fact that we live in a pluralistic society, as Cuomo argued, when the very question of *who* is part of that society (that is, whether or not it includes unborn children) is itself the point under dispute. Cuomo begged the question and lost the argument.

When the abortion-rights movement adopted the term *pro-choice*, it gave itself an effective rhetorical device. Those who oppose abortion and consider themselves pro life can also be pro-choice. You can be "personally opposed." You can have the courage of your convictions without being accused of not having the courage to act as if your convictions are true. Mrs. O'Leary down the street can be pregnant with a child that will be born in five months, while her neighbor in the condo, Ms. Blueblood, can evacuate her product of conception at the "family-planning center" at five o'clock. But the euphemism game is getting more difficult to play. The problem you rename you do not solve. The pro-lifers in OR bring home the undeniable fact that if you believe that the unborn are fully human, then the unborn carried in the wombs of pro-choice women are just as human as those carried in the wombs of pro-life women. Ideology does not change identity.

Although you may not agree with the pro-lifers, use your imagination and try to understand their position. To tell pro-lifers, as many abortion-rights activists do, that "they have a right to believe what they want to believe" is to unwittingly promote the tactics of OR. Think about it. If *you* believed that a class of persons were being murdered by methods that include dismemberment, suffocation, and burning, resulting in excruciating pain in many cases, wouldn't you be perplexed if someone tried to ease your outrage by telling you that you didn't have to participate in the murders if you didn't want to? That's exactly

what pro-lifers hear when abortion-rights supporters tell them, "Don't like abortion, don't have one" or "I'm pro-choice, but personally opposed." In the mind of the pro-lifer, this is like telling an abolitionist, "Don't like slavery, don't own a slave," or telling Dietrich Bonhoeffer, "Don't like the Holocaust, don't kill a Jew." Consequently, to request that pro-lifers "shouldn't force their pro-life belief on others," while claiming that "they have a right to believe what they want to believe," is to reveal an incredible ignorance of their position.

Contrary to popular belief, the so-called pro-choice position is not neutral. If it were, then pro-lifers, such as those who are part of OR, would be free to stop women from having abortions, since their belief that *all* the unborn are fully human would have to be tolerated in our pluralistic society. But as we know, the Rescuers' belief is not tolerated. Evidently, the pro-choicers don't take their own rhetoric of tolerance seriously.

Therefore, to say that women should have the "right to choose" to kill their unborn fetuses is tantamount to denying the pro-life position that the unborn are worthy of protection. And to affirm that the unborn are fully human with a "right to life" is tantamount to denying the abortion-rights position that women have a fundamental right to terminate their pregnancies, since such a termination would result in a homicide. It seems, then, that neutrality concerning abortion is an intellectual impossibility.

Arguments Ad Hominem

Ad hominem literally means to "attack the man (or person). . . . [T]o attack *ad hominem* is to attack the man who presents an argument rather than the argument itself."[26] Instead of dealing with what a person is actually saying, one attacks the person. This is a bad form of reasoning because it ultimately does not refute the person's argument. Hence, when the abortion-rights advocate judges, ridicules, insults, or slanders the pro-lifer as a person he does not attack the arguments for the pro-life position. Ad hominem arguments may provoke Long Island housewives on the Donahue show to howl with glee, but they are nevertheless a bad form of reasoning. The only time an ad hominem argument is not a bad form of reasoning is when a person's credibility in a relevant area is important in ascertaining the truth, such as in the case of expert or eyewitness testimony in a criminal trial. For example, it is acceptable for an attorney to point out that an expert witness who claims to be a medical doctor in fact does not have his degree, or that an alleged *eye*witness to a robbery is legally blind. However, none of the ad hominem arguments used against the pro-life movement are of this acceptable sort.

Why Don't Pro-lifers Adopt the Babies They Don't Want Aborted?

This argument seems to be popular among newspaper letter writers and abortion-rights guests on leading talk-show programs. For example, comedienne Whoopi Goldberg used this argument several years ago as part of a stand-up comedy act televised on Home Box Office (HBO). In a recent *Dear Abby* column, a letter writer states (and by her response it is evident that Abby is in agreement):

> **Dear Abby:** This is a message to those men and women who try to prevent women from entering abortion clinics and carry big signs that say "They Kill Babies Here!"
> Have you signed up to adopt a child? If not, why not? Is it because you don't want one, can't afford one or don't have the time, patience, or desire to raise a child?
> What if a woman who was about to enter a family planning clinic saw your sign, then decided not to have an abortion but chose to give her baby to you? Would you accept it? What if the mother belonged to a minority group—or was addicted to drugs, or tested positive for AIDS? . . .
> So, to those carrying those signs and trying to prevent women from entering family planning clinics, heed my message: If you must be against abortion, don't be a hypocrite—make your time and energy count.[27]

This argument can be distilled into the following assertion: unless the pro-life advocate is willing to help bring up the children she does not want aborted, she has no right to prevent a woman from having an abortion. As a principle of moral action, this seems to be a rather bizarre assertion. It begs the question by assuming that the unborn are not fully human. Wouldn't we consider the murder of a couple's children unjustified even if we were approached by the parents with the ultimatum, "Unless you adopt my three children by noon tomorrow, I will put them to death"? The fact that I may refuse to adopt these children does not mean that their parents are justified in killing them. The issue, once more, is whether the unborn are fully human.

Then, think of all the unusual precepts that would result from the moral principle put forth by the letter writer: unless I am willing to marry my neighbor's wife, I cannot prevent her husband from beating her; unless I am willing to adopt my neighbor's daughter, I cannot prevent her mother from abusing her; unless I am willing to hire ex-slaves for my business, I cannot say that the slave owner should not own slaves. Although I believe that the pro-life movement as a whole does have a moral obligation to help those in need, especially unwed mothers (and there are enough organizations dedicated to this ministry to show that the pro-lifers do practice what they preach),[28] the point is that it does not logically follow from this moral obligation that abortion ipso facto becomes a moral good simply because individual pro-life advocates are not currently involved in such a ministry (although they probably tithe to churches that do support such ministries).

To give the reader a more concrete idea of what pro-lifers are doing (see also note 28), the following are the results of an informal survey of the most active members (229 persons) of the Indiana Right to Life Organization:

81 distributed food and clothing
nearly one-fourth donated blood regularly

37 worked in support groups (drugs, alcohol, suicide)

17 worked in programs for abused women

28 worked in hospitals, clinics, and hospices

38 worked in volunteer fire and police departments and neighborhood associations

116 worked in scouting, youth work, and meals on wheels

176 worked in schools: tutoring, aiding teachers

67 worked in voter registration

52 worked in political campaigns

100 worked in Sunday schools

45 answered a crisis pregnancy phone line

75 worked distributing maternity and infant clothing

47 have shared their homes with pregnant strangers, the elderly, refugees, the sick, or foster children[29]

And finally, this argument cuts both ways. The pro-lifer can ask the abortion-rights advocate why he does not help with the upbringing of poor children whose mothers have chosen not to kill them, since the postnatal existence of these children is a result of the abortion-rights advocate's public policy of "choice." It is no small coincidence that it is not Planned Parenthood, the National Abortion Rights Action League, or the National Organization for Women that creates and runs crisis pregnancy centers and other institutions that meet the physical and spiritual needs of women who choose not to kill their unborn children. Pro-lifers are the ones who are behind such institutions. This makes it quite evident that the so-called pro-choicers in fact favor abortion, for the actions of their political organizations assume abortion as the only real choice. Otherwise they would do just as much for women who choose to keep their unborn children as do the pro-lifers.[30]

In summary, this argument is a blatant example of the ad hominem fallacy. It attacks the character of people in the pro-life movement rather than attacking the arguments for the pro-life position. We would never countenance such reasoning in other

cases of moral judgment. For example, the fact that a person during Hitler's reign was not willing to hide Jews in his home does not mean he cannot correctly say that the Holocaust was evil and should never happen again.

Aren't Pro-lifers Inconsistent If They Support Capital Punishment?

Some abortion-rights (and even pro-life) advocates have pointed out that some people who believe in capital punishment are also pro-life on the abortion issue. And since capital punishment entails the killing of another human person, these pro-lifers are inconsistent. Some people believe that this inconsistency makes the pro-life position incorrect. There are several problems with this reasoning.

First, how does this help the abortion-rights position or hurt the pro-life position on abortion? Wouldn't this argument make people who are against capital punishment and for abortion rights equally inconsistent? Second, inconsistent people can draw good conclusions. For example, a person may inconsistently believe that it is all right to murder white people and not black people. But this inconsistency in his thinking would not make his correct conclusion about the wrongness of murdering black people ipso facto incorrect. Hence, this argument is a red herring and does not deal with the ethical legitimacy of either abortion or the pro-life position. Third, a number of pro-life advocates do not believe that capital punishment is morally justified.[31] The abortion-rights advocate can't say that *these* pro-lifers are inconsistent. Why does he not then give up his abortion-rights position and embrace *this* pro-life position, since it should seem to him even more consistent than the anti-capital punishment abortion-rights position? Fourth, one can plausibly argue that the pro-life position on abortion *is* consistent with capital punishment. Pro-life advocates, for the most part, do not argue that killing is *never* justified, for many believe that there are legitimate instances in which killing is justified, such as in the cases of self-defense and capital punishment, both of which do not entail the taking of an innocent human life. But nontherapeutic abortion does entail such killing. Hence, the pro-life advocate who believes in capital punishment is saying, "It is wrong to take the life of an innocent human person, but the capital offender is not innocent. Therefore, capital punishment is morally justified."

Moreover, a murder suspect can be justly convicted only if he is provided with the constitutional right of due process, which means that the state must prove his guilt in accordance with the rules of evidence. On the other hand, the unborn, who has murdered no one, is killed without any due process. Although I have not made up my own mind on the issue of capital punishment, I do not believe it is logically inconsistent with the pro-life position.

In summary, like the previous argument, this one is a blatant example of the ad hominem fallacy, since it is a direct attack upon the character of the pro-life advocate. Instead of dealing with the pro-lifer's arguments against abortion, the abortion-rights advocate attacks the pro-lifer.

Men Don't Get Pregnant

This argument is so silly that acknowledging it may give it undeserved credibility. But it occurs so frequently in the media that it ought to be dealt with. I was confronted with this argument in a debate at the University of Nevada, Las Vegas (4 December 1989). One of the debate participants, Esther Langston, a professor of social work at UNLV, told the audience that she thought it was rather strange that two men (myself and my debate partner, David Day) were arguing against abortion. After all, men don't get pregnant; abortion is a woman's issue.

There are several problems with this argument. First, I responded to Professor Langston by pointing out that arguments don't have penises, people do. Since many pro-life women use the same arguments as we did in the debate, it was incumbent upon her to answer our arguments, which stand or fall apart from our genitalia. I pointed out that since she could not argue the same way if a woman were putting forth our arguments, therefore our gender is totally irrelevant to whether the pro-life position is correct. In a subtle and clever way she dodged our arguments and attacked us: a clear case of the ad hominem fallacy.

Second, on the same rationale, Langston would have to reject the *Roe v. Wade* decision, since it was arrived at by nine men (7–2). Third, if Langston's reasoning is correct, then mothers could never rightfully consent to have their newborn baby boy circumcised, since, after all, how can these mothers know how it feels to have a portion of their penis cut off?[32] Fourth, abortion is a human issue, not just a women's issue, for it has consequences for everybody in society. Tax dollars may be taken from men's salaries to fund abortions; men must help in child rearing or pay child support if the mother chooses not to abort; and the man's seed is one of the material causes (along with the female's ovum) of the unborn's being (there has been only one known virginal conception). Fifth, the appeal to the pregnant woman's personal involvement can be used as a two-edged sword. Could not someone argue that since men don't get pregnant, and hence are less tainted by personal involvement, their opinion concerning the morality of abortion is more objective?

Arguments from Decisive Moments and Gradualism

6

There is no nonarbitrary line separating a fetus from a child or, indeed, an adult human being.
Supreme Court Justice Byron White (1986)

To be or not to be, that is the question.
Shakespeare

Realizing that many of the popular arguments, such as those found in the last two chapters, have little logical merit, many philosophers, ethicists, and theologians have presented more sophisticated arguments for abortion rights. These abortion-rights thinkers, who run the gamut from the radical (e.g, their views include the permissibility of infanticide) to the moderate (e.g., they believe that abortion should be forbidden several months before birth), do agree with pro-life advocates that the abortion debate rests on the moral status of the unborn: if the unborn are fully human, then nearly every abortion performed is tantamount to murder. They argue, however, that although the unborn entity is *human*, insofar as belonging to the species *homo sapiens*, it is not a *person* and hence not *fully* human.

That is to say, although individual human life does begin at the moment of conception, it is at some later stage (i.e., some decisive moment in the unborn's development) that it becomes worthy of our protection. Some,[1] among them Michael Tooley, argue that this moment occurs after birth. At this moment the unborn entity becomes a person. Other philosophers take a gradualist position and argue that the unborn gradually gains more rights as it develops. Hence, a zygote has fewer rights than a six-month-old fetus, but this fetus has fewer rights than an adult woman. Those who argue in this fashion defend a decisive-moment or gradualist approach to the status of the unborn and the morality of abortion.

Other abortion-rights advocates do not see the status of the unborn as the decisive factor in whether or not abortion is morally justified. They argue that the unborn's presence in the pregnant woman's body entails a conflict of rights if the pregnant woman does not want to be pregnant. Therefore, the unborn, regardless of whether it is fully human and has a full right to life, cannot use the body of another against her will. Hence, a pregnant woman's removal of an unborn entity from her body, even though it will probably result in its death, is no more immoral than an ordinary person's refusal to donate his kidney to another in need of one, even though this refusal will probably result in the death of the prospective recipient.

Some abortion-rights theologians argue that their position is consistent with traditional Hebrew-Christian ethics. They argue, among other things, that there is no direct prohibition of abortion in the Bible, that there is no biblical evidence that the unborn are fully human, and that God's granting of free choice to his creation is stunted by anti-abortion legislation. In this chapter we will critically examine the most important arguments found in the decisive-moment and gradualist arguments. We will critically analyze the arguments from bodily rights in chapter 7 and arguments from theology in chapter 8. But it should be kept in mind that these three approaches are not necessarily mutually exclusive. One can easily defend abortion rights by a combination of arguments found in all three approaches.[2]

Decisive-Moment and Gradualist Theories: A Presentation and Critique

Because there is no doubt that the life of a human individual begins at conception (see chap. 3), defenders of abortion rights argue that although the unborn is biologically human it does not become fully human (or "a person") until some moment in its development. Consequently, throughout the recent history (from the late 1960s to the present) of the abortion controversy many have put forth criteria by which to judge whether a human organism has reached the point in its development at which it is fully human. Some criteria are based on so-called decisive moments in prenatal and neonatal development. Others are based on certain conditions any entity, born or unborn, must fulfill in order to be considered fully human. And others argue that there is no decisive moment but that the unborn's rights increase as its

body develops. I believe that all these views are flawed. I will argue that the pro-life view that full humanness begins at conception is the most coherent and is consistent with our basic moral intuitions. In order to adequately defend this position I will first critique a number of decisive-moment and gradualist theories, whose defenses contain many objections to the pro-life view. Then I will respond to other objections to this position that were not specifically dealt with in my criticisms of the decisive-moment and gradualist theories.

Agnostic Approach: "No One Knows When Life Begins"

It is often claimed by abortion-rights advocates that "no one knows when life begins," but this is inaccurate. No one who knows anything about prenatal development seriously doubts that individual biological human life is present from conception (see chap. 3). What the abortion-rights advocates probably mean when they say that "no one knows when life begins" is that no one knows when the individual in the womb attains personhood or full humanness. Thus, from a legal perspective they argue: since no one knows when full humanness is attained, abortion should remain legal. However, there are at least four problems with this argument.

1. It is a two-edged sword. If no one knows when full humanness is attained, then we cannot prevent a Satan-worshipping neighbor, who believes that full humanness begins at the age of two, from sacrificing his one-and-a-half-year-old son to the unholy one. After all, who knows when life begins? And who are we to push our "religious" views on others in a pluralistic society?

2. If it is true that we don't know when full humanness begins, this is an excellent reason not to kill the unborn, since we may be killing a human entity who has a full right to life. Furthermore, some have argued that even if the unborn are only potential persons, without full personhood, it still may be morally wrong to kill them for non-life-threatening reasons. If one killed an entity without knowing whether the entity killed (in

this case, the unborn) is either fully human with a full right to life or a potential person with a high moral status, it would be negligent to proceed with the killing, since there is a strong possibility that one is killing a being of great moral significance. If game hunters with this same philosophical mindset shot at rustling bushes, the National Rifle Association's membership would become severely depleted. Ignorance of a being's status is certainly not justification to kill it. This is called the benefit of the doubt argument, since we are giving the unborn the benefit of the doubt.

Professor Robert Wennberg, however, does not agree. He asks us to consider the following case:

> A thirty-six-year-old woman with four children, worn down and exhausted by poverty and terrible living conditions, married to an alcoholic husband, finds herself pregnant. Although not the sole source of income for her family, the woman does work and her income is desperately needed. After wrestling with her predicament, the woman decides that an abortion would be in the interests of herself and her family. . . . Concerned about whether abortion might be the killing of a being with a right to life, she consults two moralists, both of whom appeal to the benefit of the doubt argument. One is a "conservative" who warns her to avoid the possibility of a great moral evil—terminating the life of what might be a holder of a right to life. The other is a "liberal" who encourages her to secure what she knows to be good—avoiding considerable suffering for herself and her family.
>
> It seems to me that both pieces of advice are reasonable and that neither is clearly superior to the other.[3]

The point of this story is that the benefit of the doubt argument can be used by either the conservative or the liberal. For the liberal, the benefit of doubt should be given to elmi-nating the woman's predicament, since we know that she is a real person in a real predicament, whereas we are unsure of the fetus' right to life and/or full humanness. On the other hand, for the conservative, the benefit of the doubt should be given to the un-born, since the magnitude of the evil one may be committing (i.e., killing an innocent person for the sake of relieving one's own suffering) is so great that it should be avoided at all costs.

Wennberg's response, however, fails to really appreciate the pro-lifer's use of the benefit of the doubt argument. Wennberg's account does not seem to grasp the magnitude of killing an innocent human person. Consider the following revised version of the above story:

> A thirty-six-year-old woman with four children, worn down and exhausted by poverty and terrible living conditions, married to an alcoholic husband, finds herself pregnant. Although not the sole source of income for her family, the woman does work and her income is desperately needed. After wrestling with her predicament, the woman is approached by a wealthy benefactor who presents to her the following proposition: "If you detonate the building across the street, which I own, I will pay you $25,000 a year for the next 20 years, adjusting the sum every year in accordance with inflation and the cost of living, and provide you a housekeeper free of charge (this will, of course, more than make up for the burden another child places on the family). However, there is one catch: there is a 1 in 10 chance that in the basement of this building there is a perfectly healthy and innocent eight-year-old child. Thus you run the risk of killing another human being. Is your personal well-being worth the risk?"

If the woman decides to blow up the building, I believe that few if any would judge her actions as morally justified. Even if the odds were 1 in 100, it would seem incredible that anyone would even consider the risk of killing another human being so insignificant that she would take the chance.

To better understand the flaw in Wennberg's story, let us revise the story even further and suppose that the thirty-six-year-old woman is independently wealthy, childless, lives in a beautiful home, and has a wonderful, caring husband. Would Wennberg argue that the risk of homicide would be justified in this case? If not, then his position is tantamount to saying that risking homicide is morally acceptable for poor people but not for the wealthy, a stand that means relief of personal economic and familial burdens is a sufficient justification for risking homicide. This seems to be morally counterintuitive. If his answer is yes—that the risk of homicide *is* justified in the case of the well-off thirty-six-year-old—then relieving personal economic and familial burdens is not relevant in the justification for risking homicide, and Wennberg's support of a liberal use of the benefit of the doubt argument collapses.

We can revise Wennberg's argument in a different way and suppose that a family wanting to adopt a child will pay the thirty-six-year-old woman twenty thousand dollars in addition to hospital expenses so that she can bring the baby to term. Now that her burden has been lifted for the most part, is risk of homicide still justified? If it is, then relieving her economic and familial burdens is not relevant to Wennberg's case. If not, then, as in the other revised story, Wennberg's argument is essentially saying that risking homicide is morally justified for people with certain hardships. But, again this seems to be counterintuitive.

Even if the pro-lifer grants Wennberg his point, it has limited applications, since a great number of abortions do not occur due to desperate circumstances. It follows then that even Wennberg's agnostic must admit that a great number of abortions are immoral and should be banned, since they risk murder and do not relieve the parents of a burden whose elimination is worth the risk of murder. In sum, the benefit of the doubt argument still has much to merit it.

3. We have excellent reason to believe that full humanness is present from the moment of conception, and that the nature of prenatal and postuterine existence is merely the unfolding of human growth and development that does not cease until death (see chap. 3 and the remainder of this chapter). In other words, the unborn, like the rest of use, are not potential human persons, but human persons with much potential.

4. By permitting abortion for virtually any reason during the entire nine months of pregnancy, abortion-rights advocates have decided, for all practical purposes, when full humanness is attained. They have decided that this moment occurs at birth. Despite their claim that "no one knows when life begins," abortion-rights advocates act as if protectable human life begins at birth. Since actions speak louder than words, the so-called pro-choice movement is not telling the truth when it claims that "it doesn't know when life begins."

Some abortion-rights literature, which I am certain is quite embarrassing to the more sophisticated proponents of this cause, claims that "personhood at conception is a religious belief, not a provable biological fact."[4] What could possibly be meant by this assertion? Is it claiming that religious claims are in principle unprovable scientifically? If it is, it is incorrect, for many religions, such as Christianity and Islam, to believe that the physical world literally exists, which is a major assumption of contemporary science. On the other hand, some religions, such as Christian Science and certain forms of Hinduism,[5] deny the literal existence of the physical world. Moreover, the arguments used to support the view that life begins at conception (see chap. 3 and this chapter), or any other view on abortion for that matter, are not even remotely religious, since they involve the citing of scientific evidence and the use of philosophical reasoning.

But maybe this pro-choice assertion is simply claiming that biology can tell us nothing about values. If this is what is meant, it is right in one sense and wrong in another. It is right if it means that the brute facts of science, without any moral reflection on our part, cannot tell us what is right and wrong. But it is wrong if it means that the brute facts of science cannot tell us to whom we should apply the values of which we are already aware. For example, if I don't know whether the object I am driving toward in my car is a living woman, a female corpse, or a mannikin, biology is extremely important in helping me to avoid committing an act of homicide. Running over mannikins and corpses is not homicide, but running over a woman is.

Maybe the pro-choice assertion is saying that *when* human life should be valued is a philosophical belief that cannot be proven scientifically. Maybe so, but this cuts both ways. Isn't the belief that a woman has abortion rights a philosophical belief that cannot be proven scientifically and over which people obviously disagree? But if the pro-life position cannot be enacted into law because it is philosophical (or religious), then neither can the abortion-rights position. The abortion-rights advocate may respond to this by saying that this fact alone is a good reason to leave it up to each woman to choose whether she should have an abortion. But this response begs the question, for this is precisely the abortion-rights position. Furthermore, the pro-lifer could reply to this abortion-rights response by employing the abortion-rights advocate's own logic. The pro-lifer could argue that since the abortion-rights position is a philosophical position over which many people disagree, we should permit each unborn human being to be born and make up her own mind as to whether she should or should not die. In sum, it seems that the appeal to ignorance is seriously flawed.

Implantation

Some pro-life advocates, such as Bernard Nathanson,[6] argue that full humanness begins when the conceptus is implanted in her mother's womb, which occurs before two weeks after conception. There are four basic arguments for this position to which I will respond.

1. *Argument from the fact that at implantation the unborn establishes its presence by transmitting hormonal signals to its mother.* Nathanson argues that at the moment of implantation the unborn "establishes its presence to the rest of us by transmitting its own signals—by producing hormones—approximately one week after fertilization and as soon as it burrows into the alien uterine wall." For Nathanson implantation is significant because prior to this time the unborn "has the genetic structure but is incomplete, lacking the essential element that produces life: an interface with the human community and communication of the fact that it is there."[7] So for Nathanson the unborn's hormonal communication to her mother is essential for humanness.

I believe that this argument is flawed for at least two important reasons. First, how is it possible that one's essence is dependent on whether others are aware of one's existence? It seems intuitively correct to say that it is not essential to your being whether or not anyone knows you exist, for you are who you are regardless of whether others are aware of your existence. One interacts with a human being; one does not make a being human by interacting with it. In philosophical terms, Nathanson confuses epistemology (the study of how we know things) with ontology (the study of being or existence).

A second objection, which supports my first objection, is mentioned by Nathanson himself. He writes, "If implantation is biologically the decisive point for alpha's [the unborn's] existence, what do we do about the 'test-tube' conceptions? The zygote in these cases is seen in its culture dish and could be said to announce its existence even before it is implanted?" Nathanson responds to these questions by asserting, "It seems to me that when it is in the dish the zygote is already implanted, philosophically and biochemically, and has established the nexus with the human community, before it is 're'-implanted into the mother's womb."[8] This response, however, does not support Nathanson's position, for he is admitting that there is no essential difference between the implanted and the non-implanted zygote, just an accidental difference (the former's existence is known while the latter's is not). Hence, just as there is no essential difference between a Donald Trump who is an unknown hermit and a Donald Trump who is an entrepreneur and billionaire (there are only accidental differences between the two Trumps), there is no essential difference between an unknown conceptus and a known conceptus. In sum, it seems counterintuitive to assert that one's essence is dependent on another's knowledge of one's existence.

2. *Argument from the fact that some products of conception are not human beings and the fact that some human beings, such as clones, may not result from conception.* There is a second argument for implantation as the decisive moment: If we say that full humanness begins at conception, we must respond to the observation that "some entities that stem from the union of sperm and egg are not 'human beings' and never will develop into them" and that there may be some human beings who come into being without the union of sperm and egg.[9] Concerning the former, Nathanson gives examples of nonhuman entities that result from the sperm-egg union: the hydatidiform mole ("an entity which is usually just a degenerated placenta and typically has a random number of chromosomes"), the choriocarcinoma ("a 'conception-cancer' resulting from the sperm-egg union is one of gynecology's most malignant tumors"), and the "blighted ovum" ("a conception with the forty-six chromosomes but which is only a placenta, lacks an embryonic plate, and is always aborted naturally after implantation"). Concerning the latter, a clone is an example of a human entity that may come into being without benefit of an ordinary sperm-egg union conception.[10]

The problem with Nathanson's argument is that he confuses necessary and sufficient conditions. One who holds that full humanness begins at conception is not arguing that everything that results from the sperm-egg union is necessarily a conception. That is, every ordinary conception of an individual human entity is the result of a sperm-egg union, but not every sperm-egg union results in such a conception. Hence, the sperm-egg union is a necessary condition for an ordinary conception, but not a sufficient condition.

Furthermore, Nathanson is correct in asserting that it is possible that some day there may be human beings, such as clones, who come into existence without benefit of an ordinary sperm-egg union conception.[11] But this would only mean that sperm-egg union conception is not a necessary condition for full humanness, just as the sperm-egg union is not a sufficient condition for an ordinary conception. In sum, Nathanson's argument from both nonhuman products of sperm-egg unions and the possibility of clones is inadequate in overturning the pro-life position that full humanness begins at conception.

3. *Argument from spontaneous abortions.* It is estimated that 20 to 50 percent of all conceptions die before birth. Some estimate up to thirty percent die before implantation.[12] Some people argue that these facts make it difficult to believe that the unborn are fully human in at least the very earliest stage of their development prior to implantation. But this is clearly an invalid argument, for it does not logically follow from the number of unborn entities who die that these entities are by nature not fully human. To cite an example, it does not follow from the fact that underdeveloped countries have a high infant mortality rate that their babies are less human than those born in countries with a low infant mortality rate.

But suppose that the abortion-rights advocate responds to this by arguing "that if every fertilized ovum is human, then we are obligated to save all spontaneous abortions as well. But if we did, it would lead to overpopulation, death by medical neglect, and starvation." The problem with this response is that it confuses our obvious prima facie moral obligation not to commit homicide (that is, to perform an abortion) with the questionable moral obligation to interfere with natural death (that is, to permit the conceptus to spontaneously abort). "Protecting life is a moral obligation, but resisting natural death is not necessarily a moral duty. . . . There is no inconsistency between preserving natural life, opposing artificial abortion and allowing natural death by spontaneous abortion."[13]

Admittedly, the question of interference in spontaneous abortions provokes the pro-life ethicist to think more deeply and sensitively about his position and to make distinctions and nuances that may not be pleasing to all who call themselves pro-life. But just as the difficult question of whether to pull the plug on the irreversibly comatose who are machine-dependent or to withhold food and water from those in a persistent vegetative state does not count against the position that murdering healthy adults is morally wrong, the question of how we should ethically respond to spontaneous abortions does not count against the pro-life ethic, which says that we should not directly and intentionally kill the healthy and normally developing unborn. In other words, if we have good reason to believe that the early unborn are fully human, then the problem of spontaneous abortions must be addressed in light of that well-founded belief. That is to say, spontaneous abortions do not count against the unborn's full humanness.

4. *Argument from twinning and recombination.* Some people argue that since both twinning (the division of a single conceptus) and recombination (the reuniting of two concepti) may occur up to fourteen days after conception (before or after implantation), individual human life does not begin until that time. However, a careful examination of the nature of twinning and recombination reveals that there is no reason to suppose that the original pre-twinned conceptus or any pre-recombined conceptus is not fully human.

First, scientists are not agreed on many aspects of twinning. Some claim that twinning may be a nonsexual form of parthenogenesis or "parenting." This occurs in some animals and plants. Others claim that when twinning occurs an existing human being dies and gives life to two new and identical human beings like herself. Still others claim that since not all human concepti have the capacity to twin, one could argue that there exists in some concepti a basic duality prior to the split. Hence, it may be claimed that at least in some incipient form two individual lives were present from the start at conception. In any event, the fact of twinning does not seem to be a sufficient reason to give up the belief that full humanness begins at conception.[14]

Second, every conceptus, whether before twinning or recombination, is still a human individual who is genetically distinct from her parents. In other words, simply because identical twins result from a conceptus split or one individual results from two concepti that recombine, it does not logically follow

that any of the concepti prior to twinning or recombining were not fully human.[15] To help us understand this point, Robert Wennberg provides the following story:

> Imagine that we lived in a world in which a certain small percentage of teenagers replicated themselves by some mysterious natural means, splitting in two upon reaching their sixteenth birthday. We would not in the least be inclined to conclude that no human being could therefore be considered a person prior to becoming sixteen years of age; nor would we conclude that life could be taken with greater impunity prior to replication than afterward. The real oddity—to press the parallel—would be two teenagers becoming one. However, in all of this we still would not judge the individual's claim to life to be undermined in any way. We might puzzle over questions of personal identity . . . but we would not allow these strange replications and fusions to influence our thinking about an individual's right to life. Nor therefore does it seem that such considerations are relevant in determining the point at which an individual might assume a right to life in utero.[16]

Although identical twins are also genetically identical, this does not take away from my appealing to the fact that each is an individual human organism with a genetic code. It just happens to be in the case of twins (or in the case of identical triplets or quadruplets) that the genetic code each possesses is identical to the other. If such a fact counted against the full individual humanness of identical twins at the beginning, it would follow that it would also count against their full individual humanness after birth. But this is absurd. Therefore, if all my arguments against decisive-moment theories and gradualism are successful (and I believe they are), the fact that two individual human persons begin their existence with the same genetic code means very little concerning their status as persons.

The Appearance of "Humanness"

Some argue that the unborn become fully human when they take on the appearance of a child. Professor Ernest Van Den Haag[17] is sympathetic to this criterion, although he combines it with the criterion of sentience. He writes that when the unborn acquires a functioning brain and neural system soon after the first trimester (although brain waves can be detected at forty to forty-two days after conception, a fact that Van Den Haag *does not* mention), it "starts to resemble an embryonic human being." And after this point "abortion seems justifiable only by the gravest of reasons, such as the danger to the mother; for what is being aborted undeniably resembles a human being to an uncomfortable degree."[18]

There are several problems with this argument. First, although appearance can be helpful in determining what is or is not fully human, it is certainly not a sufficient or a necessary condition for doing so. After all, mannikins in department stores resemble human beings, and they are not even remotely human. On the other hand, some human oddities, such as the bearded lady or the elephant man, who more closely resemble nonhuman primates, are nonetheless fully human. And the reason why we believe that the bearded lady and the elephant man are fully human and the mannikin is not is because the former are functioning individual organisms which genetically belong to the species *homo sapiens*. The latter is an inanimate object.

Second, John Jefferson Davis points out that "this objection assumes that personhood presupposes a postnatal form. A little reflection, however, will show that the concept of a 'human form' is a dynamic and not a static one. Each of us, during normal growth and development, exhibits a long succession of different outward forms." That is to say, an early embryo, although not looking like a newborn, does look exactly like a human ought to look at this stage of her development. Thus, "the appearance of an 80-year-old adult differs greatly from that of a newborn child, and yet we speak without hesitation of both as persons. In both cases, we have learned to recognize the physical appearances associated with those developmental stages as normal expressions of human personhood."[19] In other words, the unborn at any stage of her development looks perfectly human because that is what human persons look like at that time.

It may be true that it is psychologically easier to kill something that does not resemble the human beings we see in everyday life, but it does not follow from this that the being in question is any less human or that the executioner is any more humane. Once we recognize that human development is a process that does not cease at the time of birth, "to insist that the unborn at six weeks look like the newborn infant is no more reasonable than to expect the newborn to look like a teenager. If we acknowledge as 'human' a succession of outward forms after birth, there is no reason not to extend that courtesy to the unborn, since human life is a continuum from conception to natural death."[20] Hence, Van Den Haag, by confusing appearance with reality, may have inadvertently created a new prejudice, natalism. And like other prejudices, such as sexism and racism, natalism emphasizes nonessential differences ("they have a different appearance") in order to support a favored group ("the already born").

Human Sentiment

Some abortion-rights people argue that since many parents do not grieve at the death of an embryo or fetus as they would at the death of an infant or a small child, the unborn are not fully human.

As a standard for moral action, this criterion rests on an unstable foundation. As John T. Noonan has observed, "[F]eeling is notoriously an unsure guide to the humanity of others. Many groups of humans have had difficulty in feeling that persons of another tongue, color, religion, sex, are as human as they."[21] One usually feels a greater sense of loss at the sudden death of a healthy parent than one feels for the hundreds who die daily of starvation in underdeveloped countries. Does this mean that the latter are less human than one's parent? Certainly not. Noonan points out that "we mourn the loss of a ten-year-old boy more than the loss of his one-day-old brother or his 90-year-old grandfather." The reason for this is that "the difference felt and the grief expressed vary with the potentialities extinguished, or the experience wiped out; they do not seem to point to any substantial difference in the humanity of baby, boy, or grandfather."[22]

Furthermore, if this abortion-rights argument is correct, it leads to an absurdity: by grieving the death of their unborn child, one set of parents can make their child a person, whereas another set of parents who don't grieve the death of their child can make their child a nonperson. And what about the parents of a deceased two-year-old who don't grieve their child's death; is this two-year-old suddenly not a person? It is evident that a theory of personhood contingent on the emotional reactions of others is fundamentally absurd.

Quickening

Although I have already mentioned the quickening criterion in chapter 3, a critique of it bears both repeating and enhancement at this juncture. *Quickening* has traditionally referred to the first movement of the unborn felt by her mother. It was at this time in fetal development that some medieval and common-law scholars thought it could be proven that the unborn was "alive" or that the soul had entered her body. Not having access to the biological facts or medical technology we currently possess, they reasoned that prior to quickening it could not be proven for legal purposes that the unborn entity was alive or fully human. And without proof of the fetus being alive, it was difficult if not impossible to prosecute someone for killing the unborn if an abortion occurred prior to quickening. However, current biology, which has conclusively demonstrated that a biologically living human individual is present from conception, has decisively refuted the notion of quickening, just as current astronomy has refuted the geocentric solar system. In addition, modern technology is able to detect quite easily whether or not the unborn is alive long before the mother feels any movements. Does this mean that these ancestors of ours were not pro-life? Not at all.

Legal scholar and theologian John Warwick Montgomery has pointed out that when our medieval and common-law forefathers talked about quickening as the beginning of life "they were just identifying the first evidence of life they could conclusively detect. . . . They were saying that as soon as one had life, there must be protection. Now we know that life starts at the moment of conception with nothing superadded."[23] Law professor Robert Byrn writes:

> Quickening [in common law] was never intended as a substantive standard for the beginning of human life. It evolved purely as an evidentiary device [i.e., "Was the fetus alive when expelled from the womb?"]. As a Massachusetts court observed in 1834. "The distinction between a woman being pregnant, and being quick with child is applicable mainly, not exclusively, to criminal cases" (*Hall v. Hancock*).[24]

Hence, in order to be consistent with contemporary science and technology, legal protection should be extended to the unborn entity from the moment of conception.

Furthermore, we now know that the ability to feel the unborn's movement is contingent upon the amount of the mother's body fat. It seems silly to say that one's pre-born humanness is contingent upon whether one is fortunate to have been conceived in a body that frequents aerobics classes.

Viability

Viability is the time at which the unborn can live outside her mother's womb. Some have argued that prior to this time, since the unborn cannot survive independent of her mother, she is not a completely independent human life and hence not fully human. Bioethicist Andrew Varga points out a number of problems with this criterion.

First, "how does viability transform the nature of the fetus so that the nonhuman being then turns into a human being?" That is to say, viability is a measure of the sophistication of our neonatal life-support systems. Humanity remains the same, but viability changes. Viability measures medical technology, not one's humanity. Second, "is viability not just an extrinsic criterion imposed upon the fetus by some members of society who simply declare that the fetus will be accepted at that moment as a human being?"[25] In other words, the viability criterion seems to be arbitrary and not applicable to the question of whether the unborn is fully human, since it is only a criterion that tells us when certain members of our society want to accept the humanity of the unborn. Nothing follows from this fact concerning the nature of the unborn entity.

And third, "the time of viability cannot be determined precisely, and this fact would create great practical problems for those who hold this opinion."[26] For example, in 1973, when the Supreme Court legalized abortion, viability was between 24 and 28 weeks. But now some babies have survived 20 weeks after conception. This, of course, puts the defender of abortion-rights in a morally difficult situation. For some health-care facilities are allowing viable babies to be killed by abortion in one room while in another room doctors are trying heroically to save other viable infants born prematurely (preemies). It seems only logical that if the 21-week-old preemie is fully human, then so is the 28-week-old unborn who can be legally killed by abortion. This is why philosopher Jane English, who is a moderate on the abortion issue (i.e., her position does not fit well into either the pro-life or abortion-rights camp, although she seems closer to the latter), has asserted "that the similarity of a fetus to a baby is very significant. A fetus one week before birth is so much like a newborn baby in our psychological space that we cannot allow any cavalier treatment of the former while expecting full sympathy and nurturative support for the latter. . . . An early horror story from New York about nurses who were expected to alternate between caring for six-week premature infants and disposing of viable 24-week aborted fetuses is just that—a horror story." English writes that "these beings are so much alike that no one can be asked to draw a distinction and treat them so differently."[27]

In addition to Varga's observations, one can point out that each one of us is nonviable in relation to his environment. If any one of us were to be placed naked on the moon or the earth's North Pole for just a few minutes, one would quickly become aware of one's nonviability. Therefore, the unborn entity prior to the time she can live outside her mother's womb is as nonviable in relation to her environment as we are nonviable in relation to ours.

Furthermore, it seems that many who defend the viability criterion argue in a circle. Take Supreme Court Justice Harry Blackmun's use of it in his dissenting opinion in *Webster v. Reproductive Health Services* (1989):

> For my part, I remain convinced, as six other Members of this court 16 years ago were convinced, that the *Roe* framework, and the viability standard in particular, fairly, sensibly, and effectively functions to safeguard the constitutional liberties of pregnant women while recognizing and accommodating the State's interest in potential human life. The viability line reflects the biological facts and truths of fetal development; it marks the threshold moment prior to which a fetus cannot survive separate from the woman and cannot reasonably and objectively be regarded as a subject of rights or interests distinct from, or paramount to, those of the pregnant woman. At the same time, the viability standard takes account of the undeniable fact that as the fetus evolves into its postnatal form, and as it loses its dependence on the uterine environment, the State's interest in the fetus' potential human life, and in fostering a regard for human life in general, becomes compelling.[28]

Although put forth by a Supreme Court justice, this defense of the viability criterion is completely circular (and in practice irrelevant, since the Court's "health provision" allows for abortion on demand throughout pregnancy; see chap. 2). Blackmun tells us that viability is the time at which the state has interest in protecting potential human life (not *actual* human life, since, according to the Court, this does not occur until birth; see chap. 2) because the fetus has no interests or rights prior to being able to survive outside the womb. But then we are told that viability is the best criterion because it "takes account of the undeniable fact that as the fetus evolves . . . and loses its dependence on the uterine environment, the State's interest in the fetus' potential human life . . . becomes compelling." In other words, Blackmun is claiming that the state has an interest in protecting fetal life only when that life can live outside the womb. But why is this correct? Because, we are told, prior to being able to live outside the womb the fetus has no interests or rights. But this is clearly a case of circular reasoning, for Blackmun is assuming (that the fetus has no interests or rights prior to viability) what he is trying to prove (that the fetus has no interests or rights prior to viability). This argument is no more compelling than the one given by the zealous UNLV basketball fan who argues that the Runnin' Rebels are the best team because no team is better (which, of course, is the same as being the best team). This argument, like Blackmun's, falls prey to the fallacy of circular reasoning because it assumes what it is trying to prove without providing any independent evidence or reasons for the conclusion.

It is interesting to note that even a student of the great Greek logician Aristotle, Mortimer Adler, defends viability in a circular fashion: "The crucial question here is a factual one: Is the fetus a viable organism outside the mother's body during that time? If it cannot live by itself as an independent organism, it does not have a life of its own."[29] But why is this so? Why does not being an independent organism mean that the previable fetus does not have a life of its own (or, is not a person)? Because, according to Adler, to answer the question of whether the fetus has a life of its own (or, is a person) one must first answer the crucial question of whether the fetus is a viable organism outside the mother's body. And if it is not viable, then it does not have a life of its own. Consequently for Adler, a nonviable fetus does not have a life of its own because it is not an independent organism (that is, nonviable). Thus the circularity of Adler's argument is now easy to discern: a nonviable fetus does not have a

life of its own because it is nonviable. This is no different than the sexist argument that women are inferior to men because they're women. Adler's argument fares no better than Blackmun's.

Beginning of Brain Functioning

Some bioethicists, such as Baruch Brody, believe that full humanness begins when the brain starts functioning, which can first be detected by the electroencephalogram (EEG) at about forty to forty-three days after conception.[30] Brody maintains that in order to decide when something is fully human "we must first see . . . what properties are such that their loss would mean the going out of existence (the death) of a human being."[31] He concludes that since at brain death a human being goes out of existence (at least in this mortal realm), the presence of a functioning human brain is the property which makes one fully human. Hence, it seems only logical that the start of brain functioning is the beginning of full humanness.

The fundamental difficulty with this argument "is that brain death indicates the end of human life as we know it, the dead brain having no capacity to revive itself. But the developing embryo has the natural capacity to bring on the functioning of the brain."[32] That is to say, an entity's irreversible absence of brain waves after the brain waves have come into existence indicates that the entity no longer has the natural inherent capacity to function as a human being, since our current technology is incapable of reactivating the brain. However, the unborn entity who has yet to reach the stage in her development at which brain waves can be detected, unlike the brain-dead corpse, still has the natural inherent capacity to have brain waves, like a patient with a temporarily flat EEG (that is, the cessation is reversible). Therefore, "the two stages of human life are, then, entirely different from the point of view of brain functioning. The embryo contains the natural capacity to develop all the human activities: perceiving, reasoning, willing and relating to others. Death means the end of natural growth, the cessation of these abilities."[33] An embryo, in its earliest stages, does not need a brain to live, whereas human persons at later stages do. As ethicist Stephen Schwarz points out: "There is clearly a world of difference between no brain activity in the sense of 'no more' and in the sense of 'not yet.' If a human being with irreversible 'no more' is dead, it does not follow that a human being whose lack of brain activity has the character of 'not yet' is dead, or otherwise not a human being."[34]

Brody responds to this criticism by presenting the following science-fiction case:

[I]magine that medical technology has reached the stage at which, when brain death occurs, the brain is removed, "liquified," and "recast" into a new functioning brain. The new brain bears no relation to the old one (it has none of its memory traces, and so on). If the new brain were put into the old body, would the same human being exist or a new human being who made use of the body of the old one? I am inclined to suppose the latter. But consider the entity whose brain has died. Is he not like the fetus? Both have the potential for developing into an entity with a functioning brain (we shall call this a weak potential) but it seems to me, that an entity can go out of existence even if it retains a weak potential for having a functioning brain, and that, analogously, the fetus is not a human being just because it has this weak potential. What is essential for being human is the possession of the potential for human activities that comes with having the structures required for a functioning brain. It is this potential that the fetus acquires at (or perhaps slightly before) the time that its brain starts functioning, and it is this potential that the newly conceived fetus does not have.[35]

I do not believe that this response succeeds. First, unlike the potential of the corpse's dead brain to be liquified and recast as a new brain, the unborn's potency to develop is within itself (intrinsic). "As in the case of other organisms," philosopher A. Chadwick Ray points out, the unborn's development "admittedly requires nourishment from outside and an appropriate environment (consider parasites), but still, the fetus has within itself the power to appropriate nourishment and grow." On the other hand, the potential of Brody's corpse is utterly extrinsic. That is, "it can be acted upon from the outside and brought to life, but without immediate surgery its life will not be restored, and it will simply rot."[36]

Second, the unborn has "interests of itself, in a straightforward, non-projective way, that go beyond the interests of its component parts—cells, tissues, etc.," just as I as a living organism have interests that go beyond the interests of my component parts—ears, nose, teeth, etc. On the other hand, the corpse "has no interests beyond those of its parts. The component cells may have an interest in continuing to live, but the corpse itself has none." For example, "there would be no loss in the corpse's organs all being donated to different patients (imagine donating every living cell if you prefer), whereas in a living fetus's being chopped up for spare parts its *own* interests would be sacrificed."[37]

In summary, "the growth of the fetus is in its own interest and is the realization of its intrinsic potential, in which realization of its identity is preserved." However, "the implanting of a new brain into a brainless corpse would constitute the genesis of a new organism with its own new *telos* and interests where there were none."[38] Therefore, since the pre-brain-functioning unborn entity has a natural inherent capacity for brain functioning (like the patient with the temporarily flat EEG) while the corpse does not, they do not have the same kind of weak potential Brody claims they have.

What if someone responds: "The fact is that the zygote and early embryo are not conscious, cannot think, and cannot communicate. How can such a being be a person?" First, as Schwarz points out, "That he [i.e., the zygote or early embryo] cannot think and communicate means merely that he cannot function as a person, not that he lacks the being of a person."[39] (See "The Attainment of Sentience" and "Criteria of Personhood.") Second, by saying that certain unborn human beings lack consciousness but will by nature eventually attain it, the objector implicitly affirms the personhood of the unconscious unborn, since a being who lacks a certain characteristic it will by nature eventually attain means that it is a certain sort of being, in this case, a human person, who possesses the essential structure necessary for the manifestation of certain functions. What the unconscious unborn "lacks is the immediate capacity for consciousness, which is simply an aspect of his lack of development, something entirely appropriate for a being at the beginning of his development."[40] For example, a three-month-old baby who currently lacks the immediate capacity to communicate through language is still a human person precisely because he is the sort of being that possesses the essential structure necessary for the manifestation of language skills (humanness). Yet it is entirely appropriate, because of his level of development, for a three-month-old baby to lack the immediate capacity to communicate through language. On the other hand, a stone or a piece of wood cannot be said to lack consciousness, because neither has the sort of nature necessary for this function; that is, a stone or piece of wood that is not conscious does not lack anything. "The zygote [or early embryo] is a person who is *not yet* conscious, not a being who is simply not conscious like a stone."[41]

It should be noted that even if Brody is correct about personhood beginning with brainwave activity, his view does not really help the abortion-rights position, since brain waves are first detected six weeks after conception, and a vast number of women who have abortions do not discover they are pregnant until after that time.

The Attainment of Sentience

Some ethicists argue that the unborn becomes fully human sometime later in brain development when he becomes *sentient*, capable of experiencing sensations such as pain. The reason for choosing sentience as the criterion is because a being that cannot experience anything (i.e., a presentient unborn entity) cannot be harmed. Of course, if this position is correct, then the unborn becomes fully human probably during the first

trimester and at least by the third trimester. Therefore, one does not violate anyone's rights when one aborts a non-sentient unborn entity.[42]

There are several problems with this argument. First, it seems to confuse harm with hurt as well as confusing the experience of harm with the reality of harm.[43] One can certainly be harmed without ever experiencing the hurt that sometimes follows from that harm and that we often mistake for the harm itself. For example, if my wife commits adultery but I never find out about it, and if she behaves in a manner no different than she did prior to the adultery, I am harmed by the adultery but not hurt. After all, since she made a vow to remain faithful to me, her violation of that vow, whether I am aware of it or not, harms me. Moreover, if one steals fifty cents from Donald Trump and he never discovers that it is missing, one has harmed Trump by stealing what is rightfully his, but one has certainly not hurt him. Furthermore, a temporarily comatose person who is suffocated to death "experiences no hurt," but he is nevertheless harmed. Hence, one does not have to consciously experience harm, which is sometimes manifested in hurt, in order to truly be harmed. Although not specifically talking about the argument from sentience, Wennberg provides another helpful example:

> If I were cheated out of a just inheritance that I didn't know I had, I would be harmed regardless of whether I knew about the chicanery. Deprivation of a good (be it an inheritance or self-conscious existence) constitutes harm even if one is ignorant of that deprivation.[44]

Second, if sentience is the criterion of full humanness, then the reversibly comatose, the momentarily unconscious, and the sleeping would have to be declared nonpersons, for like the presentient unborn, these individuals all have the natural inherent capacity to be sentient. Yet to countenance their executions would be morally reprehensible. Therefore, one cannot countenance the execution of some unborn entities simply because they are not currently sentient.

Someone may respond to these objections by conceding that they make important points but that there is a problem of a false analogy in the second objection. Someone could point out that although it is true that the reversibly comatose, the momentarily unconscious, and the sleeping are beings who once functioned as sentient beings and are now in a temporary state of nonsentience, the presentient unborn were never sentient. Hence, one is fully human if one was sentient "in the past" and will probably become sentient again in the future.

However, there are at least two problems with this response. First, to claim that a person can be sentient, become nonsentient, and then return to a state of sentience is to assume that there is some underlying personal unity to this individual that makes it intelligible for us to say that the person who has returned to sentience is the same person who was sentient prior to being in a state of nonsentience. But this would mean that sentience is a sufficient but not a necessary condition for personhood. Moreover, if sentience is a necessary condition for personhood, then when someone comes out of a coma or returns to consciousness a new person comes into existence. But this is absurd. Consequently, it does not make sense to say that a person comes into existence when sentience arises, but it does make sense to say that a fully human entity is a person who has the natural inherent capacity to give rise to sentience. A presentient unborn human entity does have this capacity. Therefore, an ordinary unborn human entity is a person, and hence, fully human.

Second, Ray points out that this attempt to exclude many of the unborn from the class of the fully human is "ad hoc and counterintuitive." He asks us to "consider the treatment of comatose patients. We would not discriminate against one merely for rarely or never having been sentient in the past while another otherwise comparable patient had been sentient. (That the presentient patient might have more catching up to do than the other is a difference that can be overcome in this thought experiment by our imagining our artificially equipping the disadvantaged

one with skills and memories.) In such cases, potential counts for everything."[45]

In order to understand Ray's point, consider the following example. Suppose two twins are born, Stacey and Larry. Both are born in a coma and hence have never been sentient. However, two weeks after they're born, Stacey becomes sentient for twenty-four hours and then falls back into a coma. After this occurrence, suppose their physician tells their parents that both children will remain in a coma for nine more months, after which they will both come out of it. According to the sentience criterion of personhood, Stacey is a person but Larry is not, which means that the day before they are set to come out of the coma it is morally all right to kill Larry but not Stacey. I submit that this is counterintuitive, since there does not seem to be any real difference between the moral status of Stacey and the moral status of Larry. Therefore, since there is no moral difference between "not yet sentient, but will be" (Larry) and "once was sentient, but is not" (Stacey), the attainment of sentience is an inadequate criterion for personhood.[46]

Since we have already seen that one does not have to experience hurt or harm in order to be harmed, it seems more consistent with our moral sensibilities to assert that what makes it wrong to kill the reversibly comatose, the sleeping, the momentarily unconscious, and the presentient unborn is that they all share the same nature, human personhood, which entails the natural inherent capacity to perform personal acts. And what makes it morally right to kill plants and to pull the plug on the respirator-dependent brain-dead, who were sentient "in the past," is that their deaths cannot deprive them of their natural inherent capacity to function as persons, since they do not possess such a natural inherent capacity.

Birth

Some people argue that birth is the time at which a human entity becomes fully human. They usually hold this position for at least two reasons: our society calculates the beginning of one's existence from one's day of birth; and it is only after birth that a child is named, baptized, and accepted into a family.

That our society counts one's beginning from one's birthday and that people name and baptize children after their births are simply social conventions. One is not less human if one is abandoned, unnamed, and not baptized. Some cultures, such as the Chinese, count one's beginning from the moment of conception. Does that mean that the American unborn are not fully human while the Chinese unborn are? Also, there is no essential difference between an unborn entity and a newborn baby, just a difference in location. As Wennberg writes, "surely personhood and the right to life is not a matter of location. It should be *what* you are, not *where* you are that determines whether you have a right to life."[47] In fact, abortion-rights philosophers Peter Singer and Helga Kuhse write, "The pro-life groups are right about one thing: the location of the baby inside or outside the womb cannot make such a crucial moral difference. We cannot coherently hold that it is all right to kill a fetus a week before birth, but as soon as the baby is born everything must be done to keep it alive."[48] Third, as Wennberg points out, a newborn chimpanzee can be treated like a human newborn (i.e., named, baptized, accepted into a family), but this certainly does not mean that it is fully human.[49]

Criteria of Personhood

Several ethicists, such as Michael Tooley,[50] Mary Anne Warren,[51] James Rachels,[52] and Virginia Ramey Mollenkott,[53] have put forth criteria a being must fulfill in order to be considered fully human (a person). For some, these criteria apply to any entity, whether before or after birth. In fact, according to Tooley, birth has no bearing on the moral status of the newborn.[54]

Those who defend criteria for full humanness make a distinction between being a human and being a person. They argue that although the unborn are part of the species *homo sapiens*, and in that sense are human, they are not truly persons since they

fail to fulfill a particular set of personhood criteria.

Although the defenders of personhood criteria do not agree on everything, their underlying philosophical assumptions are virtually identical. If I can show that these assumptions are significantly flawed then probably no personhood criteria theory can succeed in supporting the abortion-rights position. Since Mollenkott's view is the most clear and succinct example, I will use her article as a point of departure to critique the personhood criteria position. Although much of my critique of this view can be found in my criticisms of the other decisive-moment theories, its underlying philosophical assumptions deserve a separate critique.

In order to fully grasp Mollenkott's position, let me quote her at length:

> Kay Coles James of the National Right to Life Committee claimed that fetal personhood is a biological fact rather than a theological perception. But in all truthfulness, the most that biology can claim is that the fetus is genetically human, in the same way that a severed human hand or foot or other body part is human. The issue of *personhood* is one that must be addressed through religious reasoning. Hence, the Lutheran Church in America makes "a qualitative distinction" between the claims of the fetus and "the rights of a responsible person made in God's image who is in living relationships with God and other human beings." Except in the most materialistic of philosophies, human *personhood* has a great deal to do with feelings, awareness, and interactive experience.[55]

There are actually two arguments in this quote. The first goes something like this:

A

1. Unborn humans are genetically human.
2. Severed limbs and body parts are genetically human.
3. Severed limbs and body parts are not persons.
4. Therefore, genetic humanness cannot be a criterion of personhood.

The problem with this argument is that it shows a gross misunderstanding of the pro-life position, and probably commits the informal fallacy of equivocation. For one thing, when a pro-life advocate argues for the unborn's personhood from its genetic code, he is not arguing that anything with a human genetic code is a person. Nobody defends such an absurdity. Rather, he is arguing that the unborn human is an independent living human organism in a certain stage of development. And we know this organism to be such an entity because it has, among other characteristics, a human genetic code (different from its father's or mother's). In other words, possessing a human genetic code is a necessary but not a sufficient condition for human personhood.

Second, it seems that the phrase *genetically human* has a different meaning in premise 1 than in premise 2. In premise 1 the unborn entity in utero is genetically human in the sense that it is an independent living and developing organism that is part of the human family. But in premise 2 the phrase *genetically human* refers to a severed limb that is obviously a dead part of a former or a current living and developing organism, and is genetically human only insofar as it possesses the identical genetic code of its owner. No severed limb ever developed into a basketball star, a pianist, a philosopher, or a feminist theologian, but every basketball star, pianist, philosopher, and feminist theologian was at one stage in her development an unborn human with a human genetic code. Therefore, because this argument equivocates on the phrase *genetically human*, it is logically fallacious.

Let us now turn to Mollenkott's second argument, which I believe is the cornerstone of her position:

B

1. A person can be defined as a living being with feelings, awareness, and interactive experience (I assume she means some sort of self-consciousness).
2. An unborn entity does not possess the characteristics of a person as defined in 1.

3. Therefore, an unborn entity, although a human being, is not a person.
4. Therefore, killing an unborn entity is not seriously wrong.

Others, such as Tooley and Warren, give more elaborate criteria of personhood. For instance, Tooley claims, among other things, that a being "cannot have a right to continued existence unless he possesses the concept of a subject of experiences, the concept of a temporal order, and the concept of identity of things over time." And since "the concept of a right is such that an individual cannot have a right that *p* be the case unless the individual is capable of desiring that *p* be the case," it follows that a non-self-conscious being with no desire for its own continued existence has no right to life.[56] Hence, the unborn do not have a right to life.

Warren suggests five traits that are most central to the concept of personhood. Although she admits a person may lack as many as two or even three of these traits, she does claim that any being that satisfies none of these traits is certainly not a person:

1. consciousness (of objects and events external and/or internal to the being), and in particular the capacity to feel pain;
2. reasoning (the *developed* capacity to solve new and relatively complex problems);
3. self-motivated activity (activity that is relatively independent of either genetic or external control);
4. the capacity to communicate, by whatever means, messages of an indefinite variety of types, that is, not just with an infinite number of possible contents, but on indefinitely many possible topics;
5. the presence of self-concepts, and self-awareness, either individual or racial, or both.[57]

The underlying philosophical assumption behind Mollenkott's, Tooley's, and Warren's arguments is that only an entity that *functions* in a certain way (e.g., in the case of Tooley, "is capable of desiring that *p* be the case") is a person with a full right to life (i.e., fully human). I believe that this position has several flaws.

Abortion may be wrong even if the fetus is not a full person. It does not seem to follow from the intermediate conclusion of Mollenkott's argument (premise 3), that an unborn human is not a person, that abortion is always morally justified. Jane English has pointed out that "nonpersons do get some consideration in our moral code, though of course they do not have the same rights as persons have (and in general they do not have moral responsibilities), and though their interests may be overridden by the interests of persons. Still, we cannot just treat them in any way at all."[58] But unlike other nonpersons, for the abortion-rights supporter the fetus is at least a potential person.

English goes on to write that we consider it morally wrong to torture beings that are nonpersons, such as dogs or birds, although we do not say that these beings have the same rights as persons. And though she considers it problematic as to how we are to decide what one may or may not do to nonpersons, she nevertheless draws the conclusion that "if our moral rules allowed people to treat some person-like non-persons in ways we do not want people to be treated, this would undermine the system of sympathies and attitudes that makes the ethical system work." Based on this reasoning, English makes the important observation that "a fetus one week before birth is so much like a newborn baby in our psychological space that we cannot allow any cavalier treatment of the former while expecting full sympathy and nurturative support for the latter." She cites the fact that "an early horror story from New York about nurses who were expected to alternate between caring for six-week premature infants and disposing of viable 24-week aborted fetuses is just that—a horror story. These beings are so much alike that no one can be asked to draw a distinction and treat them so very differently."[59]

The wrong-making feature of killing adults is present in most abortions. University of Kansas philosopher Don Marquis points out that criteria for personhood, or personhood theories, such as the ones we have gone over, "cannot straightforwardly account for the wrongness of killing infants and young children," since such children satisfy few if any of the personhood criteria. Marquis believes that because it is obvious that killing such children is morally wrong, we have to come up with a theory which accounts for this. It is evident that the proposed criteria of personhood do not. Marquis suggests that what best accounts for the wrongness of killing young children and infants directly is the view that "the primary wrong-making feature of a killing is the loss to the victim of its future." But this view has "obvious consequences for the ethics of abortion," for "the future of the standard fetus includes a set of experiences, projects, activities, and such which are identical with the futures of adult human beings and are identical with futures of young children. Since the reason that is sufficient to explain why it is wrong to kill human beings after birth is a reason that also applies to fetuses, it follows that abortion is prima facie morally wrong."[60]

Marquis anticipates several objections to his thesis. Although I too respond to these objections (elsewhere in this book) in the context of the case for which I am arguing, one objection bears a separate critique: the discontinuation account rather than the future-like-ours account does a better job of explaining the wrongness of killing. The discontinuation "account is based on the obvious fact that people value the experience of living and wish for the valuable experience to continue. Therefore, it might be said what makes killing wrong is the discontinuation of that experience for the victim." Consequently, "if it is the continuation of one's activities, experiences, and projects, the loss of which makes killing wrong, then it is not wrong to kill fetuses for that reason, for fetuses do not have experiences, activities, and projects to be continued or discontinued. Accordingly, the discontinuation account does not have the anti-abortion consequences that the value of a future-like-ours account has."[61] (This argument is similar, though not identical, to an objection to my critique of the sentience criterion as well as to an objection to my critique of the "criteria of personhood" viewpoint.)

In response, Marquis argues that it is the person's future, not his or her past, that is morally relevant to deciding whether or not he or she should be killed. Apparently an advocate of active euthanasia, Marquis writes that "it makes no difference whether the patient's immediate past contains intolerable pain, or consists in being in a coma (which we can imagine is a situation of indifference), or consists in a life of value. If the patient's future is a future of value, we want our account to make it wrong to kill the patient. If the patient's future is intolerable, whatever his or her immediate past, we want our account to allow killing the patient. Obviously, then, it is the value of that patient's future which is doing the work in rendering the morality of killing the patient intelligible."[62] Although I have deep reservations about Marquis's view of euthanasia, his point is simply that what makes killing morally wrong is that the entity being killed has a future-like-ours.

Criteria of personhood arguments confuse function with being (or essence). One can question why one must accept a *functional* definition of personhood to exclude the unborn. It is not obvious that functional definitions always succeed. For example, when Michael Jordan is kissing his wife does he cease to be a basketball player because he is not functioning as one? Of course not. He does not *become* a basketball player when he functions as a basketball player, but rather, he functions as a basketball player because he *is* a basketball player. Similarly, when a person is asleep, unconscious, temporarily comatose, a newborn, or a young infant, she is not functioning as a person as defined in premise 2 of Mollenkott's argument, but nevertheless, no reasonable person would say that this individual is not a person while in any of these states. Consequently, to accept a functional definition of personhood excludes not only the unborn, but also the unconscious, the temporarily comatose, the sleeping, newborns, and young infants. Therefore, it seems more consistent with our moral intuitions to say that a person func-

tions as a person because she is a person, not that she is a person because she functions as a person. Thus defining personhood strictly in terms of function is inadequate.

Of course, the abortion-rights advocate may want to argue, as he did in our analysis of the sentience criterion, that the analogy between sleeping/unconscious/comatose persons and the unborn breaks down because the former at one time in their existence functioned as persons and will probably do so in the future, while the latter, the unborn, did not. Although the abortion-rights advocate makes an important point, he fails to grasp the significant flaw in defining personhood strictly in terms of function.

First, the abortion-rights defender still has a problem with newborns and young infants. How does he morally include them as persons and exclude the unborn? If he opts for Marquis's proposal—that newborns and infants have a future-like-ours—then he must oppose abortion, since he would have to include the unborn who also have a future-like-ours. But if he opts for a pragmatic reason to protect newborns and young infants—such as that there are people wanting to adopt them, which is Warren's stance, or that killing them would make us callous—that is still not a *moral* reason. This is like saying that slavery ought to be abolished because it is good for the economy. That is to say, the abortion-rights defender is still left incapable of claiming that newborns and young infants have an intrinsic right not to be killed, especially if there is no one who wants to adopt them and if killing them would not make us callous.

Second, as I pointed out in my criticism of the sentience criterion, to claim that a person can be functional, become nonfunctional, and then return to a state of function is to assume that there is some underlying personal unity to this individual that makes it intelligible for us to say that the person who has returned to functional capacity is the same person who was functional previously. Or else we would have to make the absurd claim that a new person has popped into existence. It follows then that human function is a sufficient but not a necessary condition for human personhood. Consequently, it does not make sense to say that a person comes into existence when human function arises, but it does make sense to say that a fully human person is an entity who has the natural inherent capacity to give rise to human functions. And since an unborn entity typically has this natural inherent capacity, she is a person. As Davis writes, "Our ability to have conscious experiences and recollections arises out of our personhood; the basic metaphysical reality of personhood precedes the unfolding of the conscious abilities inherent in it."[63] Therefore, an ordinary unborn human entity is a person, and hence, fully human. In other words, because the unborn human is a person with a certain *natural inherent* capacity (i.e., her being or essence), she will function as a person in the near future, just as the reversibly comatose and the temporarily unconscious will likewise do because of their natural inherent capacity.

Third, in a recent critique of James Rachels's position on euthanasia, philosopher J. P. Moreland discusses Rachels's distinction between biographical and biological life.[64] This distinction roughly corresponds to the pro-abortionist's distinction between person and human being. According to Moreland, Rachels argues that "the mere fact that something has biological life . . ., whether human or nonhuman, is relatively unimportant." It is biographical life that is important. Quoting Rachels, Moreland writes that one's biographical life is "'the sum of one's aspirations, decisions, activities, projects, and human relationships.'"[65] For Mollenkott a person can be defined as a living being with feelings, awareness, and interactive experience. Hence, it seems reasonable to assert that Mollenkott, and others such as Tooley and Warren, would agree with Rachels that a person is a living being who possesses biographical life, and since the unborn do not possess this sort of life, they are therefore not persons.

In response to Rachels, Moreland argues that "his understanding of biographical life, far from rendering biological life morally insignificant, presupposes the importance of biological life."[66] Applying this to the issue of abortion, one can say that an unborn human being develops into a functioning person precisely because of what he *essentially* is, a person. Employing the Aristotelian/Thomistic notion of secondary substance (natural kind, essence), Moreland points out that "it is because an entity has an essence and falls within a natural kind that it can possess a unity of dispositions, capacities, parts and properties at a given time and can maintain identity through change." Moreover, "it is the natural kind that determines what kinds of activities are appropriate and natural for that entity."[67]

Further, an organism *qua* essentially characterized particulars has second-order capacities to have first-order capacities that may or may not obtain (through some sort of lack). These second-order capacities are grounded in the nature of the organism. For example, a child may not have the first-order capacity to speak English due to a lack of education. But because the child has humanness it has the capacity to develop the capacity to speak English. The very idea of a defect presupposes these second-order capacities.

Now the natural kind "human being" or "human person" (I do not distinguish between these) is not to be understood as a mere biological concept. It is a metaphysical concept that grounds both biological functions and moral intuitions. . . .

In sum, if we ask why biographical life is both possible and morally important, the answer will be that such a life is grounded in the kind of entity, a human person in this case, that typically can have that life.[68]

Schwarz puts it rather well when he writes: "It is *being* a person that is crucial morally, not *functioning* as a person. The very existence and meaning of functioning as a person can have its basis only in the being of a person." That is to say, "it is because you have the being of a person that you can function as a person, although you might fail to function as a person and still retain your full being as a person."[69]

Along the same lines, A. Chadwick Ray has observed that the view of a human person as a natural kind that grounds certain functions, rather than as an emergence of certain functions, is more consistent with our general moral intuitions. "The recognition of the rights of the young is less dependent on their actual, current capacities than on their species and potential [i.e., their being]." For example, no one doubts that day-old human children have fewer actual capacities than day-old calves. Human infants, in terms of environmental awareness or mobility are rather unimpressive in comparison to the calves, especially if one calculates their ages from conception. But this comparison does not persuade us in believing that the calves have greater intrinsic worth and an inherent right to life. If human infants were sold to butchers (let us suppose for the high market value of their body parts) in the same way that farmers sell calves to humane butchers, we would find such a practice deeply disturbing. Yet if intrinsic worth is really contingent upon current capacities rather than natural inherent capacity (or being), we should have no problem with the selling of human infants to butchers. But Ray points out why we do find such a practice morally repugnant: "The wrongness would consist not merely in ignoring the interest that society might have in the children, but in violating the children's own rights. Yet if those rights are grounded in current capacities alone, the calves should enjoy at least the same moral status as the children, and probably higher status." What follows is that "the difference in status is plausibly explained . . . only with reference to the children's humanity, their natural kind,"[70] that is, their being.

To fully grasp Ray's point, consider the following story developed by Professor Schwarz:

> Imagine a case of two children. One is born comatose, and he will remain so until the age of nine. The other is healthy at birth, but as soon as she achieves the concept of a continuing self for a brief time, she, too, lapses into a coma, from which she will not emerge until she is nine. Can anyone seriously hold that the second child is a person with a right to life, while the first child is not? In one case, self-awareness will come

only after nine years have elapsed, in the other, it will return. In both cases, self-awareness will grow and develop. Picture the two unconscious children lying side by side. Almost nine years have passed. Would it not be absurd to say that only one of them is a person, that there is some essential, morally relevant, difference between them. Imagine someone about to kill both of them. Consistent with his theory, Tooley [as well as others who deny that the unborn are persons because they have not functioned as persons "in the past"] would have to say: "You may kill the first, for he is not a person. He is human only in the genetic sense, since he has no history of functioning as a person. You may not kill the second, since she does have such a history." If this distinction is absurd while applied to the two born human beings, is it any less absurd when applied to two human beings, one born (asleep in bed), the other pre-born (sleeping in the womb)?[71]

I agree with Schwarz when he concludes that "when it comes to functioning as a person, there is no moral difference between 'did, but does not' (the sleeping adult) and 'does not, but will' (the small child)."[72]

Therefore, since the functions of personhood (first-order capacities) are grounded in the essential nature of human personhood (second-order capacities), it follows that the unborn are human persons of great worth, and therefore should be treated with the utmost dignity. No doubt much more can be said about the problem of what constitutes personhood,[73] but what is important in this immediate discussion is that we have seen that a functional definition of personhood is riddled with serious problems and that the pro-life advocate has been given no compelling reason to dispense with his belief that the unborn are persons, and hence, fully human. Furthermore, the arguments for the full personhood of the unborn are extremely strong.

Gradualism

Some ethicists, such as Wennberg and Daniel Callahan,[74] deny that there is any decisive moment at which the unborn moves from nonpersonhood to personhood, but that the unborn's achievement of personhood is a gradual process. That is to say, as the unborn entity grows in physical stature her right to life increases. In order to fully grasp this position, let me quote Wennberg at length:

> It is my contention that the right to life possessed by the human fetus ought to be understood in a *qualified* sense, the right to life that begins at conception ought to be understood as increasing in strength as the fetus grows and develops (the gradualist thesis). The newly fertilized ovum or zygote does not possess the full moral standing of an adult, but it increasingly assumes that standing as it matures. The fetus is not without moral standing, and so the IUD (which apparently works by producing a mini-abortion) ought not be viewed as morally inconsequential; but inasmuch as the zygote lacks *full* moral standing, neither should it be viewed with the same intrinsic seriousness as would a device that caused the death of a normal adult human being. Terminating the life of a human zygote is simply not as wrong, intrinsically, as terminating the life of an adult human being.[75]

It should be kept in mind that Wennberg is not enthusiastic about abortion. And although his work is a sincere and scholarly effort to grapple with the issue, one can raise serious objections to his gradualist thesis. First, Philip Devine provides a criticism that Wennberg cites:

> If personhood or humanity admits of degrees before birth, then it would seem it must admit of degrees after birth as well. . . . But few hold and fewer still teach that a ten-year-old child can be killed on lighter grounds than an adult.[76]

Wennberg responds to this by pointing out that this criticism is not a valid criticism of his gradualist view, "since that position dictates that although the right to life is indeed a matter of degree both before and after birth, once one becomes a person, considerations of degree no longer apply: a ten-year-old child is presumed to be a person with as strong a right to life as any adult's."[77] In other words, the unborn human gradually becomes a person with a serious right to life, and then when it reaches the point at which it is a person, any other development of the individual after that point cannot increase its right to life.

This means, of course, that the gradualist position, as presented by Wennberg, is fundamentally a decisive-moment view, although it does differ insofar as the latter position considers the decisive moment an all-or-nothing event (i.e., it is at a particular moment that the unborn moves from nonpersonhood to personhood), whereas the gradualist thesis sees each level of development as increasing the personhood of the unborn until it has attained full personhood. Nevertheless, the gradualist view which Wennberg defends entails that there is a decisive moment (although we may not be able to precisely pinpoint it) at which full personhood is achieved. And for this reason, though Wennberg's response to Devine is adequate, it does not avoid the following criticism.

Second, since, as we have seen, none of the decisive moments are sufficient to eliminate the unborn entity as fully human at any stage of her development, it seems then that there are no philosophical, scientific, or moral grounds by which to say that the unborn gradually becomes fully human and then achieves full humanness at some decisive moment. For someone who is fully human cannot gradually become more fully human. Certainly it is true that the unborn human develops gradually physically, as is true of humans at latter stages (e.g., infancy, childhood, adolescence), but it does not follow from this fact that the unborn human is any less a human person than the infant, the child, or the adolescent, who are nonetheless fully human although they are gradually developing. Your "being" happens all at once, but your "doing" unfolds gradually.

Third, it follows that the defender of the gradualist thesis makes an unwarranted logical move from "gradual physical development" to "gradual increase of personhood." In other words, the defender of the gradualist thesis is arguing:

C

1. The unborn gradually develops physically
2. Therefore, the unborn's personhood gradually develops as well.

The problem with this argument is that the conclusion does not follow from the premise. For it could certainly be the case that the premise is true—that the unborn gradually develops physically—and that the conclusion is false. It is not the case that the unborn's personhood gradually develops as well. We know that the same child develops physically after birth but we don't say that its personhood develops as well. Even Wennberg recognizes this when responding to Devine's critique: "once one becomes a person, considerations of degree no longer apply." However, the question then can be raised as to why one is justified in inferring personhood development based on physical development before birth but not after birth. If the response by the gradualist is that personhood development occurs until personhood is achieved—at some time after birth, when the child is able to function in a particular way—then the gradualist is arguing that a necessary and sufficient condition for personhood is the ability to function in a certain way. In other words, the achievement of particular functions corresponds with the achievement of personhood. But this response confuses function with being. For someone can certainly be a person without functioning as a person. Consequently, the objector to the gradualist thesis, employing the same reasoning Wennberg employed in his response to Devine, can say that *once one becomes a person at conception, considerations of functional degrees no longer apply.*

Fourth, Robert Joyce has made the observation that a "major flaw in the gradualist approach is its subtle or not so subtle projection of a mechanistic model of development onto an organically developing reality." That is to say, the gradualist position "fails to distinguish between natural process and arti-

factual process. Only artifacts, such as clocks and spaceships, come into existence part by part. Living beings come into existence all at once and then gradually unfold to themselves and to the world what they already, but only incipiently, *are.*"[78] Consequently, one can only develop certain functions because that is the sort of being one is. The unborn are not potential persons but persons with great potential.

Fifth, when all is said and done Wennberg resorts to instinct (or intuition) to establish the factual elements of his position. He argues that "in considering the stages backward from newborn to fetus to embryo to zygote, most people instinctively become increasingly reluctant to recognize a strong right to life, feeling that abortion becomes less and less morally objectionable—and the gradualist theory presents a reasonable basis for supposing that this instinctive reaction may be valid."[79] In other words, Wennberg believes that his gradualist view is more consistent with most people's basic moral instincts (or intuitions) about the nature of the developing unborn entity.

There is much to be said for this approach, for many ethicists concede that an appeal to intuition is important in recognizing and establishing the values employed in moral reasoning (see chap. 1). However, Wennberg's appeal to intuition in defending his gradualist view does not point to any moral value that has since been unrecognized by all parties in the abortion debate (see chap. 1). His appeal is to the intuitions of ordinary people about the factual nature of the unborn entity. But even Wennberg must admit that these intuitions can be called into question or rendered false if there are good philosophical and/or scientific reasons to disbelieve them, just as our intuitions about the geocentric solar system, quickening and ensoulment, the inferiority of blacks and women, and the existence of the ether have been rendered false by good philosophical and/or scientific reasons. Therefore, since none of the decisive-moment theories are sufficient to exclude the unborn human from the realm of the fully human at any stage of development, we do have good philosophical and scientific reasons to believe that the intuitions of some ordinary people are not correct on this matter.

Moreover, one can argue that unlike our universal moral intuition about the prima facie wrongness of murder, there is no such universal intuition about the gradualist theory. That is to say, Wennberg overstates the instinctive (or intuitional) nature of his view. For a great number of people have a pro-life intuition, that full humanness begins at the moment of conception. Furthermore, one can argue that the reason why some people seem to have an intuition about the gradualist theory is because they confuse appearance with reality (i.e., "it doesn't look human"). This confusion may be attributed to not having carefully investigated the facts of prenatal development and to not having critically evaluated one's philosophical assumptions, just as primitives who do not know astronomy confuse appearance with reality and claim that the sun revolves around the earth. This confusion may also be attributed to the psychological need to justify a practice (abortion) that many people we know and love, including ourselves, engage in, just as people need to justify racism, sexism, and torture, and do so by dehumanizing their victims.

Suppose someone responds, "Since society grants rights to persons as they develop—for example, at age sixteen, you have a right to drive; at eighteen, the right to vote; at twenty-one, the right to drink; at thirty-five, the right to run for the presidency—why can't the right to life be granted by society at a particular time in development as well?"

This response equivocates on the word *rights*. Rights that society grants, such as the right to vote or to drink alcohol, are based on a person's assumed maturing responsibility, not on whether the person has become a different sort of being when he or she reaches a particular age of responsibility (e.g., sixteen, eighteen, twenty-one). On the other hand, the right to life, as presented in the Declaration of Independence and a number of recent human rights declarations,[80] is not granted by any society. It is a fundamental natural right that all human persons possess by virtue of being human persons. And if a gov-

ernment allows for the transgression of that right, the victimized human persons still possess it naturally. For example, the six million Jews who were murdered by Adolf Hitler in Nazi Germany possessed a natural right to life even though the government sanctioned their murders. In fact, this is what the Chief Counsel for the United States, Robert H. Jackson, argued at the Nuremberg trials.[81] Of course, if one argues that there is no such natural right or no natural rights at all, but only rights granted by governments (positive rights), then one is put in the precarious position of having no objective moral basis by which to condemn the Holocaust, since it was a government-sanctioned activity. Therefore, if the unborn are human persons, then they possess the right to life naturally by virtue of being human persons, regardless of whether or not the state acknowledges or recognizes this natural right.

Conclusion: The SLED Test

Schwarz has provided a useful anacronym (SLED) to describe the four differences between the unborn and the born, all of which are morally irrelevant in deciding whether anyone, born or unborn, has a fundamental right to life.[82] It will become apparent that all the decisive-moment and gradualist theories accept one or more of these differences as morally relevant. Since I have already detailed the flaws in these positions, the following is merely a summary.

Size. The unborn is smaller than the newborn. But a 6'5" basketball player, such as Larry Johnson, is much bigger than my wife, Frankie Beckwith, who is 4'11 3/4". It would be absurd to say that Frankie has less moral value than Larry (although he does have greater economic value, as he signed a multi-million-dollar contract with the NBA's Charlotte Hornets).

Level of development. A newborn baby is less developed than an adolescent, but that does not mean that the newborn has less of a right to life. According to Schwarz, "he is equally a person; he is the same person at his earlier stage of development as at the later stages, or else it would not be *his* development" (emphasis added).[83] Therefore, the fact that the unborn is less developed than the newborn has no moral relevancy.

Environment. *Where* one is is irrelevant to *who* one is. The fact that a child may be in her mother's womb is a geographical fact, not a value judgment. A newborn in an incubator is not worth less than one in her mother's arms or one who is a week younger and still in her mother's womb. It is easy to see that environment is not at all morally relevant.

Degree of dependency. To a great extent we are all dependent on one another, some less than others and some more than others. A person in a nursing home is more dependent on another's care than a healthy twenty-five-year old attorney. Yet it seems obvious that the nursing home patient's greater dependence does not disqualify his right to life. As Professor Schwarz points out: "I remain myself through the various changes, phases of growth and development, phases of relative dependency or independence, that pertain to my body. I am not any less *me* because my body may be in a state of greater dependency than at another time. Thus we see that dependency through connection to another person has nothing to do with being a person. It only has to do with how the body is sustained."[84] Consequently, the fact that the unborn through most of her development is physically dependent on her mother has no moral bearing as to her nature or whether she is a person with a full right to life.

Other Objections to Personhood Beginning at Conception

In my critique of the decisive-moment and gradualist theories, I dealt with a number of objections to the pro-life position that full humanness begins at conception. However, people oftentimes bring up other objections that should be dealt with. Some have to do with the legal ramifications of this view. In this concluding section, I will briefly respond to fourteen of these objections.

1. *Why don't sperm, ova, as well as other cells, have a right to life, since they are also genetically human?* Sperm and ova do not have a right to life because they are not individual genetic human beings, but are merely parts of individual genetic human beings. They are genetically human only insofar as they share the genetic codes of their owners, but this is also true of their owners' other parts (e.g., hands, feet, kidneys). Sperm and ova cease to exist at conception when the zygote, an individual genetic human being, comes into existence.

In a recent article, Peter K. McInerny argues that "a living human cell that might be stimulated into a clone of a person does not now have a personal future. A fetus similarly has only the potentiality to develop a personal future. For this reason, killing a fetus is morally very different from killing a normal adult human."[85] But this argument is no better than the one we just criticized, for the unstimulated cell (which is genetically part of a human being), as well as the thing used to stimulate it, is merely a material cause of the resulting unborn human clone. Likewise, the sperm and ovum (which are genetically each a part of an individual human being) are material causes of the resulting unborn human non-clone. But none of the material causes for either the unborn human clone or the unborn human non-clone has a natural inherent capacity for personal acts, but in fact ceases to exist as an entity when conception results. Hence, there is no similarity between an unstimulated living human cell, which has no natural inherent capacity for personal acts and is a part of another human being, and a typical unborn human being, which is a genetically human individual possessing a natural inherent capacity for personal acts.

2. *Doesn't this view absolutize biological human life and entail* speciesism? Not at all. Although the pro-life advocate believes that biological human life is important, she certainly does not believe that it is absolute. Biological human life without the natural inherent capacity to function as a person (that is, the metaphysical grounding of human personhood that makes human function possible) is probably not fully human. And it is questionable whether the taking of such a life or the permitting of such a life to die can

be classified as homicide. For example, I do not think it is homicide to pull the plug on a respirator that is sustaining the biological life of a brain-dead patient. Such a patient's natural inherent capacity for personal acts is simply not present. Of course, other questions surrounding the problem of the withdrawal of certain forms of health care are much more complex and certainly fall outside the scope of this book.[86] In any event, the pro-life advocate does not absolutize biological human life and is willing to apply his principles critically and to think reflectively in morally challenging situations.

The pro-life position does not lead to what certain animal rights proponents call "speciesism,"[87] the belief that all human life is sacred and/or special simply because it belongs to the species *homo sapiens*. Rather, pro-lifers believe that human life is sacred and/or special for all sorts of reasons, some religious,[88] others secular,[89] and some a combination of both.[90] But all at least agree that ordinary human life is sacred and/or special because it has from the moment of conception a natural inherent capacity to function in a profound and unique way; that is, the personhood present from conception grounds personality and rationality. And if another species existed, whether in this world or in another, that possessed this natural inherent capacity from the moment of conception, then we would also seek to forbid the unjustified homicide of these creatures.[91] Hence, the pro-life position is not speciesist.

3. *Aren't you absolutizing the unborn's right to life?* No, for there could be times at which abortion is justified. The pro-lifer is fully cognizant of the fact that we live in a world in which moral conflicts can occur. Consider a case in which it is highly likely that a woman's pregnancy will result in her death (e.g., a tubal pregnancy). Because it is a greater good that one human should live rather than two die, the pro-lifer believes that in this case abortion is justified, since if the pregnancy were to continue both unborn and mother would die. However, abortion is not justified in cases in which one appeals to reasons such as financial burden or the child's potential handicap, because if the unborn

entity is fully human, one must respect her life as one would respect the lives of those who are already born.

4. *Wouldn't your position mean that some forms of artificial birth control result in homicide?* Yes. For example, forms of birth control that cause the death of the unborn, such as the IUD and RU-486, would logically entail homicide if the pro-life position is correct. Because they produce abortions, they are called abortifacients. However, not every form of birth control results in the death of the unborn. For example, the condom, diaphragm, some forms of the Pill, spermicides, and sterilization would not logically entail homicide if the pro-life position is correct, for they merely prevent conception.

This is why the pro-life advocate makes a distinction between contraception and birth control. Contraception literally means "to prevent conception." Therefore, all contraception is a form of birth control, since it prevents birth. But not all forms of birth control are contraceptive, since some forms, such as the ones cited, prevent birth by killing the conceptus *after conception*. Hence, the pro-life advocate finds no problem with contraception as a form of family planning.

5. *Wouldn't your position entail that certain abortifacients, which are used exclusively for birth control, would have to be made illegal?* Yes, it would. This question is sometimes raised because it is presumed that by answering the question "yes" the pro-lifer claims something totally outrageous. But it is only presumed outrageous because those who present the question either explicitly or implicitly deny that the unborn are fully human. Therefore, the outrageousness of banning abortifacients is contingent upon the full humanness of the unborn. If the unborn is not fully human, at least in its earliest stages of development, my answer *is* outrageous. But if the unborn is fully human, then to call for its protection is certainly not outrageous at all, but something which all just governments are obligated to do. Hence, if my arguments for the unborn's full humanness in chapter 3 and this chapter are correct or more probably correct than not, then those who see nothing morally wrong in permitting the use of abor-

tifacients to kill unborn persons are the ones who support something totally outrageous.

Let me stress, however, that I do *not* oppose the use of contraceptives (that which prevents a human person from coming into existence), but only the use of abortifacients (that which kills a human being who has already come into existence). In addition, those drugs that can be beneficial to persons in other contexts, which may also function as abortifacients, obviously cannot be banned. Just as one cannot ban a butcher knife simply because it may be used to kill another person, one cannot ban a drug that is beneficial in some contexts simply because it may be used to kill another person.

6. *If the unborn is a person, would this mean that pregnant women would be forbidden to use any and all medical treatments that have an abortifacient side effect (that is, results in an abortion)?* Assuming that the unborn child is a person, it would depend on the condition from which the woman is suffering. For example, if the unborn is not viable, and if the woman's condition is life-threatening, and if the treatment in question is necessary to save the mother's life, then banning the treatment is not justified, since if the woman's life is not saved then both mother and child would die. Since it is better that one person should live rather than two die, use of a treatment with an abortifacient side effect in this situation is morally justified.

On the other hand, if the treatment in question is not intended to preserve the mother's life and the woman's condition is not life-threatening, then to risk the death of the unborn child is not morally justified. If the unborn is fully human, it is morally required that we forbid non-life-preserving medical treatment with an abortifacient side effect. As Schwarz points out, "[M]edical treatments should be proscribed if they include the killing of the child, just as any treatment, or any action, should be proscribed if it includes the killing of an innocent person."[92]

7. *Isn't it true that some of the unborn do not have forty-six chromosomes?* Yes. Although the normal number of chromsomes is forty-six, some people are born with fewer (people with Turner's syndrome have forty-five) and some people are born with more (people with Down's syndrome have forty-seven). But don't forget that the case for the unborn's humanness does not rest necessarily on the number of chromosomes an individual may have, but on the fact that the entity in question has a human genetic structure. It bears repeating that I argued that the pro-life advocate believes that full humanness begins at conception for at least four reasons:

a. At the moment of conception a separate unique human individual, with its own genetic code, comes into existence, needing only food, water, shelter, and oxygen in order to grow and develop.
b. Like the infant, the child, and the adolescent, the conceptus is a being who is in the process of becoming. He is not a becoming who is striving toward being. He is not a potential human life but a human life with great potential.
c. The conceptus is the sexual product of human parents, and a developing conceptus that is the sexual product of members of a particular mammalian species is itself an individual member of that species.
d. The same being that begins as a zygote continues to birth and adulthood. There is no decisive break in the continuous development of the human entity from conception until death that would make this entity a different individual before birth. This is why it makes perfect sense for any one of us to say, "When *I* was conceived . . ."

The Turner's or Down's syndrome child does not fail to fulfill any of these criteria, although someone may argue that the child fails to fulfill Reason a. But this argument would fail, because a human genetic structure can still subsist in an abnormal number of chromosomes (genes are contained in the chromosomes within the nuclei of a person's cells). That is to say, the Down's or Turner's syndrome child with human genes and an abnormal number of chromosomes is no more nonhuman than a child with an abnormal number of more obvious parts. For example, a person born with six fingers is human, as is a person born with one arm or one leg.

8. *Isn't an unborn human, at least in its earliest stages of development, like an acorn that is only a potential oak tree?* This analogy has been used on many ocassions by abortion-rights advocates in popular debate. In fact, Professor Frank R. Zindler, in an article that originally appeared in *American Atheist*, argues: "As for potential persons, *an acorn is not an oak tree!*"[93] Aside from the problem of claiming that the unborn are "potential persons," which we have already addressed, there are several reasons why this analogy fails.

First, philosopher Norman Geisler has made the observation that "it is a misunderstanding of botany to say an acorn is a potential oak tree. An acorn is a tiny living oak tree inside a shell. Its dormant life does not grow until properly nourished by planting and watering, but it is a tiny living oak tree nonetheless." The fact of the matter is that this analogy backfires, for "all the genetic information which comprises an oak tree is in the acorn. And all the genetic information which comprises an adult human being is in the fertilized ovum."[94]

Second, one can also argue that since a human being is a mammal and an oak tree is a plant, there really is no analogy between a human being and an oak tree. In order to provide a good analogy one would have to compare a human being to another mammal, such as a dog, a cow, or a horse. But since the unborn offspring of these mammals are developing, growing, and living members of the same species as their parents, just as are unborn humans, this sort of analogy would hurt the abortion-rights position. One newspaper letter writer, who is an admitted reader of the *Daily Racing Form*, points out that "the name of the unborn horse within its mother's womb is foal. It's also known by this name during the entire first year of life following birth. Then it becomes a yearling. So inside or outside the womb, foal is the name given to the baby horse. The pronouncement by the veterinary doctor that life has begun is used in writing contracts and other legal statements by the breeding industry. The word foal is simply the equine equivalent of baby."[95]

9. *Isn't the unborn, at least in its earliest stages of development, just a blueprint, or "information code," of a human being?* In response to the pro-life argument that full humanness begins at conception, a booklet published by the Religious Coalition for Abortion Rights, *Words of Choice*, claims that "just as a blueprint for a house is not a house, a genetic blueprint for a human body [i.e., the entity at conception] is not a person."[96] Such a claim reveals a complete ignorance of the pro-life position. The unborn from the moment of conception is a living individual human being who *possesses* a genetic code; she is not a model, or blueprint, of a human being. Dr. Daniel Callahan, a moderate advocate of abortion rights, agrees:

> It is . . . unscientific to call an embryo or fetus a mere "blueprint." Blueprints of buildings are not ordinarily mixed into the mortar; they remain in the hands of the architects. Moreover, once a building has been constructed, the blueprint can be thrown away, and the building will continue to stand. The genetic blueprint operates in an entirely different way: it exerts a directly causal action in morphological development; as an instrinsic part of the physiological structure, it can at no point be thrown away or taken out.[97]

10. *Doesn't your "life of the mother" exception involve a contradiction?* A number of people have raised this objection. They argue: If you believe that life is sacred, why do you say that the killing of the unborn child is justified to save the life of the mother?

Although I have sufficiently explained elsewhere in this text why this exception is morally justified and is not a contradiction, I will explain again in greater detail.

First, when pregnancy endangers a mother's life, medical personnel should try to save the lives of both mother and child.

Second, if that is not possible, the physician must choose the course of action that best upholds the sanctity of human life. Since the mother's body serves as the environment in which the unborn is nurtured, it is impossible to save the unborn child before viability (twenty to twenty-four weeks after conception). In fact, almost all abortions performed to save the mother's life are done long before viability and usually to end an ectopic (or tubal) pregnancy. Consequently, in such cases, the physician must save the mother's life even if it results in the death of the unborn. His intention is not to kill the child but to save the mother. But since saving both is impossible and it is better that one should live rather than two die, "abortion" to save the mother's life in this case is justified.

Third, after viability, when abortion itself is far riskier for the mother than is childbirth, there are few if any instances in which an "abortion" will save the mother's life. But when such cases do occur, the same principles apply here as prior to viability. Former Surgeon General C. Everett Koop explains:

> When the woman is pregnant, her obstetrician takes on the care of two patients—the mother-to-be and the unborn baby. If, toward the end of the pregnancy, complications arise that threaten the mother's health, he will take the child by inducing labor or performing a Caesarean section.
>
> His intention is still to save the life of both the mother and the baby. The baby will be premature and perhaps immature depending on the length of gestation. Because it has suddenly been taken out of the protective womb, it may encounter threats to its survival. The baby is never willfully destroyed because the mother's life is in danger.[98]

Fourth, the fact that the pro-life position has "an exception" no more counts against it than do libel and slander laws count against the legitimacy of free speech. All vibrant moral positions take into consideration competing values and principles that demand resolution. The fact that the pro-lifer provides a resolution to an apparent conflict in his position testifies to its sophistication, which certain critics caricature without fully appreciating it.

11. *Is a zygote equal to an adult woman?* Writes Zindler: "If the single-celled zygote is *equal* to a full-grown woman, it follows that a full-grown woman can't be worth *more* than a single cell! Anyone who values women so little is a menace to society and shouldn't be allowed to run loose without a leash."[99] There are several serious philosophical problems with this emotionally charged argument.

First, the argument equivocates on the meaning of the word *cell*. The pro-lifer is not saying that a mature adult woman is equal to *any* single cell, a statement that would imply the absurd conclusion that the single cells that make up a woman's body would each be individually equal to the total number of them together (i.e., the woman herself). Rather, the pro-lifer argues that when it comes to the right to life all human beings are on an equal footing regardless of what stage of development they are at, whether at the beginning (a single-celled zygote) or at the end (an elderly person). It just happens to be that the person is a single cell at the beginning, but it does not follow, as Zindler mistakenly assumes, that adult human beings are equal to *any* individual human cell. Zindler attacks something nobody believes, a straw man.

Second, Zindler writes: "If the single-celled zygote is *equal* to a full-grown woman, it follows that a full-grown woman can't be worth *more* than a single cell!" Unfortunately for Zindler, his conclusion does not follow from his premise. Treating persons with dignity at whatever stage of their development does not *logically* make the more developed ones worth less than they would have been worth if we had not come to value the less developed ones. Increasing the membership of the community of human persons to include the less developed ones, if in fact they deserve to belong, does not decrease the value of the more developed ones who have always been members. It simply means that the community of valuable persons is larger than we had imagined. Consequently, the fact that pro-lifers claim that human beings at whatever stage of development ought to be treated as human persons with dignity and respect no more undermines the value of a pregnant woman than does treating newborn infants as human persons undermine the value of more developed human persons such as adults. If the pro-lifer's arguments for the unborn's personhood are correct (see chap. 3 and the previous discussions in this chapter), then all human persons are valuable no matter what their stage of development. In fact, the pro-life position, in contrast to Zindler's, shows a great deal more respect for the pregnant woman's place in society. According to the pro-life view, the pregnant woman has the enormous responsibility and privilege of protecting and nurturing a developing human being, whereas according to Zindler's position, the pregnant woman is merely an incubator who serves as a temporary shelter for a blob of cells. Zindler's position also implies that unborn females have no value. I am shocked how little Zindler values female human beings.

Third, Zindler's argument equivocates on the word *equal*. When pro-lifers say that all human beings are equal in their right to life, they do not argue that all human beings are equal as to their function. When confronted with a similar question posed by Jeanne Maust, a Pro-Choice Advocacy representative, I answered: "It all depends; of course, a zygote cannot ride a bicycle as well as an adult. But insofar as possessing the nature of human personhood the zygote is equal to all other human beings with whom this nature is shared." Zygotes cannot function like older persons (as newborns cannot function like an older person), but this certainly does not mean they are not human persons.

Fourth, Zindler's argument (as well as Maust's), by emphasizing the one-celled zygote rather than the older fetus that is a small scale baby at seven weeks and can feel pain by thirteen and one-half weeks and maybe as early as eight, proves too little if he (or she) is correct. That is to say, even if this argument supports the moral rightness of killing zygotes and early embryos, it does not support the morality of killing the unborn entity when it is much more developed. As Schwarz points out, "When examined carefully, the absurdity of this argument as an attempt to justify abortion confronts us. 'It's all right to destroy a tiny [zygote], because it is so tiny.

Therefore it's all right to take a well-developed child at twelve weeks or more, burn her skin and poison her by saline, or cut her to pieces by D & E.'"[100]

Fifth, following from my fourth criticism, this abortion-rights objection ironically could be construed as a moderate *anti*abortion argument. As Schwarz explains:

Suppose [this argument] convinces a person that a [zygote] counts for virtually nothing in comparison to a mature person. The reason would be its tiny size and undeveloped status, implying that with development and a more normal size, the being in question would be valued. But that is precisely what is true of a seven-week-old baby in the womb, or that same child in later phases. Thus, if the zygote may be destroyed because it is so tiny, then precisely for this reason the child who is a victim of standard abortion techniques may not be destroyed, because he is not tiny. Therefore, abortion is wrong.[101]

Sixth, Zindler's argument has no logical content, but is merely a rhetorical device. Consider his argument again: "If the single-celled zygote is *equal* to a full-grown woman, it follows that a full-grown woman can't be worth *more* than a single cell! Anyone who values women so little is a menace to society and shouldn't be allowed to run loose without a leash." Of course, the pro-lifer can take the same data and turn it around: "If the worth of human beings is dependent on such morally irrelevant factors as size, level of development, environment, and dependency, then Zindler is claiming that big, developed, and independent people can wantonly kill tiny, less developed, dependent people. Anyone who sees the value of human life as being subject to such irrelevant factors is a menace to society and shouldn't be allowed to run loose without a leash." Zindler, someone could unkindly say, is nothing more than a natalist: a bigot who incorrectly thinks that size, level of development, environment, and dependency are morally relevant.

Seventh, the pro-lifer believes all human persons, regardless of their stage of development, are beings of great worth whose lives ought to be protected. Consequently, no human person has a right to expect another human person to forfeit his life for the other's perceived benefit. It follows then that an adult woman, as well as all other human persons, regardless of whether they are one-celled or an octogenarian, are worth much more than *any* single cell, since they all have the nature of human personhood, something that transcends the sum total of their physical parts. This is further evidence that Zindler's argument caricatures the pro-life view.

Eighth, if the arguments in this chapter are successful, or more likely successful than not, then Zindler's argument collapses. Therefore, Zindler must first dispense with the argument that full humanness begins at conception before employing his rhetoric.

12. *If the unborn, especially the zygote and early embryo, are legally recognized as human persons, would not this wreak havoc on our current legal and social structure (census counting, tax laws, legislative apportionment, government funding, and services based on population?* Not at all. First of all, treating the unborn as human persons, and protecting them from being killed, does not necessarily mean that we must overturn our current legal and social structure. In the census we can continue to count only the number of born persons, and base legislative reapportionment on that count, since it is extremely difficult and highly inefficient to count unborn persons. We cannot see them and many of them die before birth, sometimes without the mother ever being aware that she was pregnant. Consequently, there is nothing inconsistent with thinking of the census as a count of only born persons and at the same time acknowledging that the unborn are human persons who ought to be protected. This same rationale can be applied as well to the tax laws, government funding, and services based on population.

Second, prior to the legalization of abortion in the mid-1960s, when the laws in every state considered the unborn human persons,[102] our legal and social structure was relatively the same as it is today. Outlawing abortion would not change that structure.

Third, even if our legal and social structure would need to be overhauled, this has no bearing on whether the unborn are fully human. Certainly the unborn can be fully human regardless of how the legal and social structure may be set up. Consider the example of slavery. Suppose a defender of slavery argued that abolishing slavery was not a good thing because it would undermine his society's legal and social structure (e.g., there would be no free labor on the plantations, free blacks would need jobs, unemployment would increase, the census would have to be changed, and the tax code altered). Would this objection have any bearing on the question of whether black slaves were fully human? Of course not. The same is true of unborn humans.

13. *If the unborn is considered a person under the law, would it not follow that pregnant women would be forbidden to smoke, drink alcohol, or engage in other activities that may harm the unborn? Wouldn't such prohibitions violate a woman's privacy as well as be impossible to enforce?* The fact that smoking and drinking alcohol during pregnancy can harm the unborn is well-documented in the medical and scientific literature. Consequently, since such activity is harmful to the unborn, and the unborn are human persons, a mother has a moral responsibilty to make sure her child is not harmed, just as she does *after* the child's birth. However, whether or not prohibiting such harmful activity should be a law is another question.

My view is the one proposed by Schwarz, who draws an analogy with the "born child [who] has a right to good health care, proper diet, protection from harmful effects." He points out, however, that although "to some extent this right can be enshrined in law, to a large extent it cannot. We cannot have police at the family dinner table ensuring that the child gets all the nourishing food and vitamins he needs. Nor can he be protected from all harmful effects in the home, parallel to the harmful effects for the preborn child from his mother's smoking [or drinking]." Yet, Schwarz concludes, "surely the born child's right to live must be enshrined in the law, and given the same legal protection the rest of us enjoy. Exactly the same applies to that child before he is born."[103]

It should be noted that this question really does not help the abortion-rights position, since the same question can be asked of the abortion-rights supporter who argues that the being in the womb is not an actual person but only a potential person. After all, the harm caused to the fetus by the pregnant woman's smoking or drinking will still affect this being *after* it is born. That is to say, "even if he is not a person before birth, as [the abortion-rights] position holds, he is surely a person after birth, and suffers then because of the adverse effects of his mother's smoking [or drinking] before his birth."[104] Since we all have a moral obligation not to engage in activities that may harm other persons, and since drinking and smoking during pregnancy may harm another person if the pregnancy comes to term (even if the abortion-rights view of the unborn is correct), it follows then that the pregnant woman, if she intends to give birth, does have a moral obligation not to harm her future child by not drinking and smoking. Therefore, "the wrongness of smoking [or drinking] while pregnant is no way removed, or even mitigated, by adopting the view that no person is present in the womb. Correspondingly, if smoking [or drinking] is already wrong on the assumption the 'fetus' is merely a potential person, nothing significant is changed or added when we come to realize that he is already a person, an actual person."[105] Consequently, the objection raised in this question is not peculiar to the pro-life view defended in this book, but can applied to the "potential person" view as well, which is held by nearly all supporters of abortion rights.

Furthermore, if abortion is made illegal because the law considers the unborn human persons, then they will have to be treated as born children. And just as the law presumes that the parents of born children have the best interests of their children in mind, the law will presume the same about the parents of unborn children. Therefore, unless the state has a very good reason to suspect that the activities of the parents are causing harm to their unborn child (as it would have to for parents of born children), the state has to presume that the parents are acting in a way that has the best interests of their child in mind.

14. *If the unborn is considered a person under the law, wouldn't all miscarriages be suspect and women would have to prove that their miscarriages were not elective abortions?* Not at all. For one thing, this question is a crass appeal to fear. People die all the time, but we don't ask those closest to the deceased to prove that they didn't commit a murder. After all, one is innocent until proven guilty. If the unborn are considered full persons under the law, this would be true of women who have had miscarriages as well. Second, all miscarriages would not be suspect, only those for which there are reasonble grounds to suspect that deliberate killing was involved. This is how we treat the deaths of small children and babies who die from an accident at home. If there is evidence to suspect that the born child was abused and his death caused by a parent or another person, then there ought to be an official investigation. If there is no evidence, then the parents ought to be left alone to mourn their loss. The same principle would apply to the unborn who die due to miscarriage.

Arguments from Bodily Rights

In a perfect world, there would be no pregnancy.
Glynda White, J.D., in a debate against two pro-lifers on the campus of the University of Nevada, Las Vegas (1989)

Once impregnation has taken place, it is no longer a question of whether the persons concerned have responsibility for possible parenthood; they have become parents.
Helmut Thielicke

If a woman decides in the depth of her soul . . . that she doesn't want to have a child, then I think that's her right to say no, but let's not pretend that it isn't a form of killing.
Norman Mailer

In chapter 6 I noted that some abortion-rights advocates do not see the status of the unborn as the decisive factor in whether or not abortion is morally justified. They argue that the unborn's presence in the pregnant woman's body entails a conflict of rights if the pregnant woman does not want to be pregnant. Therefore, the unborn, regardless of whether it is fully human and has a full right to life, cannot use the body of another against her will. Hence, a pregnant woman's removal of an unborn entity from her body, even though it will probably result in that entity's death, is no more immoral than an ordinary person's refusal to donate his kidney to another in need of one, even though this refusal will probably result in the death of the prospective recipient. In this chapter we will discuss such arguments from rights.

The most famous and influential argument from rights is the one presented by philosopher Judith Jarvis Thomson. However, prior to analyzing that argument, I want to respond to two popular arguments that are much less sophisticated than Thomson's. These arguments, unlike Thomson's, do not assume for the sake of argument that the unborn is fully human, but ignore altogether the question of the unborn's humanness.

Argument from a Woman's Right over Her Own Body

This argument asserts that because a woman has a right to control her own body, she therefore has a right to undergo an abortion for any reason she deems fit. Although it is not obvious that either the law or sound ethical reasoning supports such a strong view of personal autonomy (e.g., laws against prostitution and suicide), this abortion-rights argument still fails logically even if we assume that such a strong view of personal autonomy is correct.

First, the unborn entity within the pregnant woman's body is not a part of her body, although many people, (even very intelligent ones) seem unaware of this fact. Consider the comments of philosopher Mortimer Adler, who claims that prior to viability the life the unborn "has is as a part of the mother's body, in the same sense that an individual's arm or leg is a part of a living organism. An individual's decision to have an arm or leg amputated falls within the sphere of privacy— the freedom to do as one pleases in all matters that do not injure others or the public welfare."[1] Even someone as knowledgeable on the abortion issue as Laurence Tribe of the Harvard Law School writes that "although the fetus at some point develops an independent identity and even an independent consciousness, it begins as a living part of the woman's body."[2] Both Adler and Tribe are completely mistaken. For one thing, the conceptus is a genetically distinct entity with its own individual gender, blood type, bone structure, and genetic code. Although the unborn entity is attached to her mother, she is not part of her mother. To say that the unborn entity is part of her mother is to claim that the mother possesses four legs, two heads, two noses, and with the case of a male fetus, a penis and two testicles. Moreover, Bernard Nathanson points out "that the modern science of immunology has shown that the unborn child is not a part of a woman's body in the sense that her kidney or heart is."[3] This, of course, contradicts the claims of Adler and Tribe. Nathanson goes on to outline the scientific basis for this claim:

Immunologic studies have demonstrated beyond cavil that when a pregnancy implants itself into the wall of the uterus at the eighth day following conception the defense mechanisms of the body, principally the white blood cells, sense that this creature now settling down for a lengthy stay is an intruder, an alien, and must be expelled. Therefore, an intense immunological attack is mounted on the pregnancy by the white blood cell elements, and through an ingenious and extraordinarily efficient defense system the unborn child succeeds in repelling the attack. In ten per cent or so of cases the defensive system fails and pregnancy is lost as a spontaneous abortion or miscarriage. Think how fundamental a lesson there is for us here: Even on the most minute microscopic scale the body has trained itself, or somehow in some inchoate way *knows*, how to recognize *self* from *non-self*.[4]

Furthermore, since scientists have been able to achieve conception in a petri dish (the "test-tube" baby), and this conceptus if it has white parents can be transferred to the body of a black woman and be born white, we know conclusively that the unborn is not part of the pregnant woman's body. Certainly a woman has a right to control her own body, but the unborn entity is not part of her body. Hence, abortion is not justified, since no one's right to personal autonomy is so strong that it permits the arbitrary execution of others.

Second, this abortion-rights argument is guilty of special pleading. The concept of a personal right over one's own body presupposes the existence of a person who possesses such a right. Such a right also presupposes that this right to personal autonomy should not interfere with another person's identical right. This is why smoking is being prohibited in more and more public places. Many studies have shown conclusively that a smoker's habit affects not only his own lungs, but also the lungs of others who choose not to smoke. The smoker's "secondary smoke" can cause the nonsmoker to be ill and quite possibly acquire lung cancer if he is exposed to such smoke over a long period of time. Since the nonsmoker has a personal right over his own body, and he chooses not to fill it with nicotine, the smoker's personal right to smoke and fill his own body with nicotine is limited by the nonsmoker's personal right to remain healthy. This is because in the process of smoking the smoker passes on harmful secondary smoke to the unwilling nonsmoker.

Suppose a smoker, in arguing against a prohibition of smoking in public places, continually appeals to his "personal right" to control his own body. And suppose he dismisses out of hand any counterargument that appeals to the possible existence of other persons (nonsmokers) whose rights his actions may obstruct. This sort of argumentation would be a case of *special pleading*, a fallacy that occurs when someone selects pieces of evidence that confirm his position (in this case, the smoker's legitimate right to personal autonomy) and ignores counterexamples that conflict with it (in this case, the nonsmoker's legitimate right to personal autonomy). Therefore, in terms of the abortion issue, when the abortion-rights advocate appeals to a woman's right to control her own body while ignoring the possibility that this control may entail the death of another, he is guilty of selecting principles that support his position (every person has a prima facie right to personal autonomy) while ignoring principles that conflict with it (every person has a prima facie obligation not to kill another). Thus the abortion-rights advocate is guilty of special pleading.

Of course, if the unborn entity is not fully human, this abortion-rights argument is successful. But this means that one begs the question when one argues for abortion rights from a woman's right to control her own body if one does not first show that the unborn entity is not fully human. Baruch Brody adds to this observation that although "it is surely true that one way in which women have been oppressed is by their being denied authority over their own bodies . . ., it seems to be that, as the struggle is carried on for meaningful amelioration of such oppression, it ought not to be carried so far that it violates the steady responsibilities all people have to one another." To cite a number of examples, "parents may not desert their children, one class may not oppress another, one race or nation may not exploit another. For parents, powerful groups in society, races or nations in ascendancy, there are penalties for refraining from these wrong actions, but those penalties can in no way be taken as the justification for such wrong actions. Similarly, if the fetus is a human being, the penalty of carrying it cannot, I believe, be used as justification for destroying it."[5]

Argument from Abortion Being Safer Than Childbirth

This argument attempts to show that the pregnant woman has no moral obligation to carry her unborn offspring to term, regardless of whether or not it is fully human. The abortion-rights advocate argues that childbirth is an act that is not morally obligatory on the part of the pregnant woman, since an abortion is statistically safer than childbirth. The statistic often quoted to support this argument is one found in the most recent edition of the *American Medical Association Encyclopedia of Medicine*: "Mortality is less than one per 100,000 when abortion is performed before the 13th week, rising to three per 100,000 after the 13th week. (For comparison, maternal mortality for full-term pregnancy is nine per 100,000.)"[6]

Virginia Ramey Mollenkott gives this argument a theological twist by attempting to ground it in the Hebrew-Christian Scriptures. She argues that Jesus asserted that risking one's life constituted exceptional love, not obligatory love (see John 15:13). Hence, since childbirth would be an act of exceptional love,[7] one is not obligated to carry the fetus to term. In any event, this argument can be outlined in the following way.

A
1. Among moral acts one is not morally obligated to perform are those that can endanger one's life (e.g., the man who dove into the Potomac in the middle of winter to save the survivors of a plane crash).
2. Childbirth is more life-threatening than having an abortion.

125

3. Therefore, childbirth is an act one is not morally obligated to perform.
4. Therefore, abortion is justified.

The problem with this argument lies in the inference from 2 to 3. First, assuming that childbirth is on the average more life-threatening than abortion, it does not follow that abortion is justified in every case. The fact that one act, A, is more life-threatening *on the average* than another act, B, does not mean that one is not justified or obligated to perform A in *specific* situations where there is no prima facie reason to believe that A would result in death or severe physical impairment. To use an uncontroversial example, it is probably on the average less life-threatening to stay at home than to leave home and buy groceries (e.g., one can be killed in a car crash, purchase and take tainted Tylenol, or be murdered by a mugger), yet it seems foolish, not to mention counterintuitive, to always act in every instance on the basis of that average. This is a form of the informal *fallacy of division*, which occurs when someone erroneously argues that what is true of a whole (the average) must also be true of its parts (every individual situation). One would commit this fallacy if one argued that because Beverly Hills is a wealthier city than Barstow, every individual person who lives in Beverly Hills is wealthier than every individual person who lives in Barstow.

Second, one can also imagine a situation in which one is obligated to perform a particular moral action although there is statistically more risk in performing it than abstaining from it. That is to say, one can challenge the inference from 2 to 3 by pointing out that just because an act, X, is "more dangerous" relative to another act, Y, does not mean that one is not morally obligated to perform X. For example, it would be statistically more dangerous for me (a swimmer) to dive into a swimming pool to save my wife (a nonswimmer) from drowning than it would be for me to abstain from acting. Yet this does not mean that I am not morally obligated to save my wife's life. Sometimes my moral obligation is such that it outweighs the

relatively insignificant chance of danger I avoid by not acting. One could then argue that although childbirth may be "more dangerous" than abortion, the special moral obligation one has to one's offspring far outweighs the relatively insignificant danger one avoids by not acting on that moral obligation (on the statistical insignificance between abortion and childbirth [see below]).

Of course, if a specific act, X, is significantly dangerous (i.e., there is a good chance that one will die or be severely harmed if one acts)—such as the act performed by that one man who dove into the freezing Potomac River to save the survivors of an airplane crash—then it would seem that an individual would not be obligated to perform X. However, if one had chosen to perform X, one would be performing an act of exceptional morality (what ethicists call a *supererogatory act*), although if one had refrained from X one would not be considered a bad or an evil person. In light of these observations, the abortion-rights argument in question can be strengthened if changed in the following way:

B

1. Among moral acts one is not morally obligated to perform are those that can endanger one's life.
2. A particular instance of childbirth, X, is more life-threatening to the pregnant woman than having an abortion.
3. Therefore, X is an act one is not morally obligated to perform.
4. Therefore, not-X via abortion is justified.

Although avoiding the pitfalls of the first argument, this one does not support the abortion-rights position. It is consistent with the pro-life assertion that abortion is justified if it is employed in order to save the life of the mother (see chap. 6 for defense of this "exception"). Therefore, whether or not abortion is statistically safer than childbirth is irrelevant to whether or not abortion is justified in particular cases where sound medical diagnosis indicates that childbirth will pose virtually no threat to the mother's life.

Two other observations can be made about the argument from abortion being safer than childbirth. First, the AMA statistics are misused and do not really establish the abortion-rights position. The statistics claim that the mortality rate for a woman in childbirth is 9 per 100,000 while mortality is less than 1 per 100,000 when abortion is performed before the thirteenth week, increasing to 3 per 100,000 after the thirteenth week. This is why abortion-rights advocates often claim that a first trimester abortion is nine times safer than childbirth. Although this assertion is technically true if one assumes that the statistics are accurate, it is statistically insignificant. This becomes apparent when one converts the odds into percentages. If the mortality of childbirth is 9 per 100,000, then a woman has a 99.991 percent chance of surviving. If the mortality of a first-trimester abortion is 1 per 100,000, then a woman has a 99.999 percent chance of surviving. But the statistical difference between 99.991 percent and 99.999 percent (00.008 percent) is moot, especially if one considers the complex nature of both childbirth and abortion, as there are so many variables that may account for the small difference in the mortality rates.

Second, one can call into question the truth of the claim that abortion is safer than childbirth. David C. Reardon points out that claims that abortion is safer than childbirth are based on dubious statistical studies, simply because "accurate statistics are scarce because the reporting of complications is almost entirely at the option of abortion providers. In other words, abortionists are in the privileged position of being able to hide any information which might damage their reputation or trade." And since "federal court rulings have sheltered the practice of abortion in a 'zone of privacy,'" therefore "any laws which attempt to require that deaths and complications resulting from abortion are recorded, much less reported, are unconstitutional." This means that the "only information available on abortion complications is the result of data which is voluntarily reported."[8] From these and other factors,[9] Reardon concludes that

complication records from outpatient clinics are virtually inaccessible, or non-existent, even though these clinics provide the vast majority of all abortions. Even in Britain where reporting requirements are much better than in the United States, medical experts believe that less than 10 percent of abortion complications are actually reported to government health agencies.[10]

Reardon's study indicates that it may be more true to say that abortion is more dangerous than childbirth. His work deals with the physical risks as well as the psychological impact of abortion on women, in addition to the impact of abortion on later children. He concludes that the harm caused by abortion to the woman and her children is grossly understated by abortion-rights advocates.[11]

It should be noted that many scholars have disputed the claim of abortion-rights advocates that early abortions are safer than childbirth. These critics argue that the data used to draw this conclusion have been misinterpreted and/or are problematic. Consider the following example of how such a misinterpretation can occur. In a highly sophisticated study on the topic of abortion-related maternal mortality, Thomas W. Hilgers, M.D., a professor of obstetrics and gynecology at Creighton University, writes,

Maternal mortality rates are generally expressed as the number of maternal deaths which occur—during the entire course of pregnancy and during the first three to six months following completion of the pregnancy—per 100,000 *live births*. The maternal mortality related to abortion, on the other hand, is expressed according to the type of procedure or the gestational age of the pregnancy per 100,000 *abortions*. In the latter case, the denominator is, in essence, the *number of cases* in which a particular procedure is carried out. With maternal mortality rates, this is not so. When the denominator is live births, a number of cases of pregnancy are automatically excluded from the denominator, while their associated maternal deaths are included in the numerator. This automatically strains the traditional comparison between the maternal mortality in natural pregnancy and that in abortion. Such comparisons lack statistical accuracy.[12]

Taking into consideration this and other statistical problems, Hilgers draws among many conclusions the following: "In comparing the relative risk of natural pregnancy versus that of legal abortion, *natural pregnancy was found to be safer in both the first and second 20 weeks of pregnancy.*"[13]

Considering that the supposed fact that childbirth is not as safe as abortion played a substantial role in the U.S. Supreme Court opinions that made abortion legal, *Roe v. Wade* (410 U.S. 113 [1973]) and *Doe v. Bolton* (410 U.S. 179 [1973]),[14] exposing the logical and factual flaws of this claim helps to undermine the foundation of the Court's opinions.

Argument from Unplugging the Violinist

In an article that by 1986 was "the most widely reprinted essay in all of contemporary philosophy,"[15] Judith Jarvis Thomson presents a philosophically sophisticated version of the argument from a woman's right to control her body.[16] Thomson argues that even if the unborn entity is a person with a right to life, this does not mean that a woman must be forced to use her bodily organs to sustain its life. Just as one does not have a right to use another's kidney if one's kidney has failed, the unborn entity, although having a basic right to life, does not have a right to life so strong that it outweighs the pregnant woman's right to personal bodily autonomy.

It should be noted that Thomson's argument was not used in any of the landmark Supreme Court decisions that have upheld the abortion-rights position, such as *Roe v. Wade* or *Doe v. Bolton*. Recently, however, Laurence Tribe, whose influence on the Court's liberal wing is well-known, has suggested that the Court should have seriously considered Thomson's argument. Tribe writes: "[P]erhaps the Supreme Court's opinion in *Roe*, by gratuitously insisting that the fetus cannot be deemed a 'person,' needlessly insulted and alienated those for whom the view

that the fetus is a person represents a fundamental article of faith or a bedrock personal commitment. . . . The Court could instead have said: Even if the fetus *is* a person, our Constitution forbids compelling a woman to carry it for nine months and become a mother."[17]

Presentation of the Argument

This argument is called "the argument from unplugging the violinist" because of a story Thomson uses to illustrate her position:

You wake up in the morning and find yourself back to back in bed with an unconscious violinist. A famous unconscious violinist. He has been found to have a fatal kidney ailment, and the Society of Music Lovers has canvassed all the available medical records and found that you alone have the right blood type to help. They have therefore kidnapped you, and last night the violinist's circulatory system was plugged into yours, so that your kidneys can be used to extract poisons from his blood as well as your own. The director of the hospital now tells you, "Look, we're sorry the Society of Music Lovers did this to you—we would never have permitted it if we had known. But still, they did it, and the violinist now is plugged into you. To unplug you would be to kill him. But never mind, it's only for nine months. By then he will have recovered from his ailment, and can safely be unplugged from you." Is it morally incumbent on you to accede to this situation? No doubt it would be very nice of you if you did, a great kindness. But do you *have* to accede to it? What if it were not nine months, but nine years? Or still longer? What if the director of the hospital says, "Tough luck, I agree, but you've now got to stay in bed, with the violinist plugged into you, for the rest of your life. Because remember this. All persons have a right to life, and violinists are persons. Granted you have a right to decide what happens in and to your body, but a person's right to life outweighs your right to decide what happens in and to your body. So you cannot ever be unplugged from him." I imagine that you would regard this as outrageous.[18]

Thomson concludes that she is "only arguing that having a right to life does not guarantee having either a right to be given the use of or a right to be allowed continued use of another person's body—even if one needs it for life itself."[19] Thomson anticipates several objections to her argument, and in the process of responding to them further clarifies it. It is not important, however, that we go over these clarifications now, for some are not germane to the pro-life position I am defending in this book,[20] and the remaining will be dealt with in the following critique. In any event, it should not be ignored by the pro-life advocate that Thomson's argument makes some important observations which have gone virtually unnoticed by the pro-life movement. In defending the relevance of her story, Thomson points out that it is "of great interest to ask what happens if, for the sake of argument, we allow the premise [that the unborn are fully human or persons]. How, precisely, are we supposed to get from there to the conclusion that abortion is morally impermissible?"[21] In other words, simply because a person is fully human it does not follow logically that it is *never* permissible to kill that person. Although I believe that I have (see chaps. 1, 4, 5, 6) and will (see chap. 9) adequately establish the premise that it is prima facie wrong to kill innocent human persons, Thomson's argument poses a special difficulty because she believes that since pregnancy constitutes an infringement on the pregnant woman's personal rights by the unborn entity, the ordinary abortion, although it results in the death of an innocent human person, is not prima facie wrong.

A Critique of Thomson's Argument

There at least nine problems with Thomson's argument. These problems can be put into three categories: ethical, legal, and ideological.

Ethical problems with Thomson's argument

1. *Thomson assumes volunteerism.* By using the story as a paradigm for all relationships, thus implying that moral obligations must be voluntarily accepted in order to have moral force, Thomson mistakenly infers that all true moral obligations to one's offspring are voluntary. But consider the following story. Suppose a couple has a sexual encounter that is fully protected by several forms of birth control short of surgical abortion (condom, the Pill, IUD), but nevertheless results in conception. Instead of getting an abortion, the mother of the conceptus decides to bring it to term, although the father is unaware of this decision. After the birth of the child, the mother pleads with the father for child support. Because he refuses, she takes legal action. Although he took every precaution to avoid fatherhood, thus showing that he did not wish to accept such a status, according to nearly all child-support laws in ths United States he would still be obligated to pay support *precisely because* of his relationship to this child.[22] As Michael Levin points out, "All child-support laws make the parental body an indirect resource for the child. If the father is a construction worker, the state will intervene unless some of his calories he expends lifting equipment go to providing food for his children."[23]

But this obligatory relationship is not based strictly on biology, for this would make sperm donors morally responsible for children conceived by their seed. Rather, the father's responsibility for his offspring stems from the fact that he engaged in an act, sexual intercourse, that he fully realized could result in the creation of another human being, although he took every precaution to avoid such a result. This is not an unusual way to frame moral obligations, for we hold drunk people whose driving results in manslaughter responsible for their actions, even if they did not intend to kill someone prior to becoming intoxicated. Such special obligations, although not directly undertaken voluntarily, are necessary in any civilized culture in order to preserve the rights of the vulnerable, the weak, and the young, who can offer very little in exchange for the rights bestowed upon them by the strong, the powerful, and the posthuman in Thomson's moral universe of the social contract. Thus, Thomson is wrong, in addition to ignoring the *natural* relationship between sexual intercourse and human reproduction,[24] when she claims that if a couple has "taken all reasonable precautions against having a child, they do not by virtue of their biological relationship to the child who comes into existence have a special responsibility for it." "Surely we do not have any such 'special responsibility' for a person unless we have assumed it, explicity or implicitly."[25] Hence, instead of providing reasons for rejecting any special responsibilities for one's offspring, Thomson simply dismisses the concept altogether.

2. Thomson's argument is fatal to family morality. It follows from the first criticism that Thomson's volunteerism is fatal to family morality, which has as one of its central beliefs that an individual has special and filial obligations to his offspring and family that he does not have to other persons. Although Thomson may not consider such a fatality as being all that terrible, since she may accept the feminist dogma that the traditional family is "oppressive" to women,[26] a great number of ordinary men and women, who have found joy, happiness, and love in family life, find Thomson's volunteerism to be counterintuitive. Philosopher Christina Sommers has come to a similar conclusion:

> For it [the volunteerist thesis] means that there is no such thing as filial duty per se, no such thing as the special duty of mother to child, and generally no such thing as morality of special family or kinship relations. All of which is contrary to what people think. For most people think that we do owe special debts to our parents even though we have not voluntarily assumed our obligations to them. Most people think that what we owe to our children does not have its origin in any voluntary undertaking, explicit or implicit, that we have made to them. And "preanalytically," many people believe that we owe special consideration to our siblings even at times when we may not *feel* very friendly to them. . . . The idea that to be committed to an individual is to have made a voluntarily implicit or explicit commitment to that individual is generally fatal to family morality. For it looks upon the network

of felt obligation and expectation that binds family members as a sociological phenomenon that is without presumptive moral force. The social critics who hold this view of family obligation usually are aware that promoting it in public policy must further the disintegration of the traditional family as an institution. But whether they deplore the disintegration or welcome it, they are bound in principle to abet it.[27]

3. A case can be made that the unborn does have a prima facie right to her mother's body. Assuming that there is such a thing as a special filial obligation, a principle that does not have to be voluntarily accepted in order to have moral force, it is not obvious that the unborn entity in ordinary circumstances (that is, with the exception of when the mother's life is in significant danger) does not have a natural prima facie claim to her mother's body. There are several reasons to suppose that the unborn entity does have such a natural claim.

a. Unlike Thomson's violinist, who is artificially attached to another person in order to save his life and is therefore not naturally dependent on any particular human being, the unborn entity is a human being who by her very nature is dependent on her mother, for this is how human beings are at this stage of their development.

b. This period of a human being's natural development occurs in the womb. This is the journey which we all must take and is a necessary condition for any human being's post-uterine existence. And this fact alone brings out the most glaring difference between the violinist and the unborn: the womb is the unborn's natural environment whereas being artificially hooked up to a stranger is not the natural environment for the violinist. It would seem, then, that the unborn has a prima facie natural claim upon her mother's body.

c. This same entity, when she becomes a newborn, has a natural claim upon her parents to care for her, regardless of whether her parents wanted her (see the story of the irresponsible father). This is why we prosecute child abusers, people who throw their babies in trash cans, and parents who abandon their children. Although it should not be ignored that pregnancy and childbirth entail certain emotional, physical, and financial sacrifices on the part of the pregnant woman, these sacrifices are also endemic of parenthood in general (which ordinarily lasts much longer than nine months), and do not seem to justify the execution of troublesome infants and younger children whose existence entails a natural claim to certain financial and bodily goods that are under the ownership of their parents. If the unborn entity is fully human, as Thomson is willing to grant, why should the unborn's natural prima facie claim to her parents' goods differ before birth? Of course, a court will not force a parent to donate a kidney to her dying offspring, but this sort of dependence on the parent's body is highly unusual and is not part of the ordinary obligations associated with the natural process of human development, just as in the case of the violinist's artificial dependency on the reluctant music lover.[28]

As Schwartz points out: "So, the very thing that makes it plausible to say that the person in bed with the violinist has no duty to sustain him; namely, that he is a stranger unnaturally hooked up to him, is precisely what is absent in the case of the mother and her child." That is to say, the mother "does have an obligation to take care of her child, to sustain her, to protect her, and especially, to let her live in the only place where she can now be protected, nourished, and allowed to grow, namely the womb."[29]

If Thomson responds to this argument by saying that birth is the threshold at which parents become fully responsible, then she has begged the question, for her argument was supposed to show us why there is no parental responsibility before birth. That is to say, Thomson cannot appeal to birth as the decisive moment at which parents become responsible in order to prove that birth is the time at which parents become responsible.

It is evident that Thomson's violinist illustration undermines the deep natural bond between mother and child by making it seem no different from that between two strangers artificially hooked up to each other so that one can "steal" the service of the other's kidneys. Never has something so human, so natural, so beautiful, and so wonderfully demanding of our human creativity and love been reduced to such a brutal caricature. Thomson's violinist story is to motherhood what Andres Serrano's "Piss Christ" is to Good Friday.

I am not saying that the unborn entity has an absolute natural claim to her mother's body, but simply that she has a prima facie natural claim. For one can easily imagine a situation in which this natural claim is outweighed by other important prima facie values, such as when a pregnancy significantly endangers the mother's life. Since the continuation of such a pregnancy would most likely entail the death of both mother and child, and since it is better that one human should live rather than two die, terminating such a pregnancy via abortion is morally justified.

Someone may respond to the three criticisms by agreeing that Thomson's illustration may not apply in cases of ordinary sexual intercourse, but only in cases in which pregnancy results from rape or incest,[30] although it should be noted that Thomson herself does not press this argument. She writes: "Surely the question of whether you have a right to life at all, or how much of it you have, shouldn't turn on the question of whether or not you are the product of rape."[31]

But those who do press the rape argument may choose to argue in the following way. Just as the sperm donor is not responsible for how his sperm is used or what results from its use (e.g, it may be stolen, or an unmarried woman may purchase it, inseminate herself, and give birth to a child), the raped woman, who did not voluntarily engage in intercourse, cannot be held responsible for the unborn human who is living inside her.

But there is a problem with this analogy: The sperm donor's relinquishing of responsibility does not result in the death of a human person. The following story should help to illustrate the differences and similarities between these two cases (for other responses to the general argument from rape and incest, see chap. 4).

Suppose that the sperm donated by the sperm donor was stolen by an unscrupulous physician and inseminated into a woman. Although he is not morally responsible for the child that results from such an insemination, the donor is nevertheless forced by an unjust court to pay a large monthly sum for child support, a sum so large that it may drive him into serious debt, maybe even bankruptcy. This would be similar to the woman who became pregnant as a result of rape. She was unjustly violated and is supporting a human being against her will at an emotional and financial cost. Is it morally right for the sperm donor to kill the child he is supporting in order to allegedly right the wrong that has been committed against him? Not at all, because such an act would be murder. Now if we assume, as does Thomson, that the raped woman is carrying a being who is fully human (or "a person"), her killing of the unborn entity by abortion, except if the pregnancy has a strong possibility of endangering her life, would be as unjust as the sperm donor killing the child he is unjustly forced to support. As the victimized man may rightly refuse to pay the child support, the raped woman may rightly refuse to bring up her child after the pregnancy has come to term. She can choose to put the child up for adoption. But in both cases, the killing of the child is not morally justified. Although neither the sperm donor nor the rape victim may have the same special obligation to their biological offspring as does the couple who voluntarily engaged in intercourse with no direct intention to produce a child, it seems that the more general obligation not to directly kill another human person does apply.

4. *Thomson ignores the fact that abortion is indeed killing and not merely the withholding of treatment.* Thomson makes an excellent point: namely, there are times when withholding and/or withdrawing medical treatment is morally justified. For instance, I am not morally obligated to donate my kidney to Fred, my next-door neighbor, simply because he needs a kidney in order to live. In other words, I am not obligated to risk my life so that Fred may live a few years longer. Fred should not expect that of me. If, however, I donate one of my kidneys to Fred, I will have acted above and beyond the call of duty, since I will have performed a supererogatory moral act. But this case is not analogous to pregnancy and abortion.

Levin argues that there is an essential difference between abortion and the unplugging of the violinist. In the case of the violinist (as well as my relationship to Fred's welfare), "the person who withdraws [or withholds] his assistance is not completely responsible for the dependency on him of the person who is about to die, while the mother *is* completely responsible for the dependency of her fetus on her. When one is completely responsible for dependence, refusal to continue to aid is indeed killing." For example, "if a woman brings a newborn home from the hospital, puts it in its crib and refuses to feed it until it has starved to death, it would be absurd to say that she simply refused to assist it and had done nothing for which she should be criminally liable."[32] In other words, just as the withholding of food kills the child after birth, in the case of abortion, the abortion kills the child. In neither case is there any ailment from which the child suffers and for which highly invasive medical treatment, with the cooperation of another's bodily organs, is necessary in order to cure this ailment and save the child's life.

Or consider the following case, which can be applied to the case of pregnancy resulting from rape or incest. Suppose a person returns home after work to find a baby at his doorstep. Suppose that no one else is able to take care of the child, but this person has only to take care of the child for nine months (after that time a couple will adopt the child). Imagine that this person, because of the child's presence, will have some bouts with morning sickness, water retention, and other minor ailments. If we assume with Thomson that the unborn child is as much a person as you or I, would "withholding treatment" from this child and its subsequent death be justified on the basis that the homeowner was only "withholding treatment" of a child he did not ask for in order to benefit himself? Is any person, born or unborn, obligated to sacrifice his life because his death would benefit another person? Consequently, there is no doubt that such "withholding" of treatment (and it seems totally false to call ordinary shelter and sustenance "treatment") is indeed murder.

But is it even accurate to refer to abortion as the "withholding of support or treatment"? Professors Schwarz and R. K. Tacelli make the important point that although "a woman who has an abortion is indeed 'withholding support' from her unborn child . . . abortion is far more than that. It is the active killing of a human person—by burning him, by crushing him, by dismembering him"[33] (see chap. 3 for information on fetal pain and abortion methods). Euphemistically calling abortion the "withholding of support or treatment" makes about as much sense as calling suffocating someone with a pillow the withdrawing of oxygen.

In summary, I agree with Professor Brody when he concludes that "Thomson has not established the truth of her claim about abortion, primarily because she has not sufficiently attended to the distinction between our duty to save X's life and our duty not to take it." But "once one attends to that distinction, it would seem that the mother, in order to regain control over her body, has no right to abort the fetus from the point at which it becomes a human being."[34]

Legal problems with Thomson's argument

There are at least two legal problems with Thomson's argument: one has to do with tort law, and the other has to do with parental responsibility and child-welfare law.

1. *Thomson's argument ignores tort law.* Judge John T. Noonan of the U.S. Ninth Circuit Court of Appeals points out that "while Thomson focuses on this fantasy [the violinist story], she ignores a real case from which American tort law has generalized."[35]

On a January night in Minnesota, a cattle buyer, Orlando Depue, asked a family of farmers, the Flateaus, with whom he had dined, if he could remain overnight at their house. The Flateaus refused and, although

Depue was sick and had fainted, put him out of the house into the cold night. Imposing liability on the Flateaus for Depue's loss of his frostbitten fingers, the court said: "In the case at bar defendants were under no contract obligation to minister to plaintiff in his distress; but humanity demanded they do so, if they understood and appreciated his condition. . . . The law as well as humanity required that he not be exposed in his helpless condition to the merciless elements." Depue was a guest for supper although not a guest after supper. The American Law Institute, generalizing, has said that it makes no difference whether the person is a guest or a trespasser. He has the privilege of staying. His host has the duty not to injure him or put him into an environment where he becomes nonviable. The obligation arises when one "understands and appreciates" the condition of the other.[36]

Noonan concludes that "although the analogy is not exact, the case is much closer to the mother's situation than the case imagined by Thomson; and the emotional response of the Minnesota judges seems to be a truer reflection of what humanity requires."[37]

2. *Thomson's argument ignores family law.* Thomson's argument is inconsistent with the body of well-established family law, which presupposes parental responsibility of a child's welfare. And, of course, assuming as Thomson does that the unborn are fully human, this body of law would also apply to parents' responsibility for their unborn children. According to legal scholars Dennis J. Horan and Burke J. Balche, "All 50 states, the District of Columbia, American Samoa, Guam, and the U.S. Virgin Islands have child abuse and neglect statutes which provide for the protection of a child who does not receive needed medical care." They further state that "a review of cases makes it clear that these statutes are properly applied to secure emergency medical treatment and sustenance (food or water, whether given orally or through intravenous or nasogastric tube) for children when parents, with or without the acquiescence of physicians, refuse to provide it."[38] Evidently, "pulling the plug" on a per-

fectly healthy unborn entity, assuming that it is a human person, would clearly violate these statutes.

For example, in a case in New York, the court ruled that the parents' actions constituted neglect when they failed to provide medical care to a child with leukemia: "The parent . . . may not deprive a child of life-saving treatment, however well-intentioned. Even when the parents' decision to decline necessary treatment is based on constitutional grounds, such as religious beliefs, it must yield to the State's interests, as parens patriae, in protecting the health and welfare of the child."[39] The fact of the matter is that the "courts have uniformly held that a parent has the legal responsibility of furnishing his dependent child with adequate food and medical care."[40]

It is evident then that child-protection laws reflect our deepest moral intuitions about parental responsibility and the utter helplessness of infants and small children. And without these moral scruples—which are undoubtedly undermined by "brave new notions" of a socially contracted "voluntaristic" family (Thomson's view)—the protection of children and the natural bonds and filial obligations that are an integral part of ordinary family life will become a thing of the past. This seems too high a price for bodily autonomy.

Ideological problems with the use of Thomson's argument

There are at least three ideological problems in the use of Thomson's argument by others. The other two problems are usually found in the books, speeches, articles, or papers, of those in the feminist and/or abortion-rights movements who sometimes uncritically use Thomson's argument or ones similar to it. In fact, Thomson may very well agree with most or all of the following critique.

1. *Inconsistent use of the burden of pregnancy.* Thomson has to paint pregnancy in the most horrific of terms in order to make her argument seem plausible. Dr. Bernard Nathanson, an obstetrician/gynecologist and former abortion provider, objects "strenuously to Thomson's portrayal of pregnancy as a nine-month involuntary imprisonment in bed. This casts an unfair and wrongheaded prejudice against the consideration of the state of pregnancy and skews the argument." Nathanson points out that "pregnancy is not a 'sickness'. Few pregnant women are bedridden and many, emotionally and physically, have never felt better. For these it is a stimulating experience, even for mothers who originally did not 'want' to be pregnant." Unlike the person who is plugged into Thomson's violinist, "alpha [the unborn entity] does not hurt the mother by being 'plugged in,' . . . except in the case of well-defined medical indications." And "in those few cases where pregnancy *is* a medical penalty, it is a penalty lasting nine months."[41]

Compare and contrast Thomson's portrayal of pregnancy with the fact that researchers have recently discovered that many people believe that a pregnant woman cannot work as effectively as a nonpregnant woman who is employed to do the same job in the same workplace. This has upset a number of feminists, and rightfully so. They argue that a pregnant woman is not incapacitated or ill, but can work just as effectively as a nonpregnant woman.[42] But why then do feminists who use Thomson's argument argue, when it comes to abortion, that pregnancy is similar to being bedridden and hooked up to a violinist for nine months? When it comes to equality in the workplace (with which I agree with the feminists) there is no problem. But in the case of morally justifying abortion rights, pregnancy is painted in the most horrific of terms. Although not logically fatal to the abortion-rights position, this sort of double-mindedness is not conducive to good moral reasoning.

2. *The libertarian principles underlying Thomson's case are inconsistent with the state-mandated agenda of radical feminism.* If Thomson's illustration works at all, it works contrary to the statist principles of radical feminism (of course, a libertarian feminist need not be fazed by this objection). Levin points out that "while appeal to an absolute right to the disposition of one's body coheres well with other strongly libertarian positions (laissez-faire in

the marketplace, parental autonomy in education of their children, freedom of private association), this appeal is most commonly made by feminists who are antilibertarian on just about every other issue." For example, "feminists who advocate state-mandated quotas, state-mandated comparable worth pay scales, the censorship of 'sexist' textbooks in the public schools, laws against 'sexually harassing speech' and legal limitations on private association excluding homosexuals, will go on to advocate abortion on the basis of an absolute libertarianism at odds with every one of those policies."[43] Although this criticism is ad hominem, as was the previous one, it serves to underscore the important political fact that many abortion-rights advocates are more than willing to hold and earnestly defend contrary principles for the sake of legally mandating their ideological agenda.

This sort of hypocrisy is evident in abortion-rights activity throughout the United States. In the state of Nevada, those who supported an abortion-rights referendum in November of 1990 told the voting public that they wanted to "get the government off of our backs and out of the bedrooms." But when the state legislature met in January these same abortion-rights supporters, under the auspices of the Nevada Women's Lobby, proposed legislation that asked for the taxpayers of the state to fund school-based sex clinics (which will refer teenage girls to abortion services and are euphemistically called health clinics) and assorted other programs. Forgetting that many of us keep our wallets in our back pockets and place them in the evening on our dressers in our bedrooms, the members of the Nevada Women's Lobby did not hesitate to do in January what they vehemently opposed in November: to get the government *on* our backs and *in* our bedrooms.

But this proposed government intervention was not to prevent people from killing their unborn children, an intervention that is considered bad, evil, anti-choice, and intrusive. Rather, it was to take our money we earn to support our own children and use it to subsidize the killing of other people's unborn children. The libertarians of November became the social engineers of March.

3. *Thomson's argument implies a macho view of bodily control, a view inconsistent with true feminism.* Some have pointed out that Thomson's argument and/or the reasoning behind it is actually quite antifeminist.[44] In response to a similar argument from a woman's right to control her own body, one feminist publication asks, "What kind of control are we talking about? A control that allows for violence against another human being is a macho, oppressive kind of control. Women rightly object when others try to have that kind of control over them, and the movement for women's rights asserts the moral right of women to be free from the control of others." After all, "abortion involves violence against a small, weak and dependent child. It is macho control, the very kind the feminist movement most eloquently opposes in other contexts."[45]

Celia Wolf-Devine observes that "abortion has something . . . in common with the behavior ecofeminists and pacifist feminists take to be characteristically masculine; it shows a willingness to use violence in order to take control. The fetus is destroyed by being pulled apart by suction, cut in pieces, or poisoned." Wolf-Devine goes on to point out that "in terms of social thought . . . it is the masculine models which are most frequently employed in thinking about abortion. If masculine thought is naturally hierarchical and oriented toward power and control, then the interests of the fetus (who has no power) would naturally be suppressed in favor of the interests of the mother. But to the extent that feminist social thought is egalitarian, the question must be raised of why the mother's interests should prevail over the child's. . . . Feminist thought about abortion has . . . been deeply pervaded by the individualism which they so ardently criticize."[46]

Arguments from Theology and the Bible

How is a married woman able to plan schooling or commit herself to a career or vocation as long as her life is continually open to the disruption of unplanned pregnancies? Unless, of course, she can fall back on an abortion when all else has failed!
Virginia Ramey Mollenkott, Christian feminist (1988)

"Daughters of Jerusalem, do not weep for me, weep instead for yourselves and your children, for indeed the days are coming when people will say, 'Blessed are the barren, the wombs that never bore and the breasts that never nursed.'"
Jesus Christ (Luke 23:28–29 NAB)

Recall that the young Mary was pregnant under circumstances that today routinely terminate in abortion. In the important theological context of Christmas, the killing of the unborn child is a symbolic killing of the Christchild.
Dr. Paul Vitz, New York University psychologist (1977)

Some people defend abortion rights by appealing to the Hebrew-Christian Scriptures. They argue either that the Bible does not specifically condemn abortion or that the Bible actually supports the abortion rights position. For those who do not consider the Bible authoritative, arguments for or against abortion based on its contents are obviously not compelling. But the material in the first seven chapters is sufficiently devoid of any theology that any reasonable nonbeliever could accept the pro-life position without sacrificing his unbelief. Many people, however, do consider the Bible authoritative and many others hold it in high respect. Thus the following critique will be important to these people.

Argument from the Claim That the Bible Does Not Specifically Forbid Abortion

Some people, such as Virginia Ramey Mollenkott, claim that "nowhere does the Bible prohibit abortion . . ."[1] This claim is untrue if one recognizes that the Bible's statements on some other matters can be used to draw an inference that is consistent with a pro-life position. For instance, it is clearly taught in the Bible that murder—the unjustified killing of a human being—is wrong (Exod. 20:13). And it follows logically from this that if the Bible teaches that the unborn are fully human, then it would be morally wrong in most circumstances to kill the unborn. So the real question is whether the Bible teaches that the unborn are fully human, not whether the Bible mentions or directly prohibits abortion. I believe that the following categories of Scripture passages are sufficient to show that the Bible clearly teaches the full humanity of the unborn, although the list is not exhaustive.[2]

Personal Language Applied to the Conceptus

A number of passages in the Bible apply personal language to the unborn from conception. Genesis 4:1 reads: "Now the man had relations with his wife Eve, and she conceived and gave birth to Cain." Commenting on this passage, theologian John Jefferson Davis has observed that "the writer's interest in Cain extends back beyond his birth, to his conception. That is when his personal history begins. The individual conceived and the individual born are one and the same, namely, Cain." What follows from this is that Cain's "conception, birth, and postnatal life form a natural continuum, with the God of the covenant involved at every stage."[3]

In Job 3:3, the author writes: "Let the day perish on which I was to be born. And the night, which said, 'A boy [geber] is conceived.'" This passage connects the individual born with the individual conceived. "Job traces his personal history back beyond his birth to the night of conception. The process of conception is described by the biblical writer in personal terms. There is no abstract language of the 'products of conception,' but the concrete language of humanity."[4] It is interesting to note that the Hebrew word geber is translated as "boy" and specifically applied to the unborn, although it is usually used to describe postnatal humans and translated

"male," "man," or "husband" (see Ps. 34:9; 52:9; 94:12; Prov. 6:34).[5]

Another passage, Psalm 51:5, states: "Behold, I was brought forth in iniquity, and in sin my mother conceived me." Again, we have evidence that one's beginning of existence can be traced back to conception.

The Unborn Are Called Children

The Bible refers to the unborn in the same way as it refers to infants and young children. In Luke 1:41, 44 the word baby (brephos) is applied to the unborn: "And it came about that when Elizabeth heard Mary's greeting, the baby leaped in her womb; and Elizabeth was filled with the Holy Spirit. 'For behold, when the sound of your greeting reached my ears, the baby leaped in my womb for joy.'" Compare this with Luke 2:12, 16 where the infant Jesus is called a baby (brephos): "And this will be a sign for you; you will find a baby wrapped in clothes, and lying in a manger.' And they came in haste and found their way to Mary and Joseph, and the baby as he lay in the manger."

The Unborn Are Known by God in a Personal Way

A number of biblical passages are clear on this point:

For Thou didst form my inward parts; Thou didst weave me in my mother's womb. I will give thanks to Thee, for I am fearfully and wonderfully made; Wonderful are Thy works. And my soul knows it very well. My frame was not hidden from Thee, When I was made in secret, And skillfully wrought in the depths of the earth. Thine eyes have seen my unformed substance; And in Thy book they were all written, The days that were ordained for me, When as yet there was not one of them. [Ps. 139: 13–16]

Listen to Me, O islands, And pay attention, you peoples from afar. The LORD called Me from the womb; From the body of My mother He named Me. [Isa. 49:1]

"Before I formed you in the womb I knew you, And before you were born I consecrated you; I have appointed you a prophet to the nations." [Jer. 1:5]

Then the angel of the Lord appeared to the woman, and said to her, "Behold now, you are barren and have borne no children, but you shall conceive and give birth to a son" . . . Then the woman came and told her husband, saying, "A man of God came to me and his appearance was like the appearance of the angel of God, very awesome. . . . But he said to me, 'Behold, you shall conceive and give birth to a son, and now you shall not drink wine or strong drink nor eat any unclean thing, for the boy shall be a Nazirite to God *from the womb to the day of his death.'"* [Judg. 13: 3, 5, 6, 7, emphasis added]

Some authors, such as Robert Wennberg,[6] have questioned the use of many passages to establish the full humanity of the unborn. Although he makes some valid points concerning some passages, a criticism that should provoke pro-lifers to clarify their exegesis, Wennberg tries to rob the right-to-lifer's biblical case of its strength by a hermeneutical slight of hand. First, concerning those passages that use personal language to describe the unborn, Wennberg writes that "such references designate individuals not only before birth but before conception . . ., and so they are not really to the point."[7] One problem with this criticism is that it is not applicable to all such passages, for some do speak exclusively of personal existence beginning at conception (e.g., Gen. 4:1; Job 3:3). Another problem is that none of these passages claim that the persons in question existed prior to their conception, but rather, that God knew them or had plans for them before conception. This is certainly possible for an eternal God, who knows all things simultaneously (see Ps. 147:5; Job 28:24; Isa. 41:21–24; 46:10) and is not bound by time or space (see Ps. 90:2, Isa. 40:28; 43:12b,13; 57:15a), since he is the creator of time and space (see Acts 17:25; Col. 1:16,17; Heb. 11:3; Rev. 4:11). That is, it is possible for him to know each and every one of us before we were conceived. Thus such foreknowledge of human persons prior to their conception can-

not be cited in order to explain away either conception as the beginning of personal existence or that personal existence is attributed to prenatal life when a passage in question specifically says, for example, that a certain individual either has personally existed from conception (e.g., Gen. 4:1) or has personally existed prior to birth (e.g., Jer. 1:5; Ps. 139:13–16; Luke 1:41–44). Moreover, the word *conception* or *to conceive* implies a genesis or a beginning, such as when I say, "This is the finest idea I have ever conceived." Hence, when God speaks of a person prior to conception, he is making an epistemological claim (a knowledge claim) not an ontological claim (a being claim). In light of these clarifications, the burden of proof is on Wennberg to show us why the more simple and clearly natural interpretation of the passages should be given up.

Wennberg puts forth a second argument:

Extending our examination, it would be a mistake to argue that since it was David who was being formed [or "brought forth" in NASB] in his mother's womb (Ps. 51:5) it must therefore have been David *the person* who was in his mother's womb. That would be to confuse "formation/creation" of a thing with the "completion/existence" of that thing. The fact is that an entity can be on the way to becoming a particular thing without it being that thing. It is quite natural for us to refer to what is in the process of becoming (the zygote or fetus in a Semite woman's womb) in terms of what it will eventually become (a King David), but we are not then speaking with technical accuracy. If a butterfly *is being formed* in a cocoon, it does not follow that there *is* a butterfly there (rather than a caterpillar or something betwixt or between).[8]

In essence, Wennberg is arguing that one cannot cite passages such as Psalm 51:5 to show that the unborn are fully human, since such passages are only saying that the person in question is "being formed," not that the human being in the womb has become *that* person. There are several problems with this argument. First, even if Wennberg's interpretation of passages such as Psalm 51:5

were correct, he would still have to deal with other passages that clearly state that individual personal existence begins at conception (e.g., Gen. 4:1). Second, Wennberg commits the hermeneutical fallacy that James Sire calls "worldview confusion."[9] This fallacy "occurs whenever a reader of Scripture fails to interpret the Bible within the intellectual and broadly cultural framework of the Bible itself and uses instead a foreign frame of reference."[10] Wennberg's distinction between person and human being is an invention of some contemporary philosophers who argue that a human being becomes a person at some stage in his or her development (see chap. 6). Since Wennberg has the burden to prove that the author of Psalms was assuming such a distinction, and since he provides no reason to believe he has satisfied this burden, it is reasonable to conclude that Wennberg is reading back into David's assertion a foreign worldview. Third, the passage does say that "in sin my mother conceived me." This clearly indicates that David's personal existence can be traced back to conception, since it was at conception that he asserts he was conceived. And if this is the case, then it seems natural to interpret the first half of Psalm 51:5 ("I was brought forth" or "I was being formed") as describing the subsequent physical development of David in the womb, development that continues after birth into infancy, childhood, adolescence, and adulthood. Although Wennberg is correct in saying that "if a butterfly *is being formed* in a cocoon, it does not follow that there *is* a butterfly there (rather than a caterpillar or something betwixt or between)," the insect that is becoming the butterfly is still the same insect that was once a caterpillar and will be a butterfly. In the same way, the being at conception is the same person who will become the infant, the child, the adolescent, the adult, and maybe even a philosopher. In sum, it is clear that passages such as Psalm 51:5 are describing *a person* who is in the process of development, not *a thing* which is in the process of developing into a person.

The Evidence of Church History

It is sometimes forgotten in the debate over the Bible and abortion that there has been a long and rich tradition in Christian church history, extending back to the early church fathers, against the practice of abortion. Since the early church fathers were much closer to the writing of the New Testament than we are today, it is reasonable to say that there is a presumption in favor of their interpretation of Scripture and their application of what they believe are its ethical teachings. Of course, the church fathers could have been wrong, but the burden of proof is on those who would bring this accusation against them.

In an early church document (second century), the *Didache* or the "Teaching of the Twelve Apostles" as it has been called, the author writes, "You shall not kill a child in the womb or murder a new-born infant. . . . You shall not *slay the child* by abortions." The second-century Christian apologist Athenagoras states, "We say that those women who use drugs to bring on abortion commit murder and will have to give an account to God for abortion." Another early church father of the second century, Clement of Alexandria, writes: "But women who resort to some sort of deadly abortion drug kill not only the embryos but, along with it, all human kindness."[11] This ethic is echoed by other Christian theologians of the same historical period:

Minucius Felix: In fact, it is among you that I see newly-born sons at times exposed to wild beasts and birds, or dispatched by the violent death of strangulation; and there are women who, by use of medical potions, destroy the nascent life in their wombs, and murder the child before they bring it forth.

Tertullian: But with us murder is forbidden once and for all. We are not permitted to destroy even the foetus in the womb, as long as blood is still being drawn to form a human being. To prevent the birth of a child is to anticipate murder. It makes no difference whether one destroys a life already born or interferes with it coming to birth. One who will be a man is already one.[12]

Among the many authorities in church history who have written against abortion are Basil the Great, John Chrysostom, Ambrose, Jerome, and Augustine. Although some church authorities, such as Thomas Aquinas and Augustine, under the influence of the erroneous biology of the Greek philosopher Aristotle, disputed as to when the unborn entity receives its soul (Thomas claimed it was at forty days for a male and eighty days for a female),[13] they nevertheless opposed abortion at any stage during prenatal development (though disputing if it was less serious prior to ensoulment), except when abortion is needed to save the life of the mother. Concerning the church's historical view of abortion, one study concludes:

> For the whole of Christian history until appreciably after 1900, so far as we can trace it, there was virtual unanimity amongst Christians, evangelical, catholic, orthodox, that, unless at the direct command of God, it was in all cases wrong directly to take innocent human life. Abortion and infanticide were grouped together as early as the writing called the *Didache* which comes from the first century after the crucifixion. These deeds were grouped with murder in that those committing or co-operating in them were, when penitent, still excluded from Communion for ten years by early Councils. . . . The absolute war was against the deliberate taking of *innocent* life, not in the sense of sinless life, but in the sense of life which was *innocens* (not harming). . . . We may note that this strictness constituted one of the most dramatic identifiable differences between Christian morality and pagan, Greek or Roman, morality.[14]

In summary, the Christian Church from its very beginnings has held firmly to a pro-life ethic. Since the early church was directly spawned by the New Testament church, it is safe to say that the interpretation of the Bible through the eyes of the early church will give contemporary scholars a better idea of what the Bible teaches about prenatal life than the

contemporary philosophical inventions that are often read back into the biblical text.

Conclusion: The Bible and Abortion

We can conclude that just as the Bible does not forbid murdering people with submachine guns, the Bible does not forbid abortion. But since one can infer that murdering persons with submachine guns is wrong from the fact that the Bible forbids murdering in general, one can also infer that the Bible teaches that abortion is not justified from the fact that the Bible refers to unborn human beings as persons and forbids the murdering of persons in general. If one were to accept the hermeneutical principle that whatever the Bible does not specifically forbid is permissible, one would be in the position of sanctioning everything from slavery to nuclear warfare to computer vandalism. Hence, the question is not whether the Bible specifically forbids abortion, but rather, whether the unborn are treated as persons. If they are, then we can infer that abortion in almost all circumstances is morally wrong.

Argument from God's Granting of Free Moral Agency

This argument is defended by Mollenkott.[15] She argues that because God created us as free moral agents, to use public policy to make abortion illegal would be to rob the pregnant woman of the opportunity to be a responsible moral agent. Mollenkott's argument can be put in the following form:

A
1. God created human persons as free moral agents.
2. Any public policy that limits free moral agency is against God's will.
3. Public policy forbidding abortion would limit the free moral agency of the pregnant woman.
4. Therefore, forbidding abortion is against God's will.

The problem with this argument lies with premise 2. It does not seem obvious that "any public policy that limits free moral agency is against God's will." For example, laws against drunk driving, murder, smoking crack, robbery, and child molesting are all intended to limit free moral agency, yet it seems counterintuitive, not to mention unbiblical, to assert that God does not approve of these laws. Such laws are instituted because the acts they are intended to limit often obstruct the free agency of other human persons (e.g., a person killed by a drunk driver is prevented from exercising his free agency) and/or cause them serious harm or hurt. Hence, it would seem consistent with biblical faith to say that God probably approves of a public policy that seeks to maintain a just and orderly society by limiting some free moral agency (e.g., drunk driving or murder), thus increasing free moral agency for a greater number (e.g., fewer people will be killed by drunk drivers and murderers, and hence there will be a greater number who will be able to act as free moral agents), and is intended to protect human beings from serious harm and/or hurt.

In fact, Mollenkott herself advocates a public policy that limits the moral free agency of those who do not believe it is their moral obligation to use their tax dollars to help the poor pay for abortions. She believes that "if Christians truly care about justice for women . . .," we will "work to assure the availability of legal, medically safe abortion services for those who need them—including the public funding without which the impoverished women cannot exert their creative responsibility."[16] In Mollenkott's world a taxpaying Christian woman has a greater moral obligation either to pay for the abortions of poor women or to support their children if they are carried to term than she does to carry her own unborn children to term. In Mollenkott's world no one who opposes abortion is forced to have an abortion, which is well and good; but the anti-abortionist is nevertheless forced to pay for the abortions of others even if she believes that the practice results in murder. For Mollenkott, the pro-lifer can believe what she wants to believe about the unborn, but she has no right to act on her

beliefs when it comes to public policy. When pro-life Christians are asked to subsidize what they believe is murder, and when such a total disrespect for their deeply held convictions is called justice, can anyone doubt that our religious freedoms are founded on a fragile political foundation? George Orwell's Big Brother (or should I say, Big Sibling) would be proud.

In sum, it seems clear that Mollenkott must assume that the unborn are not fully human in order for her argument from free agency to work. Thus she begs the question. Only if the act of abortion does not limit the free agency of another and/or does not harm and/or hurt another person would a law forbidding abortions unjustly limit the free moral agency of the pregnant woman. However, in chapters 3 and 6 we saw that there are good reasons to think of the unborn as persons. Hence, a public policy forbidding abortions would not be against the will of God as Mollenkott defines it.

Argument from Exodus 21:22–25

This is a theological argument popular among biblical scholars. It can be put in the following outline:

B

1. In Exodus 21: 22–25 a person who accidently kills a pregnant woman is given the death penalty.
2. In Exodus 21: 22–25, a person who causes a miscarriage is only fined for the crime.
3. Therefore, Exodus 21: 22–25 teaches both that the pregnant woman is of greater value than the unborn human she carries and that the unborn human does not have the status of a person.
4. Therefore, abortion is justified.

This argument can be criticized on four counts. First, assuming that the abortion-rights interpretation of Exodus 21: 22–25 is correct, does it logically follow that abortion on demand is morally justified? After all, the passage says that the unborn are worth something. In stark contrast, contemporary defenders of abortion rights seem to be saying that the unborn are worth only the value that their mothers place on them. Hence, this passage does not seem to support the subjectively grounded value of the unborn assumed by the abortion-rights movement. Furthermore, even if the abortion-rights interpretation is correct, the passage in question is not teaching that the pregnant woman can willfully kill the human contents of her womb. It merely teaches that there is a lesser penalty for accidently killing an unborn human than there is for accidently killing her mother. To move from this truth to the conclusion that abortion on demand is justified is a nonsequitur.

Second, the severity of an Old Testament penalty is not always indicative of the full humanness of a victim. For example, in his important article on the Old Testament and abortion, Bruce K. Waltke writes that "it does not necessarily follow that because the law did not apply the principle of *lex talionis*, that is 'person for person,' when the fetus was aborted through fighting that therefore the fetus is less than a human being." For "in the preceding case, the judgment did not apply the principle of *lex talionis* in the case of a debatable death of a servant at the hands of his master. But it does not follow that since 'life for life' was not exacted here that therefore the slave was less than a fully human life."[17]

Third, one can also raise the more general hermeneutical question, as John Warwick Montgomery has pointed out, "as to whether a statement of penalty in the legislation God gave to ancient Israel ought to establish the context of interpretation for the total biblical attitude to the value of the unborn child (including not only specific and nonphenomenological Old Testament assertions such as Psalm 51:5, but the general New Testament valuation of the [*brephos*], as illustrated especially in Luke 1:41, 44)." Montgomery goes on to ask: "Should a passage such as Exodus 21 properly outweigh the analogy of the Incarnation itself, in which God became man at the moment when 'conception by the Holy Ghost' occurred—not at a later time as the universally condemned and heretical adoptionists alleged?"[18] If the

abortion-rights supporter is indeed correct in his interpretation of Exodus 21, he still has to deal with the grander context of Scripture itself, which does seem in other texts to treat the unborn as persons.

Fourth, one can show at most that the word *miscarriage* in premise 2 is incorrectly interpreted to mean the "death of the fetus." At least, there is no scholarly consensus on this interpretation. Let us first look at Exodus 21:22–25 (RSV):

> When men strive together, and hurt a woman with child, so that there is a miscarriage, and yet no harm follows, the one who hurt her shall be fined, according as the woman's husband shall lay upon him; and he shall pay as the judges determine. If any harm follows, then you shall give life for life, eye for eye, tooth for tooth, hand for hand, foot for foot, burn for burn, wound for wound, stripe for stripe.

The ambiguity of this passage is sufficient to neatly divide commentators into two camps. One camp holds that the passage is teaching that the woman and the unborn are valued differently.[19] According to this group, the passage is saying that if the unborn is accidentally killed, there is only a fine, but if the pregnant woman is accidentally killed, it is a much more serious offense. Therefore, the death of the unborn is not considered the same as the death of an adult. Some translations, such as the Jerusalem Bible, seem to support that interpretation:

> If, when men come to blows, they hurt a woman who is pregnant and she suffers a miscarriage, though she does not die of it, the man responsible must pay the compensation demanded of him by the woman's master; he shall hand it over, after arbitration. But should she die, you shall give life for life, eye for eye, tooth for tooth, hand for hand, foot for foot, burn for burn, wound for wound, strike for strike.

This interpretation, however, has been called into question by many critics.[20] They argue that the Jerusalem Bible and other translations like it (e.g., TEV) are mistranslations and that in the Hebrew the passage is really saying that the mother and the unborn are to receive equal judicial treatment; that is, the mother and the unborn are both covered by the lex talionis. One such critic is Umberto Cassuto, who offers the following interpretation:

> The statute commences, *And when men strive together,* etc., in order to give an example of accidental injury to a pregnant woman, and . . . the law presents the case realistically. Details follow: *and* they *hurt* unintentionally *a woman with child*—the sense is, that one of the combatants, whichever of them it be (for this reason the verb translated 'and they hurt' is in the plural) is responsible—*and her children come forth* (i.e., there is a miscarriage) on account of the hurt she suffers (irrespective of the nature of the fetus, be it male or female, one or two; hence here, too, there is a generic plural as in the case of the verb 'they hurt'), *but no mischief happens*— that is, the woman and the children do not die—the one who hurt her *shall surely be punished* by a fine, *according as the woman's husband shall lay*—impose—*upon him,* having regard to the extent of the injuries and the special circumstances of the accident; *and he* who caused the hurt *shall pay* the amount of the fine to the woman's husband *with judges,* in accordance with the decision of the court that will confirm the husband's claim and compel the offender to pay compensation, for it is impossible to leave the determination of the amount of the fine to the husband, and, on the other hand, it is not within the husband's power to compel the assailant to pay if he refuses. But if *any mischief happen,* that is, if the woman dies or the children die, *then you shall give life for life,* eye for eye, etc.: you, O judge (or you, O Israel, through the judge who represents you) shall adopt the principle of "life for life," etc.[21]

Gleason Archer points out that Cassuto's rendering is an appropriate interpretation because the portion of the Hebrew translated in the New American Standard Bible as "so that she has a miscarriage" (*wĕyāṣĕû yĕlādêyāh*) does not necessarily entail the death of the unborn, but can also mean the expulsion of a premature infant from his mother's womb, regardless of whether his expulsion results in death.[22]

Dr. F. Michael Womack points out that "Exodus 21:22 uses a derivation of the root word *yāṣā'*. This is not the normal word for miscarriage. In fact, when used of children, the word refers to offspring and live birth. In the context of Exodus 21 it refers to the premature live birth of a child or children (it is in the plural—even multiple births are in mind)." Womack adds that "this becomes quite significant when one realizes that the normal Hebrew term for miscarriage is used in Exodus 23:26. There the word is *shakal*. It means to make childless or miscarry." Had the author of Exodus "intended to mean miscarry in Exodus 21, he would have used *shakal*. He did not! Exodus 21, therefore, based on simple lexical definitions, promotes life in the highest possible fashion."[23]

Hence, Exodus 21:22–25 is saying that if the incident in question results only in a premature birth, the perpetrator should be fined. However, if "harm follows" (that is, if either the mother or the child is injured or killed), the same should be inflicted upon the perpetrator.

In summary, since the interpretation of Exodus 21:22–25 is at best divided,[24] and since the Bible's larger context teaches that the unborn are persons, it seems rather foolish for the abortion-rights advocate to put all his ideological eggs into one dubious biblical basket.[25]

Argument from Numbers 5:11–31

This passage is quoted in a tract published by Episcopalians for Religious Freedom, "A Pro-Choice Bible Study."[26] It is from the New English Bible:

> When a married woman . . . is unfaithful to her husband, and has sexual intercourse with another man . . . and the crime is undetected . . . but when . . . a fit of jealousy comes over a husband which causes him to suspect his wife, . . . the husband shall bring his wife to the priest. . . . He [the priest] shall

144

take clean water in an earthenware vessel, and shall take dust from the floor of the Tabernacle and add it to the water. He shall set the woman before the Lord, uncover her head, . . . shall . . . put the woman on oath and say to her, '. . . may the Lord make an example of you . . . by bringing upon you *miscarriage and untimely birth* [abortion]; and this water that brings out the truth shall enter your body, bringing upon you *miscarriage and untimely birth.*' The woman shall respond, 'Amen, Amen.' . . . After this he shall make the woman drink the water. If she has been unfaithful to her husband, [and] when the priest makes her drink the water that brings out the truth . . . she will suffer a *miscarriage or untimely birth* . . . But if the woman has not let herself become defiled and is pure, . . . she will bear her child. [emphasis added]

The author of "A Pro-Choice Bible Study" claims that this passage proves that "*a planned abortion* is in the Bible as part of *God's law* given to Moses." He interprets the passage to mean that the request for abortion "comes from a husband, and his wife must agree to drink a potion prepared by a Hebrew priest. If the woman has been unfaithful, God initiates an abortion. This passage illustrates the direct intention of both potential parents plus a holy man to cause a miscarriage, an abortion."[27]

There are several problems with this interpretation. First, even if the passage were saying that abortion is justified in circumstances of infidelity, the passage is also saying that it is "the Lord" who brings upon her "miscarriage and untimely birth," not the priest, the husband, or the wife. Therefore, the passage does not support abortion on demand by a human being. Second, nothing in the passage is saying that the unborn human is not fully human. If execution by God makes one a nonperson, then everyone who died in the flood, including babies and small children, were not persons.

Third, it is peculiar that someone defending women's rights would cite a passage in which a husband who suspects his wife of having committed adultery is granted the right to take her to a male priest who ad-

ministers a drug and then prays that God cause an abortion if the pregnancy was the result of adultery. This is certainly not pro-*choice*. I doubt that this approach to a woman's infidelty would be welcomed by contemporary feminists.

Fourth, there is good reason to suppose that the translation from which this passage is quoted (NEB) is not accurate. The Jerusalem Bible translates "miscarriage and untimely birth" as "making your thigh shrivel and your body swell." The New American Standard Bible says "making your thigh waste away and your abdomen swell." Other translations are similar: "make thy thigh to rot, and thy belly to swell" (KJV); "make thy thigh to fall away, and thy body to swell" (ASB); "May he cause your genital organs to shrink and your stomach to swell up" (TEV); "he causes your thigh to waste away and your abdomen to swell" (NIV). An alternative reading in the New International Version states: "causes you to have a miscarrying womb and barrenness."

All these translations seem to be saying that if the wife had committed adultery, her sexual organs will become useless, thus resulting in a miscarrying womb and barrenness. But if she did not commit adultery, she "will be able to have children" (Num. 5:28b NIV).[28] This seems to be the most natural interpretation of this passage, since Numbers 5:11–31 is a test for a woman if her husband is unsure of her fidelity. It is not a test for a pregnancy that may or may not result from adultery. Since a vast majority of adulterous unions do not result in pregnancy, a test for adultery that procured an abortion would not be a very good test. What good would such an adultery test be if the wife had committed adultery and yet did not get pregnant? Thus it makes sense to reject the New English Bible translation.

Argument from "Breath"

Some people argue that since Adam became a living soul when God "breathed into his nostrils the breath of life" (Gen. 2:7), birth is the time at which a child becomes a living being. At birth it begins to breathe oxygen through the lungs. There are at least two problems with this argument.[29]

First, it is false to so say that the unborn from conception do not breathe in a true biological sense. As Davis points out, "while breathing in the usual sense does not begin until birth, the process of *respiration* in the more technical biological sense of the transfer of oxygen from the environment of the living organism occurs from the time of conception." Thus it is "the *mode* but not the *fact* of this oxygen transfer which changes at birth."[30] Therefore, the "breath of life" exists from the moment of conception.

Second, there is no analogy between the creation of the first man, Adam, which was a unique historical event, and the ordinary birth of a child. As theologian Harold O. J. Brown points out, "If God took inanimate matter and made a man from it, as Genesis 2:7 seems to be saying, then obviously what he created was not a human being until it was given life. But the fetus is not 'inanimate matter.' It is already alive. And it is already human." Therefore, "to apply Genesis 2:7 to human beings who were carried for nine months in a mother's womb before birth is clearly ridiculous. This argument is seldom used by people who take Scripture seriously."[31]

Miscellaneous Passages and Arguments

Since the following passages and arguments are weak biblical defenses of the abortion-rights position, my critique of them will be brief. Almost all of them come from "A Pro-Choice Bible Study." Since many people may come across this work, I believe it is necessary to address some of its arguments.

Argument from Psalm 51:5

In this passage David writes, "Behold, I was brought forth in iniquity, and in sin my mother conceived me." Strangely enough, as we have already noted, this passage is also used to defend the *pro-life* position. In any event, the abortion-rights defender argues that since David could not have been an ac-

tual sinner because he had yet to actually sin, David was only a potential sinner. But this is because he was only a potential person.

There are several problems with this argument. First, it does not address the fact that Psalm 51:5 does clearly state that it was David who came into existence at conception. Second, even if this passage were claiming that the unborn are potential sinners, this would still imply that the unborn are actual persons, since only actual persons can be potential sinners, just as only actual persons can be potential violinists, philosophers, basketball players, or deli managers. And third, the passage is not saying that David, as a zygote, performed a sin, but rather, that he was conceived a sinner by virtue of being Adam's descendant. That is to say, Adam's sin nature is passed on to all who share his human nature. But this supports the pro-life position. As Norman Geisler points out, "the very fact that humans are declared sinners from conception reveals that they are human, that is, part of the fallen human race. It is only by virtue of being part of the Adamic human race that we are conceived in sin" (see Rom. 5:12).[32]

Argument from Psalm 139:13, 16a

This passage is also used to defend the pro-life position. The passage reads: "For Thou didst form my inward parts; Thou didst weave me in my mother's womb . . . Thine eyes have seen my unformed substance." The abortion-rights advocate argues that since this passage is saying that the unborn is still being "weaved" and is "unformed," therefore it is not fully human.

There are at least two problems with this interpretation. First, "'un-formed' (v. 16) does not mean unhuman any more than de-formed does."[33] Far from casting aspersion upon the unborn's full humanness, Psalm 139 eloquently describes God's creative activity in prenatal human development, thus implying the full humanness of the unborn from the moment of conception. For in human development, "unformed" is a relational term that implies a lack a person may have in relation to a more advanced state of his development. That is to say, a pre-embryo is "unformed" in relation to an embryo; an embryo is "unformed" in relation to a fetus; a fetus is "unformed" in relation to an infant; an infant is "unformed" in relation to an adolescent, and an adolescent is "unformed" in relation to an adult. So it does not follow that since one is "unformed" one is therefore not fully human.

Second, it is bad hermeneutics (i.e., the art of intepretation) to quote this passage in isolation from other statements about the unborn found in both the Book of Psalms (e.g., Ps. 51:5) and the rest of the Bible, passages that speak of personal human existence beginning from conception (e.g., Gen. 4:1; Ps. 51:5), refer to the unborn by personal pronouns (e.g., Jer. 1:5), and apply terms to the unborn that are used of postnatal children (e.g., Luke 1:41, 44 cf. 2:12, 16).

Argument from Psalm 139:16b

The second part of Psalm 139:16 is sometimes used to deny the unborn's full humanness: "And in Thy book they were all written, The days that were ordained for me, When as yet there was not one of them." The abortion-rights advocate is arguing that this passage is saying that while in the womb the days of David's life had not yet begun ("When as yet there was not one of them"). The problem, however, with this interpretation is that the text does not say that the days of David's life exclude his prenatal existence. The passage is simply saying that all of David's days were ordained and written in God's book. And since God has known everything from all eternity, it follows that God knew of David's days "when as yet there was not one of them," a phrase that may refer to the time *prior to his conception.* Psalm 51:5 states that David's beginning can be traced back to his conception and the rest of Psalm 139 gives a detailed account of God's personal interaction with the development of the prenatal David.

Or one can argue that the passage is referring exclusively to David's postnatal days. But this would not mean that David was not

a person prior to birth or that killing him by abortion was morally justified.

Argument from Job 10:18–19

This pasage reads: "Why then hast Thou brought me out of the womb? Would that I had died and no eye had seen me! I should have been as though I had not been, carried from womb to tomb." The author of "A Pro-Choice Bible Study" interprets this passage to mean that "Job did not consider the prenatal period as an existence."[34]

This interpretation is unjustified. First, the passage says just the opposite: one does exist prenatally. Job is saying that if he were not born it would be *"as though"* he *"had not been"* (emphasis added). He is not saying that if he were not born he would have never existed, only that it would be as though he had never existed. People speak like this all the time. For example, a disenchanted husband may say that his wife treats him as though they were not married, but he is still married to her. In the same way, when Job claims that if he were stillborn it would be as though he had never existed, he still existed. One cannot use "as though" unless one "is."

Second, Job 3:3 affirms the personhood of the conceptus: "Let the day perish on which I was to be born, and the night which said, 'A boy is conceived.'" Therefore, the passage in question, and the Book of Job in particular, supports the pro-life position.

Argument from Ecclesiastes 11:5

This verse reads: "Just as you do not know the path of the wind and how bones *are formed* in the womb of the pregnant woman [or, 'how the spirit comes to the bones of a woman with child,' RSV], so you do not know the activity of God who makes all things." The author of the "Pro-Choice Bible Study" claims that "the writer of Ecclesiastes admonishes the Bible reader not to speculate about *how* or *when* the spirit of the child arrives. It could be *presumptuous* to claim that life begins at conception, which the Bible refuses to do."[35]

There are several problems with the abortion-rights intepretation of this verse. First, the verse is not commanding that "the Bible reader not speculate about how and when the spirit of the child arrives." There is no mention of *when* in the verse but only that one does not known *how* the "bones are formed in the womb of the pregnant woman." But it does not follow from my ignorance of the mechanism by which the soul or spirit is given by God that I don't know when this occurs. For example, just because a person may not know how his mind works does not mean he cannot know when his mind is working. Although we may not know how God brings human persons into existence, we do know when one's personhood begins, since so many other biblical passages clearly indicate that full humanness begins at conception.

Second, even if the abortion-rights interpretation were correct, the verse does not support abortion on demand. Certainly abortion could still be a serious moral wrong even if the unborn entity is not fully human during the entire nine months of pregnancy. Furthermore, the abortion-rights advocate is admitting that the verse is teaching that the spirit of the child arrives some time *before* birth (after all, the woman is said to be "with child," RSV). Hence, the abortion-rights view of this verse does not support the abortion-rights position.

Third, if this verse were really claiming that one does not know when the unborn becomes fully human, then it would be just as presumptuous to deny that personhood begins sometime before birth (i.e., the abortion-rights position) as it would be to affirm that personhood begins at conception. Therefore, even with an abortion-rights interpretation, this verse could still be used as a pro-life prooftext: since one does not know when life begins, therefore one should not kill the unborn entity, for it is a real possibility that if one performs an abortion one is committing a homicide. It is legal negligence to perform an act in which one does not know whether one is harming another (e.g., demolishing a building when one has not checked if anyone is inside).

Argument from 1 Corinthians 15:46

This verse reads: "However, the spiritual is not first, but the natural; then the spiritual." The abortion-rights advocate who uses this verse is arguing that the physical reality of the unborn precedes its spiritual endowment. So prior to a certain point in gestation, the unborn does not possess a spirit, and hence, it is not a person. The problem with this use of 1 Corinthians 15:46 is that the verse has nothing even remotely to do with embryology or human development. The context is clearly human salvation. As the verses before and after verse 46 reveal, the author, Paul the apostle, is contrasting the first Adam with the second Adam, Jesus: "So also it is written, 'The first *man*, Adam, *became a living soul.*' The last Adam became a life-giving spirit. However, the spiritual is not first, but the natural; then the spiritual. The first man is from the earth, earthy; the second man is from heaven. As is the earthy, so also are those who are earthy; and as is the heavenly, so also are those who are heavenly. And just as we have borne the image of the earthy, we shall also bear the image of the heavenly" (1 Cor. 15:45–49, emphasis added).

Argument from the Fact That God Calls Us by Name

Since the Bible teaches that "God calls us by name" (Isa. 43:1, 7; Rev. 3:5; Luke 10:20), and "a child is ready to be named at birth because the sex is only then normally known (Gen. 29:31–35; Eccles. 6:4),"[36] the abortion-rights advocate concludes that one is only fully human at birth.

This argument is factually and logically absurd. First, none of the verses cited establish the abortion-rights position. There is no logical problem with one accepting the "pro-choice" interpretation of these verses and still remaining pro-life. That is to say, it does not follow from not being named that one is not fully human. It would still be wrong for a parent to murder her one-year-old even if she had not given the child a name. For it is persons that are named; named things do not become persons simply because they are named. Consequently, it also does not follow that because something is named it is a person. Even abortion-rights advocates must admit this, since some parents have named their miscarried children. Will the abortion-rights advocate who denies the full humanity of such beings now concede that they were fully human simply because they were named? If I name my pet gerbil Richard G., does that make the gerbil fully human?

Second, since we now know that gender is genetically determined from conception, and that it is now in prinicple possible to know the gender of one's unborn child after conception, is it now wrong to abort the offspring of parents who name them long before their birth?

And third, although it is true that God "calls us by name," it does not follow that one who is not named by another human being, such as a parent, does not have a name known only to God (see Isa. 49:1). For if this were the case, then unnamed newborns, infants, and adults would not be fully human or capable of being called by God.

Argument from the Fact That Every Person Lives under God's Care from the Time of Birth

Since both the psalmist and the prophet Isaiah teach (Ps. 22:9, 10; 58:3; 71:6; Isa. 49:5) that "every person lives under God's care from the time of birth, instead of conception,"[37] therefore, the abortion-rights advocate argues, full humanness does not begin until birth.

To be frank, this is a strange argument. None of the passages cited support the abortion-rights position on abortion. In fact, they all lend support to the pro-life position. Psalm 22:10 says that "from my mother's womb you have been my God" (JB). Psalm 58:3 merely asserts that "wicked men . . . have been in error since birth" (JB). This hardly proves that these men had no prenatal existence. After all, if the passage was asserting that birth was the beginning of personal existence one

could reasonably argue that it would most likely not say "in error since birth," but rather, "always in error." For it is certainly possible, and quite likely, for an author to use the word *since* in reference to when a thing acquires a certain attribute, such as "being in error," while at the same time not denying that the thing in question existed before acquiring that attribute. For example, if I say that I have weighed 180 pounds since 1988, it is implied that I existed at another weight prior to 1988.

Psalm 71:6a ("I have relied on you since I was born," JB) can be understood along the same lines as Psalm 58:3, for verse 5 says, "Yahweh, I have trusted you since my youth" (JB), and the second part of verse 6 states, "you have been my portion from my mother's womb" (JB). If the Psalmist is claiming in the first part of Psalm 71:6 that there was no prenatal existence, then in verse 5 he is claiming that there is no pre-adolescent existence. But the second part of verse 6 is affirming prenatal existence. Therefore, Psalm 71:6 not only does not support the abortion-rights position, but in fact supports the pro-life view.

Isaiah 49:5a reads: "And now Yawheh has spoken, he who formed me in the womb to be his servant, to bring Jacob back to him, to gather Israel to him" (JB). Since being "formed in the womb" is consistent with, and lends support to, personhood beginning from conception, it is a mystery why this passage is cited in defense of the abortion-rights position.

Argument from the Fact That Life Begins When Blood Cells Come into Existence

Since certain biblical passages teach that "life is in the blood" (Lev. 17:11, 14; Gen. 9:4; Deut. 12:23), and since "embryologists have determined that blood cells do not develop until 20 days after fertilization," therefore, the abortion-rights advocate argues, "life" does not arrive "until three weeks after conception."[38]

Aside from the fact that these passages do not support the abortion-rights position that abortion on demand should be legal for the entire nine months of pregnancy, there is a fundamental interpretative problem with the use of these biblical passages to establish the conclusion that personhood begins three weeks after conception: not one passage refers to unborn humans, but they all refer to mammals at a stage in their development when blood is a necessary condition for their mortal existence. The pre-twenty-day-old human embryo, however, is a mammal, and a living human being in particular, who does not need blood as a necessary condition for his existence. Therefore, it does not follow from the fact that blood is a necessary condition for the existence of post-twenty-day-old humans that pre-twenty-day-old humans are not fully human.

Some Concluding Remarks  Part

Conclusion
A Positive Case for the Pro-Life Position

Remember the overused rhetoric
That life begins at birth
Now they say if you're not wanted
You have no inherent worth
When dignity becomes arbitrary
We're under an evil hex
Willing to admit our nothingness
For the politics of sex

      F. J. B. ("Politics of Sex," 1984)

No being is so important that it can usurp the rights of another.

      Captain Jean-Luc Picard, character on *Star Trek: The Next Generation* (1988)

This book has made a positive case for the pro-life position on abortion. The basic argument, which is the foundation of this position, is the following:

1. The unborn entity, from the moment of conception, is fully human.
2. It is prima facie wrong to kill an entity that is fully human.
3. Almost every act of abortion is intended to kill the unborn, an entity that is fully human.
4. Therefore, almost every act of abortion is prima facie wrong.

This argument is deductively valid. That is, if one supposes that the premises are true, the conclusion follows. And if the premises of a valid argument are true, then the argument is sound. And if the argument is sound, then the pro-life position is morally correct. But are the premises of the argument true? I believe that this text has made a good case for their truth. Let us briefly summarize this case.

First, we saw that the unborn are biologically members of the species *homo sapiens* (chap. 3). Furthermore, we concluded that since none of the decisive moments or gradualist arguments work (see chap. 6) and that none of the theological arguments (chap. 8) against the unborn's humanness are successful, it follows that the unborn entity, from the moment of conception, is fully human. Second, it seems intuitively true that it is prima facie wrong to kill an entity that is fully human (see chap. 1).

Of course, by saying that killing is prima facie wrong I am claiming that in ordinary circumstances no one is morally justified in killing another human being. This is why none of the abortion-rights arguments from pity, ad hominen, and tolerance work, for they all try to justify the killing of the unborn on the same grounds for which it would be wrong to kill someone already born (see chaps. 4, 5). Hence, the real question is whether the unborn is fully human.

This does not mean, however, that it is always wrong to kill someone who is fully human, only prima facie wrong. That is to say, there could be circumstances in which killing or letting someone die is justified because a higher good is achieved. To cite two examples, most people believe that one is justified in killing in cases of self-defense, and one is also justified in letting someone die if that someone is brain-dead and his bodily organs are kept alive by a machine. In the case of abortion, the killing of an unborn entity is justified if her presence in the womb poses a significant threat to the life of her mother. If the unborn entity is not surgically removed (which will undoubtedly result in her death if she is removed before she is viable), then both mother and child will die. The specific intention of this abortion is not to kill the child but to save the life of the mother. The child's death via abortion is an unfortunate consequence that, although anticipated, cannot be avoided unless one is willing to let both mother and child die by permitting the pregnancy to continue. Since it is a higher good that one human should live rather than two die, abortion to save the life of the mother is justified.

Some philosophers, such as Judith Jarvis Thomson, although agreeing in principle with premise 2 of my argument, have argued that even if the unborn is fully human with a full right to life, a pregnant woman still has a right to get an abortion, since no one has the right to use another's body against her will. That is to say, the killing of an unborn entity via abortion is not an example of killing that is prima facie wrong. We saw, however, that there are a number of fundamental problems with both this argument and popular arguments that are similar to it (see chap. 7). In sum, it seems

that premise 2 is correct: it is prima facie wrong to kill an entity which is fully human.

Third, there is no doubt that every act of abortion, with the exception of one performed with the intention to save the mother's life, is specifically intended to kill the unborn. It seems then that all three premises of this argument are true. And since the conclusion follows logically from the premises, this argument is sound. Therefore, the pro-life position on abortion is morally correct. And since its moral correctness involves the protection of innocent human persons, and since at least one universally recognized role of government is to protect the powerless from being unjustly treated by the powerful, and since the most morally repugnant result of a power relationship is that in which the victim is unjustly killed, there is no question that the pro-life position is just the type of moral position that ought to be legally mandated. Unlike changeable laws that prohibit some types of amusement, such as anti-gambling laws, a pro-life law would prohibit exactly the type of activity for which governments are created: an activity in which the powerful unjustly poison, burn, suffocate and/or dismember the powerless. As one medical ethicist puts it, "Suppose, in the encounter between doctor and child [in an abortion], the child won half of the time, and killed the doctor in self-defense—something he would have every right to do. Very few doctors would perform abortions. They perform them now only because of their absolute power over a small, fragile, helpless victim."[1]

In conclusion, if we couple the sound moral argument with the fact that Roe v. Wade allows for abortion on demand for virtually any reason for the entire nine months of pregnancy (see chap. 2), a fact that clearly runs contrary to most people's intuitions about the wrongness of most abortions (such as those that are late-term and performed for such reasons as sex selection, birth control, or convenience), it follows that total prohibition of abortion except possibly in a few rare circumstances is morally demanded in order to move toward becoming a just society that truly respects the value of each and every human life.

Epilogue
A Dialogue on Civil Disobedience—
Socrates to the Rescue

An unjust law is a code that is out of harmony with the moral law.
One has a moral responsibility to disobey unjust laws.

Martin Luther King, Jr.

The following dialogue will, I hope, entertain as well as inform. Operation Rescue (OR) is known for its acts of civil disobedience. Members of this group block the entrances to abortion clinics in order prevent women from having abortions. They believe that by doing this they are rescuing unborn children from certain death. For the past couple of years I have wrestled with the arguments given by those on all sides of the debate. I have concluded that the members of OR are morally justified, although I am not sure that they are always obligated, to try to save the lives of the unborn by their method of civil disobedience.

This dialogue, as well as the one in Appendix C, is inspired by the works of Boston College philosophy professor, Peter Kreeft. Some scholars may be upset that I am using Socrates to defend civil disobedience, since he seemed to rail against it in two of Plato's dialogues, *The Apology* and *The Crito*. Martin Luther King, Jr., however, cites Socrates in defense of his own civil disobedience in Birmingham, Alabama.[1]

In this dialogue Socrates is speaking in the twentieth century, which means that he's had nearly twenty-five-hundred years to evaluate his position. Consequently, the position he defends here has been well thought out.[2]

I have included an addendum that contains brief summaries of the arguments against OR in this dialogue, as well as Socrates' responses to them.

We find Socrates blocking the entrance to an abortion clinic in Las Vegas, Nevada. He is just about to be carted away by police officer Pearl Lee Gates, a well-known pro-life Christian and law-and-order advocate. Standing next to both of them, and cheering the police on, is the clinic's attorney, Hugh Jenix, a professor of law and abortion-rights activist.

Scene One

Officer Pearl Lee Gates: Excuse me, sir, you've gotta come along with me.

Socrates: As you say, Officer Gates.

Officer Gates: How do you know my name?

Socrates: I've heard you on the radio. You are a well-known Christian teacher.

Officer Gates: What's your name?

Socrates: Socrates.

Officer Gates: Interesting. Are you named after the philosopher?

Socrates: You could say that.

Officer Gates: Hmmmm?

Socrates: Excuse me, I have a question.

Officer Gates: What is it?

Socrates: I know you are pro-life and you, like the rescuers, disapprove of the brutality practiced in this clinic. But why then do you arrest us?

Officer Gates: I don't believe it is right to disobey the law.

Socrates: Ever?

Officer Gates: Sometimes.

Socrates: Such as . . .

Officer Gates: If I see someone drowning in a pool behind a fence that says "no trespassing," I believe it is all right to break the no-trespassing law to save that person's life. I also believe that the underground railroad, used to hide escaping black slaves in the nineteenth century, was morally justified. Those are two examples.

Socrates: How does clinic-blocking differ?

Officer Gates: Abortion is legal.

Socrates: So was slavery.

Officer Gates: I don't agree with the comparison. The slaves were oppressed against their will, whereas pregnant women are free to refuse abortions.

Socrates: But their unborn children are not free to refuse death. Your analogy is completely wrong. You make a fatal mistake in comparing pregnant women with slaves. It is more accurate to compare the unborn with slaves, since they are both oppressed victims of unjust laws.

In fact, your view that since abortion is legal, pro-lifers should not try to save unborn lives is similar to the pro-choice response, "Don't like abortion, don't have one." Can you imagine telling an abolitionist when slavery was legal, "Don't like slavery, don't own a slave"?

Professor Hugh Jenix: Wait a second, Socrates, abortion is a constitutional right according to the U. S. Supreme Court.

Socrates: So were slavery and segregation. Do you think that civil disobedience was justified in preventing those attrocities?

Professor Jenix: Yes.

Socrates: So your position is inconsistent.

Professor Jenix: Not at all, because those African-Americans who were oppressed under slavery and segregation were human persons. The unborn are not.

Socrates: So *that's* the issue. The question of the unborn's personhood is the only factor that distinguishes the other issues from abortion.

Professor Jenix: What are you talking about?

Socrates: Perhaps I am unclear. Let me put it this way. If the unborn are human persons, then, according to your view, civil disobedience to save them is justified.

Professor Jenix: I suppose.

Socrates: So if the Rescuers are correct about the unborn's personhood, then they are justified.

Professor Jenix: Don't trap me, Socrates.

Socrates: I have no need to trap you. Logic is doing that quite well. She is our common master, even higher than your Supreme Court.

Professor Jenix: But many people, including myself, don't think that the unborn are human persons. And since it follows that many people disagree over this issue, we should tolerate differing opinions on this topic. After all, we live in a pluralistic society.

Socrates: But many people in the nineteenth century also believed that black slaves were not human persons. Should your pluralistic society have tolerated that view?

Professor Jenix: No, because those bigoted people were wrong.

Socrates: Not very tolerant for a pluralist, is he, Officer Gates?

Professor Jenix: Don't bring him into this. The man's just trying to do his job.

Socrates: Which is?

Professor Jenix: Carting away terrorists who want to force women into compulsory pregnancy.

Socrates: Don't you mean, "Brutalizing people who rescue unborn children from being burned, crushed, dismembered, and/or suffocated to death"?

Professor Jenix: No, I don't, Socrates. You're intolerant beyond repair.

Socrates: And you are not? Aren't you intolerant of *me* putting into practice my heartfelt belief that the unborn are human persons who are being murdered by abortion?

Professor Jenix: But many people believe that the unborn are not persons.

Socrates: So, once again, *that* is the issue. It is not pluralism, tolerance, legality, or even constitutionality, or any of the other substances with which you have polluted the river of truth.

Professor Jenix: Socrates, we will not settle this today. I've got to get back to Boston. Take care of him, Officer Gates.

Socrates: Before we part ways, Professor Jenix, let me ask you to define what you mean when you say that "we live in a pluralistic society."

Professor Jenix: I mean that we live in a society of people in which different views on different topics are expressed and ought to be tolerated.

Socrates: Are the unborn members of this "pluralistic society"?

Professor Jenix: No.

Socrates: Evidently then, neither are pro-lifers, since they believe that the unborn *are* part of this pluralistic society. Your society of openness seems to include only pro-choicers.

Professor Jenix: Of course pro-lifers belong, Socrates. And they can believe what they want to believe.

Socrates: But they can't *act* as if what they believe is true. They can believe in their minds that all the unborn are human persons, but they can't *act* as if all the unborn are human persons. In practice, therefore, your idea of a "pluralistic society" turns out to be exclusively pro-choice.

Professor Jenix: That's not true.

Socrates: On the contrary, Professor. Do you think that pro-lifers ought to permit each pregnant woman to decide whether or not she wants an abortion?

Professor Jenix: Yes, of course.

Socrates: What is the pro-choice position that you espouse?

Professor Jenix: That each pregnant woman should be allowed to decide whether or not she wants an abortion.

Socrates: Hmmm. But this is exactly the stance you want pro-lifers to take.

Professor Jenix: I suppose.

Socrates: It turns out then that in your "pluralistic society" there is only one view: yours.

Professor Jenix: Why are you doing this to me, Socrates?

Socrates: I am doing nothing. It is logic that is doing it. She is our master. And one more thing, Professor.

Professor Jenix: What's that?

Socrates: The fundamental reason your argument from pluralism doesn't work is because you cannot appeal to the fact that we live in a pluralisitic society when the very question of *who* is part of that society (that is, whether or not it includes unborn children) is itself under dispute in the abortion debate.

Professor Jenix: Take him away, Officer Gates.

Officer Gates: Sure thing, Professor Jenix.

Socrates: Before you go, Professor Jenix, could you do something for me?

Officer Gates: What is it?

Socrates: When you get home, take the time to call Dr. Rex Herrod, Professor Attila Tarian, and "Pop" Syke. We've discussed abortion at length. I believe that these discussions have caused them to think more critically about and call into question your view on abortion. Also, give my best to Peter.[3]

Professor Jenix: I'll see what I can do, Socrates.

Scene Two

Officer Gates: Let's go, Socrates.

Socrates: I'm moving as fast as a twenty-five-hundred-year-old man can move.

Officer Gates: Do you want to hear a joke?

Socrates: Of course. Humor is the medicine of the soul.

Officer Gates: Did you hear about the skeptic who was both Greek and Jewish?

Socrates: No.

Officer Gates: He demanded both miraculous signs and clever arguments in order to believe (1 Cor. 1:22).[4]

Socrates: (Laughs) But maybe if we can gain wisdom about civil disobedience, then the world will see it as a sign of our seriousness about abortion being murder.

Officer Gates: Here we go again!

Socrates: Don't you want to find the truth?

Officer Gates: Yes.

Socrates: Then let's find it! Since we have already seen that your first argument is invalid, do you have another argument against rescuing?

Officer Gates: I have four more, Socrates.

Socrates: Excellent. Proceed.

Officer Gates: Here are my four arguments. First, since I am a Christian, I believe that the Bible is my normative guide in faith and practice. I believe that the Bible teaches that Christians are to obey the government (Rom. 12) up until the point at which it demands that Christians disobey a clear command of God, such as when the Jewish leaders told Jesus' apostles not to preach the gospel. The apostles were justified in disobeying that statute. However, in the case of abortion, the state is not forcing Christians to disobey God's command, although it is permitting others to do so. My second argument goes like this: If the intention of Operation Rescue is to save lives, why stop at clinic-blocking? Why not blow up the clinic and kill the doctor? Wouldn't this save more lives? My third argument is this: Since spiritual death is worse than physical death, why don't Rescuers block the entrances to churches they consider to be preaching untrue doctrines and prevent the members' innocent children from hearing those doctrines? My fourth argument goes like this: Rescuing will hurt the pro-life cause by turning off the general public as well as dividing the pro-life movement. So in the long run, if the pro-life movement fails because of Operation Rescue, more babies will die.

Socrates: Very good. Let us look at each argument one at a time, beginning with the last argument.

Officer Gates: Why this one first?

Socrates: Because it is not a moral argument and we can easily dispense with it.

Officer Gates: What kind of argument is it?

Socrates: It's a prudential argument, an argument involving which course of action will best achieve a certain goal.

Officer Gates: Please explain.

Socrates: Let us apply prudential judgment to the question of rescuing. Now follow closely. If rescuing is morally justified both ethically and biblically, your argument is merely saying that other morally justified means, which are legal, will best achieve the desired goal of rescuing: to save as many lives as possible by putting an end to as many abortions as possible. On the other hand, if rescuing is not ethically and biblically justified, then it cannot be an option in an ethical person's prudential judgment. To press this even further, if rescuing is not ethically and biblically justified but results in political success for the pro-life movement, rescuing would still remain unjustified. Hence, your argument that rescuing will hurt the pro-life movement, although raising an important point, does not settle the question of whether the rescuers are ethically and biblically justified.

Officer Gates: Can you give me an example?

Socrates: Just as giving money to a homeless person may not be prudent (on the well-grounded suspicion that he will buy whiskey) yet at the same time morally allowable, rescuing may not be the prudent thing to do (on the well-grounded suspicion that it will hurt the pro-life movement in the long run) while at the same time being morally justified.

Officer Gates: I get it. It's sort of like when your wife asks you if you think her hair is nice and you think it looks awful. Although you are morally justified in saying

"I think it looks terrible," prudential judgment dictates you say something like, "That hairstyle does not do justice to your beauty."

Socrates: Exactly. Whether or not OR is prudential in achieving the pro-life goals is a question we must leave for another day, and can only be properly answered after we answer the question of the ethical and biblical justification of rescuing. So it's important that we now move on to your first three arguments, all of which are moral arguments. Refresh my memory on the first one.

Officer Gates: My first argument goes like this: Since the Christian is justified in disobeying only the laws that command him to violate a clear command of God, OR is not justified in its civil disobedience. The government is not forcing its members to have abortions or to disobey any other command of God. That's it in a nutshell.

Socrates: What did Jesus say are the two greatest commandments?

Officer Gates: Love the Lord your God with all your heart, mind, and soul, and love your neighbor as yourself.

Socrates: Is it morally wrong to disobey any one of these commandments?

Officer Gates: Yes, of course. What a silly question.

Socrates: If a government tells you to disobey any of God's commandments, are you justified in disobeying the government?

Officer Gates: Yes.

Socrates: Does this also go for the two commandments Jesus called the two greatest?

Officer Gates: Of course.

Socrates: Is saving your neighbor's life a way to "love your neighbor as yourself"?

Officer Gates: Yes.

Socrates: Is the unborn child your neighbor?

Officer Gates: Yes.

Socrates: So the government, by forbidding the Christian to save the lives of the unborn, is telling him to not love his neighbor as himself. Isn't this a law that violates a clear command of God?

Officer Gates: Not exactly, for the government is just forbidding the Rescuers from disobeying trespassing laws. It is not telling them to not love their neighbor.

Socrates: But isn't this more insidious than a law that clearly forbids them from loving the unborn by saving their lives?

Officer Gates: Please explain, Socrates.

Socrates: The trespassing laws are being used to force Christians to disobey a clear command of God, just as the perjury laws were used in Nazi Germany to force those hiding Jews from certain death to tell the truth under oath as to the Jews' whereabouts. Based on your reasoning, wouldn't it be correct to say that the "government was just forbidding them to disobey perjury laws but not forbidding them to rescue Jews?" Therefore, according to your logic, those who rescued Jews from the Holocaust were wrong, since the state was not compelling most of them to directly kill a Jew or work in a concentration camp.

Officer Gates: There goes my first argument. But I have two more.

Socrates: Let's hear the second one.

Officer Gates: The tactics of OR will lead to violence against clinics and doctors, since anything can be justified to "save lives."

Socrates: Aren't you attacking a strawman?

Officer Gates: I don't know. It's been years since I've seen *The Wizard of Oz*.

Socrates: No, I'm referring to the logical fallacy.

Officer Gates: Explain what you mean.

Socrates: Attacking a strawman occurs when someone attacks a caricature or a distorted version of what another believes instead of the real thing.

Officer Gates: Give me an example.

Socrates: Some people attack the Christian doctrine of the Trinity by saying that Christians believe in a three-headed god. But this is clearly not the doctrine. It is a strawman, for no intelligent Christian really believes such nonsense, and no official creed has ever asserted such lunacy.

Officer Gates: I understand it, but how does my argument against rescuing attack a straw man?

Socrates: Your argument makes the assumption that Rescuers believe that any violation of the law—moral, civil, or crim-

159

inal—is justified if it results in "saving lives." But as I understand the Rescuers' view, they believe in *nonviolent* civil disobedience, which means that they would object to any violence. In fact, many of your political philosophers, such as Thomas Jefferson, call this type of civil disobedience "revolution." OR does not advocate revolution, but nonviolent civil disobedience. They are two different concepts. The moral justification of revolution is a separate issue that we can discuss later, but it is not civil disobedience and it is not endorsed by the Rescuers.

Officer Gates: So I've misrepresented their position by attacking a straw man.

Socrates: There's more.

Officer Gates: More?

Socrates: Your argument also assumes that the Rescuers believe that the end justifies the means, which is not their position. They believe, as I understand it, that they are obeying a higher law by saving lives. They believe that the command for preserving life carries with it a greater moral obligation than the command for no trespassing. Many of your great Christian philosophers—Augustine, Thomas Aquinas, and Martin Luther King, Jr.—taught similar doctrines, which they believed were supported by the Bible.

Officer Gates: What's the point, Socrates?

Socrates: The point is that blowing up clinics and commiting acts of violence against physicians would seriously compromise this higher-law view, since the acts in question seriously jeopardize innocent lives as well as making OR the judge, jury, and executioner of others, which is what physicians who perform abortions are doing to the unborn. By nonviolently blocking clinics OR is saving lives without seriously compromising its higher-law view. So it is safe to say that your argument against the Rescuers misrepresents their position.

Officer Gates: But when clinics are blocked, police are taken from their normal duties so that they can cart away Rescuers to jail. While the police are away from their normal posts, people who would otherwise be protected are put in jeopardy.

Socrates: But if the Rescuers don't rescue, the unborn are put in worse jeopardy. After all, there are 1.5 million abortions every year, a far greater number than the number of born people murdered every year; the Rescuers are doing what the police should be doing. Furthermore, it is highly unlikely that if the police were not at a rescue that there would be a huge reduction in born people being murdered. On the other hand, rescues produce tangible results of actual lives saved.[5]

Moreover, if it were legal for parents to take their eight-year-old to death centers when the parents "got tired of taking care of the kid," no moral person would consider it all that troubling that police were being detained by death-center blockers. But you consider the unborn to be just as human as the eight-year-old. Your position, then, seems to accept your opponents' view of the unborn. If you were prochoice you would be begging the question.

Officer Gates: But don't Rescuers fill up jails unnecessarily?

Socrates: Such an argument assumes the abortion-rights view that the unborn are not fully human as well as falling prey to a reductio ad absurdum.

Officer Gates: Why does my argument fall prey to a reductio ad absurdum?

Socrates: Let's first talk about the first problem.

Officer Gates: Assuming the abortion-rights position?

Socrates: Yes.

Officer Gates: What do you mean by that?

Socrates: As with your last comment about the detaining of policemen, this comment assumes that the unborn are not fully human. Again, can you imagine someone arguing that people ought not to rescue eight-year-olds from a legal killing center because it would "fill up jails"? Wouldn't that be silly?

Officer Gates: Yes, it would. But how is my argument similar?

Socrates: Prolifers believe that the unborn are just as human as the eight-year-old. Correct?

Officer Gates: Yes.

160

Socrates: So if the jail argument doesn't work for the eight-year-olds it doesn't work for the unborn. Correct?

Officer Gates: (Reluctantly) Yes. You're right, Socrates. I can't imagine using my reasoning against those blocking the death centers. If the unborn are as human as eight-year olds, the principle defended in my argument must apply equally to both age groups. Since it doesn't, my argument is absurd.

Socrates: Very impressive, Officer Gates. Your logic is impeccable.

Officer Gates: But what about the other problem you mentioned.

Socrates: A reductio ad absurdum, which literally means "to reduce to the absurd." What I was saying is that your argument can be reduced to the absurd if its reasoning is applied to similar situations that clearly contradict your argument's conclusion.

Officer Gates: For instance . . .

Socrates: If your argument is correct, then Christians in the early church who chose to obey God's command to preach the gospel but were forbidden to do so by the state were wrong. But they were right. Hence your argument is absurd.

Officer Gates: I don't understand.

Socrates: Let me explain. The early church, by its civil disobedience, burdened the Roman government and its prisons, as do the present-day Rescuers who fill jails.

Officer Gates: I'm embarrassed to admit it, but I've thought of other ways that my argument can be exposed as absurd.

Socrates: Excellent. You are truly a seeker of truth. Continue.

Officer Gates: If we apply my argument's reasoning to the civil rights protestors of the 1950s and 1960s, to those who rescued slaves in nineteenth-century America, as well as to those who have resisted apartheid in South Africa, my argument is clearly absurd, since it seems that these people were all right.

Socrates: Excellent. You are truly mastering logic.

Officer Gates: But I am afraid that I am lossing terribly.

Socrates: How can you lose if you find the truth?

Officer Gates: Good point, Socrates.

Socrates: Do you have anything else to say about this argument?

Officer Gates: No, let's move on.

Socrates: Not quite yet. There's still one more point to make about your argument, and it's an important one.

Officer Gates: And what's that?

Socrates: It has to do with prudential judgment, the point we brought up at the beginning of our discussion concerning your fourth argument.

Officer Gates: Yes, I think I understand. Can't we apply it the same way to this argument as we did to the first one?

Socrates: Excellent.

Officer Gates: Should I continue?

Socrates: Yes.

Officer Gates: The Rescuer could grant to his objector that he is morally justified in blowing up a clinic (if he is certain beyond a reasonable doubt that no innocent persons would be harmed) as well as attacking a physician who is about to, or is in the process of, killing an unborn child. However, the Rescuer could also argue that out of prudential judgment there is no reason to resort to such tactics.

Socrates: Is there an underlying principle to this reasoning?

Officer Gates: Yes, and it goes like this: Simply because something is morally permissible does not mean it is always prudent to do it. Another way of putting it is this way: Just because I can do something does not mean that I must do it.

Socrates: You have gone beyond my expectations.

Officer Gates: Thank you, Socrates. But aren't you going to ask me to provide another example of this? I'm ready!

Socrates: Of course.

Officer Gates: In the Persian Gulf war, the United States could have, if it really wanted to, find and kill Saddam Hussein, since he was technically a soldier in the Iraqi army and it is not immoral to kill an enemy soldier in war. But since his assassination would have probably precipitated an invasion by Iran (Iraq's neighboring enemy), a serious internal conflict between the Kurds and the Arabs, as well as other havoc in the Middle East, prudential judgment dictated that killing Hussein was not a good idea. Although morally permissible in the context of war, causing Hussein's death would have been imprudent.

Socrates: Excellent. So you see, even if the use of force is morally justified, prudential judgment seems to indicate that in the current stage of the abortion debate it would be severely counterproductive.

Officer Gates: I still have one more argument.

Socrates: Summarize it quickly. It's getting dark and I want to get a nice prison cell.

Officer Gates: Is comfort more important than truth?

Socrates: No, it is not. You are correct. And in this case the student is greater than his master. But do proceed.

Officer Gates: My last argument goes like this: If it's necessary to save someone from physical death, as Rescuers argue, then it must be necessary to save someone from spiritual death, which is far worse. But this would entail blocking the entrances to churches that teach doctrines that lead to spiritual death, but this is absurd. Hence, rescuing is absurd.

Socrates: Although you are correct that spiritual death is worse than physical death, don't you at least agree with the Rescuers that causing an innocent person's physical death deprives him of his God-given right to life and that a great injustice has been committed?

Officer Gates: Yes, of course. I am not minimizing the value of physical life; it is extremely valuable and a gift from God. I am just saying that spiritual life is more valuable.

Socrates: Now that we have that settled, please answer this question: If you had to choose between stopping one of the following two father/son couples, which one would you choose? Father A is taking his son to the woodshed to kill him with a 44-magnum handgun, but only after an hour of torturing him by covering his body with battery acid. Father B is taking his son to the First Church of the False God, where they will attend Sunday service and return home to eat lunch.

Officer Gates: Obviously, I would stop Father A.

Socrates: Why?

Officer Gates: That's a stupid question. If I don't stop Father A his son will be brutally tortured and mercilessly killed within a few minutes.

Socrates: Why didn't you choose Father B?

Officer Gates: Because his death is not imminent.

Socrates: But you just told me that spiritual death is worse than physical death. Have you changed your mind so quickly?

Officer Gates: No, I haven't. There's just something different about these cases.

Socrates: What is it? Think carefully.

Officer Gates: Well . . . In the case of Father A I have to act quickly and decisively because if I don't the child will suffer immensely and die a cruel death. But in the case of Father B, though he leads his child down the path of spiritual death, he does not kill the child spiritually.

Socrates: If the child spiritually dies, when does he die and who kills him?

Officer Gates: The child spiritually dies only after he has reached the age of accountability, freely chooses to reject the truth, and after physical death is judged by God.

Socrates: So even if you wanted to prevent the child's spiritual death, you couldn't, since it will result only from God's judgment based on a choice the child will freely make when he reaches the age of accountability. Correct?

Officer Gates: Yes.

Socrates: If abortion is murder, as you believe, isn't the case of Father A like abortion?

Officer Gates: I suppose it is.

Socrates: And since spiritual death is "suicidal" rather than "homicidal," what is the only way we as third parties can prevent the spiritual death of our neighbors, such as Father B and his son?

Officer Gates: Share with them the truth about God and pray that they make a correct decision.

Socrates: And what is the best way to stop someone, like Father A's son or the unborn child, from being brutally murdered if either of their parents will not listen to reason?

Officer Gates: Put yourself between death and the child, whether it is manifested in the abortion clinic or the drawer in which Father A keeps his 44-magnum.

Socrates: To get a little more technical, your argument commits what philosophers call "a category mistake."

Officer Gates: What's that?

Socrates: This mistake occurs when you apply something to one category of being that does not rightfully apply to that category. For example, it is a category mistake to ask the question, "What sound is blue?" or "How tall is the number 3?"

Officer Gates: How did my argument commit this mistake?

Socrates: You mistakenly applied that which is an appropriate response to prevent imminent murder (immediate physical interference) to the question of how to prevent spiritual death, in order to make the Rescuers look absurd. But as we have seen,

murder (a form of physical death) and spiritual death each results from completely different causes. The first is physically inflicted upon the victim by another person and is irreversible; the second is a decision made by the victim himself and can be reversed prior to his physical death.

Officer Gates: It looks like my final argument has fared no better than the other four. But I have a small problem.

Socrates: What's that?

Officer Gates: Since all my arguments against OR are unsound, I cannot arrest you.

Socrates: Very logical.

Officer Gates: I know, but very costly.

Socrates: Why do you say that?

Officer Gates: Just sit down right here next to me.

Postscript

Professor Hugh Jenix continues to teach law at a leading university. Jenix has grown fond of the German philosopher Friedrich Nietzsche, who is known for his strong dislike of Socrates. Officer Pearl Lee Gates was fired after being arrested for blocking the entrance to an abortion clinic. An unidentified Greek citizen was arrested as well.[6]

Addendum:
Outline of Arguments Against Operation Rescue and Socrates' Responses to Them

Argument 1. One has an obligation to obey the law, especially if it is constitutional.

Response A: What about breaking no-trespassing laws to save a drowning child?

Response B: What about the underground railroad, which helped black slaves escape from states where slavery was legal?

Response C: Slavery, under the U.S. Supreme Court's Dred Scott decision, was constitutional. Did one have an obligation to uphold that law?

Argument 2. Since we live in a pluralistic society, Rescuers must tolerate those who don't believe the unborn are human persons.

Response A: This is tantamount to asking abolitionists to tolerate slave owners who did not believe that blacks were persons.

Response B: This is tantamount to asking pro-lifers to act as if their belief about the unborn is false, to behave like pro-choicers.

Response C: One cannot appeal to the fact that we live in a pluralisitic society when the very question of *who* is part of that society (that is, whether or not it includes unborn children) is itself the point under dispute.

Argument 3. OR's civil disobedience is wrong because the state does not compel pro-life Christians to abort their unborn children, and the Bible only commands Christians to disobey the law when the state *commands* them to do evil.

Response A: By forbidding Rescuers to exercise Christ's command to "love your neighbor [including unborn children] as yourself," the government is in fact compelling pro-life Christians to do evil.

Response B: Based on this reasoning, those who rescued Jews from the Holocaust were wrong, since the state was not compelling most of them to kill a Jew or work in a concentration camp.

Argument 4. The tactics of OR will lead to violence against clinics and doctors, since anything can be justified to "save lives."

Response A: This is a strawman argument. OR believes in nonviolent civil disobedience.

Response B: This argument assumes that the Rescuers believe that the end justifies the means, but this is not their view. Their view is that the command to save lives is greater than the command not to trespass. It does not follow from this that they are commanded to use violence whenever they believe it is justified to achieve their end.

Response C: Even if violence against clinics and doctors were permissible in a few rare and narrowly defined circumstances, that does not mean that the Rescuer must engage in it. He may avoid it out of prudential considerations (see response to argument 8).

Argument 5. Rescuers detain police from their normal duties and put the lives of others in jeopardy.

Response A: This argument assumes that the unborn are not fully human. It accepts the abortion-rights view of abortion. Can you imagine someone arguing that rescuing eight-year-olds from death centers is wrong because police are detained from their normal duties? If for the pro-lifer the unborn are as fully human as eight-year-olds, then this argument collapses.

Response B: Assuming that the unborn are fully human, if the Rescuers don't rescue, then unborn human beings are put in worse jeopardy.

Response C: The police are at fault, since they are supposed to protect lives. By arresting Rescuers they are trying to prevent civilians from doing what they themselves should be doing. That is, the police are putting more lives in jeopardy by not preventing the 1.6 million abortions that happen every year.

Argument 6. Rescuers fill up jails unnecessarily.

Response A: Same as response A to argument 5.

Response B: Assuming that rescuing is correct on other grounds, this argument can be reduced to the absurd by pointing out that the early church filled up Roman jails for preaching the gospel. If argument 6 is correct, then the early church was wrong. But we know it was right. This same reasoning can be applied with other justified acts of civil disobedience—Reductio ad absurdum.

Argument 7. Since spiritual death is worse than physical death, why don't Rescuers block the entrances to churches that they believe lead people to spiritual death?

Response A: Physical death and spiritual death are fundamentally different. The physical death in abortion is inflicted on someone by another and is irreversible, while spiritual death is self-inflicted and reversible prior to physical death.

Response B: One prevents physical death differently than one prevents spiritual death. One cannot prevent the spiritual death of another by blocking the entrances of churches. People choose to reject God apart from entering a building. One can only prevent the spiritual death of another by telling him the truth about God and praying for him. On the other hand, one can prevent the physical death that abortion results in by physically blocking the entrances to an abortion clinic.

Argument 8. Rescuing makes the pro-life movement look bad and divides the movement.

Response: This is a prudential judgment, not a moral argument. Rescuing may hurt the pro-life movement in terms of popularity and group unity, but rescuing can still be morally justified. Prudential judgments are important for political strategy, but are not decisive in moral judgment. That is, rescuing may not be the prudent thing to do, just as giving money to a homeless person may not be prudent (on the suspicion that he will buy whiskey). Yet both acts may at the same time be morally allowable.

Appendices

List of Arguments for Abortion Rights

In this book we went over a number of arguments for abortion rights. In order to help the reader to better assess these arguments and the responses to them, I have listed each argument in this appendix, along with the page numbers where it is located in the book. Because so many of these arguments overlap each other, many of the arguments named in this appendix may be under a more general heading in the text.

Arguments from Pity

1. Argument from the dangers of illegal abortion. "If *Roe v. Wade* is overturned, then many women will die from illegal abortions" (54–59).

2. Argument from economic inequity. "If abortion is prohibited, it will not prevent rich women from having safe and legal abortions elsewhere" (59–60).

3. Argument from population, poverty, and financial burden. "If abortion is forbidden, then the poor will keep producing children to draw more welfare, which will in turn cause a population problem" (60–63).

4. Argument from unwanted children and child abuse. "Abortion eliminates unwanted children, who will most likely be abused after they are born" (63–65).

5. Argument from the deformed or mentally handicapped child. "Abortion is justified if the child will be deformed or retarded" (65–68).

6. Argument from interference in career. "Unless a woman can fall back on abortion if her contraception fails, the pregnancy and subsequent birth of a child will disrupt her advancement if she is career-minded" (68).

7. Argument from rape and incest. "Abortion is justified if a woman's pregnancy is the result of either rape or incest" (68–72).

8. Argument from pity for the woman prosecuted, convicted, and/or sentenced for murder if abortion is made illegal. "If abortion is made illegal because the unborn are human persons, then women who undergo abortions ought to be convicted for murder. However, this seems to be quite harsh and lacks compassion" (72–74).

9. Argument from the social inequality of men and women. "Women need abortion in order to fully participate in the social and political life of society" (76–77).

Arguments from Tolerance

10. Argument from non-interference with others's rights. "I am personally against abortion, but if a woman wants to get an abortion, she should have a right to do so" (20).

11. Argument from religious pluralism. "The question of when protectable human life begins is a personal religious question that one must answer for oneself. Hence, prohibiting abortion is against American pluralism" (80–81).

12. Argument from separation of church and state. "If the pro-life position becomes law, it will violate the separation of church and state, since it is a 'religious' position" (80–81).

13. Argument from the fact that pro-lifers are not forced to have abortions. "If pro-lifers don't believe abortion is right, they don't have to have abortions if they don't want to" (80–81, 86–87).

14. Argument from imposing morality. "By attempting to forbid women from having abortions, pro-lifers are forcing their morality on others" (81–82).

15. Argument against a public policy forbidding abortion. "It is not wise to make a public policy decision in one direction when there is

169

wide diversity of opinion within society. Therefore, our society should not legistlate against abortion rights" (82–83).

16. Argument from the impossibility of legally stopping abortion. "Since abortions will always occur regardless of whether or not it is illegal, we should keep it legal so that women can get medically safe abortions" (83–84).

17. Argument from "compulsory" pregnancy. "The pro-life position is tantamount to compulsory pregnancy" (84–85).

18. Argument from privacy. "The abortion decision is a very private and intimate one which should be kept between a woman, her physician, and her family" (85–86).

Arguments Ad Hominem

19. Why don't pro-lifers adopt the babies they don't want aborted? (88–89).

20. Aren't pro-lifers inconsistent if they support capital punishment? (89–90).

21. Men don't get pregnant. "Men have no right to speak out about abortion; abortion is a woman's issue" (90).

Arguments from Decisive Moments and Gradualism

22. Argument from agnosticism. "No one knows when life begins" (41–46, 92–95).

23. Argument from implantation being the beginning of life based on the unborn announcing its presence to its mother. "Full humanness is not attained until the conceptus is implanted in its mother's womb" (95–96).

24. Argument from the fact that some products of conception are not human beings and the fact that some human beings, such as clones, may not result from conception. "Some entities that stem from the sperm-egg union are not 'human beings' and never will develop into them. Furthermore, if conception resulting from a sperm-egg union is when individual human life begins, would not this mean that if human clones could be produced they would not be fully human?" (96).

25. Argument from spontaneous abortions. "Since at least 30 percent of all zygotes die, how can the unborn, at least in the earliest stages of pregnancy, be considered fully human. If they are fully human, don't we have an obligation to try to save them all?" (96–97).

26. Argument from twinning and recombination. "Since the twinning of one conceptus and the recombination of two concepti may occur prior to implantation, individual human life does not begin until that time" (97).

27. Argument from the appearance of humanness. "The unborn becomes fully human at the time at which it begins to take on the appearance of a child" (97–98).

28. Argument from human sentiment. "Since parents do not grieve at the death of an embryo or fetus as they would at the death of an infant, the unborn are not fully human" (98–99).

29. Argument from quickening. "The unborn entity is fully human when her mother can feel her move" (99).

30. Argument from viability. "Since the unborn cannot independently survive outside the womb prior to viability, the nonviable unborn is not a fully independent human life and hence not fully human" (99–101).

31. Argument from the beginning of brain function. "Since at 'brain death' a human being goes out of existence, it seems only logical that the start of brain functioning is the beginning of full humanness" (101–3).

32. Argument from the attainment of sentience. "Since a being that cannot experience anything cannot be harmed, the unborn becomes fully human when it becomes sentient, capable of experiencing sensations such as pain" (103–4).

33. Argument from birth. "Since our society calculates the beginning of one's existence from one's birth, and it is only after birth that a child is named, baptized, and accepted into a family, birth is the time at which a human entity becomes fully human" (104–5).

34. Argument from criteria of personhood. "Any human being, unborn or otherwise, must fulfill particular criteria, such as self-consciousness and rationality, in order to be declared fully human ('a person')" (105–10).

35. Argument from gradualism. "There is no decisive moment at which the unborn entity moves from nonpersonhood to personhood. But rather, as the unborn entity grows in her physical stature her right to life increases. Thus, a twenty-four-week-old fetus has a greater right to life than a zygote, and the newborn has a greater right to life than the twenty-four-week-old fetus" (110–13).

36. Argument from the gradual achievement of rights. "Since society grants people rights as they develop, why can't the right to life be granted at a particular time in a human's development as well?" (113).

Other Arguments Against Full Humanness Beginning at Conception

37. Why don't sperm and ova have a right to life? They are also genetically human (114).

38. Argument from each human cell's potential. "Since it is theoretically possible that each cell in a human being's body can be artificially stimulated to produce a human clone, each human cell in a person's body, like the fetus, is potentially a born person. But we don't believe that each cell has a right to life"? (114).

39. Doesn't this view absolutize biological human life and entail "speciesism"? (114–15).

40. Aren't you absolutizing the unborn's right to life? (115).

41. Wouldn't your position mean that some forms of birth control result in homicide? (115)

42. Wouldn't your position entail that certain abortifacients, which are used exclusively for birth control, would have to be made illegal? (115–16).

43. If the unborn is a human person, would this mean that pregnant women would be forbidden to use any and all medical treatments that have an abortifacient side effect (that is, results in an abortion)? (116).

44. Isn't it true that some zygotes do not have forty-six chromosomes? (116–17).

45. Isn't an unborn human, at least in its earlier stages of development, like an acorn that is only a potential oak tree? (117).

46. Isn't the unborn, at least in its earliest stages of development, just a blueprint, or an "information code," of a human being? (117).

47. Doesn't your "life of the mother" exception involve a contradiction? (117–18).

48. Is a zygote equal to an adult woman? (118–20).

49. If the unborn, especially the zygote and early embryo, are legally recognized as human persons, would not this wreak havoc on our current legal and social structure? (120).

50. If the unborn is considered a person under the law, would not it follow that pregnant women would be forbidden to smoke, drink alcohol, or engage in other activities that may harm the unborn? Wouldn't such prohibitions violate a woman's privacy as well as be impossible to enforce? (120–21).

51. If the unborn is considered a person under the law, wouldn't all miscarriages be suspect and women would have to prove that their miscarriages were not elective abortions? (121).

Arguments from Bodily Rights

52. Argument from a woman's right over her own body. "You cannot tell a woman not to have an abortion. She has a right to control her own body" (124–25).

53. Argument from abortion being safer than childbirth. "Since abortion is safer than childbirth, a woman is taking a risk in bringing a baby to term. And since someone is not required to take a risk for another's life, abortion is justified" (125–28).

54. Argument from unplugging the violinist. "You cannot force a woman to use her body as a life-support system for someone else, even if that someone else has a right to life and is fully human" (128–35).

Arguments from Theology and the Bible

55. Argument from the fact that the Bible does not prohibit abortion. "Since the Bible does not specifically forbid abortion, therefore abortion is justified" (137–41).

56. Argument from God's granting of free moral agency. "Since we cannot truly be the best creatures we can be without free will, it is wrong to prevent people from getting abortions, since God has granted them a free will" (141–42).

57. Argument from Exodus 21:22–25. "Since this passage teaches that it is a capital offense to accidentally kill a pregnant woman but you are only required to pay a fine if you accidentally kill her fetus, the unborn are not fully human. Therefore, abortion is justified" (142–44).

58. Argument from Numbers 5:11–31. "Since this passage seems to encourage abortion in some circumstances, one can conclude that the Bible does not condemn abortion outright" (144–45).

59. Argument from "breath." "Since Adam was not a living soul until God gave him 'breath,' the unborn are not fully human until they take their first breath at birth" (145–46).

Miscellaneous Arguments from Theology and the Bible

60. Argument from Psalm 51:5 (146).

61. Argument from Psalm 139:13, 16a (146–47).

62. Argument from Psalm 139:16b (147).

63. Argument from Job 10:18–19 (147).

64. Argument from Ecclesiastes 11:5 (147–48).

65. Argument from 1 Corinthians 15:46 (148).

66. Argument from the fact that God calls us by name. "Since God does not supposedly call people by their names until after they are born, full humanness is not attained until birth" (148–49).

67. Argument from the fact that every person lives under God's care from the time of birth. "Since the Bible allegedly teaches that we are not under God's care until birth, full humanness is not attained until birth" (149).

68. Argument from the fact that life begins when the blood comes into existence. "Since the Bible allegedly teaches that 'life is in the blood,' an embryo who does not yet have flowing blood is not fully human" (149–50).

Choice Quotes

In a debate in which I participated (April 12, 1990)—aired on the show "Real to Reel," hosted by Mitch Fox and broadcast over KLVX-TV, the southern Nevada PBS affiliate—my debate partner, Lucille Lusk of the Nevada Coalition of Conservative Citizens, and I were asked by our opponents, Susan Quig-Terry of the American Civil Liberties Union of southern Nevada and Jeanne Maust of Pro-Choice Advocacy, to comment on certain irresponsible statements made by some popular pro-life activists. Although we were certain that some of the statements were taken out of context, some could not be so easily explained away. Let's face it, some pro-lifers make stupid statements. However, the citation of such statements by abortion-rights proponents does not show the pro-life position to be implausible. It merely shows that some pro-lifers do not take into consideration people's perceptions, however mistaken, of their public statements.

The purpose of this appendix is to provide the pro-life advocate with ammunition to directly combat such statements. I have included in this appendix a number of bizarre statements made by abortion-rights activists. Although such statements do not show the abortion-rights position to be implausible or the pro-life view to be correct, if they are used properly, they will force your abortion-rights opponent to get back to the real issue, the moral question of abortion, and away from ad hominem attacks on pro-life activists. When using these "choice quotes" in response to the use of statements by pro-lifers, I usually confront the abortion-rights supporter with the following proposition: "We can go on all evening (or day) calling each other names and citing the statements of extremists on both sides of the abortion debate. However, that strategy, though it is sensational, will generate an enormous amount of heat and very little light. I know you agree with

that. If you want to go on, I've got a long list of statements made by your people that I am quite sure you don't want the audience to hear. So let's be civil and discuss the real question that underlies the abortion debate: Are the unborn truly persons? And, of course, if they are, then abortion in almost all cases is unjustified homicide. Don't you agree?"

Let me stress, however, that the use of the following quotes should never be a pro-lifer's primary strategy, for such a use does nothing, from a logical perspective, to support our case. Thus I do not approve of such a use and find it to be unethical and purely demagogic. These quotes should be used simply to deflect character assassinations by the other side so that the pro-lifer can move on to more fruitful discussions.

It should be pointed out that there are many more quotes that I could have used, but the following should suffice. The following quotes are all completely documented.

Leading Abortion-Rights Activists Deny the Uniqueness and Value of the Traditional Family

Esther Langston, professor of social work, University of Nevada, Las Vegas:

A normal family may be a mother and father; a normal family may be a single mother; may be a single female; may be a single father; *a normal family may be two lesbian women or two homosexual men.*[1] (emphasis added)

National Organization for Women (NOW)

The simple fact is that *every woman must be willing to be identified as a lesbian to be fully feminist.*[2] (emphasis added)

Shiela Cronan, radical feminist leader

Since *marriage constitutes slavery for women*, it is clear that the women's movement must concentrate on attacking this institution. *Freedom for women cannot be won without the abolition of marriage.*[3] (emphasis added)

Mary Jo Bane, assistant professor of education and director of the Center for Research on Women, Wellesley College

In order to raise children with equality, we must take them away from families and communally raise them.[4]

Leading Abortion-Rights Proponents See Nothing Wrong with Infanticide, the Killing of Infants after Birth, or Treating Newborns as Nonpersons

Margaret Sanger, founder of Planned Parenthood

The most merciful thing a large family can do for one of its infant members is *to kill it.*[5] (emphasis added)

Peter Singer, professor of philosophy and director of the Center for Human Bioethics, Monsah University

Species membership in Homo-sapiens is not morally relevant. If we compare a dog or a pig to a severely defective infant, we often find the non-human to have superior capacities.[6] (emphasis added)

Esther Langston, professor of social work, University of Nevada, Las Vegas

What we are saying is that abortion becomes one of the choices, and the person has the right to choose whatever it is that is best that they need as necessary and best for them in the situation for which they find themselves, be it abortion, to keep, to adopt, *to sell, to leave in a dumpster,* to put on your porch, whatever; it's the person's right to choose.[7] (emphasis added)

Michael Tooley, professor of philosophy, University of Western Australia

Since it is virtually certain that *an infant* at such a stage of its development does not possess the concept of a continuing self, and thus *does not possess a serious right to life, there is excellent reason to believe that infanticide is morally permissible* in most cases where it is otherwise desirable.[8] (emphasis added)

James Watson, Nobel Prize laureate

Because of the present limits of such detection methods, most birth defects are not discovered until birth . . . *If a child was not declared alive until three days after birth, then all parents could be allowed the choice . . . the doctor could allow the child to die if the parents so choose* and save a lot of misery and suffering.[9] (emphasis added)

Beverly Harrison, professor of Christian ethics, Union Theological Seminary

Infanticide is not a great wrong. I do not want to be construed as condemning women who, under certain circumstances, quietly put their infants to death.[10]

Leading Abortion-Rights Activists Reveal a Contempt for Pregnancy, Motherhood, and Romance

Alison Jaggar, Wilson Professor of Ethics, University of Cincinnati

We do not, after all, elevate "prostate leave" into a special right of men.[11]

Both men and women might be outraged at the description of their candlelight dinner as *prostitution,* but the radical feminist argues this outrage is due simply to the participant's failure or refusal to perceive the social context in which their dinner date occurs.[12] (emphasis added)

Mary S. Calderone, M.D., head of the Sex Information and Education Council of the United States (SIECUS) and former president and medical director of Planned Parenthood Federation of America

We have yet to beat our drums for birth control in the way we beat them for polio vaccine, *we are still unable to put babies in the class of dangerous epidemics, even though this is the exact truth.*[13]

Warren Hern, M. D., abortionist and an author in Planned Parenthood's journal Family Planning Perspectives

[Pregnancy] may be defined as a disease . . . [and] . . . treated by evacuation of the uterine contents.[14]

Jeffner Allen, feminist philosopher

A mother is she whose body is used as a resource to reproduce men and the world of men. . . . Motherhood is dangerous to women because it continues the structure within which females must be women and mothers . . . it denies to females the creation of a . . . world that is open and free.[15]

Catherine MacKinnon, professor of law, University of Michigan Law School

Feminism stresses the indistinguishability of prostitution, marriage, and sexual harrassment.

Compare victims reports of rape with women's reports of sex. They look a lot alike. . . . In this light *the major distinction between intercourse (normal) and rape (abnormal) is that the normal happens so often that one cannot see anyting wrong with it.*[16]

Some Abortion-Rights Supporters Deny That It Is Possible to Make Objective Moral Judgments about Sexual Behavior

Dr. Sol Gordon, Institute for Family Research and Education

All thoughts, all wishes, all dreams, all fantasies are normal! If you have a thought you're quite guilty about, you'll have that thought over and over again until it becomes a self-fulfilling prophecy. If I walk down the street and I see a pretty girl that captures my fancy, I have sex with her. Now, the girl doesn't know about it, my wife doesn't know about it, and it enhances my walk. I don't want to think that's my total repertoire, because it isn't. *I have all kinds of thoughts about men and women—and animals. Why is that funny? Who has never had a thought about an animal, stand up!*[17] (emphasis added).

From SIECUS position statements

Sexual Orientation

It is the right of all persons to enter into relationships with others regardless of their gender, and to engage in such sexual behaviors as are satisfying and nonexploitive.

Explicit sexual materials

The use of explicit sexual materials (sometimes referred to as pornography) can serve a variety of important needs in the lives of countless individuals and should be made available to adults who wish to have them.[18]

Some Abortion-Rights Supporters, Who Claim to Espouse Choice, Find Nothing Wrong with Compulsory Abortion

Molly Yard, past president of the National Organization for Women, in response to a question on the "Oprah Winfrey Show" concerning Red China's policy of compulsory abortion for some couples who already have one child

I consider *the Chinese government's policy among the most intelligent in the world. It is a policy limited to the overpopulated areas and it is an attempt to feed the people of China. I find it very intelligent.*[19] (emphasis added)

Alan Guttmacher, M. D., former president of Planned Parenthood Federation of America

Abortion and sterilization on request should certainly be introduced *before family-size coercian is attempted.*[20] (emphasis added)

Some Defenders of Abortion-Rights Argue That Women Should Not Have the Choice to Marry and Raise a Family

Simone de Beauvoir, existentialist philosopher, acknowledged founder of modern feminism, and author of The Second Sex

No woman should be authorized to stay at home and raise her children . . . Women *should not have the choice,* precisely because if there is such a choice, too many women will make that one.[21] (emphasis added)

Vivian Gornick, feminist author

Being a housewife is an illegitimate profession . . . the choice to serve and be protected and plan towards *being a family maker is a choice that shouldn't be.* The heart of radical feminism is to change that.[22] (emphasis added)

"The Declaration of Feminism" (November 1971)

Marriage has existed for the benefit of men; and has been a legally sanctioned method of control over women. . . . *We must work to destroy it. The end of the institution of marriage is a necessary condition for the liberation of women.* Therefore it is important for us to encourage women to leave their husbands and not to live individually with men. . . . All of history must be rewritten in terms of oppression of women. We must go back to ancient female religions like witchcraft.[23] (emphasis added)

Some Abortion-Rights Proponents Argue, and Others Seem to Implicitly Allow, for Children Legally Being Permitted to Engage in Sex with Other Children and Adults, Including Incest.[24]

Mary S. Calderone, M.D., head of the Sex Information and Education Council of the United States (SIECUS) and former president and medical director of Planned Parenthood Federation of America

The child has a fundamental right to know about sexuality and to be sexual.[25]

John Money, sexologist, Johns Hopkins University, and founding member of SIECUS

A childhood sexual experience, such as being the partner of a relative or of an older person, need not necessarily affect the child adversely. . . . It is almost certain that human beings, like the other primates, require a period of early sexual rehearsal play.[26]

Douglas Powell, psychologist, Harvard Health Service

I have not seen anyone harmed by this [i.e., child sex] so long as it occurs in a relationship with somebody who really cares about the child.[27]

Larry Constantine, family therapist, Tufts University; board of consultants, Penthouse/Forum Magazine:

Children really are a disenfranchised minority. They should have the right to express themselves sexually which means that they may or may not have contact with people older than themselves.[28]

Many Abortion-Rights Activists Are Sexist, Since They Believe That Without Abortion (a Form of Corrective Surgery) Women Are Naturally Inferior to Men

Kate Michelman, president of the National Abortion Rights Action League (NARAL)

We have to remind people that abortion is the guarantor of a woman's . . . right to participate fully in the social and political life of society.[29]

Nancy S. Erickson, abortion-rights attorney

This right [to abortion], of necessity *must* be absolute, for if it is not, women will never truly have the ability to plan and to control their own lives.[30]

Laurence Tribe, Tyler Professor of Constitutional Law, Harvard Law School

Laws restricting abortion so dramatically shape the lives of women, and only of women, that their denial of equality hardly needs detailed elaboration. While men retain the right to sexual and reproductive autonomy, restrictions on abortion deny that autonomy to women. *Laws restricting access to abortion thereby place a real and substantial burden on women's ability to participate in society as equals.*[31] (emphasis added)

Justice Harry Blackmun, United States Supreme Court, author of the majority opinion in Roe v. Wade

[T]he plurality [in *Webster v. Reproductive Health Services,* 1989] discards a landmark case of the last generation [*Roe v. Wade*], and casts into darkness the hopes and visions of every woman in this country who had come to believe that the Constitution guaranteed her the right to exercise some control over her unique ability to bear children. The plurality does so either oblivious or insensitive to the fact that millions of women, and their families, have ordered their lives around the right to reproductive choice, and that *this right has become vital to the full participation of women in the economic and political walks of American life.*[32] (emphasis added)

Postscript

A recent nationwide advertisement by Planned Parenthood Federation of America called those who opposed the organization's desire to keep abortion on demand legal as "extremists" and purveyors of a "holy war."[33] The ad concludes with the statement, "If the extremists win, the whole world loses." For once, I agree with Planned Parenthood. But after reviewing the "choice quotes" can anyone doubt who are the extremists and who has the unholy motives?

Socrates Meets Dukakis

The following is a dialogue, summarizing and distilling many of the arguments covered in this book, that originally appeared in the *Las Vegas Review Journal* (October 30, 1988). It was inspired by a series of fictional books (by Boston College philosophy professor Peter Kreeft) about the possible dialogues of a Socrates who arrives in the twentieth century. This imaginary dialogue is between the Greek philosopher and 1988 Democratic presidential candidate Michael Dukakis on the abortion issue.

* * *

Dukakis greets Socrates at Harvard University, October 1988:

Dukakis: Socrates, what are you doing at Harvard? Aren't you a bit too old for even graduate school? (Socrates would be 2,457 years old.)

Socrates: Not at all. Nobody, neither you nor I, is too old to learn.

D: I agree.

S: In that case, you may be able to teach me a thing or two about something of which you obviously have great wisdom: abortion and the sanctity of prenatal life.

D: I'm flattered, Socrates, but please explain.

S: You have expressed on numerous occasions that you are in favor of a woman's right to an abortion for any reason the woman deems fit. Yet recently you unveiled your $100-million-a-year federally funded prenatal program.

Now my question is this—and I'm surprised your modern-day Sophists, the media, have not asked it: If abortion is not the taking of prenatal human life, and given the fact that persons are of greater value than nonpersons, then the moral worth of your proposed program is undermined because you are in fact asking real persons (taxpayers) to sacrifice a portion of their incomes for the care of nonpersons, who in another context (abortion) possess no inherent sanctity; that is,

they can be arbitrarily exterminated by the women whose bodies serve as a temporary environment for them.

On the other hand, if abortion is the taking of prenatal human life, then your proposal for prenatal care seems to imply that the unborn do possess inherent sanctity, and therefore, a woman's choice to have an abortion is tantamount to murder. How do you reconcile this apparent contradiction?

D: An excellent question, but somewhat misguided. My position has always been that if a woman truly wants a child the government should provide the best prenatal and natal care possible, but if she does not want the child the government should provide her with the financial means by which to exercise her reproductive rights, namely, to have an abortion. Hence, Socrates, my position is perfectly consistent.

S: So the only difference between the wanted and the unwanted is that the one is wanted and the other one is not. And this obviously determines the superior worth of the former?

D: Yes.

S: So if a white racist, such as Archie Bunker, does not want a black family, such as the Jeffersons, to move in his neighborhood, then the black family has less worth than the white family that Archie would prefer to move in.

D: That's ridiculous! A person's worth is independent of what you or I think. After all, our Declaration of Independence talks about "inalienable rights endowed to us by our Creator."

S: Hence, your response to my initial question on abortion must be inadequate because, like Archie, you thought that "wantedness" determined worth.

D: To a certain extent, except in the case of Archie's racism, you are talking about treating real persons badly. A fetus may be genetically a human being, but it is certainly not a person.

S: Why do you say that?

D: A person is a self-conscious reflective individual who communicates socially with other persons by using language. A fetus does not possess these characteristics.

S: Neither do you when you are asleep or unconscious. When you are asleep or unconscious you are neither reflectively self-conscious nor do you communicate socially with other persons. Hence, there must be something wrong with your definition of personhood.

D: Could you elaborate?

S: Are you a lawyer?

D: Yes. Harvard grad. Card-carrying member of the ACLU.

S: You are not now functioning as a lawyer although you are a lawyer. You are neither in court, seeing a client, nor writing a brief. Yet you are still a lawyer.

D: Yes.

S: Do you see my point? Just as your functioning or not functioning as a lawyer is irrelevant to the fact of whether you are a lawyer, a person is a person regardless of whether he is functioning in that capacity although he possesses the potential to do so—and unborn humans obviously possess this potential.

D: That is all philosophically thought-provoking, but, Socrates, the fact that we disagree means that nobody knows what a person really is. Therefore, abortion is justified.

S: So if someone enters your house at night, and you're not sure whether it's a prowler or your teenage daughter arriving from a late party, you are justified in shooting whoever it is on the assumption that it may be a prowler?

D: No, of course not.

S: Why not?

D: I could be wrong. It may not be a prowler.

S: Applying this to abortion, can't we now say that the fact that we are not sure whether a fetus is a person is not a good reason for justifying abortion?

D: You Moral Majority types just want to impose your morality on others.

S: Are you accusing me of imposing my social morality on people by taking from them yearly $100 million because I think it is their moral obligation to fund other people's prenatal needs?

D: That's a cheap shot, Socrates. You're making fun of me.

S: On the contrary, you call me a moral majoritarian when in fact it was your social policy we were discussing. A policy I hope to Zeus is the most moral, or otherwise why would you want the rest of your fellow citizens to financially contribute with their tax dollars?

D: Socrates, I have to run. I have to debate George Bush, although you have been excellent practice.

S: Practice? Weren't we trying to find the truth?

D: Truth is just ideology.

S: Do you think that is true?

D: Uh? Well, good luck at Harvard this spring.

S: You'll be living so close, maybe we can go see some Celtic games together in February?

Defense of Legal Abortion Ignores Logic

The following article originally appeared in the *Las Vegas Review-Journal* (August 10, 1989). It is written in response to an article written in the the same newspaper by a southern Nevada obstetrician who owns an abortion clinic, Sol DeLee. DeLee defended abortion rights with many of the arguments we critiqued in this book. My response to DeLee is for the most part a brief summary of the logical problems of popular arguments for abortion rights we dealt with in chapters 4 and 5 of this book. I included this article to show the reader how to logically analyze and critically evaluate abortion-rights rhetoric in newspaper style.

Dr. Sol DeLee's defense of abortion rights (Nevada Views, July 30) was one of the more articulate, well-written pieces on this topic I have ever read.

DeLee reassures the reader that although he performs abortions, he is much more fond of childbirth. This is a very impressive and delightful fact about the doctor's personal psychology but has nothing do with the moral legitimacy of either performing or undergoing an abortion. For this reason, I will ignore DeLee's personal feelings about abortion and deal with his arguments for keeping abortion on demand legal.

I define "abortion on demand" as the view that a pregnant woman should have the choice to have an abortion for any reason she deems fit throughout the entire nine months of pregnancy.

From a logical point of view, DeLee's article is seriously flawed. He continually commits the fallacy of begging the question, which occurs when one assumes what one is trying to prove without providing any evidence or proof for that assumption.

First, DeLee argues that prior to legal abortion, women resorted to unscrupulous doctors who performed illegal abortions on them, and consequently they were harmed.

If the unborn are not fully human, DeLee has a legitimate concern. But if the unborn are fully human, his argument is tantamount to saying that because people die or are harmed while killing other people, the state should make it safe for them to do so. Hence, only by assuming that the unborn are not fully human does DeLee's argument work. Therefore, he begs the question.

Second, DeLee argues that women who did not go to unscrupulous doctors traveled to foreign nations where abortions were legal. This was an option open only for rich women who could afford such an expense.

Presumably he believes present abortion laws make the current situation fairer for poor women. But such an argument is fallacious, for it assumes abortion is a moral good that poor women were denied. But since the morality of abortion is the point under question, DeLee assumes what he is trying to prove and therefore begs the question.

Since equal opportunity to eliminate an innocent human being cannot be a moral good, the question of whether it is fair that certain rich people will have privileged access to abortion must be answered after we answer the question of whether abortion is in fact not the killing of an innocent human life. To bypass this question by appealing to "fairness" is silly.

Third, DeLee makes much of both the use of abortion as a means of population control and the financial and emotional burden a child may put on a family. However, if the unborn are fully human, then this is also a good argument for infanticide and the killing of all humans we find to be financially burdensome and emotionally taxing.

Therefore, only by assuming the unborn are not fully human does DeLee escape such horrendous consequences. Thus in order for his argument to "work," he must rely on fallacious reasoning.

Throughout his article, DeLee seems to confuse the concept of "finding a solution" with the concept of "eliminating a problem."

For example, one can eliminate poverty by executing all poor people, but this would not solve the problem, since it would directly conflict with a basic moral truth that human beings should not be gratuitously exterminated for the sake of easing economic tension . . . [T]his "solution" would undermine the very moral sentiments that ground our compassion for poor people—namely, that they are humans of great worth and should be treated with dignity regardless of their predicament.

Therefore, all of DeLee's arguments are superfluous unless he can show that the unborn are not fully human and hence do not deserve to be the recipients of our basic moral sentiments.

Fourth, DeLee argues that pro-lifers are trying to force their morality on others. Once again, he begs the question.

If the unborn are not fully human, then DeLee is correct in saying that pro-lifers are trying to force their morality on the woman who wants an abortion. But if the unborn are fully human, a woman receiving an abortion is infringing upon the right to life of an unborn human, and is thus forcing her morality upon another.

Therefore, unless DeLee assumes that the unborn are not fully human, his argument does not fly. Hence, the question of whose morality is being forced upon whom hinges on the status of the unborn.

Fifth, DeLee presents one sentence to show that the unborn are not fully human: "But up to about twenty-four weeks, such [the unborn entity] is incapable of having an extrauterine existence (it is nonviable), and one can argue it is not really a human being with the rights of a fully developed person, any more than was the single-celled egg just after it was penetrated by a single-celled sperm."

Instead of trying to argue for this thesis—that viability is the chief factor for determining full humanness (which is the underlying assumption behind all his arguments)—DeLee merely assumes its truth and goes on to write that "from this point forward one can get into a philosophical harangue that would be tedious, endless . . . and pointless in this treatise." What a fascinating concession. DeLee admits that because the task is much too tedious, he cannot be bothered with dealing with the question of when full humanness is attained.

This means that he goes on performing abortions with unmoved and admitted ignorance as to the full humanness of the entity being exterminated. If game hunters shot at rustling bushes with the same philosophical mind-set, the National Rifle Association's membership would become severely depleted.

Ignorance of a being's status is certainly not justification to kill.

"The Euphemisms of Abortion Hide the Crime"
Michael Bauman, Ph.D., professor of theology and culture
Hillsdale College (Hillsdale, Michigan)

The following article is a brief expose of the pro-abortion movement's manipulation and misuse of language. The original version of it appeared in the *Orange County Register* (9 January, 1989).

Language is a weapon. In the hands of a skilled wordsmith, it can sensitize people's consciences to injustice and motivate them to heroic virtue and reform. A propagandist, by contrast, can apply it as the verbal veneer needed to camouflage some wildly horrific crime under apparent respectability. When the Nazis, for example, resorted to genocidal barbarism in their quest for a "purer" race and nation, they called on their word warriors to help them cloak their wickedness in terms of decency in order to make the unspeakable speakable. Dachau and Buchenwald were painted with the brush of inoffensive clinical jargon. "We have implemented," the Nazis said, "the final solution."

Whereas great evils are often disguised by clinical language, accurate words call the ghosts out of the closet. That is why we must learn to call things by their real names. That is why we must beware of every euphemism.

But, even now, decades after Hitler, we fail to speak plainly.

We hide the fetal holocaust that surrounds us every day just as effectively as the Nazis hid their extermination of the Jews. And we do it the same way. We cannot bring ourselves to utter the "M" word, though we commit the "M" act. That is, we do not murder unborn children, we "abort fetuses." That terminology, we wrongly believe, helps to remove our heinous deeds from the realm of the morally reprehensible. It allows us to view ourselves and our neighbors with more self-respect and ethical complacency. After all, that nice young woman next door would never pay her doctor a handsome sum to murder her unborn baby. That is unthinkable. She merely aborted her fetus because she did not want to sentence her inconvenient offspring to a life of poverty. Described in less graphic and less accurate terms, to murder her child seems not only not evil, it seems downright virtuous.

Beware of every euphemism.

Some of the more squeamish among us are unable even to say the "A" word. Though by aborting fetuses rather than murdering babies our linguistic sleight of hand has hidden the real nature of our action (murder) and the real identity of our victim (baby), some people require a still heavier dose of verbal opium. We must tell them they are merely "terminating a pregnancy," which eliminates overt reference to any living thing. Unlike fetuses and children, which are undeniably alive, and unlike abortion and murder, which seem to imply nasty things like blood and death, simply to terminate a pregnancy sounds as innocuous as ending a radio transmission or pulling into the station after a pleasant railroad journey.

If "terminating pregnancies" is still too overt a verbal description because the word *pregnant* tends to evoke unfortunate images of happy women large with child, we can hide the crime behind an even more impersonal wall of words. We can say that the murdering of unborn children is nothing more than the voluntary extraction of the "product of conception," or, as nearly all abortion clinics have it, "removing the POC." What could be more innocent.

Nearly everything.

Beware of every euphemism.

Pleasant words can be a fraud. A sterile idiom can be a defense mechanism behind which we conceal the grossest reality. But defense mechanisms do not change that reality. They merely disguise it. The evil facts themselves remain the same. Never forget that the disease you hide you cannot heal. For jargon wizards like us, therefore, there remains no therapy.

Rather than facing the facts and owning up to this great wickedness for what it is, rather than calling an unconditional halt to the war we wage on our unborn young, rather than confessing our guilt and casting ourselves on the immense mercy of God, we mask our shame behind a veil of words and sell our souls to the verbal charlatans who tell us what we want. Beware of every euphemism.

A murder by any other name . . .

A List of Pro-Life Organizations

The following is a list of the addresses of leading pro-life organizations. I encourage the reader who is interested in pro-life involvement to contact one of these organizations. These organizations are able to provide the reader with further information about the abortion debate. This list is by no means exhaustive.

Advocates for Life
P.O. Box 13656
Portland, OR 97213

After Abortion Helpline
P.O. Box 28633
Providence, RI 02908

American Life League
P.O. Box 1350
Stafford, VA 22554

American Victims of Abortion
419 7th St. N.W., #402
Washington, DC 20004

Americans Against Abortion
P.O. Box 40
Lindale, TX 75771

Americans United for Life
343 S. Dearborn, Suite 1804
Chicago, IL 60604

Birthright
11235 S. Western Ave.
Chicago, IL 60643

Black Americans for Life
419 7th St. NW, #500
Washington, DC 20004

CARE
709B Investment Building
Pittsburgh, PA 15222

Christian Action Council
101 W. Broad St., Suite 500
Falls Church, VA 22046

Community to Protect the Family Foundation
8001 Forbes Pl., Suite 102
Springfield, VA 22151

Concerned Women for America
122 C. St., NW, Suite 800
Washington, DC 20001

Conquerors
New Life Homes and Family Service
3361 Republic Ave., #201
Minneapolis, MN 55426

Eagle Forum
P.O. Box 618
Alton, IL 62002

Family Reseach Council
515 Second St., NE
Washington, DC 20002

Fathers for Life
Fathers' Rights Legal Services
3623 Douglas Ave.
Des Moines, IA 50310

Feminists for Life
811 East 47th Street
Kansas City, MO 64110

Focus on the Family
Colorado Springs, CO 80995

Free Congress Reseach and Education Foundation
721 Second St., NE
Washington, DC 20002

Heart Light
P.O. Box 8513
Green Bay, WI 54038

Help Services Women's Center
P.O. Box 1141
Humble, TX 77338

Human Life Foundation
150 E. 35th St.
New York, NY 10157

Human Life International
7845-E Airpark Rd.
Gaithersburg, MD 20879

Libertarians for Life
13424 Hathaway Drive
Wheaton, MD 20906

Liberty Federation
505 Second St., NE
Washington, DC 20002

Liberty Godparent Foundation
P.O. Box 27000
Lynchburg, VA 24506

Life Cycle Books
P.O. Box 420
Lewiston, NY 14092

LifeNet
P.O. Box 185066
Fort Worth, TX 76181-0066

March for Life
P.O. Box 90300
Washington, DC 20090

March for Life Education and Defense Fund
P.O. Box 90330
Washington, DC 20090

National Right to Life Committee
419 7th St., NW #402
Washington, DC 20004

Open Arms
P.O. Box 7188
Federal Way, WA 98003

Operation Blessing
CBN Center
Virginia Beach, VA 23463

Operation Rescue
P.O. Box 1180
Binghamton, NY 13902

Orthodox Christians for Life
P.O. Box 805
Melville, NY 11747

PACE
701 W. Broad St., Suite 405
Falls Church, VA 22046

Project Rachel
c/o Respect Life Office
Archdiocese of Millwaukee
P.O. Box 2018
Millwaukee, WI 53201

Pro-Life Action League
6160 N. Cicero Ave., #600
Chicago, IL 60646

Pro-Life Action Ministries
1163 Payne
St. Paul, MN 55101

RETURN
Joliet Diocesan Life Center
Route 53 & Airport Rd.
Romeoville, IL 60441

The Rutherford Institute
P.O. Box 7482
Charlottsville, VA 22906-7482

Sex Respect
P.O. Box 349
Bradley, IL 60915

University Faculty for Life (UFL)
Box 2273
Georgetown University
Washington, DC 20057

Why Wait?
P.O. Box 1000
Dallas, TX 75221

Women Exploited by Abortion (WEBA)
National Headquarters
24823 Nogal Street
Moreno Valley, CA 92388

Planned Parenthood v. *Casey* (1992)

The following is an abridged version of the U. S. Supreme Court's reaffirmation of *Roe v. Wade*, *Planned Parenthood v. Casey* (1992). It contains the Court's opinion, as authored by Justices O'Connor, Kennedy, and Souter, as well as the dissenting opinions of Chief Justice Rehnquist and Justice Scalia. The opinions of Justices Blackmun and Stevens have been edited from this republication for the sake of brevity.

Justice O'Connor, Justice Kennedy, and Justice Souter announced the judgment of the Court and delivered the opinion of the Court with respect to Parts I, II, III, V-A, V-C, and VI, an opinion with respect to Part V-E, in which Justice Stevens joins, and an opinion with respect to Parts IV, V-B, and V-D.

I

Liberty finds no refuge in a jurisprudence of doubt. Yet 19 years after our holding that the Constitution protects a woman's right to terminate her pregnancy in its early stages, *Roe v. Wade*, 410 U. S. 113 (1973), that definition of liberty is still questioned. Joining the respondents as *amicus curiae*, the United States, as it has done in five other cases in the last decade, again asks us to overrule *Roe*. See Brief for Respondents 104–117; Brief for United States as *Amicus Curiae* 8.

At issue in these cases are five provisions of the Pennsylvania Abortion Control Act of 1982 as amended in 1988 and 1989. 18 Pa. Cons. Stat. §§3203–3220 (1990). Relevant portions of the Act are set forth in the appendix. *Infra*, at 60. The Act requires that a woman seeking an abortion give her informed consent prior to the abortion procedure, and specifies that she be provided with certain information at least 24 hours before the abortion is performed. §3205. For a minor to obtain an abortion, the Act requires the informed consent of one of her parents, but provides for a judicial by-

pass option if the minor does not wish to or cannot obtain a parent's consent. §3206. Another provision of the Act requires that, unless certain exceptions apply, a married woman seeking an abortion must sign a statement indicating that she has notified her husband of her intended abortion. §3209. The Act exempts compliance with these three requirements in the event of a "medical emergency," which is defined in §3203 of the Act. See §§3203, 3205(a), 3206(a), 3209(c). In addition to the above provisions regulating the performance of abortions, the Act imposes certain reporting requirements on facilities that provide abortion services. §§3207(b), 3214(a), 3214(f).

Before any of these provisions took effect, the petitioners, who are five abortion clinics and one physician representing himself as well as a class of physicians who provide abortion services, brought this suit seeking declaratory and injunctive relief. Each provision was challenged as unconstitutional on its face. The District Court entered a preliminary injunction against the enforcement of the regulations, and, after a 3-day bench trial, held all the provisions at issue here unconstitutional, entering a permanent injunction against Pennsylvania's enforcement of them. 744 F. Supp. 1323 (ED Pa. 1990). The Court of Appeals for the Third Circuit affirmed in part and reversed in part, upholding all of the regulations except for the husband notification requirement. 947 F. 2d 682 (1991). We granted certiorari. 502 U. S. ____ (1992).

The Court of Appeals found it necessary to follow an elaborate course of reasoning even to identify the first premise to use to determine whether the statute enacted by Pennsylvania meets constitutional standards. See 947 F. 2d, at 687–698. And at oral argument in this Court, the attorney for the parties challenging the statute took the position that none of the enactments can be upheld without overruling *Roe v. Wade.* Tr. of Oral Arg. 5–6. We disagree with that analysis; but we acknowledge that our decisions after *Roe* cast doubt upon the meaning and reach of its holding. Further, the CHIEF JUSTICE admits that he would overrule the central holding of *Roe* and adopt the rational relationship test as the sole criterion of constitutionality. See *post,* at ____. State and federal courts as well as legislatures throughout the Union must have guidance as they seek to address this subject in conformance with the Constitution. Given these premises, we find it imperative to review once more the principles that define the rights of the woman and the legitimate authority of the State respecting the termination of pregnancies by abortion procedures.

After considering the fundamental constitutional questions resolved by *Roe,* principles of institutional integrity, and the rule of *stare decisis,* we are led to conclude this: the essential holding of *Roe v. Wade* should be retained and once again reaffirmed.

It must be stated at the outset and with clarity that *Roe's* essential holding, the holding we affirm, has three parts. First is a recognition of the right of the woman to choose to have an abortion before viability and to obtain it without undue interference from the State. Before viability, the State's interests are not strong enough to support a prohibition of abortion or the imposition of a substantial obstacle to the woman's effective right to elect the procedure. Second is a confirmation of the State's power to restrict abortions after fetal viability, if the law contains exceptions for pregnancies which endanger a woman's life or health. And third is the principle that the State has legitimate interests from the outset of the pregnancy in protecting the health of the woman and the life of the fetus that may become a child. These principles do not contradict one another; and we adhere to each.

II

Constitutional protection of the woman's decision to terminate her pregnancy derives from the Due Process Clause of the Fourteenth Amendment. It declares that no State shall "deprive any person of life, liberty, or property, without due process of law." The controlling word in the case before us is "liberty." Although a literal reading of the Clause might suggest that it governs only the procedures by which a State may deprive persons of liberty, for at least 105 years, at least since *Mugler v. Kansas,* 123 U. S. 623, 660–661 (1887), the Clause

has been understood to contain a substantive component as well, one "barring certain government actions regardless of the fairness of the procedures used to implement them." *Daniels v. Williams,* 474 U. S. 327, 331 (1986). As Justice Brandeis (joined by Justice Holmes) observed, "[d]espite arguments to the contrary which had seemed to me persuasive, it is settled that the due process clause of the Fourteenth Amendment applies to matters of substantive law as well as to matters of procedure. Thus all fundamental rights comprised within the term liberty are protected by the Federal Constitution from invasion by the States." *Whitney v. California,* 274 U. S. 357, 373 (1927) (Brandeis, J., concurring). "[T]he guaranties of due process, though having their roots in Magna Carta's '*per legem terrae*' and considered as procedural safeguards 'against executive usurpation and tyranny,' have in this country 'become bulwarks also against arbitrary legislation.'" *Poe v. Ullman,* 367 U. S. 497, 541 (1961) (Harlan, J., dissenting from dismissal on jurisdictional grounds) (quoting *Hurtado v. California,* 110 U. S. 516, 532 (1884).

The most familiar of the substantive liberties protected by the Fourteenth Amendment are those recognized by the Bill of Rights. We have held that the Due Process Clause of the Fourteenth Amendment incorporates most of the Bill of Rights against the States. See, *e.g., Duncan v. Louisiana,* 391 U. S. 145, 147–148 (1968). It is tempting, as a means of curbing the discretion of federal judges, to suppose that liberty encompasses no more than those rights already guaranteed to the individual against federal interference by the express provisions of the first eight amendments to the Constitution. See *Adamson v. California,* 332 U. S. 46, 68–92 (1947) (Black, J., dissenting). But of course this Court has never accepted that view.

It is also tempting, for the same reason, to suppose that the Due Process Clause protects only those practices, defined at the most specific level, that were protected against government interference by other rules of law when the Fourteenth Amendment was ratified. See *Michael H. v. Gerald D.,* 491 U. S. 110, 127–128, n. 6 (1989) (opinion of SCALIA, J.). But such a view would be inconsistent with our law. It is a promise of the Constitution that there is a realm of personal liberty which the government may not enter. We have vindicated this principle before. Marriage is mentioned nowhere in the Bill of Rights and interracial marriage was illegal in most States in the 19th century, but the Court was no doubt correct in finding it to be an aspect of liberty protected against state interference by the substantive component of the Due Process Clause in *Loving v. Virginia*, 388 U. S. 1, 12 (1967) (relying, in an opinion for eight Justices, on the Due Process Clause). Similar examples may be found in *Turner v. Safley*, 482 U. S. 78, 94–99 (1987); in *Carey v. Population Services International*, 431 U. S. 678, 684–686 (1977); in *Griswold v. Connecticut*, 381 U. S. 479, 481–482 (1965), as well as in the separate opinions of a majority of the Members of the Court in that case, *id.*, at 486–488 (Goldberg J., joined by Warren, C. J., and Brennan, J., concurring) (expressly relying on due process), *id.*, at 500–502 (Harlan, J., concurring in judgment) (same), *id.*, at 502–507 (WHITE, J., concurring in judgment) (same); in *Pierce v. Society of Sisters,*, 268 U. S. 510, 534–535 (1925); and in *Meyer v. Nebraska*, 262 U. S. 390, 399–403 (1923).

Neither the Bill of Rights nor the specific practices of States at the time of the adoption of the Fourteenth Amendment marks the outer limits of the substantive sphere of liberty which the Fourteenth Amendment protects. See U. S. Const., Amend. 9. As the second Justice Harlan recognized:

"[T]he full scope of the liberty guaranteed by the Due Process Clause cannot be found in or limited by the precise terms of the specific guarantees elsewhere provided in the Constitution. This 'liberty' is not a series of isolated points pricked out in terms of the taking of property; the freedom of speech, press, and religion; the right to keep and bear arms; the freedom from unreasonable searches and seizures; and so on. It is a rational continuum which, broadly speaking, includes a freedom from all substantial arbitrary impositions and purposeless restraints, . . . and which also recognizes, what a reasonable and sensitive judgment must, that certain interests require particularly careful scrutiny of the state needs asserted to justify their abridgment." *Poe v. Ullman, supra*, at 543 (Harlan, J., dissenting from dismissal on jurisdictional grounds).

Justice Harlan wrote these words in addressing an issue the full Court did not reach in *Poe v. Ullman*, but the Court adopted his position four Terms later in *Griswold v. Connecticut, supra*. In *Griswold*, we held that the Constitution does not permit a State to forbid a married couple to use contraceptives. That same freedom was later guaranteed, under the Equal Protection Clause, for unmarried couples. See *Eisenstadt v. Baird*, 405 U. S. 438 (1972).

Constitutional protection was extended to the sale and distribution of contraceptives in *Carey v. Population Services International, supra*. It is settled now, as it was when the Court heard arguments in *Roe v. Wade*, that the Constitution places limits on a State's right to interfere with a person's most basic decisions about family and parenthood, See *Carey v. Population Services International, supra; Moore v. East Cleveland*, 431 U. S. 494 (1977); *Eisenstadt v. Baird, supra; Loving v. Virginia, supra; Griswold v. Connecticut, supra; Skinner v. Oklahoma ex rel. Williamson*, 316 U. S. 535 (1942); *Pierce v. Society of Sisters, supra; Meyer v. Nebraska, supra*, as well as bodily integrity. See, *e.g., Washington v. Harper*, 494 U. S. 210, 221–222 (1990); *Winston v. Lee*, 470 U. S. 753 (1985); *Rochin v. California*, 342 U. S. 165 (1952).

The inescapable fact is that adjudication of substantive due process claims may call upon the Court in interpreting the Constitution to exercise that same capacity which by tradition courts always have exercised: reasoned judgment. Its boundaries are not susceptible of expression as a simple rule. That does not mean we are free to invalidate state policy choices with which we disagree; yet neither does it permit us to shrink from the duties of our office. As Justice Harlan observed:

"Due process has not been reduced to any formula; its content cannot be determined by reference to any code. The best that can be said is that through the course of this Court's decisions it has represented the balance which our Nation, built upon postulates of respect for the liberty of the individual, has struck between that liberty and the demands of organized society. If the supplying of content to this Constitutional concept has of necessity been a rational process, it certainly has not been one where judges have felt free to roam where unguided speculation might take them. The balance of which I speak is the balance struck by this country, having regard to what history teaches are the traditions from which it developed as well as the traditions from which it broke. That tradition is a living thing. A decision of this Court which radically departs from it could not long survive, while a decision which builds on what has survived is likely to be sound. No formula could serve as a substitute, in this area, for judgment and restraint." *Poe v. Ullman*, 367 U. S., at 542 (Harlan, J., dissenting from dismissal on jurisdictional grounds).

See also *Rochin v. California, supra,* at 171–172 (Frankfurter, J., writing for the Court) ("To believe that this judicial exercise of judgment could be avoided by freezing 'due process of law' at some fixed stage of time or thought is to suggest that the most important aspect of constitutional adjudication is a function for inanimate machines and not for judges").

Men and women of good conscience can disagree, and we suppose some always shall disagree, about the profound moral and spiritual implications of terminating a pregnancy, even in its earliest stage. Some of us as individuals find abortion offensive to our most basic principles of morality, but that cannot control our decision. Our obligation is to define the liberty of all, not to mandate our own moral code. The underlying constitutional issue is whether the State can resolve these philosophic questions in such a definitive way that a woman lacks all choice in the matter, except perhaps in those rare circumstances in which the pregnancy is itself a danger to her own life or health, or is the result of rape or incest.

It is conventional constitutional doctrine that where reasonable people disagree the government can adopt one position or the other. See, *e.g., Ferguson v. Skrupa,* 372 U. S. 726 (1963); *Williamson v. Lee Optical of Oklahoma, Inc.,* 348 U. S. 483 (1955). That theorem, however, assumes a state of affairs in which the choice does not intrude upon a protected liberty. Thus, while some people might disagree about whether or not the flag should be saluted, or disagree about the proposition that it may not be defiled, we have ruled that a State may not compel or enforce one view or the other. See *West Virginia State Bd. of Education v. Barnette,* 319 U. S. 624 (1943); *Texas v. Johnson,* 491 U. S. 397 (1989).

Our law affords constitutional protection to personal decisions relating to marriage, procreation, contraception, family relationships, child rearing, and education. *Carey v. Population Services International,* 431 U. S., at 685. Our cases recognize "the right of the *individual,* married or single, to be free from unwarranted governmental intrusion into matters so fundamentally affecting a person as the decision whether to bear or beget a child." *Eisenstadt v. Baird, supra,* at 453 (emphasis in original). Our precedents "have respected the private realm of family life which the state cannot enter." *Prince v. Massachusetts,* 321 U. S. 158, 166 (1944). These matters, involving the most intimate and personal choices a person may make in a lifetime, choices central to personal dignity and autonomy, are central to the liberty protected by the Fourteenth Amendment. At the heart of liberty is the right to define one's own concept of existence, of meaning, of the universe, and of the mystery of human life. Beliefs about these matters could not define the attributes of personhood were they formed under compulsion of the State.

These considerations begin our analysis of the woman's interest in terminating her pregnancy but cannot end it, for this reason: though the abortion decision may originate within the zone of conscience and belief, it is more than a philosophic exercise. Abortion is a unique act. It is an act fraught with consequences for others: for the woman who must live with the implications of her decision; for the persons who perform and assist in the procedure; for the spouse, family, and society which must confront the knowledge that these procedures exist, procedures some deem nothing short of an act of violence against innocent human life; and, depending on one's beliefs, for the life or potential life that is aborted. Though abortion is conduct, it does not follow that the State is entitled to proscribe it in all instances. That is because the liberty of the woman is at stake in a sense unique to the human condition and so unique to the law. The mother who carries a child to full term is subject to anxieties, to physical constraints, to pain that only she must bear. That these sacrifices have from the beginning of the human race been endured by woman with a pride that ennobles her in the eyes of others and gives to the infant a bond of love cannot alone be grounds for the State to insist she make the sacrifice. Her suffering is too intimate and personal for the State to insist, without more, upon its own vision of the woman's role, however dominant that vision has been in the course of our history and our culture. The destiny of the woman must be shaped to a large extent on her own conception of her spiritual imperatives and her place in society.

It should be recognized, moreover, that in some critical respects the abortion decision is of the same character as the decision to use contraception, to which *Griswold v. Connecticut, Eisenstadt v. Baird,* and *Carey v. Population Services International,* afford constitutional protection. We have no doubt as to the correctness of those decisions. They support the reasoning in *Roe* relating to the woman's liberty because they involve personal decisions concerning not only the meaning of procreation but also human responsibility and respect for it. As with abortion, reasonable people will have differences of opinion about these matters. One view is based on such reverence for the wonder of creation that any pregnancy ought to be welcomed and carried to full term no matter how difficult it will be to provide for the child and ensure its well-being. Another is that the inability to provide for the nurture and care of the infant is a cruelty to the child and an anguish to the parent. These are intimate views with infinite variations, and their deep, personal character underlay our decisions in *Griswold, Eisenstadt,* and *Carey.* The same concerns are present when the woman confronts the reality that, perhaps despite her attempts to avoid it, she has become pregnant.

It was this dimension of personal liberty that *Roe* sought to protect, and its holding invoked the reasoning and the tradition of the precedents we have discussed, granting protection to substantive liberties of the person. *Roe* was, of course, an extension of those cases and, as the decision itself indicated, the separate States could act in some degree to further their own legitimate interests in protecting pre-natal life. The extent to which the legislatures of the States might act to outweigh the interests of the woman in choosing to terminate her pregnancy was a subject of debate both in *Roe* itself and in decisions following it.

While we appreciate the weight of the arguments made on behalf of the State in the case before us, arguments which in their ultimate formulation conclude that *Roe* should be overruled, the reservations any of us may have in reaffirming the central holding of *Roe* are outweighed by the explication of individual liberty we have given combined with the force of *stare decisis.* We turn now to that doctrine.

III

A

The obligation to follow precedent begins with necessity, and a contrary necessity marks its outer limit. With Cardozo, we recognize that no judicial system could do society's work if it eyed each issue afresh in every case that raised it. See B. Cardozo, The Nature of the Judicial Process 149 (1921). Indeed, the very concept of the rule of law underlying our own Constitution requires such continuity over time that a respect for precedent is, by definition, indispensable. See Powell, Stare Decisis and Judicial Restraint, 1991 Journal of Supreme Court History 13, 16. At the other extreme, a different necessity would make itself felt if a prior judicial ruling should come to be seen so clearly as error that its enforcement was for that very reason doomed.

Even when the decision to overrule a prior case is not, as in the rare, latter instance, virtually foreordained, it is common wisdom that the rule of *stare decisis* is not an "inexorable command," and certainly it is not such in every constitutional case, see *Burnet v. Coronado Oil Gas Co.,* 285 U. S. 393, 405–411 (1932) (Brandeis, J., dissenting). See also *Payne v. Tennessee,* 501 U. S. ___, ___ (1991) (slip op., at ___) (SOUTER, J., joined by KENNEDY, J., concurring); *Arizona v. Rumsey,* 467 U. S. 203, 212 (1984). Rather, when this Court reexamines a prior holding, its judgment is customarily informed by a series of prudential and pragmatic considerations designed to test the consistency of overruling a prior decision with the ideal of the rule of law, and to gauge the respective costs of reaffirming and overruling a prior case. Thus, for example, we may ask whether the rule has proved to be intolerable simply in defying practical workability, *Swift & Co. v. Wickham,* 382 U. S. 111, 116 (1965); whether the rule is subject to a kind of reliance that would lend a special hardship to the consequences of overruling and add inequity to the cost of repudiation, *e.g., United States v. Title Ins. & Trust Co.,* 265 U. S. 472, 486 (1924); whether related principles of law have so far developed as to have left the old rule no more than a remnant of abandoned doctrine, see *Patterson v. McLean Credit Union,* 491 U. S. 164, 173–174 (1989); or whether facts have so changed or come to be seen so differently, as to have robbed the old rule of significant application or justification, *e.g., Burnet, supra,* at 412 (Brandeis, J., dissenting).

So in this case we may inquire whether *Roe's* central rule has been found unworkable; whether the rule's limitation on state power could be removed without serious inequity to those who have relied upon it or significant damage to the stability of the society governed by the rule in question; whether the law's growth in the intervening years has left *Roe's* central rule a doctrinal anachronism discounted by society; and whether *Roe's* premises of fact have so far changed in the ensuing two decades as to render its central holding somehow irrelevant or unjustifiable in dealing with the issue it addressed.

1

Although *Roe* has engendered opposition, it has in no sense proven "unworkable," see *Garcia v. San Antonio Metropolitan Transit Authority,* 469 U. S. 528, 546 (1985), representing as it does a simple limitation beyond which a state law is unenforceable. While *Roe* has, of course, required judicial assessment of state laws affecting the exercise of the choice guaranteed against government infringement, and although the need for such review will remain as a consequence of today's decision, the required determinations fall within judicial competence.

2

The inquiry into reliance counts the cost of a rule's repudiation as it would fall on those who have relied reasonably on the rule's continued application. Since the classic case for weighing reliance heavily in favor of following the earlier rule occurs in the commercial context, see *Payne v. Tennessee, supra*, at ___ (slip op., at ___), where advance planning of great precision is most obviously a necessity, it is no cause for surprise that some would find no reliance worthy of consideration in support of *Roe*.

While neither respondents nor their *amici* in so many words deny that the abortion right invites some reliance prior to its actual exercise, one can readily imagine an argument stressing the dissimilarity of this case to one involving property or contract. Abortion is customarily chosen as an unplanned response to the consequence of unplanned activity or to the failure of conventional birth control, and except on the assumption that no intercourse would have occurred but for *Roe's* holding, such behavior may appear to justify no reliance claim. Even if reliance could be claimed on that unrealistic assumption, the argument might run, any reliance interest would be *de minimis*. This argument would be premised on the hypothesis that reproductive planning could take virtually immediate account of any sudden restoration of state authority to ban abortions.

To eliminate the issue of reliance that easily, however, one would need to limit cognizable reliance to specific instances of sexual activity. But to do this would be simply to refuse to face the fact that for two decades of economic and social developments, people have organized intimate relationships and made choices that define their views of themselves and their places in society, in reliance on the availability of abortion in the event that contraception should fail. The ability of women to participate equally in the economic and social life of the Nation has been facilitated by their ability to control their reproductive lives. See, *e.g.*, R. Petchesky, Abortion and Woman's Choice 109, 133, n. 7 (rev. ed. 1990). The Constitution serves human values, and while the effect of reliance on *Roe* cannot be exactly measured,

neither can the certain cost of overruling *Roe* for people who have ordered their thinking and living around that case be dismissed.

3

No evolution of legal principle has left *Roe's* doctrinal footings weaker than they were in 1973. No development of constitutional law since the case was decided has implicitly or explicitly left *Roe* behind as a mere survivor of obsolete constitutional thinking.

It will be recognized, of course, that *Roe* stands at an intersection of two lines of decisions, but in whichever doctrinal category one reads the case, the result for present purposes will be the same. The *Roe* Court itself placed its holding in the succession of cases most prominently exemplified by *Griswold v. Connecticut*, 381 U. S. 479 (1965), see *Roe*, 410 U. S., at 152–153. When it is so seen, *Roe* is clearly in no jeopardy, since subsequent constitutional developments have neither disturbed, nor do they threaten to diminish, the scope of recognized protection accorded to the liberty relating to intimate relationships, the family, and decisions about whether or not to beget or bear a child. See, *e.g.*, *Carey v. Population Services International*, 431 U. S. 678 (1977); *Moore v. East Cleveland*, 431 U. S. 678 (1977).

Roe, however, may be seen not only as an exemplar of *Griswold* liberty but as a rule (whether or not mistaken) of personal autonomy and bodily integrity, with doctrinal affinity to cases recognizing limits on governmental power to mandate medical treatment or to bar its rejection. If so, our cases since *Roe* accord with *Roe's* view that a State's interest in the protection of life falls short of justifying any plenary override of individual liberty claims. *Cruzan v. Director, Missouri Dept. of Health*, 497 U. S. 261, 278 (1990); Cf., *e.g.*, *Riggins v. Nevada*, 504 U. S. ___, ___ (1992) (slip. op., at 7); *Washington v. Harper*, 494 U. S. 210 (1990); see also, *e.g.*, *Rochin v. California*, 342 U. S. 165 (1952); *Jacobson v. Massachusetts*, 197 U. S. 11, 24–30 (1905).

Finally, one could classify *Roe* as *sui generis*. If the case is so viewed, then there clearly has been no erosion of its central determination. The original holding resting on the concurrence of seven Members of the Court in 1973 was expressly affirmed by a majority of six in 1983, see *Akron v. Akron Center for Reproductive Health, Inc.*, 462 U. S. 416 (1983) (*Akron I*), and by a majority of five in 1986, see *Thornburgh v. American College of Obstetricians and Gynecologists*, 476 U. S. 747 (1986), expressing adherence to the constitutional ruling despite legislative efforts in some States to test its limits. More recently, in *Webster v. Reproductive Health Services*, 492 U. S. 490 (1989), although two of the present authors questioned the trimester framework in a way consistent with our judgment today, see *id.*, at 518 (REHNQUIST C. J., joined by WHITE, and KENNEDY, JJ.); *id.*, at 529 (O'CONNOR, J., concurring in part and concurring in judgment), a majority of the Court either decided to reaffirm or declined to address the constitutional validity of the central holding of *Roe*. See *Webster*, 492 U. S., at 521 (REHNQUIST, C. J., joined by WHITE and KENNEDY, JJ.); *id.*, at 525–526 (O'CONNOR, J., concurring in part and concurring in judgment); *id.*, at 537, 553 (BLACKMUN, J. joined by Brennan and Marshall, JJ., concurring in part and dissenting in part); *id.*, at 561–563 (STEVENS, J., concurring in part and dissenting in part).

Nor will courts building upon *Roe* be likely to hand down erroneous decisions as a consequence. Even on the assumption that the central holding of *Roe* was in error, that error would go only to the strength of the state interest in fetal protection, not to the recognition afforded by the Constitution to the woman's liberty. The latter aspect of the decision fits comfortably within the framework of the Court's prior decisions including *Skinner v. Oklahoma ex rel. Williamson*, 316 U. S. 535 (1942), *Griswold, supra, Loving v. Virginia*, 388 U. S. 1 (1967), and *Eisenstadt v. Baird*, 405 U. S. 438 (1972), the holdings of which are "not a series of isolated points," but mark a "rational continuum." *Poe v. Ullman*, 367 U. S., at 543 (1961) (Harlan, J., dissenting). As we described in *Carey v. Population Services International, supra*, the liberty which encompasses those decisions

"includes 'the interest in independence in making certain kinds of important decisions.' While the outer limits of this aspect of [protected liberty] have not been marked by the Court, it is clear that among the decisions that an individual may make without unjustified government interference are personal decisions 'relating to marriage, procreation, contraception, family relationships, and child rearing and education.'" *Id.*, at 684–685 (citations omitted).

The soundness of this prong of the *Roe* analysis is apparent from a consideration of the alternative. If indeed the woman's interest in deciding whether to bear and beget a child had not been recognized as in *Roe*, the State might as readily restrict a woman's right to choose to carry a pregnancy to term as to terminate it, to further asserted state interests in population control, or eugenics, for example. Yet *Roe* has been sensibly relied upon to counter any such suggestions. *E.g., Arnold v. Board of Education of Escambia County, Ala.*, 880 F. 2d 305, 311 (CA11 1989) (relying upon *Roe* and concluding that government officials violate the Constitution by coercing a minor to have an abortion); *Avery v. County of Burke*, 660 F. 2d 111, 115 (CA4 1981) (county agency inducing teenage girl to undergo unwanted sterilization on the basis of misrepresentation that she had sickle cell trait); see also *In re Quinlan*, 70 N.J. 10, 355 A. 2d 647, cert. denied *sub nom. Garger v. New Jersey*, 429 U. S. 922 (1976) (relying on *Roe* in finding a right to terminate medical treatment). In any event, because *Roe*'s scope is confined by the fact of its concern with postconception potential life, a concern otherwise likely to be implicated only by some forms of contraception protected independently under *Griswold* and later cases, any error in *Roe* is unlikely to have serious ramifications in future cases.

4

We have seen how time has overtaken some of *Roe*'s factual assumptions: advances in maternal health care allow for abortions safe to the mother later in pregnancy than was true in 1973, see *Akron I, supra*, at 429, n. 11, and advances in neonatal care have advanced viability to a point somewhat earlier. Compare *Roe*, 410 U. S., at 160, with *Webster, supra*, at 515–516 (opinion of REHNQUIST, C.J.); see *Akron I, supra*, at 457, and n. 5 (O'CONNOR, J., dissenting). But these facts go only to the scheme of time limits on the realization of competing interests, and the divergences from the factual premises of 1973 have no bearing on the validity of *Roe*'s central holding, that viability marks the earliest point at which the State's interest in fetal life is constitutionality adequate to justify a legislative ban on nontherapeutic abortions. The soundness or unsoundness of that constitutional judgment in no sense turns on whether viability occurs at approximately 28 weeks, as was usual at the time of *Roe*, at 23 to 24 weeks, as it sometimes does today, or at some moment even slightly earlier in pregnancy, as it may if fetal respiratory capacity can somehow be enhanced in the future. Whenever it may occur, the attainment of viability may continue to serve as the critical fact, just as it has done since *Roe* was decided; which is to say that no change in *Roe*'s factual underpinning has left its central holding obsolete, and none supports an argument for overruling it.

5

The sum of the precedential inquiry to this point shows *Roe's* underpinnings unweakened in any way affecting its central holding. While it has engendered disapproval, it has not been unworkable. An entire generation has come of age free to assume *Roe's* concept of liberty in defining the capacity of women to act in society, and to make reproductive decisions; no erosion of principle going to liberty or personal autonomy has left *Roe's* central holding a doctrinal remnant; *Roe* portends no developments at odds with other precedent for the analysis of personal liberty; and no changes of fact have rendered viability more or less appropriate as the point at which the balance of interests tips. Within the bounds of normal *stare decisis* analysis, then, and subject to the considerations on which it customarily turns, the stronger argument is for affirming *Roe's* central holding, with whatever degree of personal reluctance any of us may have, not for overruling it.

B

In a less significant case, *stare decisis* analysis could, and would, stop at the point we have reached. But the sustained and widespread debate *Roe* has provoked calls for some comparison between that case and others of comparable dimension that have responded to national controversies and taken on the impress of the controversies addressed. Only two such decisional lines from the past century present themselves for examination, and in each instance the result reached by the Court accorded with the principles we apply today.

The first example is that line of cases identified with *Lochner v. New York*, 198 U. S. 45 (1905), which imposed substantive limitations on legislation limiting economic autonomy in favor of health and welfare regulation, adopting, in Justice Holmes' view, the theory of *laissez-faire. Id.*, at 75 (Holmes, J., dissenting). The *Lochner* decisions were exemplified by *Adkins v. Children's Hospital of D.C.*, 261 U. S. 525 (1923), in which this Court held it to be an infringement of constitutionally protected liberty of contract to require the employers of adult women to satisfy minimum wage standards. Fourteen years later, *West Coast Hotel Co. v. Parrish*, 300 U. S. 379 (1937), signalled the demise of *Lochner* by overruling *Adkins*. In the meantime, the De-

pression had come and, with it, the lesson that seemed unmistakable to most people by 1937, that the interpretation of contractual freedom protected in *Adkins* rested on fundamentally false factual assumptions about the capacity of a relatively unregulated market to satisfy minimal levels of human welfare. See *West Coast Hotel Co., supra*, at 399. As Justice Jackson wrote of the constitutional crisis of 1937 shortly before he came on the bench, "The older world of *laissez faire* was recognized everywhere outside the Court to be dead." R. Jackson, The Struggle for Judicial Supremacy 85 (1941). The facts upon which the earlier case had premised a constitutional resolution of social controversy had proved to be untrue, and history's demonstration of their untruth not only justified but required the new choice of constitutional principle that *West Coast Hotel* announced. Of course, it was true that the Court lost something by its misperception, or its lack of prescience, and the Court-packing crisis only magnified the loss; but the clear demonstration that the facts of economic life were different from those previously assumed warranted the repudiation of the old law.

The second comparison that 20th century history invites is with the cases employing the separate-but-equal rule for applying the Fourteenth Amendment's equal protection guarantee. They began with *Plessy v. Ferguson*, 163 U. S. 537 (1896), holding that legislatively mandated racial segregation in public transportation works no denial of equal protection, rejecting the argument that racial separation enforced by the legal machinery of American society treats the black race as inferior. The *Plessy* Court considered "the underlying fallacy of the plaintiff's argument to consist in the assumption that the enforced separation of the two races stamps the colored race with a badge of inferiority. If this be so, it is not by reason of anything found in the act, but solely because the colored race chooses to put that construction upon it." *Id.*, at 551. Whether, as a matter of historical fact, the Justices in the *Plessy* majority believed this or not, see *id.*, at 557, 562 (Harlan, J., dissenting), this understanding of the implication of segregation was the stated justification for the Court's opinion. But this understanding of the facts and the rule it was stated to justify were repudiated in *Brown v. Board of Education*, 347 U. S. 483 (1954). As one commentator observed, the question before the Court in *Brown* was "whether discrimination inheres in that segregation which is imposed by law in the twentieth century in certain specific states in the American Union. And that question has meaning and can find an answer only on the ground of history and of common knowledge about the facts of life in the times and places aforesaid." Black, The Lawfulness of the Segregation Decisions, 69 Yale L. J. 421, 427 (1960).

The Court in *Brown* addressed these facts of life by observing that whatever may have been the understanding in *Plessy*'s time of the power of segregation to stigmatize those who were segregated with a "badge of inferiority," it was clear by 1954 that legally sanctioned segregation had just such an effect, to the point that racially separate public educational facilities were deemed inherently unequal. 374 U. S., at 494–495. Society's understanding of the facts upon which a constitutional ruling was sought in 1954 was thus fundamentally different from the basis claimed for the decision in 1896. While we think *Plessy* was wrong the day it was decided, see *Plessy, supra*, at 552–564 (Harlan, J., dissenting), we must also recognize that the *Plessy* Court's explanation for its decision was so clearly at odds with the facts apparent to the Court in 1954 that the decision to reexamine *Plessy* was on this ground alone not only justified but required.

West Coast Hotel and *Brown* each rested on facts, or an understanding of facts, changed from those which furnished the claimed justifications for the earlier constitutional resolutions. Each case was comprehensible as the Court's response to facts that the country could understand, or had come to understand already, but which the Court of an earlier day, as its own declarations disclosed, had not been able to perceive. As the decisions were thus comprehensible they were also defensible, not merely as the victories of one doctrinal school over another by dint of numbers (victories though they were), but as applications of constitutional principle to facts as they had not been seen by the Court before. In constitutional adjudication as elsewhere in life, changed circumstances may impose new obligations, and the thoughtful part of the Nation could accept each decision to overrule a prior case as a response to the Court's constitutional duty.

Because the case before us presents no such occasion it could be seen as no such response. Because neither the factual underpinnings of *Roe*'s central holding nor our understanding of it has changed (and because no other indication of weakened precedent has been shown) the Court could not pretend to be reexamining the prior law with any justification beyond a present doctrinal disposition to come out differently from the Court of 1973. To overrule prior law for no other reason than that would run counter to the view repeated

in our cases, that a decision to overrule should rest on some special reason over and above the belief that a prior case was wrongly decided. See, *e.g., Mitchell v. W. T. Grant*, 416 U. S. 600, 636 (1974) (Stewart, J., dissenting) ("A basic change in the law upon a ground no firmer than a change in our membership invites the popular misconception that this institution is little different from the two political branches of the Government. No misconception could do more lasting injury to this Court and to the system of law which it is our abiding mission to serve"); *Mapp v. Ohio*, 367 U. S. 643, 677 (1961) (Harlan, J., dissenting).

C

The examination of the conditions justifying the repudiation of *Adkins* by *West Coast Hotel* and *Plessy* by *Brown* is enough to suggest the terrible price that would have been paid if the Court had not overruled as it did. In the present case, however, as our analysis to this point makes clear, the terrible price would be paid for overruling. Our analysis would not be complete, however, without explaining why overruling *Roe*'s central holding would not only reach an unjustifiable result under principles of *stare decisis*, but would seriously weaken the Court's capacity to exercise the judicial power and to function as the Supreme Court of a Nation dedicated to the rule of law. To understand why this would be so it is necessary to understand the source of this Court's authority, the conditions necessary for its preservation, and its relationship to the country's understanding of itself as a constitutional Republic.

The root of American governmental power is revealed most clearly in the instance of the power conferred by the Constitution upon the Judiciary of the United States and specifically upon this Court. As Americans of each succeeding generation are rightly told, the Court cannot buy support for its decisions by spending money and, except to a minor degree, it cannot independently coerce obedience to its decrees. The Court's power lies, rather, in its legitimacy, a product of substance and perception that shows itself in the people's acceptance of the Judiciary as fit to determine what the Nation's law means and to declare what it demands.

The underlying substance of this legitimacy is of course the warrant for the Court's decisions in the Constitution and the lesser sources of legal principle on which the Court draws. That substance is expressed in the Court's opinions, and our contemporary understanding is such that a decision without principled justification would be no judicial act at all. But even when justification is furnished by apposite legal principle, something more is required. Because not every conscientious claim of principled justification will be accepted as such, the justification claimed must be beyond dispute. The Court must take care to speak and act in ways that allow people to accept its decisions on the terms the Court claims for them, as grounded truly in principle, not as compromises with social and political pressures having, as such, no bearing on the principled choices that the Court is obliged to make. Thus, the Court's legitimacy depends on making legally principled decisions under circumstances in which their principled character is sufficiently plausible to be accepted by the Nation.

The need for principled action to be perceived as such is implicated to some degree whenever this, or any other appellate court, overrules a prior case. This is not to say, of course, that this Court cannot give a perfectly satisfactory explanation in most cases. People understand that some of the Constitution's language is hard to fathom and that the Court's Justices are sometimes able to perceive significant facts or to understand principles of law that eluded their predecessors and that justify departures from existing decisions. However upsetting it may be to those most directly affected when one judicially derived rule replaces another, the country can accept some correction of error without necessarily questioning the legitimacy of the Court.

In two circumstances, however, the Court would almost certainly fail to receive the benefit of the doubt in overruling prior cases. There is, first, a point beyond which frequent overruling would overtax the country's belief in the Court's good faith. Despite the variety of reasons that may inform and justify a decision to overrule, we cannot forget that such a decision is usually perceived (and perceived correctly) as, at the least, a statement that a prior decision was wrong. There is a limit to the amount of error that can plausibly be imputed to prior courts. If that limit should be exceeded, disturbance of prior rulings would be taken as evidence that justifiable reexamination of principle had given way to drives for particular results in the short term. The legitimacy of the Court would fade with the frequency of its vacillation.

That first circumstance can be described as hypothetical; the second is to the point here and now. Where, in the performance of its judicial duties, the Court decides a case in such a way as to re-

solve the sort of intensely divisive controversy reflected in *Roe* and those rare, comparable cases, its decision has a dimension that the resolution of the normal case does not carry. It is the dimension present whenever the Court's interpretation of the Constitution calls the contending sides of a national controversy to end their national division by accepting a common mandate rooted in the Constitution.

The Court is not asked to do this very often, having thus addressed the Nation only twice in our lifetime, in the decisions of *Brown* and *Roe*. But when the Court does act in this way, its decision requires an equally rare precedential force to counter the inevitable efforts to overturn it and to thwart its implementation. Some of those efforts may be mere unprincipled emotional reactions; others may proceed from principles worthy of profound respect. But whatever the premises of opposition may be, only the most convincing justification under accepted standards of precedent could suffice to demonstrate that a later decision overruling the first was anything but a surrender to political pressure, and an unjustified repudiation of the principle on which the Court staked its authority in the first instance. So to overrule under fire in the absence of the most compelling reason to reexamine a watershed decision would subvert the Court's legitimacy beyond any serious question. Cf. *Brown v. Board of Education*, 349 U. S. 294, 300 (1955) (*Brown II*) ("[I]t should go without saying that the vitality of th[e] constitutional principles [announced in *Brown v. Board of Education*, 347 U. S. 483 (1954),] cannot be allowed to yield simply because of disagreement with them").

The country's loss of confidence in the judiciary would be underscored by an equally certain and equally reasonable condemnation for another failing in overruling unnecessarily and under pressure. Some cost will be paid by anyone who approves or implements a constitutional decision where it is unpopular, or who refuses to work to undermine the decision or to force its reversal. The price may be criticism or ostracism, or it may be violence. An extra price will be paid by those who themselves disapprove of the decision's results when viewed outside of constitutional terms, but who nevertheless struggle to accept it, because they respect the rule of law. To all those who will be so tested by following, the Court implicitly undertakes to remain steadfast, lest in the end a price be paid for nothing. The promise of constancy, once given, binds its maker for as long as the power to stand by the decision survives and the understanding of the issue has not changed so fundamentally as to render the commitment obsolete. From the obligation of this promise this Court cannot and should not assume any exemption when duty requires it to decide a case in conformance with the Constitution. A willing breach of it would be nothing less than a breach of faith, and no Court that broke its faith with the people could sensibly expect credit for principle in the decision by which it did that.

It is true that diminished legitimacy may be restored, but only slowly. Unlike the political branches, a Court thus weakened could not seek to regain its position with a new mandate from the voters, and even if the Court could somehow go to the polls, the loss of its principled character could not be retrieved by the casting of so many votes. Like the character of an individual, the legitimacy of the Court must be earned over time. So, indeed, must be the character of a Nation of people who aspire to live according to the rule of law. Their belief in themselves as such a people is not readily separable from their understanding of the Court invested with the authority to decide their constitutional cases and speak before all others for their constitutional ideals. If the Court's legitimacy should be undermined, then, so would the country be in its very ability to see itself through its constitutional ideals. The Court's concern with legitimacy is not for the sake of the Court but for the sake of the Nation to which it is responsible.

The Court's duty in the present case is clear. In 1973, it confronted the already-divisive issue of governmental power to limit personal choice to undergo abortion, for which it provided a new resolution based on the due process guaranteed by the Fourteenth Amendment. Whether or not a new social consensus is developing on that issue, its divisiveness is no less today than in 1973, and pressure to overrule the decision, like pressure to retain it, has grown only more intense. A decision to overrule *Roe*'s essential holding under the existing circumstances would address error, if error there was, at the cost of both profound and unnecessary damage to the Court's legitimacy, and to the Nation's commitment to the rule of law. It is therefore imperative to adhere to the essence of *Roe*'s original decision, and we do so today.

IV

From what we have said so far it follows that it is a constitutional liberty of the woman to have some freedom to terminate her pregnancy. We conclude that the basic decision in *Roe* was based on a constitutional analysis which we cannot now repudiate. The woman's liberty is not so unlimited, however, that from the outset the State cannot show its concern for the life of the unborn, and at a later point in fetal development the State's interest in life has sufficient force so that the right of the woman to terminate the pregnancy can be restricted.

That brings us, of course, to the point where much criticism has been directed at *Roe*, a criticism that always inheres when the Court draws a specific rule from what in the Constitution is but a general standard. We conclude, however, that the urgent claims of the woman to retain the ultimate control over her destiny and her body, claims implicit in the meaning of liberty, require us to perform that function. Liberty must not be extinguished for want of a line that is clear. And it falls to us to give some real substance to the woman's liberty to determine whether to carry her pregnancy to full term.

We conclude the line should be drawn at viability, so that before that time the woman has a right to choose to terminate her pregnancy. We adhere to this principle for two reasons. First, as we have said, is the doctrine of *stare decisis*. Any judicial act of line-drawing may seem somewhat arbitrary, but *Roe* was a reasoned statement, elaborated with great care. We have twice reaffirmed it in the face of great opposition. See *Thornburgh v. American College of Obstetricians & Gynecologists*, 476 U. S., at 759; *Akron I*, 462 U. S., at 419–420. Although we must overrule those parts of *Thornburgh* and *Akron I* which, in our view, are inconsistent with *Roe*'s statement that the State has a legitimate interest in promoting the life or potential life of the unborn, see *infra*, at ___, the central premise of those cases represents an unbroken commitment by this Court to the essential holding of *Roe*. It is that premise which we reaffirm today.

The second reason is that the concept of viability, as we noted in *Roe*, is the time at which there is a realistic possibility of maintaining and nourishing a life outside the womb, so that the independent existence of the second life can in reason and all fairness be the object of state protection that now overrides the rights of the woman. See *Roe v. Wade*, 410 U. S., at 163. Consistent with other constitutional norms, legislatures may draw lines which appear arbitrary without the necessity of offering a justification. But courts may not. We must justify the lines we draw. And there is no line other than viability which is more workable. To be sure, as we have said, there may be some medical developments that affect the precise point of viability, see *supra*, at ___, but this is an imprecision within tolerable limits given that the medical community and all those who must apply its discoveries will continue to explore the matter. The viability line also has, as a practical matter, an element of fairness. In some broad sense it might be said that a woman who fails to act before viability has consented to the State's intervention on behalf of the developing child.

The woman's right to terminate her pregnancy before viability is the most central principle of *Roe v. Wade*. It is a rule of law and a component of liberty we cannot renounce.

On the other side of the equation is the interest of the State in the protection of potential life. The *Roe* Court recognized the State's "important and legitimate interest in protecting the potentiality of human life." *Roe, supra*, at 162. The weight to be given this state interest, not the strength of the woman's interest, was the difficult question faced in *Roe*. We do not need to say whether each of us, had we been Members of the Court when the valuation of the State interest came before it as an original matter, would have concluded, as the *Roe* Court did, that its weight is insufficient to justify a ban on abortions prior to viability even when it is subject to certain exceptions. The matter is not before us in the first instance, and coming as it does after nearly 20 years of litigation in *Roe*'s wake we are satisfied that the immediate question is not the soundness of *Roe*'s resolution of the issue, but the precedential force that must be accorded to its holding. And we have concluded that the essential holding of *Roe* should be reaffirmed.

Yet it must be remembered that *Roe v. Wade* speaks with clarity in establishing not only the woman's liberty but also the State's "important and legitimate interest in potential life." *Roe, supra*, at 163. That portion of the decision in *Roe* has been given too little acknowledgement and implementation by the Court in its subsequent cases. Those cases decided that any regulation touching upon the abortion decision must survive strict scrutiny, to be sustained only if drawn in narrow terms to further a compelling state interest. See, *e.g., Akron I, supra*, at 427. Not all of the cases decided under that formulation can be reconciled with the holding in *Roe* itself that the State has legitimate interests in the health of the woman and in protecting the potential life within her. In resolving this tension, we choose to rely upon *Roe*, as against the later cases.

Roe established a trimester framework to govern abortion regulations. Under this elaborate but rigid construct, almost no regulation at all is permitted during the first trimester of pregnancy; regulations designed to protect the woman's health, but not to further the State's interest in potential life, are permitted during the second trimester; and during the third trimester, when the fetus is viable, prohibitions are permitted provided the life or health of the mother is not at stake. *Roe v. Wade, supra*, at 163–166. Most of our cases since *Roe* have involved the application of rules derived from the trimester framework. See, *e.g, Thornburgh v. American College of Obstetricians and Gynecologists, supra; Akron I, supra*.

The trimester framework no doubt was erected to ensure that the woman's right to choose not become so subordinate to the State's interest in promoting fetal life that her choice exists in theory but not in fact. We do not agree, however, that the trimester approach is necessary to accomplish this objective. A framework of this rigidity was unnecessary and in its later interpretation sometimes contradicted the State's permissible exercise of its powers.

Though the woman has a right to choose to terminate or continue her pregnancy before viability, it does not at all follow that the State is prohibited from taking steps to ensure that this choice is thoughtful and informed. Even in the earliest stages of pregnancy, the State may enact rules and regulations designed to encourage her to know that there are philosophic and social arguments of great weight that can be brought to bear in favor of continuing the pregnancy to full term and that there are procedures and institutions to allow adoption of unwanted children as well as a certain degree of state assistance if the mother chooses to raise the child herself. "'[T]he Constitution does not forbid a State or city, pursuant to democratic processes, from expressing a preference for normal childbirth.'" *Webster v. Reproductive Health Services*, 492 U. S., at 511 (opinion of the Court) (quoting *Poelker v. Doe*, 432 U. S. 519, 521 (1977). It follows that States are free to enact laws to provide a reasonable framework for a woman to make a decision that has such profound and lasting meaning. This, too, we find consistent with *Roe*'s central premises, and indeed the inevitable consequence of our holding that the State has an interest in protecting the life of the unborn.

We reject the trimester framework, which we do not consider to be part of the essential holding of *Roe*. See *Webster v. Reproductive Health Services, supra*, at 518 (opinion of REHNQUIST, C. J.); *id.*, at

529 (O'CONNOR, J., concurring in part and concurring in judgment) (describing the trimester framework as "problematic"). Measures aimed at ensuring that a woman's choice contemplates the consequences for the fetus do not necessarily interfere with the right recognized in *Roe*, although those measures have been found to be inconsistent with the rigid trimester framework announced in that case. A logical reading of the central holding in *Roe* itself, and a necessary reconciliation of the liberty of the woman and the interest of the State in promoting prenatal life, require, in our view, that we abandon the trimester framework as a rigid prohibition on all previability regulation aimed at the protection of fetal life. The trimester framework suffers from these basic flaws: in its formulation it misconceives the nature of the pregnant woman's interest; and in practice it undervalues the State's interest in potential life, as recognized in *Roe*.

As our jurisprudence relating to all liberties save perhaps abortion has recognized, not every law which makes a right more difficult to exercise is *ipso facto*, an infringement of that right. An example clarifies the point. We have held that not every ballot access limitation amounts to an infringement of the right to vote. Rather, the States are granted substantial flexibility in establishing the framework within which voters choose the candidates for whom they wish to vote. *Anderson v. Celebrezze*, 460 U. S. 780, 788 (1983); *Norman v. Reed*, 502 U. S. ___ (1992).

The abortion right is similar. Numerous forms of state regulation might have the incidental effect of increasing the cost or decreasing the availability of medical care, whether for abortion or any other medical procedure. The fact that a law which serves a valid purpose, one not designed to strike at the right itself, has the incidental effect of making it more difficult or more expensive to procure an abortion cannot be enough to invalidate it. Only where state regulation imposes an undue burden on a woman's ability to make this decision does the power of the State reach into the heart of the liberty protected by the Due Process Clause. See *Hodgson v. Minnesota*, 497 U. S. 417, 458–459 (1990) (O'CONNOR, J., concurring in part and concurring in judgment in part); *Ohio v. Akron Center for Reproductive Health*, 497 U. S. 502, —— (1990) (*Akron II*) (opinion of KENNEDY, J.) *Webster v. Reproductive Health Services, supra*, at 530 (O'CONNOR J., concurring in part and concurring in judgment); *Thornburgh v. American College of Obstetricians and Gynecologists*, 476 U. S., at 828 (O'CONNOR, J., dissenting); *Simopoulos v. Virginia*,

462 U. S. 506, 520 (1983) (O'CONNOR J., concurring in part and concurring in judgment); *Planned Parenthood Assn. of Kansas City v. Ashcroft*, 462 U. S. 476, 505 (1983) (O'CONNOR, J., concurring in judgment in part and dissenting in part); *Akron I*, 462 U. S., at 464 (O'CONNOR, J., joined by WHITE and REHNQUIST, JJ., dissenting); *Bellotti v. Baird*, 428 U. S. 132, 147 (1976) (*Bellotti I*).

For the most part, the Court's early abortion cases adhered to this view. In *Maher v. Roe*, 432 U. S. 464, 473–474 (1977), the Court explained: "*Roe* did not declare an unqualified 'constitutional right to an abortion,' as the District Court seemed to think. Rather, the right protects the woman from unduly burdensome interference with her freedom to decide whether to terminate her pregnancy." See also *Doe v. Bolton*, 410 U. S. 179, 198 (1973) ("[T]he interposition of the hospital abortion committee is unduly restrictive of the patient's rights"); *Bellotti I, supra*, at 147 (State may not "impose undue burdens upon a minor capable of giving an informed consent"); *Harris v. McRae*, 448 U. S. 297, 314 (1980) (citing *Maher, supra*). Cf. *Carey v. Population Services International*, 431 U. S., at 688 ("[T]he same test must be applied to state regulations that burden an individual's right to decide to prevent conception or terminate pregnancy by substantially limiting access to the means of effectuating that decision as is applied to state statutes that prohibit the decision entirely").

These considerations of the nature of the abortion right illustrate that it is an overstatement to describe it as a right to decide whether to have an abortion "without interference from the State," *Planned Parenthood of Central Mo. v. Danforth*, 428 U. S. 52, 61 (1976). All abortion regulations interfere to some degree with a woman's ability to decide whether to terminate her pregnancy. It is, as a consequence, not surprising that despite the protestations contained in the original *Roe* opinion to the effect that the Court was not recognizing an absolute right, 410 U. S., at 154–155, the Court's experience applying the trimester framework has led to the striking down of some abortion regulations which in no real sense deprived women of the ultimate decision. Those decisions went too far because the right recognized by *Roe* is a right "to be free from unwarranted governmental intrusion into matters so fundamentally affecting a person as the decision whether to bear or beget a child." *Eisenstadt v. Baird*, 405 U. S., at 453. Not all governmental intrusion is of necessity unwarranted; and that brings us to the other basic flaw in the trimester framework: even in *Roe*'s terms, in practice it undervalues the State's interest in the potential life within the woman.

Roe v. Wade was express in its recognition of the State's "important and legitimate interest[s] in preserving and protecting the health of the pregnant woman [and] in protecting the potentiality of human life." 410 U. S., at 162. The trimester framework, however, does not fulfill *Roe's* own promise that the State has an interest in protecting fetal life or potential life. *Roe* began the contradiction by using the trimester framework to forbid any regulation of abortion designed to advance that interest before viability. *Id.*, at 163. Before viability, *Roe* and subsequent cases treat all governmental attempts to influence a woman's decision on behalf of the potential life within her as unwarranted. This treatment is, in our judgment, incompatible with the recognition that there is a substantial state interest in potential life throughout pregnancy. Cf. *Webster*, 492 U. S., at 519 (opinion of REHNQUIST, C. J.); *Akron I, supra*, at 461 (O'CONNOR, J., dissenting).

The very notion that the State has a substantial interest in potential life leads to the conclusion that not all regulations must be deemed unwarranted. Not all burdens on the right to decide whether to terminate a pregnancy will be undue. In our view, the undue burden standard is the appropriate means of reconciling the State's interest with the woman's constitutionally protected liberty.

The concept of an undue burden has been utilized by the Court as well as individual members of the Court, including two of us, in ways that could be considered inconsistent. See, *e.g., Hodgson v. Minnesota*, 497 U. S., at —— (O'CONNOR, J., concurring in part and concurring in judgment); *Akron II*, 497 U. S., at —— (opinion of KENNEDY, J.); *Thornburgh v. American College of Obstetricians and Gynecologists*, 476 U. S., at 828–829 (O'CONNOR, J., dissenting); *Akron I, supra*, at 461–466 (O'CONNOR, J., dissenting); *Harris v. McRae, supra*, at 314; *Maher v. Roe, supra*, at 473; *Beal v. Doe*, 432 U. S. 438, 446 (1977); *Bellotti I, supra*, at 147. Because we set forth a standard of general application to which we intend to adhere, it is important to clarify what is meant by an undue burden.

A finding of an undue burden is a shorthand for the conclusion that a state regulation has the purpose or effect of placing a substantial obstacle in the path of a woman seeking an abortion of a nonviable fetus. A statute with this purpose is invalid because the means chosen by the State to further the interest in potential life must be calculated to inform the woman's free choice, not hinder it. And a statute which, while furthering the interest in potential life or some other valid state interest, has the effect of placing a substantial obstacle in the path of a woman's choice cannot be considered a permissible means of serving its legitimate ends. To the extent that the opinions of the Court or of individual Justices use the undue burden standard in a manner that is inconsistent with this analysis, we set out what in our view should be the controlling standard. Cf. *McCleskey v. Zant*, 499 U. S. ——, —— (1991) (slip op., at 20) (attempting to "define the doctrine of abuse of the writ with more precision" after acknowledging tension among earlier cases). In our considered judgment, an undue burden is an unconstitutional burden. See *Akron II, supra*, at —— (opinion of KENNEDY, J.). Understood another way, we answer the question, left open in previous opinions discussing the undue burden formulation, whether a law designed to further the State's interest in fetal life which imposes an undue burden on the woman's decision before fetal viability could be constitutional. See, *e.g., Akron I, supra*, at 462–463 (O'CONNOR, J., dissenting). The answer is no.

Some guiding principles should emerge. What is at stake is the woman's right to make the ultimate decision, not a right to be insulated from all others in doing so. Regulations which do no more than create a structural mechanism by which the State, or the parent or guardian of a minor, may express profound respect for the life of the unborn are permitted, if they are not a substantial obstacle to the woman's exercise of the right to choose. See *infra*, at ___-___ (addressing Pennsylvania's parental consent requirement). Unless it has that effect on her right of choice, a state measure designed to persuade her to choose childbirth over abortion will be upheld if reasonably related to that goal. Regulations designed to foster the health of a woman seeking an abortion are valid if they do not constitute an undue burden.

Even when jurists reason from shared premises, some disagreement is inevitable. Compare *Hodgson*, 497 U. S., at ___-___ (opinion of KENNEDY, J.) with *id.*, at ___-___ (O'CONNOR, J., concurring in part and concurring in judgment in part). That is to be expected in the application of any legal standard which must accommodate life's complexity. We do not expect it to be otherwise with respect to the undue burden standard. We give this summary:

(a) to protect the central right recognized by *Roe v. Wade* while at the same time accommodating the State's profound interest in potential life, we will employ the undue burden analysis as explained in this opinion. An undue burden exists, and therefore a provision of law is invalid, if its purpose or effect is to place a substantial obstacle in the path of a woman seeking an abortion before the fetus attains viability.

(b) We reject the rigid trimester framework of *Roe v. Wade*. To promote the State's profound interest in potential life, throughout pregnancy the State may take measures to ensure that the woman's choice is informed, and measures designed to advance this interest will not be invalidated as long as their purpose is to persuade the woman to choose childbirth over abortion. These measures must not be an undue burden on the right.

(c) As with any medical procedure, the State may enact regulations to further the health or safety of a woman seeking an abortion. Unnecessary health regulations that have the purpose or effect of presenting a substantial obstacle to a woman seeking an abortion impose an undue burden on the right.

(d) Our adoption of the undue burden analysis does not disturb the central holding of *Roe v. Wade*, and we reaffirm that holding. Regardless of whether exceptions are made for particular circumstances, a State may not prohibit any woman from making the ultimate decision to terminate her pregnancy before viability.

(e) We also reaffirm *Roe*'s holding that "subsequent to viability, the State in promoting its interest in the potentiality of human life may, if it chooses, regulate, and even proscribe, abortion except where it is necessary, in appropriate medical judgment, for the preservation of the life or health of the mother." *Roe v. Wade*, 410 U. S., at 164–165.

These principles control our assessment of the Pennsylvania statutes, and we now turn to the issue of the validity of its challenged provisions.

V

The Court of Appeals applied what it believed to be the undue burden standard and upheld each of the provisions except for the husband notification requirement. We agree generally with this conclusion, but refine the undue burden analysis in accordance with the principles articulated above. We now consider the separate statutory sections at issue.

A

Because it is central to the operation of various other requirements, we begin with the statute's definition of medical emergency. Under the statute, a medical emergency is

"[t]hat condition which, on the basis of the physician's good faith clinical judgment, so complicates the medical condition of a pregnant woman as to necessitate the immediate abortion of her pregnancy to avert her death or for which a delay will create serious risk of substantial and irreversible impairment of a major bodily function." 18 Pa. Cons. Stat. (1990). §3203.

Petitioners argue that the definition is too narrow, contending that it forecloses the possibility of an immediate abortion despite some significant health risks. If the contention were correct, we would be required to invalidate the restrictive operation of the provision, for the essential holding of *Roe* forbids a State from interfering with a woman's choice to undergo an abortion procedure if continuing her pregnancy would constitute a threat to her health. 410 U. S., at 164. See also *Harris v. McRae*, 448 U. S., at 316.

The District Court found that there were three serious conditions which would not be covered by the statute: preeclampsia, inevitable abortion, and premature ruptured membrane. 744 F. Supp., at 1378. Yet, as the Court of Appeals observed, 947 F. 2d, at 700–701, it is undisputed that under some circumstances each of these conditions could lead to an illness with substantial and irreversible consequences. While the definition could be interpreted in an unconstitutional manner, the Court of Appeals construed the phrase "serious risk" to include those circumstances. *Id.*, at 701. It stated: "we read the medical emergency exception as intended by the Pennsylvania legislature to assure that compliance with its abortion regulations would not in any way pose a significant threat to the life or health of a woman." *Ibid.* As we said in *Brockett v. Spokane Arcades, Inc.*, 472 U. S. 491, 499–500 (1985): "Normally, . . . we defer to the construction of a state statute given it by the lower federal courts." Indeed, we have said that we will defer to lower court interpretations of state law unless they amount to "plain" error. *Palmer v. Hoffman*, 318 U. S. 109, 118 (1943). This "'reflect[s] our belief that district courts and courts of appeals are better schooled in and more able to interpret the laws of their respective States.'" *Frisby v. Schultz*, 487 U. S. 474, 482 (1988) (citation omitted). We adhere to that course today, and conclude that, as construed by the Court of Appeals, the medical emergency definition imposes no undue burden on a woman's abortion right.

B

We next consider the informed consent requirement. 18 Pa. Cons. Stat. Ann. §3205. Except in a medical emergency, the statute requires that at least 24 hours before performing an abortion a physician inform the woman of the nature of the procedure, the health risks of the abortion and of childbirth, and the "probable gestational age of the unborn child." The physician or a qualified nonphysician must inform the woman of the availability of printed materials published by the State describing the fetus and providing information about medical assistance for childbirth, information about child support from the father, and a list of agencies which provide adoption and other services as alternatives to abortion. An abortion may not be performed unless the woman certifies in writing that she has been informed of the availability of these printed materials and has been provided them if she chooses to view them.

Our prior decisions establish that as with any medical procedure, the State may require a woman to give her written informed consent to an abortion. See *Planned Parenthood of Central Mo. v. Danforth*, 428 U. S., at 67. In this respect, the statute is unexceptional. Petitioners challenge the statute's definition of informed consent because it includes the provision of specific information by the doctor and the mandatory 24-hour waiting period. The conclusions reached by a majority of the Justices in the separate opinions filed today and the undue burden standard adopted in this opinion require us to overrule in part some of the Court's past decisions, decisions driven by the trimester framework's prohibition of all previability regulations designed to further the State's interest in fetal life.

In *Akron I*, 462 U. S. 416 (1983), we invalidated an ordinance which required that a woman seeking an abortion be provided by her physician with specific information "designed to influence the woman's informed choice between abortion or childbirth." *Id.*, at 444. As we later described the *Akron I* holding in *Thornburgh v. American College of Obstetricians and Gynecologists*, 476 U. S., at 762, there were two purported flaws in the Akron ordinance: the information was designed to dissuade the woman from having an abortion and the ordinance imposed "a rigid requirement that a specific body of information be given in all cases, irrespective of the particular needs of the patient . . . ." *Ibid.*

To the extent *Akron I* and *Thornburgh* find a constitutional violation when the government requires, as it does here, the giving of truthful, non-misleading information about the nature of the procedure, the attendant health risks and those of childbirth, and the "probable gestational age" of the fetus, those cases go too far, are inconsistent with *Roe*'s acknowledgment of an important interest in potential life, and are overruled. This is clear even on the very terms of *Akron I* and *Thornburgh*. Those decisions, along with *Danforth*, recognize a substantial government interest justifying a requirement that a woman be apprised of the health risks of abortion and childbirth. *E.g., Danforth, supra*, at 66–67. It cannot be questioned that psychological well-being is a facet of health. Nor can it be doubted that most women considering an abortion would deem the impact on the fetus relevant, if not dispositive, to the decision. In attempting to ensure that a woman apprehend the full consequences of her decision, the State furthers the legitimate purpose of reducing the risk that a woman may elect an abortion, only to discover later, with devastating psychological consequences, that her decision was not fully informed. If the information the State requires to be made available to the woman is truthful and not misleading, the requirement may be permissible.

We also see no reason why the State may not require doctors to inform a woman seeking an abortion of the availability of materials relating to the consequences to the fetus, even when those consequences have no direct relation to her health. An example illustrates the point. We would think it constitutional for the State to require that in order for there to be informed consent to a kidney transplant operation the recipient must be supplied with information about risks to the donor as well as risks to himself or herself. A requirement that the physician make available information similar to that mandated by the statute here was described in *Thornburgh* as "an outright attempt to wedge the Commonwealth's message discouraging abortion into the privacy of the informed-consent dialogue between the woman and her physician." 476 U. S., at 762. We conclude, however, that informed choice need not be defined in such narrow terms that all considerations of the effect on the fetus are made irrelevant. As we have made clear, we depart from the holdings of *Akron I* and *Thornburgh* to the extent that we permit a State to further its legitimate goal of protecting the life of the unborn by enacting legislation aimed at ensuring a decision that is mature and informed, even when in so doing the State expresses a preference for childbirth over abortion. In short, requiring that the woman be informed of the availability of information relating to fetal development and the assistance available should she decide to carry the pregnancy to full term is a reasonable measure to insure an informed choice, one which might cause the woman to choose childbirth over abortion. This requirement cannot be considered a substantial obstacle to obtaining an abortion, and, it follows, there is no undue burden.

Our prior cases also suggest that the "straitjacket," *Thornburgh, supra*, at 762 (quoting *Danforth, supra*, at 67, n. 8), of particular information which must be given in each case interferes with a constitutional right of privacy between a pregnant woman and her physician. As a preliminary matter, it is worth noting that the statute now before us does not require a physician to comply with the informed consent provisions "if he or she can demonstrate by a preponderance of the evidence, that he or she reasonably believed that furnishing the information would have resulted in a severely adverse effect on the physical or mental health of the patient." 18 Pa. Cons. Stat. §3205 (1990). In this respect, the statute does not prevent the physician from exercising his or her medical judgment.

Whatever constitutional status the doctor-patient relation may have as a general matter, in the present context it is derivative of the woman's position. The doctor-patient relation does not underlie or override the two more general rights under which the abortion right is justified: the right to make family decisions and the right to physical autonomy. On its own, the doctor-patient relation here is entitled to the same solicitude it receives in other contexts. Thus, a requirement that a doctor give a woman certain information as part of obtaining her consent to an abortion is, for constitutional purposes, no different from a requirement that a doctor give certain specific information about any medical procedure.

All that is left of petitioners' argument is an asserted First Amendment right of a physician not to provide information about the risks of abortion, and childbirth, in a manner mandated by the State. To be sure, the physician's First Amendment rights not to speak are implicated, see *Wooley v. Maynard*, 430 U. S. 705 (1977), but only as part of the practice of medicine, subject to reasonable licensing and regulation by the State. Cf. *Whalen v. Roe*, 429 U. S. 589, 603 (1977). We see no constitutional infirmity in the requirement that the physician provide the information mandated by the State here.

The Pennsylvania statute also requires us to reconsider the holding in *Akron I* that the State may

not require that a physician, as opposed to a qualified assistant, provide information relevant to a woman's informed consent. 462 U. S., at 448. Since there is no evidence on this record that requiring a doctor to give the information as provided by the statute would amount in practical terms to a substantial obstacle to a woman seeking an abortion, we conclude that it is not an undue burden. Our cases reflect the fact that the Constitution gives the States broad latitude to decide that particular functions may be performed only by licensed professionals, even if an objective assessment might suggest that those same tasks could be performed by others. See *Williamson v. Lee Optical of Oklahoma, Inc.*, 348 U. S. 483 (1955). Thus, we uphold the provision as a reasonable means to insure that the woman's consent is informed.

Our analysis of Pennsylvania's 24-hour waiting period between the provision of the information deemed necessary to informed consent and the performance of an abortion under the undue burden standard requires us to reconsider the premise behind the decision in *Akron I* invalidating a parallel requirement. In *Akron I* we said: "Nor are we convinced that the State's legitimate concern that the woman's decision be informed is reasonably served by requiring a 24-hour delay as a matter of course." 462 U. S., at 450. We consider that conclusion to be wrong. The idea that important decisions will be more informed and deliberate if they follow some period of reflection does not strike us as unreasonable, particularly where the statute directs that important information become part of the background of the decision. The statute, as construed by the Court of Appeals, permits avoidance of the waiting period in the event of a medical emergency and the record evidence shows that in the vast majority of cases, a 24-hour delay does not create any appreciable health risk. In theory, at least, the waiting period is a reasonable measure to implement the State's interest in protecting the life of the unborn, a measure that does not amount to an undue burden.

Whether the mandatory 24-hour waiting period is nonetheless valid because in practice it is a substantial obstacle to a woman's choice to terminate her pregnancy is a closer question. The findings of fact by the District Court indicate that because of the distances many women must travel to reach an abortion provider, the practical effect will often be a delay of much more than a day because the waiting period requires that a woman seeking an abortion make at least two visits to the doctor. The District Court also found that in many instances this will increase the exposure of women seeking abortions to "the harassment and hostility of anti-abortion protestors demonstrating outside a clinic." 744 F. Supp., at 1351. As a result, the District Court found that for those women who have the fewest financial resources, those who must travel long distances, and those who have difficulty explaining their whereabouts to husbands, employers, or others, the 24-hour waiting period will be "particularly burdensome." Id., at 1352.

These findings are troubling in some respects, but they do not demonstrate that the waiting period constitutes an undue burden. We do not doubt that, as the District Court held, the waiting period has the effect of "increasing the cost and risk of delay of abortions," id., at 1378, but the District Court did not conclude that the increased costs and potential delays amount to substantial obstacles. Rather, applying the trimester framework's strict prohibition of all regulation designed to promote the State's interest in potential life before viability, see id., at 1374, the District Court concluded that the waiting period does not further the state "interest in maternal health" and "infringes the physician's discretion to exercise sound medical judgment." Id., at 1378. Yet, as we have stated, under the undue burden standard a State is permitted to enact persuasive measures which favor childbirth over abortion, even if those measures do not further a health interest. And while the waiting period does limit a physician's discretion, that is not, standing alone, a reason to invalidate it. In light of the construction given the statute's definition of medical emergency by the Court of Appeals, and the District Court's findings, we cannot say that the waiting period imposes a real health risk.

We also disagree with the District Court's conclusion that the "particularly burdensome" effects of the waiting period on some women require its invalidation. A particular burden is not of necessity a substantial obstacle. Whether a burden falls on a particular group is a distinct inquiry from whether it is a substantial obstacle even as to the women in that group. And the District Court did not conclude that the waiting period is such an obstacle even for the women who are most burdened by it. Hence, on the record before us, and in the context of this facial challenge, we are not convinced that the 24-hour waiting period constitutes an undue burden.

We are left with the argument that the various aspects of the informed consent requirement are unconstitutional because they place barriers in the way of abortion on demand. Even the broad-est reading of Roe, however, has not suggested that there is a constitutional right to abortion on demand. See, e.g., Doe v. Bolton, 410 U. S., at 189. Rather, the right protected by Roe is a right to decide to terminate a pregnancy free of undue interference by the State. Because the informed consent requirement facilitates the wise exercise of that right it cannot be classified as an interference with the right Roe protects. The informed consent requirement is not an undue burden on that right.

C

Section 3209 of Pennsylvania's abortion law provides, except in cases of medical emergency, that no physician shall perform an abortion on a married woman without receiving a signed statement from the woman that she has notified her spouse that she is about to undergo an abortion. The woman has the option of providing an alternative signed statement certifying that her husband is not the man who impregnated her; that her husband could not be located; that the pregnancy is the result of spousal sexual assault which she has reported; or that the woman believes that notifying her husband will cause him or someone else to inflict bodily injury upon her. A physician who performs an abortion on a married woman without receiving the appropriate signed statement will have his or her license revoked, and is liable to the husband for damages.

The District Court heard the testimony of numerous expert witnesses, and made detailed findings of fact regarding the effect of this statute. These included:

"273. The vast majority of women consult their husbands prior to deciding to terminate their pregnancy. . . .

"279. The 'bodily injury' exception could not be invoked by a married woman whose husband, if notified, would, in her reasonable belief, threaten to (a) publicize her intent to have an abortion to family, friends or acquaintances; (b) retaliate against her in future child custody or divorce proceedings; (c) inflict psychological intimidation or emotional harm upon her, her children or other persons; (d) inflict bodily harm on other persons such as children, family members or other loved ones; or (e) use his control over finances to deprive of necessary monies for herself or her children. . . .

"281. Studies reveal that family violence occurs in two million families in the United States. This figure, however, is a conservative one that substantially understates (because battering is usually not reported until it reaches life-threatening proportions) the actual number of families affected by domestic violence. In fact, researchers estimate that one of every two women will be battered at some time in their life. . . .

"282. A wife may not elect to notify her husband of her intention to have an abortion for a variety of reasons, including the husband's illness, concern about her own health, the imminent failure of the marriage, or the husband's absolute opposition to the abortion. . . .

"283. The required filing of the spousal consent form would require plaintiff-clinics to change their counseling procedures and force women to reveal their most intimate decision-making on pain of criminal sanctions. The confidentiality of these revelations could not be guaranteed, since the woman's records are not immune from subpoena. . . .

"284. Women of all class levels, educational backgrounds, and racial, ethnic and religious groups are battered. . . .

"285. Wife-battering or abuse can take on many physical and psychological forms. The nature and scope of the battering can cover a broad range of actions and be gruesome and torturous. . . .

"286. Married women, victims of battering, have been killed in Pennsylvania and throughout the United States. . . .

"287. Battering can often involve a substantial amount of sexual abuse, including marital rape and sexual mutilation. . . .

"288. In a domestic abuse situation, it is common for the battering husband to also abuse the children in an attempt to coerce the wife. . . .

"289. Mere notification of pregnancy is frequently a flashpoint for battering and violence within the family. The number of battering incidents is high during the pregnancy and often the worst abuse can be associated with pregnancy. . . . The battering husband may deny parentage and use the pregnancy as an excuse for abuse. . . .

"290. Secrecy typically shrouds abusive families. Family members are instructed not to tell anyone, especially police or doctors, about the abuse and violence. Battering husbands often threaten their wives or her children with further abuse if she tells an outsider of the violence and tells her that nobody will believe her. A battered woman, therefore, is highly unlikely to disclose the violence against her for fear of retaliation by the abuser. . . .

"291. Even when confronted directly by medical personnel or other helping professionals, battered women often will not admit to the battering because they have not admitted to themselves that they are battered. . . .

"294. A woman in a shelter or a safe house unknown to her husband is not 'reasonably likely' to have bodily harm inflicted upon her by her batterer, however her attempt to notify her husband pursuant to section 3209 could accidentally disclose her whereabouts to her husband. Her fear of future ramifications would be realistic under the circumstances.

"295. Marital rape is rarely discussed with others or reported to law enforcement authorities, and of those reported only few are prosecuted. . . .

"296. It is common for battered women to have sexual intercourse with their husbands to avoid being battered. While this type of coercive sexual activity would be spousal sexual assault as defined by the Act, many women may not consider it to be so and others would fear disbelief. . . .

"297. The marital rape exception to section 3209 cannot be claimed by women who are victims of coercive sexual behavior other than penetration. The 90-day reporting requirement of the spousal sexual assault statute, 18 Pa. Con. Stat. Ann. §3218(c), further narrows the class of sexually abused wives who can claim the exception, since many of these women may be psychologically unable to discuss or report the rape for several years after the incident. . . .

"298. Because of the nature of the batttering relationship, battered women are unlikely to avail themselves of the exceptions to section 3209 of the Act, regardless of whether the section applies to them." 744 F. Supp., at 1360–1362.

These findings are supported by studies of domestic violence. The American Medical Association (AMA) has published a summary of the recent research in this field, which indicates that in an average 12-month period in this country, approximately two million women are the victims of severe assaults by their male partners. In a 1985 survey, women reported that nearly one of every eight husbands had assaulted their wives during the past year. The AMA views these figures as "marked underestimates," because the nature of these incidents discourages women from reporting them, and because surveys typically exclude the very poor, those who do not speak English well, and women who are homeless or in institutions or hospitals when the survey is conducted. According to the AMA, "[r]esearchers on family violence agree that the true incidence of partner violence is probably *double* the above estimates; or four million severely assaulted women per year. Studies suggest that from one-fifth to one-third of all women will be physically assaulted by a partner or ex-partner during their lifetime." AMA Council on Scientific Affairs, Violence Against Women 7 (1991) (emphasis in original). Thus on an average day in the United States, nearly 11,000 women are severely assaulted by their male partners. Many of these incidents involve sexual assault. *Id.*, at 3–4; Shields & Hanneke, Battered Wives' Reactions to Marital Rape, in The Dark Side of Families: Current Family Violence Research 131, 144 (D. Finkelhor, R. Gelles, G. Hataling, & M. Straus eds. 1983). In families where wife-beating takes place, moreover, child abuse is often present as well. Violence Against Women, *supra*, at 12.

Other studies fill in the rest of this troubling picture. Physical violence is only the most visible form of abuse. Psychological abuse, particularly forced social and economic isolation of women, is also common. L. Walker, The Battered Woman Syndrome 27–28 (1984). Many victims of domestic violence remain with their abusers, perhaps because they perceive no superior alternative. Herbert, Sil-

ver, & Ellard, Coping with an Abusive Relationship: I. How and Why do Women Stay?, 53 J. Marriage & the Family 311 (1991). Many abused women who find temporary refuge in shelters return to their husbands, in large part because they have no other source of income. Aguirre, Why Do They Return? Abused Wives in Shelters, 30 J. Nat. Assn. of Social Workers 350, 352 (1985). Returning to one's abuser can be dangerous. Recent Federal Bureau of Investigation statistics disclose that 8.8% of all homicide victims in the United States are killed by their spouse. Mercy & Saltzman, Fatal Violence Among Spouses in the United States, 1976–85, 79 Am. J. Public Health 595 (1989). Thirty percent of female homicide victims are killed by their male partners. Domestic Violence: Terrorism in the Home, Hearing before the Subcommittee on Children, Family, Drugs and Alcoholism of the Senate Committee on Labor and Human Resources, 101st Cong., 2d Sess., 3 (1990).

The limited research that has been conducted with respect to notifying one's husband about an abortion, although involving samples too small to be representative, also supports the District Court's findings of fact. The vast majority of women notify their male partners of their decision to obtain an abortion. In many cases in which married women do not notify their husbands, the pregnancy is the result of an extramarital affair. Where the husband is the father, the primary reason women do not notify their husbands is that the husband and wife are experiencing marital difficulties, often accompanied by incidents of violence. Ryan & Plutzer, When Married Women Have Abortions: Spousal Notification and Marital Interaction, 51 J. Marriage & the Family 41, 44 (1989).

This information and the District Court's findings reinforce what common sense would suggest. In well-functioning marriages, spouses discuss important intimate decisions such as whether to bear a child. But there are millions of women in this country who are the victims of regular physical and psychological abuse at the hands of their husbands. Should these women become pregnant, they may have very good reasons for not wishing to inform their husbands of their decision to obtain an abortion. Many may have justifiable fears of physical abuse, but may be no less fearful of the consequences of reporting prior abuse to the Commonwealth of Pennsylvania. Many may have a reasonable fear that notifying their husbands will provoke further instances of child abuse; these women are not exempt from §3209's notification requirement. Many may fear devastating forms of psychological abuse from their husbands, including verbal harassment, threats of future violence, the destruction of possessions, physical confinement to the home, the withdrawal of financial support, or the disclosure of the abortion to family and friends. These methods of psychological abuse may act as even more of a deterrent to notification than the possibility of physical violence, but women who are the victims of the abuse are not exempt from §3209's notification requirement. And many women who are pregnant as a result of sexual assaults by their husbands will be unable to avail themselves of the exception for spousal sexual assault, §3209(b)(3), because the exception requires that the woman have notified law enforcement authorities within 90 days of the assault, and her husband will be notified of her report once an investigation begins. §3128(c). If anything in this field is certain, it is that victims of spousal sexual assault are extremely reluctant to report the abuse to the government; hence, a great many spousal rape victims will not be exempt from the notification requirement imposed by §3209.

The spousal notification requirement is thus likely to prevent a significant number of women from obtaining an abortion. It does not merely make abortions a little more difficult or expensive to obtain; for many women, it will impose a substantial obstacle. We must not blind ourselves to the fact that the significant number of women who fear for their safety and the safety of their children are likely to be deterred from procuring an abortion as surely as if the Commonwealth had outlawed abortion in all cases.

Respondents attempt to avoid the conclusion that §3209 is invalid by pointing out that it imposes almost no burden at all for the vast majority of women seeking abortions. They begin by noting that only about 20 percent of the women who obtain abortions are married. They then note that of these women about 95 percent notify their husbands of their own volition. Thus, respondents argue, the effects of §3209 are felt by only one percent of the women who obtain abortions. Respondents argue that since some of these women will be able to notify their husbands without adverse consequences or will qualify for one of the exceptions, the statute affects fewer than one percent of women seeking abortions. For this reason, it is asserted, the statute cannot be invalid on its face. See Brief or Respondents 83–86. We disagree with respondents' basic method of analysis.

The analysis does not end with the one percent of women upon whom the statute operates; it be-

gins there. Legislation is measured for consistency with the Constitution by its impact on those whose conduct it affects. For example, we would not say that a law which requires a newspaper to print a candidate's reply to an unfavorable editorial is valid on its face because most newspapers would adopt the policy even absent the law. See *Miami Herald Publishing Co. v. Tornillo*, 418 U. S. 241 (1974). The proper focus of constitutional inquiry is the group for whom the law is a restriction, not the group for whom the law is irrelevant.

Respondent's argument itself gives implicit recognition to this principle, at one of its critical points. Respondents speak of the one percent of women seeking abortions who are married and would choose not to notify their husbands of their plans. By selecting as the controlling class women who wish to obtain abortions, rather than all women or all pregnant women, respondents in effect concede that §3209 must be judged by reference to those for whom it is an actual rather than irrelevant restriction. Of course, as we have said, §3209's real target is narrower even than the class of women seeking abortions identified by the State: it is married women seeking abortions who do not wish to notify their husbands of their intentions and who do not qualify for one of the statutory exceptions to the notice requirement. The unfortunate yet persisting conditions we document above will mean that in a large fraction of the cases in which §3209 is relevant, it will operate as a substantial obstacle to a woman's choice to undergo an abortion. It is an undue burden, and therefore invalid.

This conclusion is in no way inconsistent with our decisions upholding parental notification or consent requirements. See, *e.g.*, *Akron II*, 497 U. S., at ——; *Bellotti v. Baird*, 443 U. S. 622 (1979) (*Bellotti II*); *Planned Parenthood of Central Mo. v. Danforth*, 428 U. S., at 74. Those enactments, and our judgment that they are constitutional, are based on the quite reasonable assumption that minors will benefit from consultation with their parents and that children will often not realize that their parents have their best interests at heart. We cannot adopt a parallel assumption about adult women.

We recognize that a husband has a "deep and proper concern and interest . . . in his wife's pregnancy and in the growth and development of the fetus she is carrying." *Danforth, supra*, at 69. With regard to the children he has fathered and raised, the Court has recognized his "cognizable and substantial" interest in their custody. *Stanley v. Illinois*, 405 U. S. 645, 651–652 (1972); see also *Quilloin v.*

Walcott, 434 U. S. 246 (1978); *Caban v. Mohammed*, 441 U. S. 380 (1979); *Lehr v. Robertson*, 463 U. S. 248 (1983). If this case concerned a State's ability to require the mother to notify the father before taking some action with respect to a living child raised by both, therefore, it would be reasonable to conclude as a general matter that the father's interest in the welfare of the child and the mother's interest are equal.

Before birth, however, the issue takes on a very different cast. It is an inescapable biological fact that state regulation with respect to the child a woman is carrying will have a far greater impact on the mother's liberty than on the father's. The effect of state regulation on a woman's protected liberty is doubly deserving of scrutiny in such a case, as the State has touched not only upon the private sphere of the family but upon the very bodily integrity of the pregnant women. Cf. *Cruzan v. Director, Missouri Dept. of Health*, 497 U. S., at 281. The Court has held that "when the wife and the husband disagree on this decision, the view of only one of the two marriage partners can prevail. Inasmuch as it is the woman who physically bears the child and who is the more directly and immediately affected by the pregnancy, as between the two, the balance weighs in her favor." *Danforth, supra*, at 71. This conclusion rests upon the basic nature of marriage and the nature of our Constitution: "[T]he marital couple is not an independent entity with a mind and heart of its own, but an association of two individuals each with a separate intellectual and emotional makeup. If the right of privacy means anything, it is the right of the *individual*, married or single, to be free from unwarranted governmental intrusion into matters so fundamentally affecting a person as the decision whether to bear or beget a child." *Eisenstadt v. Baird*, 405 U. S., at 453 (emphasis in original). The Constitution protects individuals, men and women alike, from unjustified state interference, even when that interference is enacted into law for the benefit of their spouses.

There was a time, not so long ago, when a different understanding of the family and of the Constitution prevailed. In *Bradwell v. Illinois*, 16 Wall. 130 (1873), three Members of this Court reaffirmed the common-law principle that "a woman had no legal existence separate from her husband, who was regarded as her head and representative in the social state; and, notwithstanding some recent modifications of this civil status, many of the special rules of law flowing from and dependent upon this cardinal principle still exist in full force in most States." *Id.*, at 141 (Bradley J., joined by Swayne and Field, JJ., concurring in judgment). Only one generation has passed since this Court observed that "woman is still regarded as the center of home and family life," with attendant "special responsibilities" that precluded full and independent legal status under the Constitution. *Hoyt v. Florida*, 368 U. S. 57, 62 (1961). These views, of course, are no longer consistent with our understanding of the family, the individual, or the Constitution.

In keeping with our rejection of the common-law understanding of a woman's role within the family, the Court held in *Danforth* that the Constitution does not permit a State to require a married woman to obtain her husband's consent before undergoing an abortion. 428 U. S., at 69. The principles that guided the Court in *Danforth* should be our guides today. For the great many women who are victims of abuse inflicted by their husbands, or whose children are the victims of such abuse, a spousal notice requirement enables the husband to wield an effective veto over his wife's decision. Whether the prospect of notification itself deters such women from seeking abortions, or whether the husband, through physical force or psychological pressure or economic coercion, prevents his wife from obtaining an abortion until it is too late, the notice requirement will often be tantamount to the veto found unconstitutional in *Danforth*. The women most affected by this law—those who most reasonably fear the consequences of notifying their husbands that they are pregnant—are in the gravest danger.

The husband's interest in the life of the child his wife is carrying does not permit the State to empower him with this troubling degree of authority over his wife. The contrary view leads to consequences reminiscent of the common law. A husband has no enforceable right to require a wife to advise him before she exercises her personal choices. If a husband's interest in the potential life of the child outweighs a wife's liberty, the State could require a married woman to notify her husband before she uses a postfertilization contraceptive. Perhaps next in line would be a statute requiring pregnant married women to notify their husbands before engaging in conduct causing risks to the fetus. After all, if the husband's interest in the fetus' safety is a sufficient predicate for state regulation, the State could reasonably conclude that pregnant wives should notify their husbands before drinking alcohol or smoking. Perhaps married women should notify their husbands before using contraceptives or before undergoing any type of surgery that may have complications affecting the husband's interest in his wife's reproductive organs. And if a husband's interest justifies notice in any of these cases, one might reasonably argue that it justifies exactly what the *Danforth* Court held it did not justify—a requirement of the husband's consent as well. A State may not give to a man the kind of dominion over his wife that parents exercise over their children.

Section 3209 embodies a view of marriage consonant with the common-law status of married women but repugnant to our present understanding of marriage and of the nature of the rights secured by the Constitution. Women do not lose their constitutionally protected liberty when they marry. The Constitution protects all individuals, male or female, married or unmarried, from the abuse of governmental power, even where that power is employed for the supposed benefit of a member of the individual's family. These considerations confirm our conclusion that §3209 is invalid.

D

We next consider the parental consent provision. Except in a medical emergency, an unemancipated young woman under 18 may not obtain an abortion unless she and one of her parents (or guardian) provides informed consent as defined above. If neither a parent nor a guardian provides consent, a court may authorize the performance of an abortion upon a determination that the young woman is mature and capable of giving informed consent and has in fact given her informed consent, or that an abortion would be in her best interests.

We have been over most of this ground before. Our cases establish, and we reaffirm today, that a State may require a minor seeking an abortion to obtain the consent of a parent or guardian, provided that there is an adequate judicial bypass procedure. See, *e.g., Akron II*, 497 U. S., at ——; *Hodgson*, 497 U. S., at ——; *Akron I, supra*, at 440; *Bellotti II, supra*, at 643–644 (plurality opinion). Under these precedents, in our view, the one-parent consent requirement and judicial bypass procedure are constitutional.

The only argument made by petitioners respecting this provision and to which our prior decisions do not speak is the contention that the parental consent requirement is invalid because it requires informed parental consent. For the most part, petitioners' argument is a reprise of their argument with respect to the informed consent requirement in general, and we reject it for the reasons given above. Indeed, some of the provisions regarding informed consent have particular force with respect to minors: the waiting period, for example, may provide the parent or parents of a pregnant young woman the opportunity to consult with her in private, and to discuss the consequences of her decision in the context of the values and moral or religious principles of their family. See *Hodgson, supra*, at—.

E

Under the recordkeeping and reporting requirements of the statute, every facility which performs abortions is required to file a report stating its name and address as well as the name and address of any related entity, such as a controlling or subsidiary organization. In the case of state funded institutions, the information becomes public.

For each abortion performed, a report must be filed identifying: the physician (and the second physician where required); the facility; the referring physician or agency; the woman's age; the number of prior pregnancies and prior abortions she has had; gestational age; the type of abortion procedure; the date of the abortion; whether there were any pre-existing medical conditions which would complicate pregnancy; medical complications with the abortion; where applicable, the basis for the determination that the abortion was medically necessary; the weight of the aborted fetus; and whether the woman was married, and if so, whether notice was provided or the basis for the failure to give notice. Every abortion facility must also file quarterly reports showing the number of abortions performed broken down by trimester. See 18 Ps. Cons. Stat. §§3207, 3214 (1990). In all events, the identity of each woman who has had an abortion remains confidential.

In *Danforth*, 428 U. S., at 80, we held that recordkeeping and reporting provisions "that are reasonably directed to the preservation of maternal health and that properly respect a patient's confidentiality and privacy are permissible." We think that under this standard, all the provisions at issue here except that relating to spousal notice are constitutional. Although they do not relate to the State's interest in informing the woman's choice, they do relate to health. The collection of information with respect to actual patients is a vital element of medical research, and so it cannot be said that the requirements serve no purpose other than to make abortions more difficult. Nor do we find that the requirements impose a substantial obstacle to a woman's choice. At most they might increase the cost of some abortions by a slight amount. While at some point increased cost could become a substantial obstacle, there is no such showing on the record before us.

Subsection (12) of the reporting provision requires the reporting of, among other things, a married woman's "reason for failure to provide notice" to her husband. §3214(a)(12). This provision in effect requires women, as a condition of obtaining an abortion, to provide the Commonwealth with the precise information we have already recognized that many women have pressing reasons not to reveal. Like the spousal notice requirement itself, this provision places an undue burden on a woman's choice and must be invalidated for that reason.

VI

Our Constitution is a covenant running from the first generation of Americans to us and then to future generations. It is a coherent succession. Each generation must learn anew that the Constitution's written terms embody ideas and aspirations that must survive more ages than one. We accept our responsibility not to retreat from interpreting the full meaning of the covenant in light of all of our precedents. We invoke it once again to define the freedom guaranteed by the Constitution's own promise, the promise of liberty.

* * *

The judgment in No. 91–902 is affirmed. The judgment in No. 91–744 is affirmed in part and reversed in part, and the case is remanded for proceedings consistent with this opinion, including consideration of the question of severability.

It is so ordered. . . .

* * *

Chief Justice Rehnquist, with whom Justice White, Justice Scalia, and Justice Thomas join, concurring in the judgment in part and dissenting in part.

The joint opinion, following its newly-minted variation on *stare decisis,* retains the outer shell of *Roe* v. *Wade,* 410 U. S. 113 (1973), but beats a wholesale retreat from the substance of that case. We believe that *Roe* was wrongly decided, and that it can and should be overruled consistently with our traditional approach to *stare decisis* in consti-

tutional cases. We would adopt the approach of the plurality in *Webster* v. *Reproductive health Services,* 492 U. S. 490 (1989), and uphold the challenged provisions of the Pennsylvania statute in their entirety.

I

In ruling on this case below, the Court of Appeals for the Third Circuit first observed that "this appeal does not directly implicate *Roe;* this case involves the regulation of abortions rather than their outright prohibition." 947 F. 2d 682, 687 (1991). Accordingly, the court directed its attention to the question of the standard of review for abortion regulations. In attempting to settle on the correct standard, however, the court confronted the confused state of this Court's abortion jurisprudence. After considering the several opinions in *Webster* v. *Reproductive Health Services, supra,* and *Hodgson* v. *Minnesota,* 497 U. S. 417 (1990), the Court of Appeals concluded that JUSTICE O'CONNOR's "undue burden" test was controlling, as that was the narrowest ground on which we had upheld recent abortion regulations. 947 F. 2d, at 693–697 ("'When a fragmented court decides a case and no single rationale explaining the result enjoys the assent of five Justices, the holding of the Court may be viewed as that position taken by those Members who concurred in the judgments on the narrowest grounds'" (quoting *Marks* v. *United States,* 430 U. S. 188, 193 (1977) (internal quotation marks omitted)). Applying this standard, the Court of Appeals upheld all of the challenged regulations except the one requiring a woman to notify her spouse of an intended abortion.

In arguing that this Court should invalidate each of the provisions at issue, petitioners insist that we reaffirm our decision in *Roe* v. *Wade, supra,* in which we held unconstitutional a Texas statute making it a crime to procure an abortion except to save the life of the mother. We agree with the Court of Appeals that our decision in *Roe* is not directly implicated by the Pennsylvania statute, which does not prohibit, but simply regulates, abortion. But, as the Court of Appeals found, the state of our post-*Roe* decisional law dealing with the regulation of abortion is confusing and uncertain, indicating that a reexamination of that line of cases is in order. Unfortunately for those who must apply this Court's decisions, the reexamination undertaken today leaves the Court no less divided than beforehand. Although they reject the trimester framework that formed the underpinning of *Roe,* JUSTICES O'CONNOR, KENNEDY, and

SOUTER adopt a revised undue burden standard to analyze the challenged regulations. We conclude, however, that such an outcome is an unjustified constitutional compromise, one which leaves the Court in a position to closely scrutinize all types of abortion regulations despite the fact that it lacks the power to do so under the Constitution.

In *Roe,* the Court opined that the State "does have an important and legitimate interest in preserving and protecting the health of the pregnant woman, . . . and that it has still another important and legitimate interest in protecting the potentiality of human life." 410 U. S., at 162 (emphasis omitted). In the companion case of *Doe v. Bolton,* 410 U. S. 179 (1973), the Court referred to its conclusion in *Roe* "that a pregnant woman does not have an absolute constitutional right to an abortion on her demand." 410 U. S., at 189. But while the language and holdings of these cases appeared to leave States free to regulate abortion procedures in a variety of ways, later decisions based on them have found considerably less latitude for such regulations than might have been expected.

For example, after *Roe,* many States have sought to protect their young citizens by requiring that a minor seeking an abortion involve her parents in the decision. Some States have simply required notification of the parents, while others have required a minor to obtain the consent of her parents. In a number of decisions, however, the Court has substantially limited the States in their ability to impose such requirements. With regard to parental *notice* requirements, we initially held that a State could require a minor to notify her parents before proceeding with an abortion. *H. L. v. Matheson,* 450 U. S. 398, 407–410 (1981). Recently, however, we indicated that a State's ability to impose a notice requirement actually depends on whether it requires notice of one or both parents. We concluded that although the Constitution might allow a State to demand that notice be given to one parent prior to an abortion, it may not require that similar notice be given to *two* parents, unless the State incorporates a judicial bypass procedure in that two-parent requirement. *Hodgson v. Minnesota, supra.*

We have treated parental *consent* provisions even more harshly. Three years after *Roe,* we invalidated a Missouri regulation requiring that an unmarried woman under the age of 18 obtain the consent of one her parents before proceeding with an abortion. We held that our abortion jurisprudence prohibited the State from imposing such a "blanket provision . . . requiring the consent of a parent." *Planned Parenthood of Central Mo. v. Danforth,* 428 U. S. 52, 74 (1976). In *Bellotti v. Baird,* 443 U. S. 622 (1979), the Court struck down a similar Massachusetts parental consent statute. A majority of the Court indicated, however, that a State could constitutionally require parental consent, if it alternatively allowed a pregnant minor to obtain an abortion without parental consent by showing either that she was mature enough to make her own decision, or that the abortion would be in her best interests. See *id.,* at 643–644 (plurality opinion); *id.,* at 656-657 (WHITE, J., dissenting). In light of *Bellotti,* we have upheld one parental consent regulation which incorporated a judicial bypass option we viewed as sufficient, see *Planned Parenthood Assn. of Kansas City, Mo., Inc. v. Ashcroft,* 462 U. S. 476 (1983), but have invalidated another because of our belief that the judicial procedure did not satisfy the dictates of *Bellotti.* See *Akron v. Akron Center for Reproductive Health, Inc.,* 462 U. S. 416, 439–442 (1983). We have never had occasion, as we have in the parental notice context, to further parse our parental consent jurisprudence into one-parent and two-parent components.

In *Roe,* the Court observed that certain States recognized the right of the father to participate in the abortion decision in certain circumstances. Because neither *Roe* nor *Doe* involved the assertion of any paternal right, the Court expressly stated that the case did not disturb the validity of regulations that protected such a right. *Roe v. Wade,* 410 U. S., at 165, n. 67. But three years later, in *Danforth,* the Court extended its abortion jurisprudence and held that a State could not require that a woman obtain the consent of her spouse before proceeding with an abortion. *Planned Parenthood of Central Mo. v. Danforth,* 428 U. S., at 69–71.

States have also regularly tried to ensure that a woman's decision to have an abortion is an informed and well-considered one. In *Danforth,* we upheld a requirement that a woman sign a consent form prior to her abortion, and observed that "it is desirable and imperative that [the decision] be made with full knowledge of its nature and consequences." *Id.,* at 67. Since that case, however, we have twice invalidated state statutes designed to impart such knowledge to a woman seeking an abortion. In *Akron,* we held unconstitutional a regulation requiring a physician to inform a woman seeking an abortion of the status of her pregnancy, the development of her fetus, the date of possible viability, the complications that could result from an abortion, and the availability of agencies providing assistance and information with respect to adoption and childbirth. *Akron v. Akron Center for Reproductive Health, supra,* at 442–445. More recently, in *Thornburgh v. American College of Obstetricians and Gynecologists,* 476 U. S. 747 (1986), we struck down a more limited Pennsylvania regulation requiring that a woman be informed of the risks associated with the abortion procedure and the assistance available to her if she decided to proceed with her pregnancy, because we saw the compelled information as "the antithesis of informed consent." *Id.,* at 764. Even when a State has sought only to provide information that, in our view, was consistent with the *Roe* framework, we concluded that the State could not require that a physician furnish the information, but instead had to alternatively allow non-physician counselors to provide it. *Akron v. Akron Center for Reproductive Health,* 462 U. S., at 448–449. In *Akron* as well, we went further and held that a State may not require a physician to wait 24 hours to perform an abortion after receiving the consent of a woman. Although the State sought to ensure that the woman's decision was carefully considered, the Court concluded that the Constitution forbade the State from imposing any sort of delay. *Id.,* at 449–451.

We have not allowed States much leeway to regulate even the actual abortion procedure. Although a State can require that second-trimester abortions be performed in outpatient clinics, see *Simopoulos v. Virginia,* 462 U. S. 506 (1983), we concluded in *Akron* and *Ashcroft* that a State could not require that such abortions be performed only in hospitals. See *Akron v. Akron Center for Reproductive Health, supra,* at 437–439; *Planned Parenthood Assn. of Kansas City, Mo., Inc. v. Ashcroft, supra,* at 481–482. Despite the fact that *Roe* expressly allowed regulation after the first trimester in furtherance of maternal health, "'present medical knowledge,'" in our view, could not justify such a hospitalization requirement under the trimester framework. *Akron v. Akron Center for Reproductive health, supra,* at 437 (quoting *Roe v. Wade, supra,* at 163). And in *Danforth,* the Court held that Missouri could not outlaw the saline amniocentesis method of abortion, concluding that the Missouri Legislature had "failed to appreciate and to consider several significant facts" in making its decision. 428 U. S., at 77.

Although *Roe* allowed state regulation after the point of viability to protect the potential life of the fetus, the Court subsequently rejected attempts to regulate in this manner. In *Colautti v. Franklin,* 439 U. S. 379 (1979), the Court struck down a statute that governed the determination of viability. *Id.,* at 390–397. In the process, we made clear that the trimester framework incorporated only one definition of viability—ours—as we forbade States from deciding that a certain objective indicator—"be it weeks of gestation or fetal weight or any other single factor"—should govern the definition of viability. *Id.,* at 389. In that same case, we also invalidated a regulation requiring a physician to use the abortion technique offering the best chance for fetal survival when performing postviability abortions. See *id.,* at 397–401; see also *Thornburgh v. American College of Obstetricians and Gynecologists, supra,* at 768–769 (invalidating a similar regulation). In *Thornburgh,* the Court struck down Pennsylvania's requirement that a second physician be present at postviability abortions to help preserve the health of the unborn child, on the ground that it did not incorporate a sufficient medical emergency exception. *Id.,* at 769–771. Regulations governing the treatment of aborted fetuses have met a similar fate. In *Akron,* we invalidated a provision requiring physicians performing abortions to "insure that the remains of the unborn child are disposed of in a humane and sanitary manner." 462 U. S., at 451 (internal quotation marks omitted).

Dissents in these cases expressed the view that the Court was expanding upon *Roe* in imposing ever greater restrictions on the States. See *Thornburgh v. American College of Obstetricians and Gynecologists,* 476 U. S., at 783 (Burger, C. J., dissenting) ("The extent to which the Court has departed from the limitations expressed in *Roe* is readily apparent"); *id.,* at 814 (WHITE, J., dissenting) ("[T]he majority indiscriminately strikes down statutory provisions that in no way contravene the right recognized in *Roe*"). And, when confronted with State regulations of this type in past years, the Court has become increasingly more divided: the three most recent abortion cases have not commanded a Court opinion. See *Ohio v. Akron Center for Reproductive health,* 497 U. S. 502 (1990); *Hodgson v. Minnesota,* 497 U. S. 417 (1990); *Webster v. Reproductive Health Services,* 492 U. S. 490 (1989).

The task of the Court of Appeals in the present case was obviously complicated by this confusion and uncertainty. Following *Marks v. United States,* 430 U. S. 188 (1977), it concluded that in light of *Webster* and *Hodgson,* the strict scrutiny standard enunciated in *Roe* was no longer applicable, and that the "undue burden" standard adopted by JUSTICE O'CONNOR was the governing principle. This state of confusion and disagreement warrants reexamination of the "fundamental right" accorded to a woman's decision to abort a fetus in *Roe*, with its concomitant requirement that any state regulation of abortion survive "strict scrutiny." See *Payne* v. *Tennessee*, 501 U. S. ——, —— – —— (1991) (slip op., at 17–20) (observing that reexamination of constitutional decisions is appropriate when those decisions have generated uncertainty and failed to provide clear guidance, because "correction through legislative action is practically impossible" (internal quotation marks omitted)); *Garcia* v. *San Antonio Metropolitan Transit Authority*, 469 U. S. 528, 546–547, 557 (1985).

We have held that a liberty interest protected under the Due Process Clause of the Fourteenth Amendment will be deemed fundamental if it is "implicit in the concept of ordered liberty." *Palko* v. *Connecticut*, 302 U. S. 319, 325 (1937). Three years earlier, in *Snyder* v. *Massachusetts*, 291 U. S. 97 (1934), we referred to a "principle of justice so rooted in the traditions and conscience of our people as to be ranked as fundamental." *Id.,* at 105; see also *Michael H.* v. *Gerald D.*, 491 U. S. 110, 122 (1989) (plurality opinion) (citing the language from *Snyder*). These expressions are admittedly not precise, but our decisions implementing this notion of "fundamental" rights do not afford any more elaborate basis on which to base such a classification.

In construing the phrase "liberty" incorporated in the Due Process Clause of the Fourteenth Amendment, we have recognized that its meaning extends beyond freedom from physical restraint. In *Pierce* v. *Society of Sisters*, 268 U. S. 510 (1925), we held that it included a parent's right to send a child to private school; in *Meyer* v. *Nebraska*, 262 U. S. 390 (1923), we held that it included a right to teach a foreign language in a parochial school. Building on these cases, we have held that that the term "liberty" includes a right to marry, *Loving* v. *Virginia*, 388 U. S. 1 (1967); a right to procreate, *Skinner* v. *Oklahoma ex rel. Williamson*, 316 U. S. 535 (1942); and a right to use contraceptives. *Griswold* v. *Connecticut*, 381 U. S. 479 (1965); *Eisenstadt* v. *Baird*, 405 U. S. 438 (1972). But a reading of these opinions makes clear that they do not endorse any all-encompassing "right of privacy."

In *Roe* v. *Wade*, the Court recognized a "guarantee of personal privacy" which "is broad enough to encompass a woman's decision whether or not to terminate her pregnancy." 410 U. S., at 152–153. We are now of the view that, in terming this right fundamental, the Court in *Roe* read the earlier opinions upon which it based its decision much too broadly. Unlike marriage, procreation and contraception, abortion "involves the purposeful termination of potential life." *Harris* v. *McRae*, 448 U. S. 297, 325 (1980). The abortion decision must therefore "be recognized as *sui generis*, different in kind from the others that the Court has protected under the rubric of personal or family privacy and autonomy." *Thornburgh* v. *American College of Obstetricians and Gynecologists, supra,* at 792 (WHITE, J., dissenting). One cannot ignore the fact that a woman is not isolated in her pregnancy, and that the decision to abort necessarily involves the destruction of a fetus. See *Michael H.* v. *Gerald D., supra,* at 124, n. 4 (To look "at the act which is assertedly the subject of a liberty interest in isolation from its effect upon other people [is] like inquiring whether there is a liberty interest in firing a gun where the case at hand happens to involve its discharge into another person's body").

Nor do the historical traditions of the American people support the view that the right to terminate one's pregnancy is "fundamental." The common law which we inherited from England made abortion after "quickening" an offense. At the time of the adoption of the Fourteenth Amendment, statutory prohibitions or restrictions on abortion were commonplace; in 1868, at least 28 of the then-37 States and 8 Territories had statutes banning or limiting abortion. J. Mohr, Abortion in America 200 (1978). By the turn of the century virtually every State had a law prohibiting or restricting abortion on its books. By the middle of the present century, a liberalization trend had set in. But 21 of the restrictive abortion laws in effect in 1868 were still in effect in 1973 when *Roe* was decided, and an overwhelming majority of the States prohibited abortion unless necessary to preserve the life or health of the mother. *Roe* v. *Wade*, 410 U. S., at 139–140; id., at 176–177, n. 2 (REHNQUIST, J., dissenting). On this record, it can scarcely be said that any deeply rooted tradition of relatively unrestricted abortion in our history supported the classification of the right to abortion as "fundamental" under the Due Process Clause of the Fourteenth Amendment.

We think, therefore, both in view of this history and of our decided cases dealing with substantive liberty under the Due Process Clause, that the Court was mistaken in *Roe* when it classified a woman's decision to terminate her pregnancy as a "fundamental right" that could be abridged only in a manner which withstood "strict scrutiny." In so concluding, we repeat the observation made in *Bowers* v. *Hardwick*, 478 U. S. 186 (1986):

"Nor are we inclined to take a more expansive view of our authority to discover new fundamental rights imbedded in the Due Process Clause. The Court is most vulnerable and comes nearest to illegitimacy when it deals with judge-made constitutional law having little or no cognizable roots in the language or design of the Constitution." *Id.,* at 194.

We believe that the sort of constitutionally imposed abortion code of the type illustrated by our decisions following *Roe* is inconsistent "with the notion of a Constitution cast in general terms, as ours is, and usually speaking in general principles, as ours does." *Webster* v. *Reproductive Health Services,* 492 U. S., at 518 (plurality opinion). The Court in *Roe* reached too far when it analogized the right to abort a fetus to the rights involved in *Pierce, Meyer, Loving,* and *Griswold,* and thereby deemed the right to abortion fundamental.

II

The joint opinion of Justices O'Connor, Kennedy, and Souter cannot bring itself to say that *Roe* was correct as an original matter, but the authors are of the view that "the immediate question is not the soundness of *Roe's* resolution of the issue, but the precedential force that must be accorded to its holding." *Ante,* at 29. Instead of claiming that *Roe* was correct as a matter of original constitutional interpretation, the opinion therefore contains an elaborate discussion of *stare decisis.* This discussion of the principle of *stare decisis* appears to be almost entirely dicta, because the joint opinion does not apply that principle in dealing with *Roe. Roe* decided that a woman had a fundamental right to an abortion. The joint opinion rejects that view. *Roe* decided that abortion regulations were to be subjected to "strict scrutiny" and could be justified only in the light of "compelling state interests." The joint opinion rejects that view. *Ante,* at 29–30; see *Roe* v. *Wade, supra,* at 162–164. *Roe* analyzed abortion regulation under a rigid trimester framework, a framework which has guided this Court's decision making for 19 years. The joint opinion rejects that framework. *Ante,* at 31.

Stare decisis is defined in Black's Law Dictionary as meaning "to abide by, or adhere to, decided cases." Black's Law Dictionary 1406 (6th ed. 1990). Whatever the "central holding" of *Roe* that is left after the joint opinion finishes dissecting it is surely not the result of that principle. While purporting

to adhere to precedent, the joint opinion instead revises it. *Roe* continues to exist, but only in the way a storefront on a western movie set exists: a mere facade to give the illusion of reality. Decisions following *Roe,* such as *Akron* v. *Akron Center for Reproductive Health, Inc.,* 462 U. S. 416 (1983), and *Thornburgh* v. *American College of Obstetricians and Gynecologists,* 476 U. S. 747 (1986), are frankly overruled in part under the "undue burden" standard expounded in the joint opinion. *Ante,* at 39–42.

In our view, authentic principles of *stare decisis* do not require that any portion of the reasoning in *Roe* be kept intact. "*Stare decisis* is not . . . a universal, inexorable command," especially in cases involving the interpretation of the Federal Constitution. *Burnet* v. *Coronado Oil & Gas Co.,* 285 U. S. 393, 405 (1932) (Brandeis, J., dissenting). Erroneous decisions in such constitutional cases are uniquely durable, because correction through legislative action, save for constitutional amendment, is impossible. It is therefore our duty to reconsider constitutional interpretations that "depar[t] from a proper understanding" of the Constitution. *Garcia* v. *San Antonio Metropolitan Transit Authority,* 469 U. S., at 557; see *United States* v. *Scott,* 437 U. S. 82, 101 (1978) ("'[I]n cases involving the Federal Constitution, . . . [t]he Court bows to the lessons of experience and the force of better reasoning, recognizing that the process of trial and error, so fruitful in the physical sciences, is appropriate also in the judicial function.'" (quoting *Burnet* v. *Coronado Oil & Gas Co., supra,* at 406–408 (Brandeis, J., dissenting))); *Smith* v. *Allwright,* 321 U. S. 649, 665 (1944). Our constitutional watch does not cease merely because we have spoken before on an issue; when it becomes clear that a prior constitutional interpretation is unsound we are obliged to reexamine the question. See, *e.g., West Virginia State Bd. of Education* v. *Barnette,* 319 U. S. 624, 642 (1943); *Erie R. Co.* v. *Tompkins,* 304 U. S. 64, 74–78 (1938).

The joint opinion discusses several *stare decisis* factors which, it asserts, point toward retaining a portion of *Roe.* Two of these factors are that the main "factual underpinning" of *Roe* has remained the same, and that its doctrinal foundation is no weaker now than it was in 1973. *Ante,* at 14–18. Of course, what might be called the basic facts which gave rise to *Roe* have remained the same— women become pregnant, there is a point somewhere, depending on medical technology, where a fetus becomes viable, and women give birth to children. But this is only to say that the same facts which gave rise to *Roe* will continue to give rise to similar cases. It is not a reason, in and of itself, why those cases must be decided in the same incorrect manner as was the first case to deal with the question. And surely there is no requirement, in considering whether to depart from *stare decisis* in a constitutional case, that a decision be more wrong now than it was at the time it was rendered. If that were true, the most outlandish constitutional decision could survive forever, based simply on the fact that it was no more outlandish later than it was when originally rendered.

Nor does the joint opinion faithfully follow this alleged requirement. The opinion frankly concludes that *Roe* and its progeny were wrong in failing to recognize that the State's interests in maternal health and in the protection of unborn human life exist throughout pregnancy. *Ante,* 29–31. But there is no indication that these components of *Roe* are any more incorrect at this juncture than they were at its inception.

The joint opinion also points to the reliance interests involved in this context in its effort to explain why precedent must be followed for precedent's sake. Certainly it is true that where reliance is truly at issue, as in the case of judicial decisions that have formed the basis for private decisions, "[c]onsiderations in favor of *stare decisis* are at their acme." *Payne* v. *Tennessee,* 501 U. S., at—(slip op., at 18). But, as the joint opinion apparently agrees, *ante,* at 13–14, any traditional notion of reliance is not applicable here. The Court today cuts back on the protection afforded by *Roe,* and no one claims that this action defeats any reliance interest in the disavowed trimester framework. Similarly, reliance interests would not be diminished were the Court to go further and acknowledge the full error of *Roe,* as "reproductive planning could take virtually immediate account of" this action. *Ante,* at 14.

The joint opinion thus turns to what can only be described as an unconventional—and unconvincing—notion of reliance, a view based on the surmise that the availability of abortion since *Roe* has led to "two decades of economic and social developments" that would be undercut if the error of *Roe* were recognized. *Ibid.* The joint opinion's assertion of this fact is undeveloped and totally conclusory. In fact, one can not be sure to what economic and social developments the opinion is referring. Surely it is dubious to suggest that women have reached their "places in society" in reliance upon *Roe,* rather than as a result of their determination to obtain higher education and compete with men in the job market, and of society's increasing recognition of their ability to fill

positions that were previously thought to be reserved only for men. *Ibid.*

In the end, having failed to put forth any evidence to prove any true reliance, the joint opinion's argument is based solely on generalized assertions about the national psyche, on a belief that the people of this country have grown accustomed to the *Roe* decision over the last 19 years and have "ordered their thinking and living around" it. *Ibid.* As an initial matter, one might inquire how the joint opinion can view the "central holding" of *Roe* as so deeply rooted in our constitutional culture, when it so casually uproots and disposes of that same decision's trimester framework. Furthermore, at various points in the past, the same could have been said about this Court's erroneous decisions that the Constitution allowed "separate but equal" treatment of minorities, see *Plessy* v. *Ferguson,* 163 U. S. 537 (1896), or that "liberty" under the Due Process Clause protected "freedom of contract." See *Adkins* v. *Children's Hospital of D. C.,* 261 U. S. 525 (1923); *Lochner* v. *New York,* 198 U. S. 45 (1905). The "separate but equal" doctrine lasted 58 years after *Plessy,* and *Lochner's* protection of contractual freedom lasted 32 years. However, the simple fact that a generation or more had grown used to these major decisions did not prevent the Court from correcting its errors in those cases, nor should it prevent us from correctly interpreting the Constitution here. See *Brown* v. *Board of Education,* 347 U. S. 483 (1954) (rejecting the "separate but equal" doctrine); *West Coast Hotel Co.* v. *Parrish,* 300 U. S. 379 (1937) (overruling *Adkins* v. *Children's Hospital, supra,* in upholding Washington's minimum wage law).

Apparently realizing that conventional *stare decisis* principles do not support its position, the joint opinion advances a belief that retaining a portion of *Roe* is necessary to protect the "legitimacy" of this Court. *Ante,* at 19–27. Because the Court must take care to render decisions "grounded truly in principle," and not simply as political and social compromises, *ante,* at 23, the joint opinion properly declares it to be this Court's duty to ignore the public criticism and protest that may arise as a result of a decision. Few would quarrel with this statement, although it may be doubted that Members of this Court, holding their tenure as they do during constitutional "good behavior," are at all likely to be intimidated by such public protests.

But the joint opinion goes on to state that when the Court "resolve[s] the sort of intensely divisive controversy reflected in *Roe* and those rare, comparable cases," its decision is exempt from reconsideration under established principles of *stare decisis* in constitutional cases. *Ante,* at 24. This is so, the joint opinion contends, because in those "intensely divisive" cases the Court has "call[ed] the contending sides of a national controversy to end their national division by accepting a common mandate rooted in the Constitution," and must therefore take special care not to be perceived as "surrender[ing] to political pressure" and continued opposition. *Ante,* at 24–25. This is a truly novel principle, one which is contrary to both the Court's historical practice and to the Court's traditional willingness to tolerate criticism of its opinions. Under this principle, when the Court has ruled on a divisive issue, it is apparently prevented from overruling that decision for the sole reason that it was incorrect, *unless opposition to the original decision has died away.*

The first difficulty with this principle lies in its assumption that cases which are "intensely divisive" can be readily distinguished from those that are not. The question of whether a particular issue is "intensely divisive" enough to qualify for special protection is entirely subjective and dependent on the individual assumptions of the members of this Court. In addition, because the Court's duty is to ignore public opinion and criticism on issues that come before it, its members are in perhaps the worst position to judge whether a decision divides the Nation deeply enough to justify such uncommon protection. Although many of the Court's decisions divide the populace to a large degree, we have not previously on that account shied away from applying normal rules of *stare decisis* when urged to reconsider earlier decisions. Over the past 21 years, for example, the Court has overruled in whole or in part 34 of its previous constitutional decisions. See *Payne* v. *Tennessee, supra,* at——, and n. 1 (slip op., at 19–19, and n. 1) (listing cases).

The joint opinion picks out and discusses two prior Court rulings that it believes are of the "intensely divisive" variety, and concludes that they are of comparable dimension to *Roe. Ante,* at 19–22 (discussing *Lochner* v. *New York, supra,* and *Plessy* v. *Ferguson, supra*). It appears to us very odd indeed that the joint opinion chooses as benchmarks two cases in which the Court chose *not* to adhere to erroneous constitutional precedent, but instead enhanced its stature by acknowledging and correcting its error, apparently in violation of the joint opinion's "legitimacy" principle. See *West Coast Hotel Co.* v. *Parrish, supra; Brown* v. *Board of Education, supra.* One might also wonder how it is that the joint opinion puts these, and not others,

in the "intensely divisive" category, and how it assumes that these are the only two lines of cases of comparable dimension to *Roe.* There is no reason to think that either *Plessy* or *Lochner* produced the sort of public protest when they were decided that *Roe* did. There were undoubtedly large segments of the bench and bar who agreed with the dissenting views in those cases, but surely that cannot be what the Court means when it uses the term "intensely divisive," or many other cases would have to be added to the list. In terms of public protest, however, *Roe,* so far as we know, was unique. But just as the Court should not respond to that sort of protest by retreating from the decision simply to allay the concerns of the protesters, it should likewise not respond by determining to adhere to the decision at all costs lest it *seem* to be retreating under fire. Public protests should not alter the normal application of *stare decisis,* lest perfectly lawful protest activity be penalized by the Court itself.

Taking the joint opinion on its own terms, we doubt that its distinction between *Roe,* on the one hand, and *Plessy* and *Lochner,* on the other, withstands analysis. The joint opinion acknowledges that the Court improved its stature by overruling *Plessy* in *Brown* on a deeply divisive issue. And our decision in *West Coast Hotel,* which overruled *Adkins* v. *Children's Hospital, supra,* and *Lochner,* was rendered at a time when Congress was considering President Franklin Roosevelt's proposal to "reorganize" this Court and enable him to name six additional Justices in the event that any member of the Court over the age of 70 did not elect to retire. It is difficult to imagine a situation in which the Court would face more intense opposition to a prior ruling than it did at that time, and, under the general principle proclaimed in the joint opinion, the Court seemingly should have responded to this opposition by stubbornly refusing to reexamine the *Lochner* rationale, lest it lose legitimacy by appearing to "overrule under fire." *Ante,* at 25.

The joint opinion agrees that the Court's stature would have been seriously damaged if in *Brown* and *West Coast Hotel* it had dug in its heels and refused to apply normal principles of *stare decisis* to the earlier decisions. But the opinion contends that the Court was entitled to overrule *Plessy* and *Lochner* in those cases, despite the existence of opposition to the original decisions, only because both the Nation and the Court had learned new lessons in the interim. This is at best a feebly supported, *post hoc* rationalization for those decisions.

For example, the opinion asserts that the Court could justifiably overrule its decision in *Lochner* only because the Depression had convinced "most people" that constitutional protection of contractual freedom contributed to an economy that failed to protect the welfare of all. *Ante*, at 19. Surely the joint opinion does not mean to suggest that people saw this Court's failure to uphold minimum wage statues as the cause of the Great Depression! In any event, the *Lochner* Court did not base its rule upon the policy judgment that an unregulated market was fundamental to a stable economy; it simple believed, erroneously, that "liberty" under the Due Process Clause protected the "right to make a contract." *Lochner* v. *New York*, 198 U. S., at 53. Nor is it the case that the people of this Nation only discovered the dangers of extreme laissez faire economics because of the Depression. State laws regulating maximum hours and minimum wages were in existence well before that time. A Utah statute of that sort enacted in 1896 was involved in our decision in *Holden* v. *Hardy*, 169 U. S. 366 (1898), and other states followed suit shortly afterwards. See, e.g., *Muller* v. *Oregon*, 208 U. S. 412 (1908); *Bunting* v. *Oregon*, 243 U. S. 426 (1917). These statutes were indeed enacted because of a belief on the part of their sponsors that "freedom of contract" did not protect the welfare of workers, demonstrating that that belief manifested itself more than a generation before the Great Depression. Whether "most people" had come to share it in the hard times of the 1930's is, insofar as anything the joint opinion advances, entirely speculative. The crucial failing at that time was not that workers were not paid a fair wage, but that there was no work available at *any* wage.

When the Court finally recognized its error in *West Coast Hotel,* it did not engage in the *post hoc* rationalization that the joint opinion attributes to it today; it did not state that *Lochner* had been based on an economic view that had fallen into disfavor, and that it therefore should be overruled. Chief Justice Hughes in his opinion for the Court simply recognized what Justice Holmes had previously recognized in his *Lochner* dissent, that "[t]he Constitution does not speak of freedom of contract." *West Coast Hotel Co.* v. *Parrish*, 300 U. S., at 391; *Lochner* v. *New York, supra,* at 75 (Holmes, J., dissenting) ("[A] Constitution is not intended to embody a particular economic theory, whether of paternalism and the organic relation of the citizen to the State or of *laissez faire*"). Although the Court did acknowledge in the last paragraph of its opinion the state of affairs during the then-current Depression, the theme of the opinion is that the Court had been mistaken as a matter of constitutional law when it embraced "freedom of contract" 32 years previously.

The joint opinion also agrees that the Court acted properly in rejecting the doctrine of "separate but equal" in *Brown*. In fact, the opinion lauds *Brown* in comparing it to *Roe. Ante*, at 25. This is strange, in that under the opinion's "legitimacy" principle the Court would seemingly have been forced to adhere to its erroneous decision in *Plessy* because of its "intensely divisive" character. To us, adherence to *Roe* today under the guise of "legitimacy" would seem to resemble more closely adherence to *Plessy* on the same ground. Fortunately, the Court did not choose that option in *Brown,* and instead frankly repudiated *Plessy*. The joint opinion concludes that such repudiation was justified only because of newly discovered evidence that congregation had the effect of treating one race as inferior to another. But it can hardly be argued that this was not urged upon those who decided *Plessy,* as Justice Harlan observed in his dissent that the law at issue "puts the brand of servitude and degradation upon a large class of our fellow-citizens, our equals before the law." *Plessy* v. *Ferguson*, 163 U. S., at 562 (Harlan, J., dissenting). It is clear that the same arguments made before the Court in *Brown* were made in *Plessy* as well. The Court in *Brown* simply recognized, as Justice Harlan had recognized beforehand, that the Fourteenth Amendment does not permit racial segregation. The rule of *Brown* is not tied to popular opinion about the evils of segregation; it is a judgment that the Equal Protection Clause does not permit racial segregation, no matter whether the public might come to believe that it is beneficial. On that ground it stands, and on that ground alone the Court was justified in properly concluding that the *Plessy* Court had erred.

There is also a suggestion in the joint opinion that the propriety of overruling a "divisive" decision depends in part on whether "most people" would now agree that it should be overruled. Either the demise of opposition or its progression to substantial popular agreement apparently is required to allow the Court to reconsider a divisive decision. How such agreement would be ascertained, short of a public opinion poll, the joint opinion does not say. But surely even the suggestion is totally at war with the idea of "legitimacy" in whose name it is invoked. The Judicial Branch derives its legitimacy, not from following public opinion, but from deciding by its best lights whether legislative enactments of the popular branches of Government comport with the Constitution. The doctrine of *stare decisis* is an adjunct of this duty, and should be no more subject to the vagaries of public opinion than is the basic judicial task.

There are other reasons why the joint opinion's discussion of legitimacy is unconvincing as well. In assuming that the Court is perceived as "surrender[ing] to political pressure" when it overrules a controversial decision, *ante,* at 25, the joint opinion forgets that there are two sides to any controversy. The joint opinion asserts that, in order to protect its legitimacy, the Court must refrain from overruling a controversial decision lest it be viewed as favoring those who oppose the decision. But a decision to *adhere* to prior precedent is subject to the same criticism, for in such a case one can easily argue that the Court is responding to those who have demonstrated in favor of the original decision. The decision in *Roe* has engendered large demonstrations, including repeated marches on this Court and on Congress, both in opposition to and in support of that opinion. A decision either way on *Roe* can therefore be perceived as favoring one group or the other. But this perceived dilemma arises only if one assumes, as the joint opinion does, that the Court should make its decisions with a view toward speculative public perceptions. If one assumes instead, as the Court surely did in both *Brown* and *West Coast Hotel,* that the Court's legitimacy is enhanced by faithful interpretation of the Constitution irrespective of public opposition, such self-engendered difficulties may be put to one side.

Roe is not this Court's only decision to generate conflict. Our decisions in some recent capital cases, and in *Bowers* v. *Hardwick,* 478 U. S. 186 (1986), have also engendered demonstrations in opposition. The joint opinion's message to such protesters appears to be that they must cease their activities in order to serve their cause, because their protests will only cement in place a decision which by normal standards of *stare decisis* should be reconsidered. Nearly a century ago, Justice David J. Brewer of this Court, in an article discussing criticism of its decisions, observed that "many criticisms may be, like their authors, devoid of good taste, but better all sorts of criticism than no criticism at all." Justice Brewer on "The Nation's Anchor," 57 Albany L. J. 166, 169 (1898). This was good advice to the Court then, as it is today. Strong and often misguided criticism of a decision should not render the decision immune from reconsideration, lest a fetish for legitimacy penalize freedom of expression.

The end result of the joint opinion's paeans of praise for legitimacy is the enunciation of a brand new standard for evaluating state regulation of a woman's right to abortion—the "undue burden" standard. As indicated above, *Roe* v. *Wade* adopted a "fundamental right" standard under which state regulations could survive only if they met the requirement of "strict scrutiny." While we disagree with that standard, it at least had a recognized basis in constitutional law at the time *Roe* was decided. The same cannot be said for the "undue burden" standard, which is created largely out of whole cloth by the authors of the joint opinion. It is a standard which even today does not command the support of a majority of this Court. And it will not, we believe, result in the sort of "simple limitation," easily applied, which the joint opinion anticipates. *Ante,* at 13. In sum, it is a standard which is not built to last.

In evaluating abortion regulations under that standard, judges will have to decide whether they place a "substantial obstacle" in the path of a woman seeking an abortion. *Ante,* at 34. In that this standard is based even more on a judge's subjective determinations than was the trimester framework, the standard will do nothing to prevent "judges from roaming at large in the constitutional field" guided only by their personal views. *Griswold* v. *Connecticut,* 381 U. S., at 502 (Harlan, J., concurring in judgment). Because the undue burden standard is plucked from nowhere, the question of what is a "substantial obstacle" to abortion will undoubtedly engender a variety of conflicting views. For example, in the very matter before us now, the authors of the joint opinion would uphold Pennsylvania's 24–hour waiting period, concluding that a "particular burden" on some women is not a substantial obstacle. *Ante,* at 44. But the authors would at the same time strike down Pennsylvania's spousal notice provision, after finding that in a "large fraction" of cases the provision will be a substantial obstacle. *Ante,* at 53. And, while the authors conclude that the informed consent provisions do not constitute an "undue burden," JUSTICE STEVENS would hold that they do. *Ante,* at 9–11.

Furthermore, while striking down the spousal *notice* regulation, the joint opinion would uphold a parental *consent* restriction that certainly places very substantial obstacles in the path of a minor's abortion choice. The joint opinion is forthright in admitting that it draws this distinction based on a policy judgment that parents will have the best interests of their children at heart, while the same is not necessarily true of husbands as to their wives. *Ante,* at 53. This may or may not be a correct judgment, but it is quintessentially a legislative one. The "undue burden" inquiry does not in any way supply the distinction between parental consent and spousal consent which the joint opinion adopts. Despite the efforts of the joint opinion, the undue burden standard presents nothing more workable than the trimester framework which it discards today. Under the guise of the Constitution, this Court will still impart its own preferences on the States in the form of a complex abortion code.

The sum of the joint opinion's labors in the name of *stare decisis* and "legitimacy" is this: *Roe v. Wade* stands as a sort of judicial Potemkin Village, which may be pointed out to passers by as a monument to the importance of adhering to precedent. But behind the facade, an entirely new method of analysis, without any roots in constitutional law, is imported to decide the constitutionality of state laws regulating abortion. Neither *stare decisis* nor "legitimacy" are truly served by such an effort.

We have stated above our belief that the Constitution does not subject state abortion regulations to heightened scrutiny. Accordingly, we think that the correct analysis is that set forth by the plurality opinion in *Webster*. A woman's interest in having an abortion is a form of liberty protected by the Due Process Clause, but States may regulate abortion procedures in ways rationally related to a legitimate state interest. *Williamson* v. *Lee Optical of Okla., Inc.*, 348 U. S. 483, 491 (1955); cf. *Stanley* v. *Illinois*, 405 U. S. 645, 651–653 (1972). With this rule in mind, we examine each of the challenged provisions.

III

A

section 3205 of the Act imposes certain requirements related to the informed consent of a woman seeking an abortion. 18 Pa. Cons. Stat. §3205 (1990). Section 3205(a)(1) requires that the referring or performing physician must inform a woman contemplating an abortion of (i) the nature of the procedure, and the risks and alternatives that a reasonable patient would find material; (ii) the fetus' probable gestational age; and (iii) the medical risks involved in carrying her pregnancy to term. Section 3205(a)(2) requires a physician or a nonphysician counselor to inform the woman that (i) the state health department publishes free materials describing the fetus at different stages and listing abortion alternatives; (ii) medical assistance benefits may be available for prenatal, childbirth, and neonatal care; and (iii)

the child's father is liable for child support. The Act also imposes a 24–hour waiting period between the time that the woman receives the required information and the time that the physician is allowed to perform the abortion. See Appendix, *ante*, at 61–63.

This Court has held that it is certainly within the province of the States to require a woman's voluntary and informed consent to an abortion. See *Thornburgh* v. *American College of Obstetricians and Gynecologists*, 476 U. S., at 760. Here, Pennsylvania seeks to further its legitimate interest in obtaining informed consent by ensuring that each woman "is aware not only of the reasons for having an abortion, but also of the risks associated with an abortion and the availability of assistance that might make the alternative of normal childbirth more attractive than it might otherwise appear." *Id.*, at 798–799 (WHITE, J., dissenting).

We conclude that this provision of the statute is rationally related to the State's interest in assuring that a woman's consent to an abortion be a fully informed decision.

Section 3205(a)(1) requires a physician to disclose certain information about the abortion procedure and its risks and alternatives. This requirement is certainly no large burden, as the Court of Appeals found that "the record shows that the clinics, without exception, insist on providing this information to women before an abortion is performed." 947 F. 2d, at 703. We are of the view that this information "clearly is related to maternal health and to the State's legitimate purpose in requiring informed consent." *Akron* v. *Akron Center for Reproductive Health*, 462 U. S., at 446. An accurate description of the gestational age of the fetus and of the risks involved in carrying a child to term helps to further both those interests and the State's legitimate interest in unborn human life. See *id.*, at 445–446, n. 37 (required disclosure of gestational age of the fetus "certainly is not objectionable"). Although petitioners contend that it is unreasonable for the State to require that a physician, as opposed to a nonphysician counselor, disclose this information, we agree with the Court of Appeals that a State "may rationally decide that physicians are better qualified than counselors to impart this information and answer questions about the medical aspects of the available alternatives." 947 F. 2d, at 704.

Section 3205(a)(2) compels the disclosure, by a physician or a counselor, of information concerning the availability of paternal child support and state-funded alternatives if the woman decides to proceed with her pregnancy. Here again, the Court of Appeals observed that "the record indicates that most clinics already require that a counselor consult in person with the woman about alternatives to abortion before the abortion is performed." *Id.,* at 704–705. And petitioners do not claim that the information required to be disclosed by statute is in any way false or inaccurate; indeed, the Court of Appeals found it to be "relevant, accurate, and non-inflammatory." *Id.,* at 705. We conclude that this required presentation of "balanced information" is rationally related to the State's legitimate interest in ensuring that the woman's consent is truly informed, *Thornburgh* v. *American College of Obstetricians and Gynecologists,* 476 U. S., at 830 (O'CONNOR, J., dissenting), and in addition furthers the State's interest in preserving unborn life. That the information might create some uncertainty and persuade some women to forgo abortions does not lead to the conclusion that the Constitution forbids the provision of such information. Indeed, it only demonstrates that this information might very well make a difference, and that it is therefore relevant to a woman's informed choice. Cf. *id.,* at 801 (WHITE, J., dissenting) ("[T]he ostensible objective of *Roe* v. *Wade* is not maximizing the number of abortions, but maximizing choice"). We acknowledge that in *Thornburgh* this Court struck down informed consent requirements similar to the ones at issue here. See *id.,* at 760–764. It is clear, however, that while the detailed framework of *Roe* led to the Court's invalidation of those informational requirements, they "would have been sustained under any traditional standard of judicial review, . . . or for any other surgical procedure except abortion." *Webster* v. *Reproductive Health Services,* 492 U. S., at 517 (plurality opinion) (citing *Thornburgh* v. *American College of Obstetricians and Gynecologists,* 476 U. S., at 802 (WHITE, J., dissenting); *id.,* at 783 (Burger, C. J., dissenting)). In light of our rejection of *Roe's* "fundamental right" approach to this subject, we do not regard *Thornburgh* as controlling.

For the same reason, we do not feel bound to follow this Court's previous holding that a State's 24–hour mandatory waiting period is unconstitutional. See *Akron* v. *Akron Center for Reproductive health,* 462 U. S., at 449–451. Petitioners are correct that such a provision will result in delays for some women that might not otherwise exist, therefore placing a burden on their liberty. But the provision in no way prohibits abortions, and the informed consent and waiting period requirements do not apply in the case of a medical emergency. See 18 Pa. Cons. Stat. §§3205(a),(b) (1990). We are

of the view that, in providing time for reflection and reconsideration, the waiting period helps ensure that a woman's decision to abort is a well-considered one, and reasonably furthers the State's legitimate interest in maternal health and in the unborn life of the fetus. It "is surely a small cost to impose to ensure that the woman's decision is well considered in light of its certain and irreparable consequences on fetal life, and the possible effects on her own." *Id.,* at 474 (O'CONNOR, J., dissenting).

B

In addition to providing her own informed consent, before an unemancipated woman under the age of 18 may obtain an abortion she must either furnish the consent of one of her parents, or must opt for the judicial procedure that allows her to bypass the consent requirement. Under the judicial bypass option, a minor can obtain an abortion if a state court finds that she is capable of giving her informed consent and has indeed given such consent, *or* determines that an abortion is in her best interests. Records of these court proceedings are kept confidential. The Act directs the state trial court to render a decision within three days of the woman's application, and the entire procedure, including appeal to Pennsylvania Superior Court, is to last no longer than eight business days. The parental consent requirement does not apply in the case of a medical emergency. 18 Pa. Cons. Stat. §3206 (1990). See Appendix, *ante,* at 64–65.

This provision is entirely consistent with this Court's previous decisions involving parental consent requirements. See *Planned Parenthood Association of Kansas City, Mo., Inc.* v. *Ashcroft,* 462 U. S. 476 (1983) (upholding parental consent requirement with a similar judicial bypass option); *Akron* v. *Akron Center for Reproductive Health, supra,* at 439–440 (approving of parental consent statutes that include a judicial bypass option allowing a pregnant minor to "demonstrate that she is sufficiently mature to make the abortion decision herself or that, despite her immaturity, an abortion would be in her best interests"); *Bellotti* v. *Baird,* 443 U. S. 622 (1979).

We think it beyond dispute that a State "has a strong and legitimate interest in the welfare of its young citizens, whose immaturity, inexperience, and lack of judgment may sometimes impair their ability to exercise their rights wisely." *Hodgson* v. *Minnesota,* 497 U. S., at 444 (opinion of STEVENS, J.) A requirement of parental consent to abortion, like myriad other restrictions placed upon minors in other contexts, is reasonably designed to further this important and legitimate state interest. In our view, it is entirely "rational and fair for the State to conclude that, in most instances, the family will strive to give a lonely or even terrified minor advice that is both compassionate and mature." *Ohio v. Akron Center for Reproductive health,* 497 U. S., at 520 (opinion of KENNEDY, J.); see also *Planned Parenthood of Central Mo. v. Danforth,* 428 U. S., at 91 (Stewart, J., concurring) ("There can be little doubt that the State furthers a constitutionally permissible end by encouraging an unmarried pregnant minor to seek the help and advice of her parents in making the very important decision whether or not to bear a child"). We thus conclude that Pennsylvania's parental consent requirement should be upheld.

C

Section 3209 of the Act contains the spousal notification provision. It requires that, before a physician may perform an abortion on a married woman, the woman must sign a statement indicating that she has notified her husband of her planned abortion. A woman is not required to notify her husband if (1) her husband is not the father, (2) her husband, after diligent effort, cannot be located, (3) the pregnancy is the result of a spousal sexual assault that has been reported to the authorities, or (4) the woman has reason to believe that notifying her husband is likely to result in the infliction of bodily injury upon her by him or by another individual. In addition, a woman is exempted from the notification requirement in the case of a medical emergency. 18 Pa. Cons. Stat. §3209 (1990). See Appendix, *ante,* at 68–69.

We first emphasize that Pennsylvania has not imposed a spousal *consent* requirement of the type the Court struck down in *Planned Parenthood of Central Mo. v. Danforth,* 428 U. S., at 67–72. Missouri's spousal consent provision was invalidated in that case because of the Court's view that it unconstitutionally granted to the husband "a veto power exercisable for any reason whatsoever or for no reason at all." *Id.,* at 71. But this case involves a much less intrusive requirement of spousal *notification,* not consent. Such a law requiring only notice to the husband "does not give any third party the legal right to make the [woman's] decision for her, or to prevent her from obtaining an abortion should she choose to have one performed." *Hodgson v. Minnesota, supra,* at

496 (KENNEDY, J., concurring in judgment in part and dissenting in part); see *H. L. v. Matheson,* 450 U. S., at 411, n. 17. *Danforth* thus does not control our analysis. Petitioners contend that it should, however; they argue that the real effect of such a notice requirement is to give the power to husbands to veto a woman's abortion choice. The District Court indeed found that the notification provision created a risk that some woman who would otherwise have an abortion will be prevented from having one. 947 F. 2d, at 712. For example, petitioners argue, many notified husbands will prevent abortions through physical force, psychological coercion, and other types of threats. But Pennsylvania has incorporated exceptions in the notice provision in an attempt to deal with these problems. For instance, a woman need not notify her husband if the pregnancy is result of a reported sexual assault, or if she has reason to believe that she would suffer bodily injury as a result of the notification. 18 Pa. Cons. Stat. §3209(b) (1990). Furthermore, because this is a facial challenge to the Act, it is insufficient for petitioners to show that the notification provision "might operate unconstitutionally under some conceivable set of circumstances." *United States v. Salerno,* 481 U. S. 739, 745 (1987). Thus, it is not enough for petitioners to show that, in some "worst-case" circumstances, the notice provision will operate as a grant of veto power to husbands. *Ohio v. Akron Center for Reproductive Health,* 497 U. S., at 514. Because they are making a facial challenge to the provision, they must "show that no set of circumstances exists under which the [provision] would be valid." *Ibid.* (internal quotation marks omitted). This they have failed to do.

The question before us is therefore whether the spousal notification requirement rationally furthers any legitimate state interests. We conclude that it does. First, a husband's interests in procreation within marriage and in the potential life of his unborn child are certainly substantial ones. See *Planned Parenthood of Central Mo. v. Danforth,* 428 U. S., at 69 ("We are not unaware of the deep and proper concern and interest that a devoted and protective husband has in his wife's pregnancy and in the growth and development of the fetus she is carrying"); *id.,* at 93 (WHITE, J., concurring in part and dissenting in part); *Skinner v. Oklahoma ex rel. Williamson,* 316 U. S., at 541. The State itself has legitimate interest both in protecting these interests of the father and in protecting the potential life of the fetus, and the spousal notification requirement is reasonably related to advancing those state interests. By providing that a husband will usually know of his spouse's intent to have an abortion, the provision makes it more likely that the husband will participate in deciding the fate of his unborn child, a possibility that might otherwise have been denied him. This participation might in some cases result in a decision to proceed with the pregnancy. As Judge Alito observed in his dissent below, "[t]he Pennsylvania legislature could have rationally believed that some married women are initially inclined to obtain an abortion without their husbands' knowledge because of perceived problems—such as economic constraints, future plans, or the husbands' previously expressed opposition—that may be obviated by discussion prior to the abortion." 947 F. 2d, at 726 (Alito, J., concurring in part and dissenting in part).

The State also has a legitimate interest in promoting "the integrity of the marital relationship." 18 Pa. Cons. Stat. §3209(a) (1990). This Court has previously recognized "the importance of the marital relationship in our society." *Planned Parenthood of Central Mo.* v. *Danforth, supra,* at 69. In our view, the spousal notice requirement is a rational attempt by the State to improve truthful communication between spouses and encourage collaborative decision making, and thereby fosters marital integrity. See *Labine* v. *Vincent,* 401 U. S. 532, 538 (1971) ("[T]he power to make rules to establish, protect, and strengthen family life" is committed to the state legislatures). Petitioners argue that the notification requirement does not further any such interest; they assert that the majority of wives already notify their husbands of their abortion decisions, and the remainder have excellent reasons for keeping their decisions a secret. In the first case, they argue, the law is unnecessary, and in the second case it will only serve to foster marital discord and threats of harm. Thus, petitioners see the law as a totally irrational means of furthering whatever legitimate interest the State might have. But, in our view, it is unrealistic to assume that every husband-wife relationship is either (1) so perfect that this type of truthful and important communication will take place as a matter of course, or (2) so imperfect that, upon notice, the husband will react selfishly, violently, or contrary to the best interests of his wife. See *Planned Parenthood of Central Mo.* v. *Danforth, supra,* at 103–104 (Stevens, J., concurring in part and dissenting in part) (making a similar point in the context of a parental consent statute). The spousal notice provision will admittedly be unnecessary in some circumstances, and possibly harmful in others, but "the existence of particular cases in

which a feature of a statute performs no function (or is even counterproductive) ordinarily does not render the statute unconstitutional or even constitutionally suspect." *Thornburgh* v. *American College of Obstetricians and Gynecologists,* 476 U. S., at 800 (White, J., dissenting). The Pennsylvania Legislature was in a position to weigh the likely benefits of the provision against its likely adverse effects, and presumably concluded, on balance, that the provision would be beneficial. Whether this was a wise decision or not, we cannot say that it was irrational. We therefore conclude that the spousal notice provision comports with the Constitution. See *Harris* v. *McRae,* 448 U. S., at 325–326 ("It is not the mission of this Court or any other to decide whether the balance of competing interests . . . is wise social policy").

D

The Act also imposes various reporting requirements. Section 3214(a) requires that abortion facilities file a report on each abortion performed. The reports do not include the identity of the women on whom abortions are performed, but they do contain a variety of information about the abortions. For example, each report must include the identities of the performing and referring physicians, the gestational age of the fetus at the time of abortion, and the basis for any medical judgment that a medical emergency existed. See 18 Pa. Cons. Stat. §3214(a)(1), (5), (10) (1990). See Appendix, *ante,* at 69–71. The District Court found that these reports are kept completely confidential. 947 F. 2d, at 716. We further conclude that these reporting requirements rationally further the State's legitimate interests in advancing the state of medical knowledge concerning maternal health and prenatal life, in gathering statistical information with respect to patients, and in ensuring compliance with other provisions of the Act.

Section 3207 of the Act requires each abortion facility to file a report with its name and address, as well as the names and addresses of any parent, subsidiary or affiliated organizations. 18 Pa. Cons. Stat. §3207(b) (1990). Section 3214(f) further requires each facility to file quarterly reports stating the total number of abortions performed, broken down by trimester. Both of these reports are available to the public only if the facility received state funds within the preceding 12 months. See Appendix, *ante,* at 65–66, 71. Petitioners do not challenge the requirement that facilities provide this information. They contend, however, that the forced public disclosure of the information given by facilities receiving public funds serves no legitimate state interest. We disagree. Records relating to the expenditure of public funds are generally available to the public under Pennsylvania law. See P. Stat. Ann., Tit. 65, §§66.1, 66.2 (Purdon 1959 and Supp. 1991–1992). As the Court of Appeals observed, "[w]hen a state provides money to a private commercial enterprise, there is a legitimate public interest in informing taxpayers who the funds are benefiting and what services the funds are supporting." 947 F. 2d, at 718. These reporting requirements rationally further this legitimate state interest.

E

Finally, petitioners challenge the medical emergency exception provided for by the Act. The existence of a medical emergency exempts compliance with the Act's informed consent, parental consent, and spousal notice requirements. See 18 Pa. Cons. Stat. §§3205(a), 3206(a), 3209(c) (1990). The Act defines a "medical emergency" as

"[t]hat condition which, on the basis of the physician's good faith clinical judgment, so complicates the medical condition of a pregnant woman as to necessitate the immediate abortion of her pregnancy to avert her death or for which a delay will create serious risk of substantial and irreversible impairment of major bodily function." §3203.

Petitioners argued before the District Court that the statutory definition was inadequate because it did not cover three serious conditions that pregnant women can suffer—preeclampsia, inevitable abortion, and prematurely ruptured membrane. The District Court agreed with petitioners that the medical emergency exception was inadequate, but the Court of Appeals reversed this holding. In construing the medical emergency provision, the Court of Appeals first observed that all three conditions do indeed present the risk of serious injury or death when an abortion is not performed, and noted that the medical profession's uniformly prescribed treatment for each of the three conditions is an immediate abortion. See 947 F. 2d, at 700–701. Finding that "[t]he Pennsylvania legislature did not choose the wording of its medical emergency exception in a vacuum," the court read the exception as intended "to assure that compliance with its abortion regulations would not in any way pose a significant threat to the life or

health of a woman." *Id.,* at 701. It thus concluded that the exception encompassed each of the three dangerous conditions pointed to by petitioners.

We observe that Pennsylvania's present definition of medical emergency is almost an exact copy of that State's definition at the time of this Court's ruling in *Thornburgh,* one which the Court made reference to with apparent approval. 476 U. S., at 771 ("It is clear that the Pennsylvania Legislature knows how to provide a medical-emergency exception when it chooses to do so"). We find that the interpretation of the Court of Appeals in this case is eminently reasonable, and that the provision thus should be upheld. When a woman is faced with any condition that poses a "significant threat to [her] life or health," she is exempted from the Act's consent and notice requirements and may proceed immediately with her abortion.

IV

For the reasons stated, we therefore would hold that each of the challenged provisions of the Pennsylvania statute is consistent with the Constitution. It bears emphasis that our conclusion in this regard does not carry with it any necessary approval of these regulations. Our task is, as always, to decide only whether the challenged provisions of a law comport with the United States Constitution. If, as we believe, these do, their wisdom as a matter of public policy is for the people of Pennsylvania to decide. . . .

* * *

JUSTICE SCALIA, with whom THE CHIEF JUSTICE, JUSTICE WHITE, and JUSTICE THOMAS join, concurring in the judgment in part and dissenting in part.

My views on this matter are unchanged from those I set forth in my separate opinions in *Webster* v. *Reproductive Health Services,* 492 U. S. 490, 532 (1989) (SCALIA, J., concurring in part and concurring in judgment), and *Ohio* v. *Akron Center for Reproductive Health,* 497 U. S. 502, 520 (1990) (*Akron II*) (SCALIA, J., concurring). The States may, if they wish, permit abortion-on-demand, but the Constitution does not *require* them to do so. The permissibility of abortion, and the limitations upon it, are to be resolved like most important questions in our democracy: by citizens trying to persuade one another and then voting. As the Court acknowledges, "where reasonable people disagree the government can adopt one position or the other." *Ante,* at 8. The Court is correct in adding the qualification that this "assumes a state of affairs in which the choice does not intrude upon a protected liberty," *ante,* at 9—but the crucial part of that qualification is the penultimate word. A State's choice between two positions on which reasonable people can disagree is constitutional even when (as is often the case) it intrudes upon a "liberty" in the absolute sense. Laws against bigamy, for example—which entire societies of reasonable people disagree with—intrude upon men and women's liberty to marry and live with one another. But bigamy happens not to be a liberty specially "protected" by the Constitution.

That is, quite simply, the issue in this case: not whether the power of a woman to abort her unborn child is a "liberty" in the absolute sense; or even whether it is a liberty of great importance to many women. Of course it is both. The issue is whether it is a liberty protected by the Constitution of the United States. I am sure it is not. I reach that conclusion not because of anything so exalted as my views concerning the "concept of existence, of meaning, of the universe, and of the mystery of human life." *Ibid.* Rather, I reach it for the same reason I reach the conclusion that bigamy is not because of anything so exalted as my views concerning the [concept of existence, of meaning, of the universe, and of the mystery of human life." *Ibid.* Rather, I reach it for the same reason I reach the conclusion that bigamy is not constitutionally protected—because of two simple facts: (1) the Constitution says absolutely nothing about it, and (2) the longstanding traditions of American society have permitted it to be legally proscribed. *Akron II, supra,* at 520 (SCALIA, J., concurring).

The Court destroys the proposition, evidently meant to represent my position, that "liberty" includes "only those practices, defined at the most specific level, that were protected against government interference by other rules of law when the Fourteenth Amendment was ratified," *ante,* at 5 (citing *Michael H. v. Gerald D.,* 491 U. S. 110, 127, n. 6 (1989) (opinion of SCALIA, J.). That is not, however, what *Michael H.* says; it merely observes that, in defining "liberty," we may not disregard a specific, "relevant tradition protecting, or denying protection to, the asserted right," 491 U. S., at 127, n. 6. But the Court does not wish to be fettered by any such limitations on its preferences. The Court's statement that it is "tempting" to acknowledge the authoritativeness of tradition in order to "cur[b] the discretion of federal judges," *ante,* at 5, is of course rhetoric rather than reality; no government official is "tempted" to place restraints upon his own freedom of action, which is why

Lord Acton did not say "Power tends to purify." The Court's temptation is in the quite opposite and more natural direction—towards systematically eliminating checks upon its own power; and it succumbs.

Beyond that brief summary of the essence of my position, I will not swell the United States Reports with repetition of what I have said before; and applying the rational basis test, I would uphold the Pennsylvania statute in its entirety. I must, however, respond to a few of the more outrageous arguments in today's opinion, which it is beyond human nature to leave unanswered. I shall discuss each of them under a quotation from the Court's opinion to which they pertain.

"The inescapable fact is that adjudication of substantive due process claims may call upon the Court in interpreting the Constitution to exercise that same capacity which by tradition courts always have exercised: reasoned judgment."

Ante, at 7.

Assuming that the question before us is to be resolved at such a level of philosophical abstraction, in such isolation from the traditions of American society, as by simply applying "reasoned judgment," I do not see how that could possibly have produced the answer the Court arrived at in *Roe* v. *Wade,* 410 U. S. 113 (1973). Today's opinion describes the methodology of *Roe,* quite accurately, as weighing against the woman's interest the State's "'important and legitimate interest in protecting the potentiality of human life.'" *Ante,* at 28–29 (quoting *Roe, supra,* at 162). But "reasoned judgment" does not begin by begging the question, as *Roe* and subsequent cases unquestionably did by assuming that what the State is protecting is the mere "potentiality of human life." See, *e.g., Roe, supra,* at 162; *Planned Parenthood of Central Mo.* v. *Danforth,* 428 U. S. 52, 61 (1976); *Colautti* v. *Franklin,* 439 U. S. 379, 386 (1979); *Akron* v. *Akron Center for Reproductive Health, Inc.,* 462 U. S. 416, 428 (1983) (*Akron I*); *Planned Parenthood Assn. of Kansas City, Mo., Inc.* v. *Ashcroft,* 462 U. S. 476, 482 (1983). The whole argument of abortion opponents is that what the Court calls the fetus and what others call the unborn child *is a human life.* Thus, whatever answer *Roe* came up with after conducting its "balancing" is bound to be wrong, unless it is correct that the human fetus is in some critical sense merely potentially human. There is of course no way to determine that as a legal matter; it is in fact a value judgment. Some societies have considered newborn children not yet human, or the incompetent elderly no longer so.

The authors of the joint opinion, of course, do not squarely contend that *Roe v. Wade* was a *correct* application of "reasoned judgment"; merely that it must be followed, because of *stare decisis*. *Ante,* at 11, 18–19, 29. But in their exhaustive discussion of all the factors that go into the determination of when *stare decisis* should be observed and when disregarded, they never mention "how wrong was the decision on its face?" Surely, if "[t]he Court's power lies . . . in its legitimacy, a product of substance and perception," *ante,* at 23, the "substance" part of the equation demands that plain error be acknowledged and eliminated. *Roe* was plainly wrong—even on the Court's methodology of "reasoned judgment," and even more so (of course) if the proper criteria of text and tradition are applied.

The emptiness of the "reasoned judgment" that produced *Roe* is displayed in plain view by the fact that, after more than 19 years of effort by some of the brightest (and most determined) legal minds in the country, after more than 10 cases upholding abortion rights in this Court, and after dozens upon dozens of *amicus* briefs submitted in this and other cases, the best the Court can do to explain how it is that the word "liberty" *must* be thought to include the right to destroy human fetuses is to rattle off a collection of adjectives that simply decorate a value judgment and conceal a political choice. The right to abort, we are told, inheres in "liberty" because it is among "a person's most basic decisions," *ante,* at 7; it involves a "most intimate and personal choic[e]," *ante,* at 9; it is "central to personal dignity and autonomy," *ibid.;* it "originate[s] within the zone of conscience and belief," *ibid.;* it is "too intimate and personal" for state interference, *ante,* at 10; it reflects "intimate views" of a "deep, personal character," *ante,* at 11; it involves "intimate relationships," and notions of "personal autonomy and bodily integrity," *ante,* at 15; and it concerns a particularly "'important decisio[n],'" *ante,* at 16 (citation omitted). But it is obvious to anyone applying "reasoned judgment" that the same adjectives can be applied to many forms of conduct that this Court including one of the Justices in today's majority, see *Bowers* v. *Hardwick,* 478 U. S. 186 (1986)) has held are *not* entitled to constitutional protection—because, like abortion, they are forms of conduct that have long been criminalized in American society. Those adjectives might be applied, for example, to homosexual sodomy, polygamy, adult incest, and suicide, all of which are equally "intimate" and "deep[ly] personal" decisions involving "personal autonomy and bodily integrity," and all of which can constitutionally be proscribed because it is our unquestionable constitutional tradition that they are proscribable. It is not reasoned judgment that supports the Court's decision; only personal predilection. Justice Curtis's warning is as timely today as it was 135 years ago:

> "[W]hen a strict interpretation of the Constitution, according to the fixed rules which govern the interpretation of laws, is abandoned, and the theoretical opinions of individuals are allowed to control its meaning, we have no longer a Constitution; we are under the government of individual men, who for the time being have power to declare what the Constitution is, according to their own views of what it ought to mean." *Dred Scott* v. *Sandford,* 19 How. 393, 621 (1857) (Curtis, J., dissenting).

"Liberty finds no refuge in a jurisprudence of doubt."

Ante, at 1.

One might have feared to encounter this august and sonorous phrase in an opinion defending the real *Roe* v. *Wade,* rather than the revised version fabricated today by the authors of the joint opinion. The shortcomings of *Roe* did not include lack of clarity: Virtually all regulation of abortion before the third trimester was invalid. But to come across this phrase in the joint opinion—which calls upon federal district judges to apply an "undue burden" standard as doubtful in application as it is unprincipled in origin—is really more than one should have to bear.

The joint opinion frankly concedes that the amorphous concept of "undue burden" has been inconsistently applied by the Members of this Court in the few brief years since that "test" was first explicitly propounded by JUSTICE O'CONNOR in her dissent in *Akron I, supra.* See *Ante,* at 34. Because the three Justices now wish to "set forth a standard of general application," the joint opinion announces that "it is important to clarify what is meant by an undue burden," *ibid.* I certainly agree with that, but I do not agree that the joint opinion succeeds in the announced endeavor. To the contrary, its efforts at clarification make clear only that the standard is inherently manipulable and will prove hopelessly unworkable in practice.

The joint opinion explains that a state regulation imposes an "undue burden" if it "has the purpose or effect of placing a substantial obstacle in the path of a woman seeking an abortion of a nonviable fetus." *Ibid.;* see also *ante,* at 35–36. An obstacle is "substantial," we are told, if it is "calculated[,] [not] to inform the woman's free choice, [but to] hinder it." *Ante,* at 34. This latter statement cannot possibly mean what it says. *Any* regulation of abortion that is intended to advance what the joint opinion concedes is the State's "substantial" interest in protecting unborn life will be "calculated [to] hinder" a decision to have an abortion. It thus seems more accurate to say that the joint opinion would uphold abortion regulations only if they do not *unduly* hinder the woman's decision. That, of course, brings us right back to square one: Defining an "undue burden" as an "undue hindrance" (or a "substantial obstacle") hardly "clarifies" the test. Consciously or not, the joint opinion's verbal shell game will conceal raw judicial policy choices concerning what is "appropriate" abortion legislation.

The ultimately standardless nature of the "undue burden" inquiry is a reflection of the underlying fact that the concept has no principled or coherent legal basis. As THE CHIEF JUSTICE points out, *Roe's* strict-scrutiny standard "at least had a recognized basis in constitutional law at the time *Roe* was decided," *ante,* at 22, while "[t]he same cannot be said for the 'undue burden' standard, which is created largely out of whole cloth by the authors of the joint opinion," *ibid.* The joint opinion is flatly wrong in asserting that "our jurisprudence relating to all liberties save perhaps abortion has recognized" the permissibility of laws that do not impose an "undue burden." *Ante,* at 31. It argues that the abortion right is similar to other rights in that a law "not designed to strike at the right itself, [but which] has the incidental effect of making it more difficult or more expensive to [exercise the right,]" is not invalid. *Ante,* at 31–32. I agree, indeed I have forcefully urged, that a law of general applicability which places only an incidental burden on a fundamental right does not infringe that right, see *R. A. V. v. St. Paul,* 505 U. S. ___, ___ (1992) (slip op., at 11); *Employment Division, Dept. of Human Resources of Ore. v. Smith,* 494 U. S. 872, 878–882 (1990), but that principle does not establish the quite different (and quite dangerous) proposition that a law which *directly* regulates a fundamental right will not be found to violate the Constitution unless it imposes an "undue burden." It is that, of course, which is at issue here: Pennsylvania has *consciously and directly* regulated conduct that our cases have held is constitutionally protected. The appropriate

analogy, therefore, is that of a state law requiring purchasers of religious books to endure a 24–hour waiting period, or to pay a nominal additional tax of 1¢. The joint opinion cannot possibly be correct in suggesting that we would uphold such legislation on the ground that it does not impose a "substantial obstacle" to the exercise of First Amendment rights. The "undue burden" standard is not at all the generally applicable principle the joint opinion pretends it to be; rather, it is a unique concept created specially for this case, to preserve some judicial foothold in this ill-gotten territory. In claiming otherwise, the three Justices show their willingness to place all constitutional rights at risk in an effort to preserve what they deem the "central holding in *Roe,*" *ante,* at 31.

The rootless nature of the "undue burden" standard, a phrase plucked out of context from our earlier abortion decisions, see n. 3, *supra,* is further reflected in the fact that the joint opinion finds it necessary expressly to repudiate the more narrow formulations used in JUSTICE O'CONNOR's earlier opinions. *Ante,* at 35. Those opinions stated that a statute imposes an "undue burden" if it imposes "*absolute* obstacles or *severe* limitations on the abortion decision," *Akron I,* 462 U. S., at 464 (O'CONNOR, J., dissenting) (emphasis added); see also *Thornburgh* v. *American College of Obstetricians and Gynecologists,* 476 U. S. 747, 828 (1986) (O'CONNOR, J., dissenting). Those strong adjectives are conspicuously missing from the joint opinion, whose authors have for some unexplained reason now determined that a burden is "undue" if it merely imposes a "substantial" obstacle to abortion decisions. See, *e.g., ante,* at 53, 59. JUSTICE O'CONNOR has also abandoned (again without explanation) the view she expressed in *Planned Parenthood Assn. of Kansas City, Mo., Inc. v. Ashcroft,* 462 U. S. 476 (1983) (dissenting opinion), that a medical regulation which imposes an "undue burden" could nevertheless be upheld if it "reasonably relate[s] to the preservation and protection of maternal health," *id.,* at 505 (citation and internal quotation marks omitted). In today's version, even health measures will be upheld only "*if they do not constitute an undue burden,*" *ante,* at 35 (emphasis added). Gone too is JUSTICE O'CONNOR's statement that "the State possesses *compelling* interests in the protection of potential human life . . . throughout pregnancy," *Akron I, supra,* at 461 (emphasis added); see also *Ashcroft, supra,* at 505 (O'CONNOR, J., concurring in judgment in part and dissenting in part); instead, the state's interest in unborn human life is stealthily downgraded to a merely "substantial" or "profound" interest, *ante,* at 34, 36. (That had to be done, of course, since designating the interest as "compelling" throughout pregnancy would have been, shall we say, a "substantial obstacle" to the joint opinion's determined effort to reaffirm what it views as the "central holding" of *Roe.* See *Akron I,* 462 U. S., at 420, n. 1.) And "viability" is no longer the "arbitrary" dividing line previously decried by JUSTICE O'CONNOR in *Akron I, id.,* at 461; the Court now announces that "the attainment of viability may continue to serve as the critical fact," *ante,* at 18. It is difficult to maintain the illusion that we are interpreting a Constitution rather than inventing one, when we amend its provisions so breezily.

Because the portion of the joint opinion adopting and describing the undue-burden test provides no more useful guidance than the empty phrases discussed above, one must turn to the 23 pages applying that standard to the present facts for further guidance. In evaluating Pennsylvania's abortion law, the joint opinion relies extensively on the factual findings of the District Court, and repeatedly qualifies its conclusions by noting that they are contingent upon the record developed in this case. Thus, the joint opinion would uphold the 24-hour waiting period contained in the Pennsylvania statute's informed consent provision, 18 Pa. Cons. Stat §3205 (1990), because "the record evidence shows that in the vast majority of cases, a 24-hour delay does not create any appreciable health risk," *ante,* at 43. The three Justices therefore conclude that "on the record before us, . . . we are not convinced that the 24-hour waiting period constitutes an undue burden." *Ante,* at 44–45. The requirement that a doctor provide the information pertinent to informed consent would also be upheld because "there is no evidence on this record that [this requirement] would amount in practical terms to a substantial obstacle to a woman seeking an abortion," *ante,* at 42. Similarly, the joint opinion would uphold the reporting requirements of the Act, §§3207, 3214, because "there is no . . . showing on the record before us" that these requirements constitute a "substantial obstacle" to abortion decisions. *Ante,* at 59. But at the same time the opinion pointedly observes that these reporting requirements may increase the costs of abortions and that "at some point [that fact] could become a substantial obstacle," *ibid.* Most significantly, the joint opinion's conclusion that the spousal notice requirement of the Act, see §3209, imposes an "undue burden" is based in large measure on the District Court's "detailed findings of fact," which the joint opinion sets out at great length. *Ante,* at 45–49.

I do not, of course, have any objection to the notion that, in applying legal principles, one should rely only upon the facts that are contained in the record or that are properly subject to judicial notice. But what is remarkable about the joint opinion's fact-intensive analysis is that it does not result in any measurable clarification of the "undue burden" standard. Rather, the approach of the joint opinion is, for the most part, simply to highlight certain facts in the record that apparently strike the three Justices as particularly significant in establishing (or refuting) the existence of an undue burden; after describing these facts, the opinion then simply announces that the provision either does or does not impose a "substantial obstacle" or an "undue burden." See, *e.g., ante,* at 38, 42, 44–45, 52, 53, 59. We do not know whether the same conclusions could have been reached on a different record, or in what respects the record would have had to differ before an opposite conclusion would have been appropriate. The inherently standardless nature of this inquiry invites the district judge to give effect to his personal preferences about abortion. By finding and relying upon the right facts, he can invalidate, it would seem, almost any abortion restriction that strikes him as "undue"—subject, of course, to the possibility of being reversed by a Circuit Court of Supreme Court that is as unconstrained in reviewing his decision as he was in making it.

To the extent I can discern *any* meaningful content in the "undue burden" standard as applied in the joint opinion, it appears to be that a State may not regulate abortion in such a way as to reduce significantly its incidence. The joint opinion repeatedly emphasizes that an important factor in the "undue burden" analysis is whether the regulation "prevent[s] a significant number of women from obtaining an abortion," *ante,* at 52; whether a "significant number of women . . . are likely to be deterred from procuring an abortion," *ibid.*; and whether the regulation often "deters" women from seeking abortions, *ante,* at 55–56. We are not told, however, what forms of "deterrence" are impermissible or what degree of success in deterrence is too much to be tolerated. If, for example, a State required a woman to read a pamphlet describing, with illustrations, the facts of fetal development before she could obtain an abortion, the effect of such legislation might be to "deter" a "significant number of women" from procuring abortions, thereby seemingly allowing a district judge to invalidate it as an undue burden. Thus, despite flowery rhetoric about the State's "substantial" and "profound" interest in "potential human life," and criticism of *Roe* for undervaluing that interest, the joint opinion permits the State to pursue that interest only so long as it is not too successful. As JUSTICE BLACKMUN recognizes (with evident hope), *ante,* at 5, the "undue burden" standard may ultimately require the invalidation of each provision upheld today if it can be shown, on a better record, that the State is too effectively "express[ing] a preference for childbirth over abortion," *ante,* at 41. Reason finds no refuge in this jurisprudence of confusion.

"While we appreciate the weight of the arguments . . . that *Roe* should be overruled, the reservations any of us may have in reaffirming the central holding of *Roe* are outweighed by the explication of individual liberty we have given combined with the force of *stare decisis*."
Ante, at 11.

The Court's reliance upon *stare decisis* can best be described as contrived. It insists upon the necessity of adhering not to all of Roe, but only to what it calls the "central holding." It seems to me that *stare decisis* ought to be applied even to the doctrine of *stare decisis,* and I confess never to have heard of this new, keep-what-you-want-and-throw-away-the-rest version. I wonder whether, as applied to *Marbury* v. *Madison,* 1 Cranch 137 (1803), for example, the new version of *stare decisis* would be satisfied if we allowed courts to review the constitutionality of only those statutes that (like the one in *Marbury*) pertain to the jurisdiction of the courts.

I am certainly not in a good position to dispute that the Court *has saved* the "central holding" of *Roe,* since to do that effectively I would have to know what the Court has saved, which in turn would require me to understand (as I do not) what the "undue burden" test means. I must confess, however, that I have always thought, and I think a lot of other people have always thought, that the arbitrary trimester framework, which the Court today discards, was quite as central to *Roe* as the arbitrary viability test, which the Court today retains. It seems particularly ungrateful to carve the trimester framework out of the core of Roe, since its very rigidity (in sharp contrast to the utter indeterminability of the "undue burden" test) is probably the only reason the Court is able to say, in urging *stare decisis,* that *Roe* "has in no sense proven 'unworkable,'" *ante,* at 13. I suppose the Court is entitled to call a "central holding" whatever it wants to call a "central holding"—which is, come to think of it, perhaps one of the

difficulties with this modified version of *stare decisis.* I thought I might note, however, that the following portions of *Roe* have not been saved:

•Under *Roe,* requiring that a woman seeking an abortion be provided truthful information about abortion before giving informed written consent is unconstitutional, if the information is designed to influence her choice, *Thornburgh,* 476 U. S., at 759–765; *Akron I,* 462 U. S., at 442–445. Under the joint opinion's "undue burden" regime (as applied today, at least) such a requirement is constitutional, *ante,* at 38–42.

•Under *Roe,* requiring that information be provided by a doctor, rather than by nonphysician counselors, is unconstitutional, *Akron I, supra,* at 446–449. Under the "undue burden" regime (as applied today, at least) it is not, *ante,* at 42.

•Under *Roe,* requiring a 24–hour waiting period between the time the woman gives her informed consent and the time of the abortion is unconstitutional, *Akron I, supra,* at 449–451. Under the "undue burden" regime (as applied today, at least) it is not, *ante,* at 43–45.

•Under *Roe,* requiring detailed reports that include demographic data about each woman who seeks an abortion and various information about each abortion is unconstitutional, *Thornburgh, supra,* at 465–768. Under the "undue burden" regime (as applied today, at least) it generally is not, *ante,* at 58–59.

"Where, in the performance of its judicial duties, the Court decides a case in such a way as to resolve the sort of intensely divisive controversy reflected in *Roe* . . . , its decision has a dimension that the resolution of the normal case does not carry. It is the dimension present whenever the Court's interpretation of the Constitution calls the contending sides of a national controversy to end their national division by accepting a common mandate rooted in the Constitution."
Ante, at 24.

The Court's description of the place of *Roe* in the social history of the United States is unrecognizable. Not only did *Roe* not, as the Court suggests, *resolve* the deeply divisive issue of abortion; it did more than anything else to nourish it, by elevating it to the national level where it is infinitely more difficult to resolve. National politics were not plagued by abortion protests, national abortion lobbying, or abortion marches on Congress, before *Roe* v. *Wade* was decided. Profound disagreement existed among our citizens over the issue—

as it does over other issues, such as the death penalty—but that disagreement was being worked out at the state level. As with many other issues, the division of sentiment within each State was not as closely balanced as it was among the population of the Nation as a whole, meaning not only that more people would be satisfied with the results of state-by-state resolution, but also that those results would be more stable. Pre-*Roe*, moreover, political compromise was possible.

Roe's mandate for abortion-on-demand destroyed the compromises of the past, rendered compromise impossible for the future, and required the entire issue to be resolved uniformly, at the national level. At the same time, *Roe* created a vast new class of abortion consumers and abortion proponents by eliminating the moral opprobrium that had attached to the act. ("If the Constitution *guarantees* abortion, how can it be bad?"—not an accurate line of thought, but a natural one.) Many favor all of those developments, and it is not for me to say that they are wrong. But to portray *Roe* as the statesmanlike "settlement" of a divisive issue, a jurisprudential Peace of Westphalia that is worth preserving, is nothing less than Orwellian. *Roe* fanned into life an issue that has inflamed our national politics in general, and has obscured with its smoke the selection of Justices to this Court in particular, ever since. And by keeping us in the abortion-umpiring business, it is the perpetuation of that disruption, rather than of any *pax Roeana*, that the Court's new majority decrees.

"[T]o overrule under fire . . . would subvert the Court's legitimacy . . . .

"To all those who will be . . . tested by following, the Court implicitly undertakes to remain steadfast. . . . The promise of constancy, once given, binds its maker for as long as the power to stand by the decision survives and . . . the commitment [is not] obsolete. . . .

"[The American people's] belief in themselves as . . . a people [who aspire to live according to the rule of law] is not readily separable from their understanding of the Court invested with the authority to decide their constitutional cases and speak before all others for their constitutional ideals. If the Court's legitimacy should be undermined, then, so would the country be in its very ability to see itself through its constitutional ideals."

Ante, at 25–26.

The Imperial Judiciary lives. It is instructive to compare this Nietzschean vision of us unelected, life-tenured judges—leading a Volk who will be "tested by following," and whose very "belief in themselves" is mystically bound up in their "understanding" of a Court that "speak[s] before all others for their constitutional ideals"—with the somewhat more modest role envisioned for these lawyers by the Founders.

"The judiciary . . . has . . . no direction either of the strength or of the wealth of the society, and can take no active resolution whatever. It may truly be said to have neither FORCE nor WILL but merely judgment. . . . ." The Federalist No. 78, pp. 393–394 (G. Wills ed. 1982).

Or, again, to compare this ecstasy of a Supreme Court in which there is, especially on controversial matters, no shadow of change or hint of alteration ("There is a limit to the amount of error that can plausibly be imputed to prior courts," *ante,* at 24), with the more democratic views of a more humble man:

"[T]he candid citizen must confess that if the policy of the Government upon vital questions affecting the whole people is to be irrevocably fixed by decisions of the Supreme Court, . . . the people will have ceased to be their own rulers, having to that extent practically resigned their Government into the hands of that eminent tribunal." A. Lincoln, First Inaugural Address (Mar. 4, 1861), reprinted in Inaugural Addresses of the Presidents of the United States, S. Doc. No. 101–10, p. 139 (1989).

It is particularly difficult, in the circumstances of the present decision, to sit still for the Court's lengthy lecture upon the virtues of "constancy," *ante,* at 26, of "remain[ing] steadfast," *id.,* at 25, and adhering to "principle," *id., passim.* Among the five Justices who purportedly adhere to *Roe,* at most three agree upon the *principle* that constitutes adherence (the joint opinion's "undue burden" standard)—and that principle is inconsistent with *Roe,* see 410 U. S., at 154–156. To make matters worse, two of the three, in order thus to remain steadfast, had to abandon previously stated positions. See n. 4 *supra;* see *supra,* at 11–12. It is beyond me how the Court expects these accommodations to be accepted "as grounded truly in principle, not as compromises with social and political pressures having, as such, no bearing on the principled choices that the Court is obliged to make." *Ante,* at 23. The only principle the Court "adheres" to, it seems to me, is the principle that the Court must be seen as standing by *Roe.* That is not a principle of law (which is what I thought the Court was talking about), but a principle of *Realpolitik*—and a wrong one at that.

I cannot agree with, indeed I am appalled by, the Court's suggestion that the decision whether to stand by an erroneous constitutional decision must be strongly influenced—*against* overruling, no less—by the substantial and continuing public opposition the decision has generated. The Court's judgment that any other course would "subvert the Court's legitimacy" must be another consequence of reading the error-filled history book that described the deeply divided country brought together by *Roe.* In my history book, the Court was covered with dishonor and deprived of legitimacy by *Dred Scott* v. *Sandford,* 19 How. 393 (1857), an erroneous (and widely opposed) opinion that it did not abandon, rather than by *West Coast Hotel Co.* v. *Parrish,* 300 U. S. 379 (1937), which produced the famous "switch in time" from the Court's erroneous (and widely opposed) constitutional opposition to the social measures of the New Deal. (Both *Dred Scott* and one line of the cases resisting the New Deal rested upon the concept of "substantive due process" that the Court praises and employs today. Indeed, *Dred Scott* was "very possibly the first application of substantive due process in the Supreme Court, the original precedent for *Lochner* v. *New York* and *Roe* v. *Wade."* D. Currie, The Constitution in the Supreme Court 271 (1985) (footnotes omitted).)

But whether it would "subvert the Court's legitimacy" or not, the notion that we would decide a case differently from the way we otherwise would have in order to show that we can stand firm against public disapproval is frightening. It is a bad enough idea, even in the head of someone like me, who believes that the text of the Constitution, and our traditions, say what they say and there is no fiddling with them. But when it is in the mind of a Court that believes the Constitution has an evolving meaning, see *ante,* at 6; that the Ninth Amendment's reference to "othe[r]" rights is not a disclaimer, but a charter for action, *ibid.*; and that the function of this Court is to "speak before all others for [the people's] constitutional ideals" unrestrained by meaningful text or tradition—then the notion that the Court must adhere to a decision for as long as the decision faces "great opposition" and the Court is "under

fire" acquires a character of almost czarist arrogance. We are offended by these marchers who descend upon us, every year on the anniversary of *Roe,* to protest our saying that the Constitution requires what our society has never thought the Constitution requires. These people who refuse to be "tested by following" must be taught a lesson. We have no Cossacks, but at least we can stubbornly refuse to abandon an erroneous opinion that we might otherwise change—to show how little they intimidate us.

Of course, as THE CHIEF JUSTICE points out, we have been subjected to what the Court calls "political pressure" by *both* sides of this issue. *Ante,* at 21. Maybe today's decision *not* to overrule *Roe* will be seen as buckling to pressure from *that* direction. Instead of engaging in the hopeless task of predicting public perception—a job not for lawyers but for political campaign managers—the Justices should do what is *legally* right by asking two questions: (1) Was *Roe* correctly decided? (2) Has *Roe* succeeded in producing a settled body of law? If the answer to both questions is no, *Roe* should undoubtedly be overruled.

In truth, I am as distressed as the Court is—and expressed my distress several years ago, see *Webster,* 492 U. S., at 535—about the "political pressure" directed to the Court: the marches, the mail, the protests aimed at inducing us to change our opinions. How upsetting it is, that so many of our citizens (good people, not lawless ones, on both sides of this abortion issue, and on various sides of other issues as well) think that we Justices should properly take into account their views, as though we were engaged not in ascertaining an objective law but in determining some kind of social consensus. The Court would profit, I think, from giving less attention to the *fact* of this distressing phenomenon, and more attention to the *cause* of it. That cause permeates today's opinion: a new mode of constitutional adjudication that relies not upon text and traditional practice to determine the law, but upon what the Court calls "reasoned judgment," *ante,* at 7, which turns out to be nothing but philosophical predilection and moral intuition. All manner of "liberties," the Court tells us, inhere in the Constitution and are enforceable by this Court—not just those mentioned in the text or established in the traditions of our society. *Ante,* at 5–6. Why even the Ninth Amendment—which says only that "[t]he enumeration in the Constitution of certain rights shall not be construed to deny or disparage others retained by the people"—is, despite our contrary understanding for almost 200 years, a literally boundless source of additional, unnamed, un-hinted-at "rights," definable and enforceable by us, through "reasoned judgment." *Ante,* at 6–7.

What makes all this relevant to the bothersome application of "political pressure" against the Court are the twin facts that the American people love democracy and the American people are not fools. As long as this Court thought (and the people thought) that we Justices were doing essentially lawyers' work up here—reading text and discerning our society's traditional understanding of that text—the public pretty much left us alone. Texts and traditions are facts to study, not convictions to demonstrate about. But if in reality our process of constitutional adjudication consists primarily of making *value judgments*; if we can ignore a long and clear tradition clarifying an ambiguous text, as we did, for example, five days ago in declaring unconstitutional invocations and benedictions at public-high-school graduation ceremonies, *Lee* v. *Weisman,* 505 U. S. ___ (1992); if, as I say, our pronouncement of constitutional law

rests primarily on value judgments, then a free and intelligent people's attitude towards us can be expected to be (*ought* to be) quite different. The people know that their value judgments are quite as good as those taught in any law school—maybe better. If, indeed, the "liberties" protected by the Constitution are, as the Court says, undefined and unbounded, then the people *should* demonstrate, to protest that we do not implement *their* values instead of *ours*. Not only that, but confirmation hearings for new Justices *should* deteriorate into question-and-answer sessions in which Senators go through a list of their constituents' most favored and most disfavored alleged constitutional rights, and seek the nominee's commitment to support or oppose them. Value judgments, after all, should be voted on, not dictated; and if our Constitution has somehow accidently committed them to the Supreme Court, at least we can have a sort of plebiscite each time a new nominee to that body is put forward. Justice Blackmun

Select Bibliography

Books

Adler, Mortimer, *Haves Without Have-Nots*. New York: Macmillan, 1991.

Alcorn, Randy. *Is Rescuing Right?* Downers Grove, Ill.: InterVarsity Press, 1990.

American Medical Association Encyclopedia of Medicine. Edited by Charles B. Clayman. New York: Random House, 1989.

Beauchamp, Tom L. *Philosophical Ethics: An Introduction to Moral Philosophy*. New York: McGraw-Hill, 1982.

Beckwith, Francis J., and Michael A. Bauman, eds. *Are You Politically Correct? Debating America's Cultural Standards*. Buffalo, N.Y.: Prometheus, 1993.

Beckwith, Francis J. and Norman L. Geisler. *Matters of Life and Death: Calm Answers to Tough Questions about Abortion and Euthanasia*. Grand Rapids: Baker, 1991.

Bloom, Allan. *The Closing of the American Mind*. New York: Simon and Schuster, 1987.

Bork, Robert H. *The Tempting of America: The Political Seduction of the Law*. New York: Simon and Schuster, 1989.

Brody, Baruch. *Abortion and the Sanctity of Human Life: A Philosophical View*. Cambridge, Mass.: M.I.T. Press, 1975.

Brown, Harold O. J. *Death Before Birth*. Nashville: Nelson, 1975.

Burtchaell, James T. *Rachel Weeping: The Case Against Abortion*. San Francisco: Harper and Row, 1982.

Callahan, Daniel. *Abortion: Law, Choice, and Morality*. New York: Macmillan, 1970.

Cameron, Nigel M. de S. and Pamela F. Sims. *Abortion: The Crisis in Morals and Medicine*. Leicester: InterVarsity, 1986.

Collins, Vincent J., Stephen R. Zielinski, and Thomas J. Marzen, *Fetal Pain and Abortion: The Medical Evidence*. Studies in Law and Medicine, no. 18. Chicago: Americans United for Life Legal Defense Fund, 1984.

Davidson, Nicholas. *The Failure of Feminism*. Buffalo: Prometheus, 1988.

Davis, John Jefferson. *Abortion and the Christian*. Phillipsburg, N.J.: Presbyterian and Reformed, 1984.

Dobson, James, and Gary Bauer. *Children at Risk*. Dallas: Word, 1990.

Drucker, Dan. *Abortion Decisions of the Supreme Court, 1973 through 1989: A Comphrehensive Review with Historical Commentary*. Jefferson, N.C.: McFarland and Company, 1990.

Feinberg, Joel, ed. *The Problem of Abortion*. 2d ed. Belmont, Calif.: Wadsworth, 1984.

Garfield, Jay L. and Patricia Hennessey, eds. *Abortion: Moral and Legal Perspectives*. Amherst: University of Massachusetts Press, 1984.

Geisler, Norman L. *Christian Ethics: Options and Issues*. Grand Rapids: Baker, 1989.

Glessner, Thomas A. *Achieving an Abortion-Free America by 2001*. Portland: Multnomah, 1990.

Grant, George. *Grand Illusions: The Legacy of Planned Parenthood*. Brentwood, Tenn.: Wolgemuth and Hyatt, 1988.

Grisez, Germain. *Abortion: the Myths, the Realties, and the Arguments*. New York: Corpus, 1970.

Hensley, Jeff Lee, ed. *The Zero People*. Ann Arbor, Mich.: Servant, 1983.

Hern, Warren M. *Abortion Practice*. 2d ed. Philadelphia: Lippincott, 1990.

Hilgers, Thomas, and Dennis J. Horan, eds. *Abortion and Social Justice*. New York: Sheed and Ward, 1972.

Hilgers, Thomas, Dennis J. Horan, and David Mall, eds. *New Perspectives on Human Abortion*. Frederick, Md: University Publications of America, 1981.

Horan, Dennis J., and Burke J. Balch, *Infant Doe and Baby Jane Doe: Medical Treatment of the*

Handicapped Newborn. Studies in Law and Medicine, no. 20. Chicago: Americans United for Life Legal Defense Fund, 1985.

Horan, Dennis J., Edward R. Grant, and Paige C. Cunningham, eds. *Abortion and the Constitution: Reversing* Roe v. Wade *Through the Courts*. Washington, D.C.: Georgetown University Press, 1987.

Kamm, F. M. *Creation and Abortion: A Study in Moral and Legal Philosophy*. New York: Oxford University Press, 1992.

Koop, C. Everett. *The Right to Live: The Right to Die*. Wheaton: Tyndale House, 1976.

Koop, C. Everett, and Francis A. Schaeffer. *Whatever Happened to the Human Race?* Old Tappan, N.J.: Revell, 1979.

Krason, Stephen M. *Abortion: Politics, Morality, and the Constitution*. Lanham, Md: University Press of America, 1984.

Kreeft, Peter. *The Unaborted Socrates*. Downers Grove, Ill.: InterVarsity, 1983.

Levin, Michael. *Feminism and Freedom*. New Brunswick, N.J.: Transaction, 1987.

Mall, David, and Walter F. Watts, eds. *The Psychological Aspects of Abortion*. Washington, D.C.: University Publications of America, 1979.

Mappes, Thomas A., and Jane S. Zembaty, eds. *Biomedical Ethics*. New York: Macmillan, 1981.

____, eds. *Biomedical Ethics*. 3rd ed. New York: Macmillan, 1991.

Marshall, Robert, and Charles Donovan. *Blessed are the Barren: The Social Policy of Planned Parenthood*. San Francisco: Ignatius, 1991.

Martin, Walter. *Abortion: Is it Always Murder?* Santa Ana, Calif:: Vision House, 1977.

McCormick, Richard A. *How Brave a New World?: Dilemmas in Bioethcs*. Washington, D.C.: Georgetown University Press, 1981.

Montgomery, John Warwick. *Slaughter of the Innocents*. Westchester, Ill.: Crossway, 1981.

Moreland, J. P., and Norman L. Geisler. *The Life and Death Debate: Moral Issues of Our Time*. Westport, Conn.: Praeger, 1990.

Nathanson, Bernard. *Aborting America*. New York: Doubleday, 1979.

____. *The Abortion Papers: Inside the Abortion Mentality*. New York: Frederick Fell, 1983.

Noonan, John T., Jr. ed. *The Morality of Abortion*. Cambridge: Harvard University Press, 1970.

North, Gary. *Trespassing for Dear Life: What is Operation Rescue Up To?*, Ft. Worth: Dominion, 1989.

Olasky, Marvin. *Abortion Rites: A Social History of Abortion in America*. Wheaton, Ill.: Crossway, 1992.

____. *The Press and Abortion: 1838-1988*. Hillsdale, N.J.: Lawrence Erlbaum Associates, 1988.

Rachels, James, ed. *The Right Thing to Do: Basic Readings in Moral Philosophy*. New York: Random House, 1989.

Reardon, David C. *Aborted Women: Silent No More*. Westchester, Ill.: Crossway, 1987.

Schwarz, Stephen D. *The Moral Question of Abortion*. Chicago: Loyola University Press, 1990.

Sider, Ron. *Completely Pro-Life: Building a Consistent Stance*. Downers Grove, Ill.: InterVarsity, 1987.

Smith, F. LeGard. *When Choice Becomes God*. Eugene, Ore.: Harvest House, 1990.

Sproul, R. C. *Abortion: A Rational Look at an Emotional Issue*. Colorado Springs: NavPress, 1990.

Swindoll, Charles. *The Sanctity of Life*. Waco, Tex.: Word, 1990.

Szumski, Bonnie, ed. *Abortion: Opposing Viewpoints*. St. Paul: Greenhaven, 1986.

Tooley, Michael. *Abortion and Infanticide*. Oxford: Clarendon, 1983.

Tribe, Laurence. *Abortion: The Clash of Absolutes*. New York: Norton, 1990.

Varga, Andrew. *The Main Issues in Bioethics*. 2d ed. New York: Paulist, 1984.

Wardle, Lynn and Mary Anne Q. Wood. *A Lawyer Looks at Abortion*. Provo, Utah: Brigham Young University Press, 1982.

Wennberg, Robert. *Life in the Balance: Exploring the Abortion Controversy*. Grand Rapids: Eerdmans, 1985.

Wilke, Dr., and Mrs. J. C. Wilke. *Abortion: Questions and Answers*. Rev. ed. Cincinnati: Hayes Publishing, 1988.

Articles, Reviews, and Papers

Beckwith, Francis J. "A Critical Appraisal of Theological Arguments for Abortion Rights." *Bibliotheca Sacra* 148 (July–September 1991). An edited version of this article was released as a two-part series: "How Pro-life is the Bible?" *Focus on the Family Citizen,* (16 March 1992) and (20 April 1992).

____. "Abortion and Argument: A Response to Mollenkott." *Journal of Biblical Ethics in Medicine* 3 (Summer 1989).

____. "Abortion and Public Policy: A Response to Some Arguments." *Journal of the Evangelical Theological Society* 32 (December 1989).

____. "Abortion, Public Policy and Religious Conviction." Paper presented at the annual Far West Region meeting of the Evangelical Theological Society. The Master's Seminary. Sun Valley, California, 7 April 1989.

———. "Abortion Rights and Utilitarian Arguments: A Philosophical Analysis." Paper presented at the annual meeting of the Evangelical Philosophical Society. Bethel Theological Seminary West. San Diego, California. 16–18 November 1989. Also presented at the sesquicentennial symposium, "Health Care Ethics." Sponsored by Loras College's Bioethics Resource Center. Loras College. 5–7 April 1990.

———. "Answering the Arguments for Abortion Rights, Part One: The Appeal to Pity." *Christian Research Journal* 13 (Fall 1990).

———. "Answering the Arguments for Abortion Rights, Part Two: Arguments from Pity, Tolerance, and Ad Hominem." *Christian Research Journal* 13 (Winter 1991)

———. "Answering the Arguments for Abortion Rights, Part Three: Is the Unborn Human Less than Human?" *Christian Research Journal* 13 (Spring 1991).

———. "Answering the Arguments for Abortion Rights, Part Four: When Does a Human Become a Person?" *Christian Research Journal* 14 (Summer 1991).

———. "Brave New Bible: A Reply to the Moderate Evangelical Position on Abortion." *Journal of the Evangelical Theological Society* 33 (December 1990).

———. "The Misuse of Maternal Mortality Statistics in the Abortion Debate." *Ethics & Medicine* 7 (Summer 1991).

———. "Personal Bodily Rights, Abortion, and Unplugging the Violinist." *International Philosophical Quarterly* 32 (March 1992).

———. "Reply to Keenan: Thomson's Argument and Academic Feminism" *International Philosophical Quarterly* 32 (September 1992).

———. "Rights, Filial Obligations, and Medical Risks." *APA Newsletter on Philosophy and Medicine* 89:2 (Winter 1990).

———. "Sound Bites and Unsound Reasoning: Critical Thinking and Popular Moral Rhetoric." Lecture given at the University Forum Lecture Series. University of Nevada, Las Vegas. Beam Hall, 30 October 1989.

———. "Unplugging the Violinist: A Critique of Thomson's Argument for Abortion Rights." Paper presented at the 65th annual meeting of the American Philosophical Association, Pacific Division. San Francisco, California. 27–30 March 1991. Also presented at the first annual meeting of University Faculty for Life. Kennedy Institute for Ethics, Georgetown University. Washington, D.C. 8–10 June 1991.

———. "Tolerance, Religious Pluralism, and Abortion Rights." Paper presented at the annual meeting of the Evangelical Philosophical Society. Airport Hilton. San Francisco, California, 19–21 November 1992.

———. "Utilitarian Arguments, Abortion Rights, and Justce Blackmun's Dissent in *Webster*: Some Philosophical Observations. *Simon Greenleaf Review of Law and Religion* 8 (1988–89).

Clark, David. "The Quality of Life Argument for Infanticide." *Simon Greenleaf Law Review* 5 (1985-86)

Crutcher, Mark. "Abortion Questions They'd Rather Duck." *Focus on the Family Citizen* (20 May 1991).

Gordon, Doris. "Abortion and Thomson's Violinst: Unplugging a Bad Analogy." Paper published by Libertarians for Life, 1991.

Hall, Elizabeth. "When Does Life Begin? An Embryologist Looks at the Abortion Debate." Interview of Dr. Clifford Grobstein. *Psychology Today* (September 1989).

Joyce, Robert. "Personhood and the Conception Event." *The New Scholasticism* 52 (Winter 1978).

Keenan, James. "Reply to Beckwith: Abortion— Whose Agenda Is it Anyway?" *International Philosophical Quarterly* 32 (June 1992).

Kreeft, Peter. "Human Personhood Begins at Conception." *Journal of Biblical Ethics in Medicine* 4 (Winter 1990).

LaRue, Janet. "Abortion: Justice Harry A. Blackmun and the *Roe v. Wade* Decision." *Simon Greenleaf Law Review* 2 (1982-83).

Levin, Michael. Review of *Life in the Balance* by Robert Wennberg. *Constitutional Commentary* 3 (Summer 1986).

Marquis, Donald. "Why Abortion Is Immoral." *Journal of Philosophy* 86 (April 1989).

Mavrodes, Georges. "Abortion and Imagination: Reflections on Mollenkott's 'Reproductive Choice'". *Christian Scholar's Review* 18 (December 1988).

McInerney, Peter. "Does a Fetus Already Have a Future-Like-Ours?" *Journal of Philosophy* 87 (May 1990).

Mollenkott, Virginia Ramey. "Reproductive Choice: Basic to Justice for Women." *Christian Scholar's Review* 17 (March 1988).

Montgomery, John Warwick. "The Rights of Unborn Children." *Simon Greenleaf Law Review* 5 (1985–86).

Select Bibliography

Moreland, J. P. "James Rachels and the Active Euthanasia Debate." *Journal of the Evangelical Theological Society* 31 (March 1988).

Norcross, Alastair. "Killing, Abortion, and Contraceptian: A Reply to Marquis." *Journal of Philosophy* 87 (May 1990).

Olasky, Marvin. "The Village's Prolife Voice." *Christianity Today*. 24 June 1991.

Rachels, James. "A Critique of Ethical Relativism." In *Philosophy: The Quest for Truth*, edited by Louis P. Pojman. Belmont, Calif.: Wadsworth, 1989.

Ray, A. Chadwick. "Humanity, Personhood, and Abortion." *International Philosophical Quarterly* 25 (1985).

Schwarz, Stephen D., and R.K. Tacelli, "Abortion and Some Philosophers: A Critical Examination." *Public Affairs Quarterly* 3 (April 1989).

Sommers, Christina. "Philosophers Against the Family." In *Vice and Virtue in Everyday Life: Readings in Ethics*, edited by Christina Sommers. San Diego, Calif.: Harcourt Brace Jovanovich, 1989.

Waltke, Bruce. "Reflections From the Old Testament on Abortion." *Journal of the Evangelical Theological Society* 19 (1976).

Wilcox, John T. "Nature as Demonic in Thomson's Defense of Abortion." *The New Scholasticism* 63 (Autumn 1989).

Wolf-Devine, Celia. "Abortion and the 'Feminine Voice.'" *Public Affairs Quarterly* 3 (July 1989).

Notes

Introduction

1. See Fred Barnes, "Republicans Miscarry Abortion," in *The American Spectator* 23 (January 1990): 14-15.

2. See Dinesh D'Souza, *Illiberal Education: The Politics of Race and Sex on Campus* (New York: Free Press, 1991); Francis J. Beckwith and Michael A. Bauman, eds., *Are You Politically Correct?: Debating America's Cultural Standards* (Buffalo: Prometheus, 1993).

3. For an overview of the history and of the moral and legal nuances in the debates over assisted suicide and passive and active euthanasia, see Victor G. Rosenblum and Clarke D. Forsythe, "The Right to Assisted Suicide: Protection of Autonomy or an Open Door to Social Killing?" *Issues in Law & Medicine* 6 (Summer 1990): 3-31. For ethical discussions of euthanasia and suicide, see J. P. Moreland and Norman L. Geisler, *The Life and Death Debate: Moral Issues of Our Time* (Westport, Conn.: Praeger, 1990), 63-102; Francis J. Beckwith and Norman L. Geisler, *Matters of Life and Death: Calm Answers to Tough Questions about Abortion and Euthanasia* (Grand Rapids: Baker, 1991), 131-163; and Robert N. Wennberg, *Terminal Choices: Euthanasia, Suicide, and the Right to Die* (Grand Rapids: Eerdmans, 1989).

4. For an excellent scholarly survey of the history of the press and abortion, see Marvin Olasky, *The Press and Abortion, 1838–1988* (Hillsdale, N.J.: Lawrence Erlbaum Associates, 1988).

5. This is the position held by almost all the pro-abortion groups who filed briefs in *Roe v. Wade*. For a summary and overview of the main pro-abortion briefs filed in this case, see Stephen Krason, *Abortion: Politics, Morality, and the Constitution* (Lanham, Md: University Press of America, 1984), 181-223.

Furthermore, according to *Roe*, the only time at which a state may prohibit abortion if it so chooses is in the last three months of pregnancy unless the *health* of the mother is in danger. However, in *Doe v. Bolton*, 410 U.S. 179, 192 (1973), the Supreme Court defined *health* in a very broad sense when it asserted that an abortion can be performed "in light of all factors—physical, emotional, psychological, familial, and the woman's age— relevant to the well-being of the patient. All these factors relate to health." This is why a study by the Senate Judiciary Committee, which evaluated the legal and social ramifications of the Supreme Court's abortion decisions, concluded that "no significant legal barriers of any kind whatsoever exist today in the United States for a woman to obtain an abortion for any reason during any stage of her pregnancy" (7 June 1983).

For a more detailed presentation, see chapter 2: "Why Abortion on Demand Is Legal in America."

6. Included among the hundreds of works that criticize the legal reasoning of *Roe* are the following: Stephen M. Krason and William B. Hollberg, "The Law and History of Abortion: The Supreme Court Refuted," in *Abortion, Medicine, and the Law*, 3d rev. ed., eds. J. Douglas Butler and David F. Walbert (New York: Facts on File Publications, 1986); Dennis J. Horan and Thomas J. Balch, "*Roe v. Wade*: No Justification in History, Law, or Logic," in *Abortion and the Constitution: Reversing Roe v. Wade Through the Courts*, ed. Dennis J. Horan, Edward R. Grant, and Paige C. Cunningham (Washington, D.C.: Georgetown University Press, 1987); Joseph W. Dellapenna, "Abortion and the Law: Blackmun's Distortion of the Historical Record," in *Abortion and the Constituion*; Joseph W. Dellapenna, "The History of Abortion: Technology, Morality, and Law," in *University of Pittsburg Law Review* 40 (1979); Jacqueline Nolan Haley, "Haunting Shadows from the Rubble of *Roe's* Right to Privacy," *Suffolk University Law Review* 9 (1974); John Hart Ely, "The Wages of Crying Wolf: A Comment on *Roe v. Wade*," *Yale Law Journal* 82 (1973); Thomas O'Meara, "Abortion: The Court Decides a Non-Case," *The Supreme Court Review* (1974); Stanley M. Harrison, "The Supreme Court and Abortional Reform: Means to an End," *New York Law Forum* 19 (1974); Robert A. Destro, "Abortion and the Constitution: The Need for a Life-Protective Amendment," *California Law Review* 63 (1975); John T. Noonan, Jr., "Raw Judicial Power," in *The Zero People*, ed. Jeff Lane Hensley (Ann Arbor, Mich.: Servant, 1983); Charles E. Rice, "Overruling *Roe v. Wade*: An Analysis of the Proposed Constitutional Amendments," *Boston College Industrial and Commercial Law Review* 15 (December 1973); Lynn D. Wardle and Mary Anne Q. Wood, *A Lawyer Looks at Abortion* (Provo, Utah: Brigham Young University Press, 1982); William R. Hopkin, Jr., "*Roe v. Wade* and the Traditional Legal Standards Concerning Pregnancy," *Tem-*

ple Law Quarterly 47 (1974); John Warwick Montgomery, "The Rights of Unborn Children," *Simon Greenleaf Law Review* 5 (1985–86); James S. Witherspoon, "Reexamining *Roe*: Nineteenth-Century Abortion Statutes and the Fourteenth Amendment," *St. Mary's Law Journal* 17 (1985); Krason, *Abortion*; and Marvin Olasky, *Abortion Rites: A Social History of Abortion in America* (Wheaton, Ill.: Crossway, 1992).

7. For example, see Dr. and Mrs. J. C. Wilke, *Abortion: Questions and Answers*, rev. ed. (Cincinnati: Hayes Publishing, 1988), 305–13.

8. See Jay Kantor, "The Right to Life," *APA Newsletter on Philosophy and Medicine* 88:3 (Spring 1989): 80–82; and Judith Jarvis Thomson, "A Defense of Abortion," *Philosophy and Public Affairs* 1 (1971): 47–66.

9. See Krason's excellent presentation of the history of the contemporary abortion-rights movement in *Abortion*, 7–75.

10. See Krason, *Abortion*; Peter Kreeft, *The Unaborted Socrates* (Downers Grove, Ill.: InterVarsity, 1982), and C. Everett Koop and Francis A. Schaeffer, *Whatever Happened to the Human Race?* (Old Tappan, NJ: Revell, 1979).

11. For example, abortion-rights philosopher Mary Anne Warren clearly recognizes that her position on abortion cannot rest on the arguments of popular abortion-rights rhetoric if it is not first demonstrated that the unborn entity is not fully human. She writes that "the fact that restricting access to abortion has tragic side effects does not, in itself, show that the restrictions are unjustified, since murder is wrong regardless of the consequences of prohibiting it; and the appeal to the right to control one's body, which is generally construed as a property right, is at best a rather feeble argument for the permissibility of abortion. Mere ownership does not give me the right to kill innocent people whom I find on my property, and indeed I am apt to be held responsible if such people injure themselves while on my property. It is equally unclear that I have any moral right to expel an innocent person from my property when I know that doing so will result in his death." Mary Anne Warren, "On the Moral and Legal Status of Abortion," in *The Problem of Abortion*, 2d ed., ed. Joel Feinberg (Belmont, Calif.: Wadsworth, 1984), 103.

12. See the devastating and scholarly critique of Planned Parenthood and its abortion policy in Robert Marshall and Charles Donovan, *Blessed are the Barren: The Social Policy of Planned Parenthood* (San Francisco: Ignatius, 1992).

Chapter 1: The Possibility of Moral Reasoning

1. Allan Bloom, *The Closing of the American Mind* (New York: Simon and Schuster, 1987), 25.

2. See C. S. Lewis, *Mere Christianity* (New York: Macmillan, 1948), chap. 1–5, and James Rachels, "A Critique of Ethical Relativism," in *Philosophy: The Quest for Truth*, ed. Louis P. Pojman (Belmont, Calif.: Wadsworth, 1989), 317–25.

3. Rachels, "A Critique," 318–25.

4. *Ibid.*, 322–23.

5. James Rachels, "Some Basic Points about Arguments," in *The Right Thing to Do: Basic Readings in Moral Philosophy*, ed. James Rachels (New York: Random House, 1989), 40.

6. Tom L. Beauchamp, *Philosophical Ethics: An Introduction to Moral Philosophy* (New York: McGraw-Hill, 1982), 42.

7. For a philosophical defense of particular universal values, see C. S. Lewis, *The Abolition of Man* (New York: Macmillan, 1947), 95–121; Lewis, *Mere Christianity*, chaps. 1–5; Rachels, "A Critique," 322–24; and J. P. Moreland, *Scaling the Secular City* (Grand Rapids: Baker, 1987), chap. 4.

8. For a greater elaboration of the view put forth here, see Norman L. Geisler, *Christian Ethics: Options and Issues* (Grand Rapids: Baker, 1989), 113–32.

9. Rachels's "Some Basic Points about Arguments" (in *The Right Thing to Do*, 33–47) gave me the idea for this section.

10. See Lewis, *The Abolition of Man*, 95–121.

11. Judith Jarvis Thomson, "A Defense of Abortion," in *Public Affairs Quarterly* 1 (1971): 57–66. For a similar argument, see Jay Kantor, "The Right to Life," *APA Newsletter on Philosophy and Medicine* 88:3 (Spring 1989): 80–82.

Chapter 2: Why Abortion on Demand Is Legal in America

1. Mortimer J. Adler, *Haves Without Have-Nots* (New York: Macmillan, 1991), 210.

2. Dorothy C. Wertz and John C. Fletcher, "Fatal Knowledge?: Prenatal Diagnosis and Sex Selection," *Hastings Center Report* (May/June 1989): 21–27. I would like to thank James Damron, J.D., of Americans United for Life (Chicago) for providing me with a bibliography on sex-selection abortions.

3. *Ibid.*, 21.

4. Joyce Price, "Prenatal Test of Sex Sometimes Triggers Abortion Decisions," *Washington Times* (13 February 1987): 6D.

5. Gina Kolata, "Fetal Sex Test Used as Step to Abortion," *The New York Times* (25 December 1988): A1.

6. Christopher Farley, "The Debate Over Uses of Prenatal Testing," *USA Today* (2 February 1989): 1D.

7. Jo McGowan, "In India, They Abort Females," *Newsweek* (30 January 1989): 12.

8. Farley, "The Debate," 1D.

9. Anne Koeing, "Abortion for Gender is Debated," *Lancaster Pennsylvania News* (22 January 1989): A4.

10. Kolota, "Fetal Sex Test," A1.

11. *Ibid.*

12. *Akron v. Akron Center for Reproductive Health, Inc.* 462 U.S. 416, 459 (1983) (O'Connor, J., dissenting).

13. Nevada Revised Statute, 442.250, subsection 3.

14. *Doe v. Bolton* 410 U.S. 179, 192 (1973).

15. Report, Committee on the Judiciary, U.S. Senate, on Senate Resolution 3, 98th Congress, 98–149, 7 June 1983, 6.

16. *Thornburg v. American College of Obstetricians and Gynecologists* 476 U.S. 747 (1986).

17. Victor G. Rosenblum and Thomas J. Marzen, "Strategies for Reversing *Roe v. Wade* through the Courts," in *Abortion and the Constitution*, eds. Dennis Horan, Edward R. Grant, and Paige C. Cunningham (Washington, D.C.: Georgetown University Press, 1987), 199–200.

18. Report on the Human Life Bill—S. 158; Committee on the Judiciary, United States Senate, December 1981, p. 5.

19. Thomas O'Meara, "Abortion: The Court Decides a Non-Case," *The Supreme Court Review* (1974): 344.

20. Stanely M. Harrison, "The Supreme Court and Abortional Reform: Means to an End," *New York Law Forum* 19 (1974): 690.

21. Robert A. Destro, "Abortion and the Constitution: The Need for a Life-Protective Amendment," *California Law Review* 63 (1975): 1250.

22. Jacqueline Nolan Haley, "Haunting Shadows from the Rubble of *Roe's* Right to Privacy," *Suffolk University Law Review* 9 (1974): 152–53.

23. John Hart Ely, "The Wages of Crying Wolf: A Comment on *Roe v. Wade*," *Yale Law Journal* 82 (1973): 921. Emphasis in original.

24. John T. Noonan, Jr., "Raw Judicial Power," in *The Zero People*, ed. Jeff Lane Hensley (Ann Arbor, Mich.: Servant 1983), 18. This article originally appeared in *National Review*.

25. Charles E. Rice, "Overruling *Roe v. Wade*: An Analysis of the Proposed Constitutional Amendments," *Boston College Industrial and Commercial Law Review* 15 (December 1973): 309.

26. Lynn D. Wardle and Mary Anne Q. Wood, *A Lawyer Looks at Abortion* (Provo, Utah: Brigham Young University Press, 1982), 12.

27. William R. Hopkin, Jr., "*Roe v. Wade* and the Traditional Legal Standards Concerning Pregnancy," *Temple Law Quarterly* 47 (1974): 729–730.

28. John Warwick Montgomery, "The Rights of Unborn Children," *Simon Greenleaf Law Review* 5 (1985–86): 40.

29. Stephen M. Krason, *Abortion: Politics, Morality, and the Constitution* (Lanham, Md.: University Press of America, 1984), 103–4.

30. Roger Wertheimer, "Understanding Blackmun's Argument: The Reasoning of *Roe v. Wade*," in *Abortion: Moral and Legal Perspectives* (Amherst: University of Massachusetts Press, 1984), 120–21.

31. For verification of this statistic, see Colin Fracome, *Abortion Practice in Britain and the United States* (New York: Allen and Unwin, 1986), 104.

32. See *American Medical Association Encyclopedia of Medicine*, ed. Charles B. Clayman, M.D. (New York: Random House, 1989), 58.

33. Francis J. Beckwith, affidavit submitted in support of plantiffs in *Choose Life v. Del Papa* (1990) to the First Judicial District Court of the State of Nevada (Carson City) and in the appeal to the Nevada Supreme Court.

Although not an attorney, I helped the plantiffs' attorneys—Joel Hansen, Michael Peters and his paralegal assistant, Beth Moulton, and Conrad Hafen—in writing their pleadings. It was a pleasure to work with such fine, intelligent, and hardworking advocates of the pro-life position.

34. Justice William Rehnquist in *Webster v. Reproduction Health Services* (1989) No. 88–605, as found in Beckwith and Geisler, *Matters of Life and Death: Calm Answers to Tough Questions about Abortion and Euthanasia* (Grand Rapids: Baker, 1991), 282–83.

35. *Planned Parenthood v. Casey* nos. 91–744 and 91–902 (1992): I (Syllabus).

36. Ibid., p. II.

37. Ibid., p. VIII.

38. Ibid., p. 12 (Rehnquist, dissenting).

39. According to one poll taken by the *Boston Globe* and WBZ Broadcasting, the vast majority of Americans would ban abortions in the following circumstances (in parentheses is the percentage of Americans who would want it illegal): "a woman is a minor" (50), "wrong time in life to have a child" (82), "fetus not desired sex" (93), "woman cannot afford a child" (75), "as a means of birth control" (89), "pregnancy would cause too much emotional strain" (64), "father unwilling to help raise the child" (83), "father absent" (81), "mother wants abortion/father wants baby" (72), "father wants abortion/mother wants baby" (75). This is why the journalist who reported this poll concluded that "most Americans would ban the vast majority of abortions performed in this country. . . . While 78 percent of the nation would keep abortion legal in limited circumstances, according to the poll, *those circumstances account for a tiny percentage of the reasons*" (emphasis added). (Ethan Bronner, "Most in U.S. Favor Ban on Majority of Abortions, Poll Finds," in *The Boston Globe* 235 [31 March 1989]: 1, 12).

40. From *Motion and Brief Amicus Curiae of Certain Physicians, Professors and Fellows of the American College of Obstetrics and Gynecology in Support of the Appellees*, submitted to the Supreme Court of the United States, October Term, 1971, No. 70–18, Roe v. Wade, and No. 70–40, Doe v. Bolton. Prepared by Dennis J. Horan, et al. (the list of amici contains the names of more than two hundred physicians), as quoted in Stephen D. Schwarz, *The Moral Question of Abortion* (Chicago: Loyola University Press, 1990), 3.

41. See Vincent J. Collins, M.D., Steven R. Zielinski, M.D., and Thomas J. Marzen, Esq., *Fetal Pain and Abortion: The Medical Evidence*, Studies in Law & Medicine, no. 18 (Chicago: Americans United for Life Legal Defense Fund, 1984).

42. This point is argued for by the president of the Los Angeles chapter of the National Organization for Women, Kathy Spillar: "Fetal Viability Should Not Dictate Abortion Rights," in *Abortion: Opposing Viewpoints*, ed. Bonnie Szumski (St. Paul: Greenhaven, 1986), 34–37. This opinion piece originally appeared in the *Los Angeles Times* (6 April 1985).

Chapter 3: Prenatal Development, Abortion Methods, and Fetal Pain

1. The facts in this section are taken from the following works that deal with fetal development, two of which are standard medical school textbooks: F. Beck, D. B. Moffat, and D. P. Davies, *Human Embryology*, 2d ed. (Oxford: Blackwell, 1985); Keith L. Moore, *The Developing Human: Clinically Oriented Embryology*, 2d ed. (Philadelphia: W. B. Saunders, 1977); Andre E. Hellegers, "Fetal Development," in *Biomedical Ethics*, eds. Thomas A. Mappes and Jane S. Zembaty (New York: Macmillan, 1981), 405–9; Stephen M. Krason, *Abortion: Politics, Morality, and the Constitution* (Lanham, Md.: University Press of America, 1984), 337–49; Vincent J. Collins, M.D., Steven R. Zielinski, M.D., and Thomas J. Marzen, Esq., *Fetal Pain and Abortion: The Medical Evidence*, Studies in Law & Evidence, no. 18 (Chicago: Americans United for Life Legal Defense Fund, 1984); Bart T. Hefferman, "The Early Biography of Everyman," in *Abortion and Social Justice*, ed. Thomas W. Hilgers, M.D., and Dennis J. Horan, Esq. (New York: Sheed and Ward, 1972), 3–25; and *Motion and Brief Amicus Curiae of Certain Physicians, Professor and Fellows of the American College of Obstetrics and Gynecology in Support of Appellees*, submitted to the Supreme Court of the United States, October Term, 1971, No. 70–18, Roe v. Wade, and No. 70–40, Doe v. Bolton, prepared by Dennis J. Horan, et al. (The list of amici contains the names of more than two hundred physicians), as quoted extensively in Stephen D. Schwarz, *The Moral Question of Abortion* (Chicago: Loyola University Press, 1990), 2–6.

2. *The Human Life Bill: Hearings on S. 158 Before the Subcommittee on Separation of Powers of the Senate Judiciary Committee*, 97th Congress, 1st Session (1981), as quoted in Norman L. Geisler, *Christian Ethics: Options and Issues* (Grand Rapids: Baker, 1989), 149.

3. *The Human Life Bill—S. 158, Report together with Additional and Minority Views to the Committee on the Judiciary, United States Senate, made by its Subcommittee on Separation of Powers*, 97th Congress, 1st Session (1981): 9.

4. Ibid., 7–8.

5. Ibid., 8.

6. Ibid.

7. Ibid., 11.

8. Mortimer J. Adler, *Haves Without Have-Nots* (New York: Macmillan 1991), 210.

9. Hefferman, "The Early Biography of Everyman," 4.

10. From Hymie Gordon, M.D., "Genetical, Social, and Medical Aspects of Abortion," *South African Medical Journal* (20 July 1968), as quoted in Ibid., 5.

11. James J. Diamond, M.D., "Abortion, Animation and Biological Hominization," *Theological Studies* (June 1975): 305–42.

12. Krason, *Abortion*, 341.

13. Ibid.

14. Amicus curiae, as cited in Schwarz, *The Moral Question of Abortion*, 3.

15. Ibid., 3–4.

16. Ibid., 5.

17. See Mortimer Rosen, "The Secret Brain: Learning Before Birth," *Harper's* (April 1978): 46–47.

18. C. Everett Koop, M.D., and Francis A. Schaeffer, *Whatever Happend to the Human Race?* (Old Tappan, N.J.: Revell, 1979), 41. These abortion techniques are presented in a more clinical fashion by the director of the Boulder (Colorado) Abortion Clinic, Warren M. Hern, M.D., in *Abortion Practice*, 2d ed. (Philadelphia: Lippincott, 1990).

19. Ibid.

20. Ibid.

21. Ibid., 42.

22. Schwarz, *The Moral Question of Abortion*, 20.

23. Gary Bergel, *When You Were Formed in Secret* (Elyria, Ohio: Intercessors for America, 1980), II-4, as quoted in ibid., 21–22.

24. Collins, Zielinski, and Marzen, *Fetal Pain and Abortion*, 8.

25. Ibid., 8.

26. Ibid.

27. Ibid., 9. These statistics are based on calculations from the Centers for Disease Control—Abortion Surveillance, Annual Summary 1979–80. U.S. Department of Health and Human Services, May 1983.

28. John T. Noonan, "The Experience of Pain by the Unborn," in *The Zero People*, ed. Jeff Lane Hensley (Ann Arbor, Mich.: Servant, 1983), 151–52.

29. Objection 2 is brought up as well as responded to in the form of two objections in Schwarz, *The Moral Question of Abortion*, pp. 39–40.

30. This objection has been raised in a small booklet by the Religious Coalition for Abortion Rights, *Words of Choice* (Washington, D.C.: Religious Coalition for Abortion Rights, 1991), 14. It is interesting that this booklet's objection relies on a statement by the American College of Obstetricians and Gynecologists, "Statement on Pain of the Fetus" (13 February 1984) rather than on the views of neurologists and anesthesiologists, physicians who are trained specifically to deal with pain and the physiological factors necessary to experience it.

31. Collins, Zielinski and Marzen, *Fetal Pain and Abortion*, 6. In substantiating this view, the following are a few of the works the authors cite in the footnotes: A. C. Guyton, *Textbook of Medical Physiology* (Philadelphia: W. B. Saunders, 1976), 666; and H. D. Patton, J. W. Sundsten, W. E. Crill, P. D. Swanson, eds. *Introduction to Basic Neurology* (Philadelphia: W. B. Saunders, 1976), 198.

32. Noonan, "The Experience of Pain by the Unborn," 149.

33. Schwarz, *The Moral Question of Abortion*, 23–25.

Chapter 4: Arguments from Pity

1. James B. Freeman, *Thinking Logically: Basic Concepts for Reasoning* (Englewood Cliffs, N.J.: Prentice-Hall, 1988), 74.

2. From the *Informal Logic Newsletter*, vol. 2, supplement, June 1980, as quoted in ibid.

3. Mary Anne Warren, "On the Moral and Legal Status of Abortion," in *The Problem of Abortion*, 2d ed., ed. Joel Feinberg (Belmont, Calif.: Wadsworth, 1984), 103.

4. See Daniel Callahan, *Abortion: Law, Choice, and Morality* (New York: Macmillan, 1970), 132–36; and Stephen Krason, *Abortion: Politics, Morality, and the Constitution* (Lanham, Md.: University Press of America, 1984), 301–10. For a history of the nineteenth century and illegal abortion, see Marvin Olasky, *Abortion Rites: A Social History of Abortion in America* (Wheaton, Ill.: Crossway, 1992).

5. Bernard Nathanson, M.D., *Aborting America* (New York: Doubleday, 1979), 193.

6. Laurence Lader, *Abortion* (Indianapolis: Bobbs-Merrill, 1966), 3.

7. James T. Burtchaell, *Rachel Weeping: The Case Against Abortion* (San Francisco: Harper and Row, 1982), 93.

8. From the U.S. Bureau of Vital Statistics Center for Disease Control, as cited in Dr. and Mrs. J. C. Wilke, *Abortion: Questions and Answers*, rev. ed. (Cincinnati: Hayes Publishing, 1988), 101–2.

9. From Dr. Hellegers' testimony before the U.S. Senate Judiciary Committee on Constitutional Amendments, April 25, 1974, as cited in John Jefferson Davis, *Abortion and the Christian* (Phillipsburg, N.J.: Presbyterian and Reformed, 1984), 75.

10. From the U. S. Bureau of Vital Statistics Center for Disease Control, as cited in Willke, *Abortion*, 101–2.

11. As cited by moderate abortion-rights bioethicist Callahan in *Abortion*, 134.

12. The figure of ten thousand maternal deaths as well as the number of one to two million illegal abortions per year come from F. J. Taussig's 1936 book, *Abortion Spontaneous and Induced*. These figures have been called into question by a great number of scholars. And for this reason, I have found no contemporary scholar willing to stand by them. Davis cites some of the many reasons for this stance: Taussig's "estimate presupposed a 1934 study by M. E. Kopp of women who had attended the Margaret Sanger Birth Control Clinic in New York between 1925 and 1929. The Sanger Clinic sample from which the figures originated was hardly representative of the population as a whole, since 41.7 percent of the women were Jewish, and 26.1 were Catholic" (Davis, *Abortion*, 75).

13. Planned Parenthood of New York City fundraising letter, "A Century of Progress in Peril," referencing the 21 October 1989 veto of an abortion funding bill by President Bush received during the winter of 1989 (with attachments), as quoted in Robert Marshall and Charles Donovan, *Blessed are the Barren: The Social Policy of Planned Parenthood* (San Francisco: Ignatius, 1991), 203.

14. Consider the following claims. In 1967 Dr. Robert Hall, president and cofounder of the Association for the Study of Abortion, claimed that there were one million illegal abortions annually ("Abortion in American Hospitals," *American Journal of Public Health* [November 1967]: 1933-1966). In the same year, Harriet Pilpel, an abortion-rights attorney, said that there were from one

to one and a half million illegal abortions per year ("The Abortion Crisis," in *The Case for Legalized Abortion Now*, ed. Alan Guttmacher, M.D. [Berkeley, Calif.: Diablo, 1967], pp. 87–113). Also in 1967, Alan Guttmacher suggested that the number of illegal abortions was between five hundred thousand and two million (*Pregnancy, Birth, and Family Planning, A Guide for Expectant Parents in the 1970s* [New York: Viking, 1967], 165). Margaret Sanger, founder of Planned Parenthood, claimed there were two million illegal abortions per year in the United States in 1912 and 1913 (Fourth International Conference on Planned Parenthood, Stockholm, 1953, "The History of the Birth Control Movement in the English Speaking World," unedited translation from Sound-Mirror, by Margaret Sanger, 6, SSCSC). These claims and their references are taken from Marshall and Donovan, *Blessed are the Barren*, 240, 249.

15. *Vital Statistics of the United States for 1965*, mortality table 7–3, 7–78, as cited in Marshall and Donovan, *Blessed are the Barren*, 203.

16. *Washington Post*, 14 February 1990.

17. Marshall and Donovan, *Blessed are the Barren*, 203.

18. In their critical analysis of the social policy of Planned Parenthood (*Blessed are the Barren*), Marshall and Donovan present numerous other statistical absurdities put forth by abortion-rights supporters and Planned Parenthood partisans.

19. See n. 12; Callahan, *Abortion*, 132–36; Krason, *Abortion*, 301–10.

20. Barbara J. Syska, Thomas W. Hilgers, M.D., and Dennis O'Hare, "An Objective Model for Estimating Criminal Abortions and Its Implications for Public Policy," in *New Perspectives on Human Abortion*, ed. Thomas Hilgers, M.D., Dennis J. Horan, and David Mall (Frederick, Md.: University Publications of America, 1981), 78.

21. Chart taken from Marshall and Donovan, *Blessed Are the Barren*, 264.

22. Willard Cates, Jr., and Roger Rochat, "Illegal Abortion Deaths in the United States: 1972–74," *Family Planning Perspectives* 8 (March–April 1976): 86–88, 91–92, as cited in Marshall and Donovan, *Blessed Are the Barren*, 264.

23. Christopher Tietze, "The Effect of Legalization of Abortion on Population Growth and Public Health," *Family Planning Perspectives* 7 (May–June 1975): 86, as cited in Marshall and Donovan, *Blessed Are the Barren*, 264.

24. Tietze, "The Effect of Legalization of Abortion," 87, as cited in Marshall and Donovan, *Blessed are the Barren*, 264.

25. Steven Polgar and Ellen S. Freid, "The Bad Old Days: Clandestine Abortions among the Poor in New York City before Liberalization of the Abortion Law," *Family Planning Perspectives* 8 (May–June 1976): 125–127, as cited in Marshall and Donovan, *Blessed Are the Barren*, 264.

26. Marshall and Donovan, *Blessed Are the Barren*, 264.

27. Ibid.

28. Laurence Tribe, *Abortion: The Clash of Absolutes* (New York: Norton, 1990), 137, 41.

29. James Mohr, *Abortion in America: The Origins and Evolution of National Policy, 1800–1900* (New York: Oxford, 1978), 254. Tribe refers to Mohr's book in *Abortion*, 245, n. 57.

30. David C. Reardon, *Aborted Women: Silent No More* (Westchester, Ill.: Crossway, 1987), 13, 15.

31. Mary Calderone, "Illegal Abortion as a Public Health Problem," in *American Journal of Public Health* 50 (July 1960): 948–54.

32. Faye Wattleton, circular letter to members of Congress, 22 January 1979, as cited in Marshall and Donovan, *Blessed Are the Barren*, 262.

33. Sally Quinn, "Our Choices, Our Selves," *Las Vegas Review-Journal* (14 April 1992): 9B. Kathryn Kolbert, a Planned Parenthood attorney, perpetuated this statistical myth while arguing before the U.S. Supreme Court against Pennsylvania's abortion law (22 April 1992), though she cited no studies, research, or data: "In the days before Roe, *thousands of women lost their lives* and more were subjected to physical and emotional scars from back-alley and self-induced abortions. Recognizing that, this court established Roe. . . ." (Aaron Epstein, "High Court Gets Case on Abortion," *Las Vegas Review-Journal* [23 April 1992]: 1A).

34. Nathanson, *Aborting America*, 194.

35. Philosopher Craig Walton alludes to this argument in his Socratic dialogue, "Socrates Comes to His Senses During Meeting With Bush," *Las Vegas Review-Journal* (3 November 1988): 11B.

36. P. T. Bauer, *Equality, the Third World, and Economic Delusion* (Cambridge: Harvard University Press, 1981), 43–44. Among the many works that support Bauer's thesis as well as dismiss the population explosion as ludicrous are Jaqueline Kasun, "The Population Bomb Threat: A Look at the Facts," in *The Zero People*, ed. Jeff Lane Hensley (Ann Arbor, Mich.: Servant, 1983), 33–41 (this article, written by a professor of economics at Humboldt State University [Arcata, California], was originally published in *Intellect* [June 1977]); Colin Clark, *Population Growth: The Advantages* (Santa Ana, Calif.: A Life Quality Paperback, 1975); and Rousas J. Rushdoony, *The Myth of Over-Population* (Fairfax, Va.: Thoburn, 1975).

37. E. Calvin Beisner, *Prospects for Growth* (Westchester, Ill.: Crossway, 1990), 189–90.

38. Ibid., 190.

39. Ibid., 190–91.

40. Kasun, "The Population Bomb Threat," 35–36. See Clark, *Population Growth*.

41. Francis P. Felice, "Population Growth," *The Compass*, 1974, as quoted in Kasun, ibid., 38.

42. See chap. 2.

43. Baruch Brody, *Abortion and the Sanctity of Human Life: A Philosophical View* (Cambridge, Mass.: M.I.T. Press, 1975), 36–37.

44. See the arguments in the Planned Parenthood Federation of America brief (for *Roe v. Wade*), as cited in Krason, *Abortion*, 315–19.

45. C. Everett Koop and Francis A. Schaeffer, *Whatever Happened to the Human Race?* (Old Tappan, N.J.: Revell, 1979), 29–30.

46. Reardon, *Aborted Women*, 225. The statistics of increased child abuse that Reardon cites are from Philip G. Ney, "Infant Abortion and Child Abuse: Cause and Effect," *The Psychological Aspects of Abortion*, ed. David Mall and Dr. Walter Watts (Washington, D.C.: University Publications of America, 1979), 25.

47. As reported in *The Providence Journal* (29 March 1989): A–10, as cited in Stephen D. Schwarz, *The Moral Question of Abortion* (Chicago: Loyola University Press, 1990), 180.

48. See Philip G. Ney, "Relationship Between Abortion and Child Abuse," *Canadian Journal of Psychiatry* 24 (November 1979): 610–20; and Ney, "A Consideration of Abortion Survivors," in *The Zero People*, 123–38. For a critical response to Ney's position, see W. W. Walters, "Mental Health Consequences of Abortion and Refused Abortion," *Canadian Journal of Psychiatry* 25 (February 1980): 68–73.

49. Edward F. Lenoski, M.D., "Translating Injury Data into Preventative Health Care Services," University of Southern California Medical School, unpublished, 1976, as cited in Krason, *Abortion*, 320.

50. See B. D. Schmitt and C. H. Kempe, *Child Abuse: Management and Prevention of the Battered Child Syndrome* (Basle: Ciba-Geigy, 1975).

51. Krason, *Abortion*, 320. See Rosemary S. Hunter, M.D., et al., "Antecedents of Child Abuse and Neglect in Premature Infants: A Prospective Study in a Newborn Intensive Care Unit," in *Pediatrics* 61 (1978): 629, 634; Vincent J. Fontana, M.D., and Douglas J. Besharov, *The Maltreated Child*, 4th ed. (Springfield, Ill.: Charles C. Thomas, 1979), 12–13, 27; Richard Gelles, "A Profile of Violence Toward Children in the United States," in *Child Abuse: An Agenda for Action*, ed. George Gebner, Catherine J. Ross, and Edward Ziegler (New York: Oxford University Press, 1980), 102–3.

52. Sidney Callahan, "Talk of 'Wanted Child' Makes for Doll Objects," *National Catholic Reporter* (3 December 1971): 7, as quoted in Burtchaell, *Rachel Weeping*, 80.

53. For an excellent overview of the major birth defects, their causes, and the chances of them occurring (for every hundred thousand babies born alive), see "Birth Defects," in *The American Medical Association Encyclopedia of Medicine*, ed. Charles B. Clayman, M.D. (New York: Random House, 1989), 172–73.

54. See chap. 2.

55. Peter Singer and Helen Kuhse, "On Letting Handicapped Infants Die," in *The Right Thing to Do: Basic Readings in Moral Philosophy*, ed. James Rachels (New York: Random House, 1989), 146.

56. As quoted in Nathanson, *Aborting America*, 235.

57. Ibid., 235–36.

58. See Peter Kreeft, *The Unaborted Socrates* (Downers Grove, Ill.: InterVarsity, 1982), 140.

59. C. Everett Koop, *The Right to Live: The Right to Die* (Wheaton: Tyndale House, 1976), 51–52.

60. Krason, *Abortion*, 295. Hellegers' study is cited by Robert L. Sassone in Karl Binding and Ilfred Hoche, *The Release of the Destruction of Life Devoid of Value*, comments by Robert L. Sassone (Santa Ana, Calif.: A Life Quality Paperback, 1975), 65.

61. Eugene F. Diamond, M.D., "The Deformed Child's Right to Life," in *Death, Dying, and Euthanasia*, ed. Dennis J. Horan and David Mall (Washington, D.C.: University Publications of America, 1977), 133.

62. George Will, "The Killing Will Not Stop," in *The Zero People*, 206–7. This article originally appeared as a syndicated column in the *Washington Post* (22 April, 1982).

63. *AMA Encyclopedia*, 971.

64. Ibid., 104.

65. Krason, *Abortion*, 386–87. See Germain Grisez, *Abortion: the Myths, the Realities, and the Arguments* (New York: Corpus 1970), 30.

66. Krason, *Abortion*, 387. See Grisez, *Abortion*, 29-30.

67. Virginia Ramey Mollenkott, "Reproductive Choice: Basic to Justice for Women," *Christian Scholar's Review* 17 (March 1988): 286–93.

68. Ibid., 289.

69. Concerning this, Krason writes: "A number of studies have shown that pregnancy resulting from rape is very uncommon. One, looking at 2190 victims, reported pregnancy in only 0.6 percent (Charles R. Hayman, M.D., and Charlene Lanza, "Sexual Assault in Women and Girls," *American Journal of Obstetrics and Gynecology* 109 [1971]: 480–486). Barbara M. Sims, who once served as an assistant district attorney in Erie County, New York (Buffalo and vicinity) wrote in 1969 that the district attorney's office in her county "contain[ed] no reported complaints of pregnancy from forcible rape or incest for the past thirty years" (Barbara M. Sims, "A District Attorney Looks at Abortion," *Child and Family* 8 [1969]: 176, 178). In one study of 117 rape victims in Oklahoma City over a one-year period, there were no pregnancies reported (Royice B. Everett, M.D., and Gordon K. Jimmerson, M.D., "The Rape Victim: A Review of 117 cases," *Obstetrics and Gynecology* 50 [1977]: 88, 89). The Cook County, Illinois (which includes Chicago), state's attorney's office could not recall a single instance of pregnancy in about nine years of prosecuting for rape (Eugene F. Diamond, M.D., "ISMS Symposium on Medical Implications of the Current Abortion in Illinois," *Illinois Medical Journal* 131 [May 1967]: 678). St. Paul, Minnesota, did not record a single pregnancy from rape in over ten years (Fred E. Mecklenburg, M.D., "The Indications for Induced Abortion: A Physician's Perspective," in *Abortion and Social Justice*, ed. Thomas W. Hilgers and Dennis J. Horan [New York: Sheed and Ward, 1972], p. 48)." (Krason, *Abortion*, 281).

70. See Andrew Varga, *The Main Issues in Bioethics*, rev. ed. (New York: Paulist, 1984), 67–68. Varga himself, however, does not believe that abortion is morally justified in the cases of rape and incest.

71. See chap. 2.

72. Nathanson, *Aborting America*, 238.

73. Schwarz, *The Moral Question of Abortion*, 146, 151.

74. Ibid., 148.

75. Michael Bauman, "Verbal Plunder: Combatting the Feminist Encroachment on the Language of Religion and Morality," paper presented at the 42nd annual meeting of the Evangelical Theological Society, New Orleans Baptist Theological Seminary, New Orleans, Lousiana, 15–17 November 1990, 16.

76. Ibid., 16–17.

77. Ibid., 17.

78. Krason, *Abortion*, 284. For an overview of the research, see Sandra K. Mahkorn, "Pregnancy and Sexual Assault," in David Mall and Walter F. Watts, M.D., *The Psychological Aspects of Abortion* (Washington, D.C.: University Publications of America, 1979), 67–68.

79. Krason, *Abortion*, 284.

80. Mahkorn, "Pregnancy and Sexual Assault," 65. See also Curt Young, *The Least of These: What Everyone Should Know about Abortion* (Chicago: Moody, 1983).

81. Reardon, *Aborted Women*, 204–5.

82. As quoted in Ibid., 169. Abortionist Warren M. Hern apparently comments, "[T]he abortion counselor should recognize that the emotional trauma experienced by the rape or incest victim cannot be treated adequately, if at all, in the abortion clinic setting." (Warren M. Hern, *Abortion Practice*, 2d. ed. [Philadelphia: Lippincott, 1990], 84).

83. As quoted in John and Barbara Willke, *Handbook on Abortion* (Cincinnati: Hayes Publishing, 1979), 52.

84. James Witherspoon, "Reexamining *Roe*: Nineteenth Abortion Statutes and the Fourteenth Amendment," *St. Mary's Law Journal* 17:1 (1985): 31–50, 61–71. See also Dennis J. Horan and Thomas J. Balch, "*Roe v. Wade*: No Justification in History, Law, or Logic," in *Abortion and the Constitution: Reversing* Roe v. Wade *Through the Courts*, ed. Dennis J. Horan, Edward R. Grant, and Paige C. Cunningham (Washington, D.C.: Georgetown University Press, 1987), 57–88; Joseph W. Dellapenna, "Abortion and the Law: Blackmun's Distortion of the Historical Record," in *Abortion and the Constitution*, 137–58; and Krason, *Abortion*, 119–79.

85. See *Roe v. Wade*, 410 U.S. 113, 151–58 (1973), as cited in Witherspoon, "Reexamining *Roe*," 58.

86. Ibid., 58–59.

87. Marvin Olasky, *Abortion Rites: A Social History of Abortion in America* (Wheaton, Ill.: Crossway, 1992), 99.

88. Although the state penalties for an abortionist killing an unborn person were less severe than for somebody killing a born person, the lesser severity of the penalties does not mean that the unborn were seen as less than born persons under the law. Rather, like the immunity granted to pregnant women in most states, the punishments for abortionists may have taken into consideration several variables, none of which takes away from the full personhood of the unborn. For a brief survey of the legal punishments for those who attempted to produce abortions, and why these punishments did not contradict the personhood of the unborn, see Witherspoon, "Reexaming *Roe*," 51-56.

89. See Reardon, *Aborted Women*.

90. For example, see Elizabeth Hall's interview of embryologist Clifford Grobstein, "When Does Life Begin?:

An Embryologist Looks at the Abortion Debate," in *Psychology Today* (September 1989): 43–46; Mollenkott, "Reproductive Choice," 286–93; Michael Tooley, *Abortion and Infanticide* (Oxford: Clarendon, 1983), 50–86; and Warren, "On the Moral and Legal Status of Abortion," 102–119.

91. *Webster v. Reproductive Health Services* (1989) as found in *The United States Law Week* 57, no. 50 (27 July 1989): 5035–45.

92. See Stanley I. Benn, "Rights," in *Encyclopedia of Philosophy*, ed. Paul Edwards, 8 vols. (New York: Macmillan and the Free Press, 1967), 7:195–99; Ronald Dworkin, *Taking Rights Seriously* (Cambridge: Harvard University Press, 1978); and Clarence Thomas, "The Higher Law Background of the Privileges and Immunities Clause of the Fourteenth Amendment," *Harvard Journal of Law & Public Policy* 12 (Winter 1989): 63–70.

93. "The Declaration of Independence," in *The Constitutional Convention: The Constitution of the United States and Related Documents*, ed. Martin Shapiro (Northbrook, Ill.: AHM Publishing, 1966), 78–79.

94. "The Constitution of the United States," in *The Constitutional Convention*, 1.

95. Justice Harry Blackmun, in "The 1973 Supreme Court Decisions on State Abortion Laws: Excerpts from Opinion in Roe v. Wade," in *The Problem of Abortion*, 2d ed., ed. Joel Feinberg (Belmont, Calif.: Wadsworth, 1984), 194–95.

96. Ibid. For the reasons why abortion on demand is legal, see chap. 2.

97. I am not arguing that the abortion-rights movement is really defending a "natural law" view of rights. Rather, I am simply pointing out that if abortion is defended as a fundamental constitutional right, it must be seen as a natural right that cannot be legitimately changed, altered, or justified on the basis of utilitarian arguments. See Gary E. Glenn, "Abortion and Inalienable Rights in Classical Liberalism," in *American Journal of Jurisprudence* 20 (1975).

On the issue of whether *Roe v. Wade* asserts that the right to choose abortion is a fundamental right, Constitutional scholars Lynn Wardle and Mary Anne Q. Wood have this to say: "Previous Supreme Court decisions had interpreted the [liberty] to include constitutional protection for certain 'zones of privacy' including personal decisions relating to marriage, procreation, childrearing, and contraception. The Court in *Roe v. Wade* concluded that a woman's decision whether or not to have an abortion was an equally important matter that deserved special judicial protection under the Fourteenth Amendment as a *fundamental constitutional right*" (emphasis added). Lynn Wardle and Mary Anne Q. Wood, *A Lawyer Looks at Abortion* (Provo, Utah: Brigham University Press, 1982), 50.

98. *Webster*, 5041. See the appropriate section in this chapter where this is dealt with as well as Krason's (*Abortion*, 301–10), Callahan's (*Abortion*, 132–36), and Donovan's and Marshall's (*Blessed Are the Barren*, chaps. 6, 7, and 9) critiques of the statistics used to ver-

ify the number of illegal abortions prior to *Roe v. Wade*. In addition, it is conceded by sophisticated abortion-rights advocates that 90 percent of the back-alley abortions of which Blackmun speaks were, according to former Planned Parenthood president Mary Calderone, performed by licensed physicians in good standing (Calderone, "Illegal Abortion as a Public Health Problem," 948–54). Moreover, as I pointed out earlier in this chapter, arguments from the dangers of illegal abortions, beg the question as to the full personhood of the unborn.

99. Tribe, *Abortion*, 105.

100. As quoted in *The New York Times* (10 May 1988).

101. "Women and the Supreme Court: Anatomy Is Destiny," *Brooklyn Law Review* 41 (1974): 242.

102. n.a., *Sound Advice for All Prolife Activists and Candidates Who Wish to Include a Concern for Women's Rights in Their Prolife Advocacy: Feminists for Life Debate Handbook* (Kansas City, Mo.: Feminists for Life of America, n.d.), 17.

103. See Hall, "When Does Life Begin?"; Mollenkott, "Reproductive Choice," pp. 286–93; Tooley, *Abortion*, 50–86; and Warren, "On the Moral and Legal Status of Abortion," 102–19.

104. For example, see Judith Jarvis Thomson, "A Defense of Abortion," in *The Problem of Abortion*, 173–87; and Jay Kantor, "The Right to Life," *APA Newsletter on Philosophy and Medicine* 88:3 (Spring 1989): 80–82.

105. Blackmun in "Excerpts from Opinion in Roe v. Wade," 195.

Chapter 5: Arguments from Tolerance and Ad Hominem

1. Justice Harry Blackmun, "The 1973 Supreme Court Decisions on State Abortion Laws: Excerpts from Opinion in Roe v. Wade," in *The Problem of Abortion*, 2d ed., ed. Joel Feinberg (Belmont, Calif.: Wadsworth, 1984), 195.

2. Ibid., 196.

3. *Webster v. Reproductive Health Services* (1989), as found in *The United States Law Week* 57, no. 50 (27 July 1989): 5044–45.

4. Virginia Ramey Mollenkott, "Reproductive Choice: Basic to Justice for Women," *Christian Scholar's Review* 17 (March 1988): 291.

5. See the results of *The Boston Globe*/WBZ-TV nationwide poll published in *The Globe*, which concluded that "most Americans would ban the vast majority of abortions performed in this country. . . . While 78 percent of the nation would keep abortion legal in limited circumstances, according to the poll, these circumstances account for a tiny percentage of the reasons cited by women having abortions." (Ethan Bronner, "Most in US Favor Ban on Majority of Abortions, Poll Finds," in *The Boston Globe* 235 [31 March 1989]: 1, 12).

6. *Webster*, 5044, n. 16. See also the official statements of denominations and religious groups that are pro-

choice: *We Affirm: National Religious Organizations' Statements on Abortion Rights* (Washington, D.C.: Religious Coalition for Abortion Rights, n.d.).

7. See especially the nontheological defense of the pro-life position by former abortion-rights activist Bernard Nathanson, M.D. (*Aborting America* [New York: Doubleday, 1979] and *The Abortion Papers: Inside the Abortion Mentality* [New York: Frederick Fell, 1983]). For other examples of nontheological defenses of the pro-life position, see Francis J. Beckwith and Norman L. Geisler, *Matters of Life and Death: Calm Answers to Tough Questions about Abortion and Euthanasia* (Grand Rapids: Baker, 1991), 15–127; Baruch Brody, *Abortion and the Sanctity of Human Life: A Philosophical View* (Cambridge, Mass.: M.I.T. Press, 1975); David Clark, "The Quality of Life Argument for Infanticides," in *Simon Greenleaf Law Review* 5 (1985–86): 91–112; Peter Kreeft, *The Unaborted Socrates* (Downers Grove, Ill.: InterVarsity Press, 1984); Don Marquis, "Why Abortion Is Immoral," *Journal of Philosophy* 86 (April 1989): 183–202; A. Chadwick Ray, "Humanity, Personhood, and Abortion," *International Philosophical Quarterly* 25 (1985): 233–45; Stephen D. Schwarz, *The Moral Question of Abortion* (Chicago: Loyola University Press, 1990); Andrew Varga, *The Main Issues in Bioethics*, rev. ed. (New York: Paulist, 1984), 59–65; and the literature published by the group Feminists for Life (811 East 47th Street, Kansas City, Mo. 64110; phone [816] 753–2130).

8. Mollenkott, "Reproductive Choice." See also *We Affirm*.

9. Laurence Tribe, *Abortion: The Clash of Absolutes* (New York: Norton, 1990), 116.

10. George Mavrodes, "Abortion and Imagination: Reflections on Mollenkott's 'Reproductive Choice,'" in *Christian Scholar's Review* 18 (December 1988): 168–69.

11. Bronner, "Most in US Favor Ban on Majority of Abortions, Poll Finds," 1, 12.

12. Ibid., 12.

13. Ibid., 1.

14. David C. Reardon, *Aborted Women: Silent No More* (Westchester, Ill.: Crossway, 1987), 13, 15.

15. Barbara J. Syska, Thomas W. Hilgers, M.D., and Dennis O'Hare, "An Objective Model for Estimating Criminal Abortions and Its Implications for Public Policy," in *New Perspectives on Human Abortion*, ed. Thomas Hilgers, M.D., Dennis J. Horan, and David Mall (Frederick, Md.: University Publications of America, 1981), 178. For a summary of the scholarly dispute over the pre-legalization statistics, see Daniel Callahan, *Abortion: Law, Choice and Morality* (New York: Macmillan, 1970), 132–36; Stephen Krason, *Abortion: Politics, Morality and the Constitution* (Lanham, Md., University Press of America, 1984) 301–10; and Robert Marshall and Charles Donovan, *Blessed are the Barren: The Social Policy of Planned Parenthood* (San Francisco: Ignatius, 1991), chap. 6, 7, and 9.

16. Reardon, *Aborted Women*, 319.

17. Ibid., 319–20. For studies showing the plausibility of this view see the works cited by Reardon.

18. Nathanson, *Aborting America*, 267.

19. Frank R. Zindler, "Human Life Does Not Begin at Conception," in *Abortion: Opposing Viewpoints*, ed. Bonnie Szumski (St. Paul: Greenhaven, 1986), 24.

20. Schwarz, *The Moral Question of Abortion*, 197.

21. Ibid.

22. Ibid., 197–98.

23. See, for example, Mollenkott, "Reproductive Choice," 286–93; Michael Tooley, *Abortion and Infanticide* (Oxford: Clarendon, 1983), 50–86; and Warren, "On the Moral and Legal Status of Abortion," 102–19.

24. For example, see Judith Jarvis Thomson, "A Defense of Abortion," in *The Problem of Abortion*, 173–87; and Jay Kantor, "The Right to Life," *APA Newsletter on Philosophy and Medicine* 88:3 (Spring 1989): 80–82.

25. Blackmun in "Excerpts from Opinion in Roe v. Wade," 195.

26. Nicholas Capaldi, *The Art of Deception: An Introduction to Critical Thinking*, rev. ed. (Buffalo: Prometheus, 1987), 92.

27. "Abortion Foes Challenged to Help," in *Dear Abby* column, in *Las Vegas Review-Journal* (4 October, 1989): 4F.

28. Among the many organizations that help unwed mothers and women in crisis pregnancies are Crisis Pregnancy Centers (branches are found in many cities across North America), Pregnancy Crisis Center (Virginia), and Bethany Lifeline (1-800-234-4269). See the interview of the administrator of an Assembly of God adoption agency in "Alternative to Abortion," *Pentecostal Evangel* (11 February, 1990): 14–15.

29. Ruth Ann Hanley, "Do Right-to-Lifers Care Only About the Unborn?" editorial, *The Communicator* (Indiana Right-to-Life newsletter) 5, no. 5 (June 1980): 2, as quoted in James T. Burtchaell, *Rachel Weeping: The Case Against Abortion* (San Francisco: Harper and Row, 1982), 129.

30. Special thanks to my good friend, Dan Green, for sharing with me this important observation.

31. For example, see Ron Sider, *Completely Pro-Life: Building a Consistent Stance* (Downers Grove, Ill.: InterVarsity, 1987).

32. Example taken from Nathanson, *Aborting America*, 189.

Chapter 6: Arguments from Decisive Moments and Gradualism

1. See Michael Tooley, *Abortion and Infanticide* (Oxford: Clarendon, 1983); and Peter Singer and Helga Kuhse, "On Letting Handicapped Infants Die," in *The Right Thing to Do*, ed. James Rachels (New York: Random House, 1989).

2. Virginia Ramey Mollenkott comes closest to this eclectic approach in "Reproduction Choice: Basic Justice For Women," *Christian Scholars' Review* 17 (March 1988): 286–93. Robert Wennberg also seems to take an eclectic approach in *Life in the Balance: Exploring the Abortion Controversy* (Grand Rapids: Eerdmans, 1985).

3. Wennberg, *Life in the Balance*, 59.

4. This is from a pamphlet distributed by the National Abortion Rights Action League, *Choice—Legal Abortion: Abortion Pro & Con,* prepared by Polly Rothstein and Marian Williams (White Plains, N.Y.: Westchester Coalition for Legal Abortion, 1983).

5. On Christian Science, see Walter R. Martin, *Kingdom of the Cults,* 3d ed. (Minneapolis: Bethany House, 1985), 126–65. On Hinduism and New Age thinking, see Elliot Miller, *A Crash Course on the New Age Movement* (Grand Rapids: Baker, 1989), 16–18, 22.

6. Bernard Nathanson, M.D., *Aborting America* (New York: Doubleday, 1979), 213–15, 216–17.

7. Ibid., 216.

8. Ibid., 217.

9. Ibid., 214.

10. Ibid.

11. For a summary of the philosophical and scientific problems surrounding human cloning, see Andrew Varga, *The Main Issues in Bioethics,* 2d. ed. (New York: Paulist, 1984), 119–26.

12. As cited in John Jefferson Davis, *Abortion and the Christian* (Phillipsburg, N.J.: Presbyterian and Reformed, 1984), 60. It should be noted that Davis is critical of these statistics (see 60–61). For a more detailed critical evaluation of these statistics, see Thomas W. Hilgers, M.D., "Human Reproduction," *Theological Studies* 38 (1977): 136–52.

13. Norman L. Geisler, *Christian Ethics: Options and Issues* (Grand Rapids: Baker, 1989), 153.

14. See Varga, *Issues in Bioethics,* 64–65.

15. Ibid., 65.

16. Wennberg, *Life in the Balance,* 71.

17. Ernest Van Den Haag, "Is There a Middle Ground?" *National Review* (12 December, 1989): 29–31.

18. Ibid., 30.

19. Davis, *Abortion and the Christian,* 58.

20. Ibid., 59.

21. John T. Noonan, "An Almost Absolute Value in History," in *The Morality of Abortion,* ed. and intro. John T. Noonan (Cambridge: Harvard University Press, 1970), 53.

22. Ibid.

23. John Warwick Montgomery, *Slaughter of the Innocents* (Westchester, Ill.: Crossway, 1981), 37. This is not to say that there was no disagreement over quickening or that many who employed the quickening criterion for recognizing life's beginning did not think that abortion was immoral prior to that moment. My purpose is simply to address the quickening criterion as a criterion but not necessarily in terms of its historical context. For more on the historical and legal background of quickening, see ibid., 103–19; and David W. Louisell and John T. Noonan, "Constitutional Balance," in *The Morality of Abortion,* 223–26.

24. Robert M. Byrn, "Goodbye to the Judeo-Christian Era in Law," *America* (2 June 1973): 512. The case *Hall v. Hancock* was decided in 1834.

25. Varga, *Issues in Bioethics,* 62–63.

26. Ibid, 63.

27. Jane English, "Abortion and the Concept of a Person," in *Biomedical Ethics,* ed. Thomas A. Mappes and Jane S. Zembaty (New York: McGraw-Hill, 1981), 430.

28. *Webster v. Reproductive Health Services* (1989), as found in *The United States Law Week* 57, no. 50 (27 July 1989): 5040. I would like to thank my friend, Larry Moore, a southern Nevada attorney, for providing me with a copy of this decision. The book I co-authored with Norman L. Geisler, *Matters of Life and Death: Calm Answers to Tough Questions about Abortion and Euthanasia* (Grand Rapids: Baker, 1991), contains as appendices the three major U.S. Supreme Court decisions on abortion: *Roe v. Wade, Doe v. Bolton,* and *Webster.*

29. Mortimer J. Adler, *Haves Without Have-Nots* (New York: Macmillan, 1991), 210.

30. Baruch Brody, *Abortion and the Sanctity of Human Life: A Philosophical View* (Cambridge, Mass.: M.I.T. Press, 1975).

31. Ibid., 102.

32. Varga, *Issues in Bioethics,* 61–62.

33. Ibid., 62.

34. Stephen D. Schwarz, *The Moral Question of Abortion* (Chicago: Loyola University Press, 1990), 52.

35. Brody, *Abortion,* 113–14.

36. A. Chadwick Ray, "Humanity, Personhood, and Abortion," *International Philosophical Quarterly* 25 (1985): 238.

37. Ibid.

38. Ibid.

39. Schwarz, *The Moral Question of Abortion,* 72.

40. Ibid., 73.

41. Ibid.

42. For a defense of this view, see Richard Werner, "Abortion: The Ontological and Moral Status of the Unborn," *Social Policy and Practice* 3 (1974): 201–22.

43. For a philosophical defense of these distinctions, see Joel Feinberg, "Grounds for Coercion," in *Ethical Theory and Social Issues,* ed. David Theo Goldberg (New York: Holt, Rinehart, and Winston, 1989), 307–15. This article is taken from Feinberg's *Social Philosophy* (Englewood Cliffs, N.J.: Prentice-Hall, 1973), 20–22, 27–29, 33, 34, 36–37, 42–45.

44. Wennberg, *Life in the Balance,* 98.

45. Ray, "Humanity, Personhood and Abortion," 240.

46. This example is similar to one presented by Schwarz in a different context (see *The Moral Question of Abortion,* 90). I use Schwarz's example when dealing with the "Criteria of Personhood."

47. Wennberg, *Life in the Balance,* 77.

48. Singer and Kuhse, "On Letting Handicapped Infants Die," 146.

49. Wennberg, *Life in the Balance,* 77–78.

50. Tooley, *Abortion and Infanticide.*

51. Mary Anne Warren, "On the Moral and Legal Status of Abortion," in *Biomedical Ethics,* 417–23.

52. James Rachels, *The End of Life* (Oxford: Oxford University Press, 1986). For a critical analysis of this book, see J. P. Moreland's review in *The Thomist* 53 (October 1989): 714–22.

53. Mollenkott, "Reproductive Choice."

54. See Tooley, *Abortion and Infanticide.*

55. Mollenkott, "Reproductive Choice," 291.

56. Tooley, *Abortion and Infanticide,* 167. Although our critique of "critieria of personhood" views in general, is sufficient to refute Tooley's argument from desire, since it rests on a functional defintion of personhood ("desire"), I refer the reader to critiques which specifically deal with Tooley's position: David Clark, "An Evaluation of the Quality of Life Argument for Infanticide," *Simon Greenleaf Law Review* 5 (1985–86): 104–8; and Richard A. McCormick, S.J., *How Brave a New World?: Dilemmas in Bioethics* (Washington, D.C.: Georgetown University Press, 1981), 157–59.

57. Warren, "On the Moral and Legal Status of Abortion," in *Biomedical Ethics,* 419. It is interesting to note that Warren lists under her criterion of consciousness the ability to feel pain, a criterion that, she admits in her article, if linked with her second criterion, may be sufficient to establish personhood. When she originally published this argument in *The Monist* in 1973, much less was known about the unborn's ability to feel pain than we know today. As I pointed out in chapter 3, citing the work of Vincent J. Collins, M.D., University of Illinois and Northwestern University Professor of Anesthesiology, it is highly probable that the unborn can feel pain by thirteen and a half weeks after conception and maybe as early as eight weeks (for more on this, see chap. 3). Consequently, the unborn child, according to Warren's criteria, is much more a person than she supposed in 1973.

58. English, "Abortion," 429.

59. Ibid., 430.

60. Don Marquis, "Why Abortion Is Immoral," *Journal of Philosophy* 86 (April 1989): 192.

61. Ibid., 195, 196.

62. Ibid., 197.

63. Davis, *Abortion and the Christian,* 57.

64. J. P. Moreland, "James Rachels and the Active Euthanasia Debate," *Journal of the Evangelical Theological Society* 31 (March, 1988): 81–90.

65. Ibid., 85.

66. Ibid., 86.

67. Ibid.

68. Ibid., 87. See also Rebecca Pentz, "Potentiality, Possibility, and Persons," *APA Newsletter on Philosophy and Medicine* 88:1 (November 1988): 38–39.

69. Schwarz, *The Moral Question of Abortion,* 94.

70. Ray, "Humanity, Personhood and Abortion," 240–41.

71. Schwarz, *The Moral Question of Abortion,* 90.

72. Ibid.

73. See the fourteen articles in Section B ("Persons and Their Lives") of part 2 of *Bioethics: Readings & Cases,* ed. Baruch A. Brody and H. Tristram Englehardt, Jr. (Englewood Cliffs, N.J.: Prentice-Hall, 1987), 132–84.

74. Daniel Callahan, *Abortion: Law, Choice, and Morality* (New York: Macmillan, 1970).

75. Wennberg, *Life in the Balance,* 98.

76. Philip Devine, *The Ethics of Homicide* (Ithaca, N.Y.: Cornell University Press, 1979), 79–80, as quoted in ibid., 117.

77. Wennberg, *Life in the Balance,* 170.

78. Robert E. Joyce, "Personhood and the Conception Event," *The New Scholasticism* 52 (Winter 1978): 106, 113.

79. Wennberg, *Life in the Balance,* 117.

80. John Warwick Montgomery, in his *Human Rights and Human Dignity* (Grand Rapids: Zondervan, 1986), reprints in appendices 1, 2, 3a and 3b four contemporary declarations on human rights.

81. See John Warwick Montgomery, "The Case for 'Higher Law,'" in *The Law above the Law* (Minneapolis: Dimension, 1975), 17–57.

82. Schwarz, *Moral Question of Abortion,* 15–19.

83. Ibid., 15.

84. Ibid., 17.

85. Peter K. McInerny, "Does a Fetus Have a Future-Like-Ours?" *Journal of Philosophy* 87 (May 1990): 266. Professor Frank R. Zindler makes the same mistake as McInerny in his article, "Human Life Does Not Begin at Conception," in *Abortion: Opposing Viewpoints,* ed. Bonnie Szumski (St. Paul: Greenhaven, 1986), 27. This article originally appeared under the title "An Acorn is Not an Oak Tree," in *American Atheist* (August 1985).

86. On the question of euthanasia and the withdrawal/withholding of health care, see J. P. Moreland and Norman L. Geisler, *The Life and Death Debate: Moral Issues of Our Time* (Westport, Conn.: Praeger, 1990), 43–102; Francis J. Beckwith and Norman L. Geisler, *Matters of Life and Death: Calm Answers to Tough Questions about Abortion and Euthanasia* (Grand Rapids: Baker, 1991), part 2; Robert N. Wennberg, *Terminal Choices: Euthanasia, Suicide, and the Right to Die* (Grand Rapids: Eerdmans, 1989); President's Commission for the Study of Ethical Problems in Medicine and Biomedical and Behavioral Research, *Deciding to Forego Life-Sustaining Treatment* (Washington, D.C.: GPO, 1983); and President's Commission for the Study of Ethical Problems in Medicine and Biomedical and Behavioral Research, *Defining Death: Medical, Legal, and Ethical Issues in the Determination of Death* (Washington, D.C.: GPO, 1983).

87. For example, see Peter Singer, *Animal Liberation* (New York: Avon, 1977).

88. For example, see Charles Swindoll, *The Sanctity of Life* (Waco: Word, 1990); and chap. 8 of this book.

89. For example, see Nathanson, *Aborting America;* Beckwith and Geisler, *Matters of Life and Death,* 15–127; and the first 7 chapters of this book.

90. For example, see Geisler, *Christian Ethics;* Davis, *Abortion and the Christian;* and Harold O. J. Brown, *Death Before Birth* (Nashville: Nelson, 1975).

91. Marquis presents a similar argument in "Why Abortion is Immoral," 190–91.

92. Schwarz, *Moral Question of Abortion,* 214.

93. Zindler, "Human Life Does Not Begin at Conception," 27.

94. Geisler, *Christian Ethics,* 147.

95. Coulter Irwin, "Of Foals and Fetuses," *Las Vegas Sun* (23 March 1989): letter to the editor.

96. *Words of Choice* (Washington, D.C.: Religious Coalition for Abortion Rights, 1991), 11.

97. Daniel Callahan, "Abortion: Some Ethical Issues," in *Abortion, Medicine, and the Law*, 3d ed., ed. J. Douglas Butler and David F. Walbert (New York: Facts on File Publications, 1986), 345.

98. C. Everett Koop, "Deception on Demand," *Moody Monthly* 80 (May 1980): 26.

99. Zindler, "Human Life Does Not Begin at Conception," 27.

100. Schwarz, *Moral Question of Abortion*, 85.

101. Ibid.

102. See James Witherspoon, "Reexaming *Roe*: Nineteenth-Century Abortion Statutes and the Fourteenth Amendment," *St. Mary's Law Journal* 17 (1985): 29–77; Joseph W. Dellapenna, "Abortion and the Law: Blackmun's Distortion of the Historical Record," in *Abortion and the Constitution: Reversing* Roe v. Wade *Through the Courts*, ed. Dennis J. Horan, Edward R. Grant, and Paige C. Cunningham (Washington, D.C.: Georgetown University Press, 1987), 137–58; Dennis J. Horan and Thomas J. Balch, "*Roe v. Wade*: No Justification in History, Law, or Logic," in *Abortion and the Constitution*, 57–88; and Beckwith and Geisler, *Matters of Life and Death*, 41–44.

103. Schwarz, *Moral Question of Abortion*, 212.

104. Ibid., 213.

105. Ibid.

Chapter 7: Arguments from Bodily Rights

1. Mortimer J. Adler, *Haves Without Have-Nots: Essays for the 21st Century on Democracy and Socialism* (New York: Macmillan, 1991), 210.

2. Laurence H. Tribe, *Abortion: The Clash of Absolutes* (New York: Norton, 1990), 102.

3. Bernard N. Nathanson, M.D., *The Abortion Papers: Inside the Abortion Mentality* (New York: Frederick Fell, 1983), 150.

4. Ibid., 150–51.

5. Baruch Brody, *Abortion and the Sanctity of Human Life: A Philosophical View* (Cambridge, Mass.: M.I.T. Press, 1975).

6. *American Medical Association Encyclopedia of Medicine*, ed. Charles B. Clayman, M.D. (New York: Random House, 1989), 58.

7. Virginia Ramey Mollenkott, "Reproductive Choice: Basic to Justice for Women," *Christian Scholar's Review* 17 (March 1988): 293.

8. David C. Reardon, *Aborted Women: Silent No More* (Westchester, Ill.: Crossway, 1987), 90. Reardon cites a *Chicago Sun Times* piece ("The Abortion Profiteers," 12 November 1978), in which writers Pamela Zekman and Pamela Warrick "reveal how undercover investigators in abortion clinics found that clinic employees routinely checked 'no complications' before the abortion was even performed." (Reardon, *Aborted Women*, 343).

9. Some other reasons for underreporting could be the following: few outpatient clinics provide follow-up examinations; long-term complications may develop (e.g., sterility, incompetent uterus) that cannot be detected without prolonged surveillance; of the women who require emergency treatment after an outpatient abortion, more than 60 percent go to a local hospital rather than returning to the abortion clinic; some women who are receiving treatment for such long-term complications as infertility may either hide their abortion or not know that it is relevant. (Ibid., 91).

10. Ibid.

11. See ibid., 89–160, 219–31.

12. Thomas W. Hilgers, M.D. and Dennis O'Hare, "Abortion Related Maternal Mortality: An In-Depth Analysis," in *New Perspectives on Human Abortion*, ed. Thomas W. Hilgers, M.D., Dennis J. Horan, and David Mall (Frederick, Md.: University Publications of America, 1981), pp. 69–70. See also Robert Marshall and Charles Donovan, *Blessed Are the Barren: The Social Policy Planned Parenthood* (San Francisco: Ignatius, 1991), 187–210.

13. Hilgers and O'Hare, "Morality," 90.

14. This argument was presented to the Court by members of the medical profession in the following brief: Amicus curiae brief filed on behalf of the American College of Obstetricians and Gynecologists, the American Medical Women's Association, the American Psychiatric Association, the New York Academy of Medicine, medical school deans and professors, and certain individual physicians, in *Doe v. Bolton*, 410 U.S. 179 (1973).

15. According to her editor, William Parent, in Judith Jarvis Thomson, *Rights, Restitution, and Risk* (Cambridge: Harvard University Press, 1986), vii.

16. Judith Jarvis Thomson, "A Defense of Abortion," in *The Problem of Abortion*, 2d ed., ed. Joel Feinberg (Belmont, Calif.: Wadsworth, 1984), 173–87. This article was originally published in *Philosophy and Public Affairs* 1 (1971): 47–66.

17. Tribe, *Abortion*, 135.

18. Thomson, "Defense of Abortion," 174–75.

19. Ibid., 180.

20. For example, in clarifying her own view, Thomson criticizes the absolutist position on abortion that it is morally impermissible to have an abortion even if the life of the mother is in significant danger. Needless to say, I agree with Thomson that this view is seriously flawed, and have spelled out my reasons for this in the introduction, chap. 1 and chap. 6.

21. Thomson, "Defense of Abortion," 174.

22. See *In the Best Interest of the Child: A Guide to State Child Support and Paternity Laws*, ed. Carolyn Royce Kastner and Lawrence R. Young (n.p.: Child Support Enforcement Beneficial Laws Project, National Conference of State Legislatures, 1981).

23. Michael Levin, review of *Life in the Balance* by Robert Wennberg, *Constitutional Commentary* 3 (Summer 1986): 511.

24. The lengths to which Thomson will go in order to deny the natural relationship between sex, reproduction, and filial obligations is evident in her use of the following analogy: "If the room is stuffy, and I therefore open a window to air it, and a burglar climbs in, it would

be absurd to say, 'Ah, now he can stay, she's given him a right to use her house—for she is partially responsible for his presence there, having voluntarily done what enabled him to get in, in full knowledge that there are such things as burglars, and that burglars burgle'" (Thomson, "Defense of Abortion," 182). Since there is no natural dependency between burglar and homeowner, as there is between child and parent, Thomson's analogy is way off the mark. Burglers don't belong in other people's homes, whereas preborn children belong in no other place *except* their mother's womb.

25. Ibid., 186.

26. For critiques of the radical feminist view of the family, see Christina Sommers, "Philosophers Against the Family," in *Vice and Virtue in Ereveryday Life: Readings in Ethics*, ed. Christina Sommers and Fred Sommers (San Diego, Calif.: Harcourt Brace Jovanovich, 1989), 720 51; George Gilder, *Men and Marriage* (Gretna, La.: Pelican, 1986); Michael Levin, *Feminism and Freedom* (New Brunswick, N.J.: Transaction, 1987); and Midge Decter, *The New Chastity and Other Arguments Against Women's Liberation* (New York: Coward, McCann, and Geoghegan, 1972).

27. Sommers, "Philosophers Against the Family," 744–45.

28. In order to strengthen Thomson's case, Robert Wennberg asks us to imagine that the violinist is the music lover's son. But, according to Wennberg, why should this make a legal difference? For "even though turning the stranger into a son may alter our *moral* evaluation of the case, I don't think it would alter our conviction that we should not legally force the mother to remain hooked up to the violinist." (Robert Wennberg, *Life in the Balance: Exploring the Abortion Controversy* [Grand Rapids: Eerdmans, 1985], 159). By making the adult violinist (who needs to be artificially attached to *any healthy person* for survival) the woman's son, Wennberg does not really address my objection that a mother has an obligation not to detach her offspring during pregnancy when that detachment will result in its death, since she, as with any other person, has an obligation not to kill another who is solely and naturally dependent on her and whose dependence does not cause significant harm; and as its mother, she has a special filial obligation to nurture her child during this stage of its development.

29. Stephen D. Schwarz, *The Moral Question of Abortion* (Chicago: Loyola University Press, 1990), 118.

30. Mary Anne Warren brings up this point when she writes: "The plausibility of such an argument is enough to show that the Thomson analogy can provide a clear and persuasive defense of a woman's right to obtain an abortion only with respect to those cases in which the woman is in no way responsible for her pregnancy, e.g., where it is due to rape." (Mary Anne Warren, "On the Moral and Legal Status of Abortion," in *The Problem of Abortion*, 108).

31. Thomson, "Defense of Abortion," 175.

32. Levin, *Feminism*, 288–89.

33. Stephen D. Schwarz and R. K. Tacelli, "Abortion and Some Philosophers: A Critical Examination," *Public Affairs Quarterly* 3 (April 1989): 85.

34. Brody, *Abortion*, 30.

35. John T. Noonan, "How to Argue About Abortion," in *Morality in Practice*, 2d ed., ed. James P. Sterba (Belmont, Calif.: Wadsworth, 1988), 150. This article is from Noonan's "Responding to Persons: Methods of Moral Argument in Debate over Abortion," *Theology Digest* (1973): 291–307.

36. Ibid.

37. Ibid.

38. Dennis J. Horan and Burke J. Balch, *Infant Doe and Baby Jane Doe: Medical Treatment of the Handicapped Newborn*, Studies in Law & Medicine Series (Chicago: Americans United for Life, 1985), 2.

39. *In re Storar*, 53 N.Y. 2d 363, 380-381, 420 N.E. 2d 64, 73, 438 N.Y.S. 2d 266, 275 (1981), as quoted in ibid., 3 3.

40. Horan and Balch, *Infant Doe*, 3–4.

41. Bernard Nathanson, M.D., *Aborting America* (New York: Doubleday, 1979), 220.

42. Michelle Healy, "At Work: Maternity Bias," *USA Today* (30 July 1990): 1A. Conducted by researcher Hal Grueutal of State University of New York, Albany, this survey found that 41 percent of those interviewed (133 women and 122 men at eight businesses in the Northeast) "said they think pregnancy hurts a woman's job performance."

43. Levin, review of *Life in the Balance*, 507–8.

44. Although not dealing exclusively with Thomson's argument, Celia Wolf-Devine's article is quite helpful: "Abortion and the 'Feminine Voice,'" *Public Affairs Quarterly* 3 (July 1989): 181–97. See also Doris Gordon, "Abortion and Thomson's Violinist," a paper published by Libertarians for Life, 1991 (13424 Hathaway Drive, Wheaton, Md. 20906; 301-460-4141); Janet Smith, "Abortion as a Feminist Concern," in *The Zero People*, ed. Jeffe Lane Hensley (Ann Arbor, Mich.: Servant, 1983), 77–95; and John T. Wilcox, "Nature as Demonic in Thomson's Defense of Abortion," *The New Scholasticism* 63 (Autumn 1989): 463–84.

45. n.a., *Sound Advice for All Prolife Activists and Candidates Who Wish to Include a Concern for Women's Rights in Their Prolife Advocacy: Feminists for Life Debate Handbook* (Kansas City, Mo.: Feminists for Life of America, n.d.), 15–16.

46. Wolf-Devine, "Abortion," 86, 87.

Chapter 8: Arguments from Theology and the Bible

1. Virginia Ramey Mollenkott, "Reproductive Choice: Basic to Justice for Women," *Christian Scholar's Review* 17 (March 1988): 291.

2. For greater detail and defense of the biblical case against abortion rights, see John Jefferson Davis, *Abortion and the Christian* (Phillipsburg, N.J.: Presbyterian and Reformed, 1984), 35–62; and Norman L. Geisler, *Chris-*

tian Ethics: Options and Issues (Grand Rapids: Baker, 1989), 142–46, 148.

3. Davis, *Abortion and the Christian*, 40.

4. Ibid., 41.

5. Ibid.

6. Robert Wennberg, *Life in the Balance: Exploring the Abortion Controversy* (Grand Rapids: Eerdmans, 1985), 60–63.

7. Ibid., 62.

8. Ibid., 63.

9. James Sire, *Scripture Twisting* (Downers Grove, Ill.: InterVarsity, 1980), 23–30, 127–44.

10. Ibid., 26.

11. As quoted in Nigel M. de S. Cameron and Pamela F. Sims, *Abortion: The Crisis in Morals and Medicine* (Leicester: InterVarsity, 1986), 14, 28. The early church material Cameron and Sims cite is acquired from citations compiled in David Braine, *Medical Ethics and Human Life* (Aberdeen, 1982). For more on the Early Church's view on abortion, see Michael Gorman, *Abortion and the Early Church* (Downers Grove, Ill.: InterVarsity, 1982).

12. Cited in Cameron and Sims, *Abortion*, 29–30.

13. See John T. Noonan, Jr., "Aquinas on Abortion," in *St. Thomas Aquinas on Politics and Ethics* trans. and ed. Paul E. Sigmund (New York: Norton, 1988), 245–48.

14. Braine, *Medical Ethics*, as cited in Cameron and Sims, *Abortion*, 29.

15. Mollenkott, "Reproductive Choice," 288–89.

16. Ibid., 293.

17. Bruce K. Waltke, "Reflections From the Old Testament on Abortion," *Journal of the Evangelical Theological Society* 19 (1976): 3. Although appearing to accept the pro-choice interpretation of the Exodus passage, Waltke takes a strong pro-life position and denies the abortion-rights inference that this passage supports legalized abortion on demand.

For a journalistic, though somewhat misleading, review of the theological debate, see Jefferey L. Sheler, "The Theology of Abortion," *U.S. News & World Report* (9 March 1992): 54–55. I would like to thank Dr. F. Michael Womack, Pastor of Calvary Baptist Church (Erwin, Tennessee), for bringing this article to my attention.

18. John Warwick Montgomery, "The Christian View of the Fetus," in *Jurisprudence: A Book of Readings*, ed. John Warwick Montgomery (Strasbourg, France: International Scholarly Publishers, 1974), 585.

19. For example, see Ronald E. Clements, *Exodus*, Cambridge Commentaries on the New English Bible (Cambridge: Cambridge University Press, 1972), 138; J. Phillip Hyatt, *Exodus*, New Century Bible (London: Oliphants, 1971), 233; Walter R. Martin, *Abortion: Is It Always Murder?* (Santa Ana, Calif.: Vision House, 1977); Martin Noth, *Exodus: A Commentary*, trans. J. S. Bowden (Philadelphia: Westminster, 1962), 181; J. Coert Rylaarsdam, "Exodus," in *The Interpreter's Bible*, ed. George Arthur Buttrick, et al. (New York: Cokesbury-Abingdon, 1951–57), 1:999; and Bruce K. Waltke, "Old Testament Texts Bearing on Abortion," *Christianity Today* (8 Nov. 1968): 99–105.

20. For example, see Gleason Archer, *Encyclopedia of Bible Difficulties* (Grand Rapids: Zondervan, 1982), 246–49; Umberto Cassuto, *A Commentary on the Book of Exodus*, trans. Israel Abrahams (Jerusalem: Magnes, 1967), 275; C. F. Keil and F. Delitzsch, "The Second Book of Moses: Exodus," in *The Pentateuch*, vol. 1 of *Commentary on the Old Testament* (Grand Rapids: Eerdmans, 1980; reprint of 1864–1901 ed.), 135; Meredith G. Kline, "*Lex Talionis* and the Human Fetus," *Simon Greenleaf Law Review* 5 (1985–86): 73–89; and Montgomery, "The Christian View of the Fetus," 585–87.

21. Cassuto, *Commentary on the Book of Exodus*, 275.

22. Archer, *Encyclopedia*, 247.

23. Personal letter from Dr. F. Michael Womack (13 March 1992).

24. There is a third interpretation of this verse, defended by both Davis (*Abortion and the Christian*) and Kline ("*Lex Talionis* and the Human Fetus"), two pro-life theologians. Since, however, my main focus is simply to call into question the so-called pro-choice interpretation of Exodus 21:22–25, it is not necessary for me to bring up yet another view that undermines the abortion-rights position.

25. A portion of Wennberg's work on abortion (*Life in the Balance*) was instrumental in my discovery of the differing views on Exodus 21:22–25.

26. "A Pro-Choice Bible Study" (Seattle, Wash.: Episcopalians for Religious Freedom, 1989).

27. Ibid.

28. Other translations render this passage in the following way: "she will then be free to conceive children" (NASB); "she will bear children" (JB); "and shall conceive seed" (KJV); "and will be able to bear children" (TEV).

29. For more detailed critiques of this argument, see Harold O. J. Brown, *Death Before Birth* (Nashville: Nelson, 1977), 123–24; and Davis, *Abortion and the Christian*, 101–2.

30. Davis, *Abortion and the Christian*, 101.

31. Brown, *Death Before Birth*, 124.

32. Geisler, *Christian Ethics*, 145.

33. Ibid.

34. "A Pro-Choice Bible Study," n.p.

35. Ibid.

36. Ibid.

37. Ibid.

38. Ibid.

Conclusion: A Positive Case for the Pro-Life Position

1. Stephen D. Schwarz, *The Moral Question of Abortion* (Chicago: Loyola University Press, 1990), 143.

Epilogue: A Dialogue on Civil Disobedience

1. See Martin Luther King, Jr., "Letter from the Birmingham City Jail," in *The Right Thing to Do: Basic Readings in Moral Philosophy*, ed. James Rachels (New York: Random House, 1989), 236–53.

2. I would like to thank Bob and Gretchen Passantino for helping me to think more critically about the arguments against Operation Rescue. Without their intellectual input, this epilogue would have never been written. I would like to also thank my wife, Frankie R. D. Beckwith, who had always told me I was wrong about Operation Rescue.

3. The dialogues with Rex Herrod, Atilla Tarian, and "Pop" Syke are found in Peter Kreeft, *The Unaborted Socrates* (Downers Grove, Ill.: InterVarsity, 1983).

4. This joke was created by my former student and UNLV graduate, Dennis Monokroussos.

5. For documentation of this, see Randy Alcorn, *Is Rescuing Right?* (Downers Grove, Ill.: InterVarsity, 1990), 150–65.

6. For those readers interested in further study of all sides of the debate over Operation Rescue, I suggest the following: Alcorn, *Is Rescuing Right?*; Gary North, *Trespassing for Dear Life: What Is Operation Rescue Up To?* (Ft. Worth: Dominion, 1989); Gary North, *When Justice Is Aborted—Biblical Standards for Non-violent Resistance* (Ft. Worth: Dominion, 1989); Francis J. Beckwith and Norman L. Geisler, *Matters of Life and Death: Calm Answers to Tough Questions about Abortion and Euthanasia* (Grand Rapids: Baker, 1991), chap. 7; Norman L. Geisler, *Christian Ethics: Options and Issues* (Grand Rapids: Baker, 1989), 239–55; Norman L. Geisler, *Operation Unbiblical: Should Christians Ever Break the Law?* (Lynchburg, Va: Quest, 1989); Randall Terry, *Operation Rescue* (Springdale, Pa.: Whitaker House, 1988); and Donald P. Shoemaker, *Operation Rescue: A Critical Analysis* (Seal Beach, Calif.: Grace Community Church, n.d.). This last work, by the senior pastor of Grace Community Church of Seal Beach, is very helpful in evaluating the many views concerning Operation Rescue. To get a copy, send $2 to Grace Community Church, 138 8th St., Seal Beach, Calif. 90740.

Appendix B: Choice Quotes

1. Spoken in a public debate on the campus of the University of Nevada, Las Vegas at the Hendrix Auditorium, December 4, 1989. Participants in the debate were myself and David Day (a UNLV graduate student in the M.A. in ethics and policy studies program) taking the pro-life position and Professor Langston and Glynda White (a southern Nevada attorney) taking the abortion-rights position. The debate, sponsored by UNLV's Black Student Association, was taped by many people in the audience. The tape from which this statement is taken was recorded by my brother-in-law, Mark Wiegand. I would like to thank him for providing me with this tape.

2. From *National N.O.W. Times* (January 1988), as quoted in *New Dimensions* 4 (October 1990): 42.

3. As quoted in ibid.

4. As quoted in ibid., 43.

5. *Woman and the New Race* (New York: Brentano's, 1920), 63.

6. "Sanctity of Life or Quality of Life?" *Pediatrics* 73 (July 1973): 128–29.

7. Spoken in debate cited in n. 1.

8. "Abortion and Infanticide: Abortion on Demand," in *Ethics for Modern Life*, eds. Raziel Abelson and Marie-Louise Friquegnon (New York: St. Martin's, 1987), 122–23.

9. *AMA Prism*, chap. 3 (May 1973), 2.

10. Quoted in *Policy Review* (Spring 1985): 15.

11. "On Sex Equality," in *Sex Equality*, ed. Jane English (Englewood Cliffs, N.J.: Prentice-Hall, 1977), 102.

12. "Prostitution," in *Women and Values: Readings in Recent Feminist Philosophy*, ed. Marilyn Pearsell (Belmont, Calif.: Wadsworth, 1986), 117, as quoted in Christina Sommers, "Do These Feminists Like Women?" *Journal of Social Philosophy* 21 (Fall/Winter 1990): 70.

13. Quoted in Robert Marshall and Charles Donovan, *Blessed Are the Barren: The Social Policy of Planned Parenthood* (San Francisco: Ignatius, 1991), 182.

14. Warren Hern, "Is Pregnancy Normal?" *Family Planning Perspectives* 3 (January 1971): 9–12, as cited in Marshall and Donovan, *Blessed Are the Barren*, 182.

15. Jeffner Allen, "Motherhood: The Annihilation of Women," in *Mothering: Essays in Feminist Theory*, ed. Joyce Trebilcot (Totowa, N.J.: Rowman and Allanheld, 1984), 315, as quoted in Sommers, "Do These Feminists Like Women?" 67.

16. As quoted in Christina Sommers, "Hard-Line Feminists Guilty of Ms.-Representation," *Wall Street Journal* (7 November 1991): A-14.

17. Sol Gordon, "It's Not OK to Be Antigay," address to the American Library Assocation, in *The Sexual Adolescent* by Sol Gordon, Peter Scales, and Kathleen Everly (North Scituate, Mass.: Duxbury, 1979), 232, as quoted in Marshall and Donovan, *Blessed Are the Barren*, 112.

18. "SIECUS Position Statements," *SIECUS Report*, vol. 2, no. 5 (May 1974): 2, as quoted in Marshall and Donovan, *Blessed Are the Barren*, 78.

19. As quoted in *Focus on the Family Citizen* (October 1989): 12. Yard's comment on the Oprah Winfrey show is also quoted by Gary Bauer, "Abetting Coercion in China," *The Washington Times* (10 October 1989).

20. Alan Guttmacher, *Presidential Letter*, no. 35 (4 October 1968): 3.

21. As quoted in *Saturday Review* (1975), as cited in Christina Hoff Sommers, "Feminism and the College Curriculum," *Imprimis* 19 (June 1990): 3.

22. As quoted in *New Dimensions* (October 1990): 43.

23. From *The Daily Illini* (25 April 1981), as quoted in ibid.

24. For a brief summary of the "pro-incest lobby" and its leadership and goals, see Mildred Daley Pagelow (with Lloyd W. Pagelow), *Family Violence*, Praeger Special Studies (New York: Praeger, 1984), 410–12; John Leo, "Cradle-to-grave Intimacy," *Time* (7 September 1981): 69; Benjamin DeMott, "The Pro-incest Lobby," *Psychology Today* (March 1980): 12; and Marshall and Donovan, *Blessed Are the Barren*, 125–29.

25. As quoted in Leo, "Cradle," 69.

26. As quoted in ibid.

27. As quoted in ibid.

28. As quoted in ibid.

29. As quoted in *The New York Times* (10 May 1988).

30. "Women and the Supreme Court: Anatomy Is Destiny," *Brooklyn Law Review* 41 (1974): 242.

31. *Abortion: The Clash of Absolutes* (New York: Norton, 1990), 105.

32. *Webster v. Reproductive Health Services* 492 U.S. 490, 557 (1989). (J. Blackmun, dissenting). By discounting the evidence for the unborn's personhood from the outset, Blackmun's argument is reduced to a highly emotional appeal that merely begs the question, just as it would beg the question as to the black man's humanness if it were employed in a defense of slavery:

The Congress in passing the 14th Amendment discards a landmark case of the last generation (*Dred Scott*), and casts into darkness the hopes and visions of every property owner in the South who had come to believe that the Constitution guaranteed him the right to exercise some control over his God-given right to own property. The plurality does so either oblivious or insensitive to the fact that millions of property owners, and their families, have ordered their lives around the right to ownership of property, and that this right has become vital to the full participation of Southern gentlemen in the economic and political walks of American life.

33. This advertisement is reproduced in *New Dimensions* (October 1990): 58.

Index

Index

Index

Index